DATE DUE

EXPLORATIONS IN
SHAKESPEARE'S LANGUAGE

Explorations in
Shakespeare's Language

*Some Problems of Lexical Meaning
in the Dramatic Text*

HILDA M. HULME

NEW YORK

BARNES & NOBLE INC.

Publishers · Booksellers · Since 1873

© HILDA M. HULME 1962
FIRST PUBLISHED 1962
THIS EDITION FIRST PUBLISHED 1963

PRINTED IN GREAT BRITAIN AT
THE UNIVERSITY PRESS
ABERDEEN

To the memory of my father and mother
Samuel and Mary Hulme

The full titles of works to which incidental reference is made are given at the time. Works more frequently consulted are referred to by short titles only, the expansion of which may be sought in the list below. Other abbreviations, signs, etc. (mainly those used in the *New English Dictionary*) are as follows:

a. (as *a.* 1300)	*ante*, before	*Obs.*	obsolete
a., adj.	adjective	OE	Old English (Anglo-
adv.	adverb		Saxon)
arch.	archaic	ON	Old Norse
attrib.	attributive, -ly	OTeut.	Original Teutonic
c. (as *c.* 1300)	*circa*, about	*poet.*	poetic
comb.	combined, -ing	*sb.*	substantive
dial.	dialect, -al	*Sc.*	Scotch
fig.	figurative, -ly	*trans.*	transitive
ME	Middle English	*transf.*	transferred sense
north.	northern (dialect)	*v.*	verb
		vbl. sb.	verbal substantive

IN THE LIST OF FORMS:

   1 = before 1100
   2 = 12th c. (1100-1200)
   5-7 = 15th to 17th century

IN THE ETYMOLOGY:

* indicates a word or form not actually found, but of which the existence is inferred

> becomes
< derives from

CONTENTS

ix

PREFACE

This book is an offshoot of a more comprehensive Shakespeare glossary on which I have been long engaged. It describes a series of experiments to add to our knowledge of the language of Shakespeare's time and attempts an interpretation of some of the more difficult words and phrases of his dramatic text.

All references to Shakespeare's plays are to the act, scene and line numbering of the Globe edition (1891) as given in Bartlett's *Concordance*. For all passages quoted (except in a very few instances where the language problem or language evidence extends through several lines) a single line reference is given: the number of the line containing the language problem or relevant linguistic evidence; where a longer passage is cited as evidence of dramatic context, the line number given is that of the last line of the quoted passage. Quotations are from the First Folio unless otherwise stated; proper names within this text are given in roman type; italics are introduced for emphasis and ease of exposition; names of speaking characters are expanded. In quotations from Latin and French dictionaries grammatical detail is silently omitted. Manuscript contractions are silently expanded; money references are usually formalised (e.g. 00-05-08).

My thanks are due to Professor C. J. Sisson of University College, London, for much help and encouragement especially in earlier stages of the work; also to Professor A. H. Smith and Professor J. R. Sutherland; to Professor J. R. Firth, of the School of Oriental and African Studies in the University of London, I am greatly indebted for his suggesting to me, as to all who attended his Wednesday morning lectures, that there are always new ways of looking at language. Other friends and colleagues of London University and elsewhere have given generously of time and knowledge. I am grateful to my husband for advice on the form and structure of the book, for useful criticism on many points of detail, and, above all, for urging me on to make an end.

I acknowledge with thanks the receipt of generous grants from the Central Research Fund of the University of London which helped to make possible the earlier work on manuscript materials and on the Shakespeare glossary, and I am glad also to have this opportunity of thanking Mr. J. H. P. Pafford, Goldsmith's Librarian, and members of his staff in the London University Library, for most valuable assistance and service over many years.

Some few of the interpretations here put forward have already been discussed in *William Shakespeare: The Complete Works*, ed. by C. J. Sisson, London, 1954 and in short papers and articles in *English Studies, Essays in Criticism, Journal of English and Germanic Philology, Modern Language Review, Neophilologus, Notes and Queries, Review of English Studies* and *Shakespeare Quarterly*, and I thank Professor Sisson and the editors of these periodicals for their kind permission to reproduce some of this material which is here incorporated in more finished form.

London
January 1961   H. M. H.

CHAPTER I

Introductory

I

My purpose in this book is to explore the meaning of some of the words and phrases in Shakespeare's plays, and, in so doing, to suggest what further knowledge we may yet obtain both about the language of Shakespeare's England and the language of Shakespeare's art. Such a study is necessarily discursive, tentative and incomplete; I would claim that it is, nonetheless, disciplined and systematic. By the term 'meaning' I intend, roughly, 'translation equivalent', and I take the word or phrase as the unit of meaning for convenience of handling only; that we cannot understand the word until we have understood the 'sentence' I readily concede. I have preferred to work with the language of the plays rather than the poems, partly because problems of meaning seem to present themselves more clearly, more challengingly, in the dramatic text; partly too from the feeling that the essential clues are there in the cut and thrust of dramatic dialogue in a way in which they are not there in the more musically organised, or more secret language of the poems and sonnets. In Shakespeare's plays I include the thirty-six plays of the First Folio (1623) and also *Pericles* (1609); my quotations are from the First Folio unless otherwise stated. I assume that 'Shakespeare' may have been responsible for the wording of either the First Folio or the good Quarto texts and when, in the passages which I am seeking to interpret, these texts are at variance, I try to consider, in the light of our twentieth-century knowledge of Elizabethan English, what meaning each version might have had for Shakespeare's first audience. Rather than say too frequently 'in the latter half of the sixteenth century and the early years of the seventeenth', I shall often, for ease of reference, use the term 'Elizabethan' as if Shakespeare and Queen Elizabeth were contemporaries, i.e. as if the Queen died not in 1603, but in 1616, the year of Shakespeare's death.

My approach to the problem of Shakespeare's meaning may be reckoned, I suppose, at once linguistic and literary, since I need to deal with both external and internal evidence, with the common currency of Elizabethan speech and the heightened language of dramatic art. I should, however, make clear at once that my academic training has been on the language side and it is as a linguist that I began to be concerned with the less literary English of Shakespeare's time. By drawing attention to some of this external evidence I hope to show how we may increase our linguistic equipment, and also how we may better use the equipment already available to us, so as to bring ourselves, here and there, a step or two nearer to the language world in which Shakespeare's plays were written and first performed. For in feeding our memories more information about Elizabethan English, we may deepen our sensitivity to the potential meaning of Shakespeare's words and phrases, and, at the same time, we may become more alert to those clues within the text by which Shakespeare himself has circumscribed that potentiality, has limited our freedom of response.

2

Of the language of art, it has been said, two things, apparently contradictory, are plainly true: first, that there is no single way of responding to its meaning; what one finds depends on what one brings. And equally, what one finds is there already; the meaning is there in the language. That no two individuals will experience a play or poem in quite the same way is readily recognised; where we feel intensely we apprehend partially, selectively. Different

societies too are of different tempers; the time and place in which
we live will condition what we bring to our understanding of
the artist's purposes. Shakespeare's meaning, in this sense of the
term, is something that is continually recreated between himself
and his reader, his audience. Who that reader is will determine, to
some extent, what Shakespeare the dramatist can mean. As
applied to the total meaning of any one of his plays such a statement has an obvious truth; that it may be applied also to some of
the tiny units of language of which the single play is composed,
it has been the special distinction of recent criticism to reaffirm
and re-emphasise. For we do not now expect to find plain
meaning, clear and unclouded, of a limited and uniform intelligi-
bility, either in the effortless talk of ordinary men or in the finely
structured language of drama and poetry. Whereas the eighteenth
century admired Shakespeare rather '*in spite of* his language',[1]
so that Dr. Johnson praises only the 'ease and simplicity' of the
dialogue, finding his 'ruggedness or difficulty' a fault, his conceits
'idle', and his equivocations 'contemptible', the twentieth century,
as we are all aware, has shifted back to earlier values. In our views
of language and of the arts of language, in the pleasure we
find in all the various modes of complex meaning, we feel
ourselves nearer to Shakespeare's first public than to his first
critical and scholarly editors, those pioneering giants five
generations after his day, whose industry and taste were to leave
so firm an imprint on his text. Shakespeare 'regarded more the
series of ideas, than of words', says Johnson; we admire in
Shakespeare's writing the different kinds of progression that he
can simultaneously control; that this progression be always
linear or forward-moving we do not stipulate. In the intricacy
of his dramatic meaning we appreciate that there may be always
a little more to understand. As T. S. Eliot said on his seventieth
birthday, 'It takes a lifetime to grow up to Shakespeare.'

---

[1] 'The fact is that Shakespeare succeeded in pleasing the eighteenth century
in spite of his language . . .'. See 'Shakespeare's Imitators in the Eighteenth
Century', by J. R. Sutherland, *Modern Language Review*, Jan. 1933, Vol. XXVIII,
No. 1, p. 25.

So too, it has been pointed out, when the first collected edition of Shakespeare's plays was set before the reading public, some such estimate of Shakespeare's language had already been made by two of the actors in his company. As early as 1623, Heminge and Condell, Shakespeare's first 'editors', recognise the variability of reader response and the possible enrichment of that response as the reader is able to attend more and more closely to the meaning that is there in the printed text. The fate of all books, they acknowledge, depends upon the capacities of those who read them; their volume is addressed 'To the great Variety of Readers. From the most able, to him that can but spell.' To them, as editors, it is the financial rather than the intellectual capacity of their potential public that is of primary importance; to all whose purses are heavy enough to buy the book, they concede full liberty of criticism. Individual quirks of judgment are freely allowed : 'read and censure' so runs their invitation, '. . . how odde soeuer your braines be, or your wisedomes'. For Shakespeare's work, as they well know, can stand up to criticism; on the public stage 'these Playes haue had their triall alreadie'. They too praise Shakespeare's 'easinesse', but it is an easiness in him of a special kind:

> what he thought, he vttered with that easinesse, that wee haue scarse receiued from him a blot in his papers.

Shakespeare's final draft, they say, the copy as it came into their hands, was free of erasures and alterations; he had no need of second thoughts. How much of this springs from the exaggerated respect of layman for professional, how much is literal truth, we can make no estimate; no single fragment of the papers from which the First Folio was printed is known to have survived. The comment suggests however both the standard which Shakespeare set himself and his confidence in the expression he achieved, his awareness that the artist's purpose is accomplished when nothing can be other than it is. And his actors too, it seems, could recognise in his language that fullness of meaning which it was their business to bring out in a stage performance; they do not expect the

Shakespearean reader to reach at once a final understanding. It
is for each to make his own exploration, his own discoveries.

> And there we hope, to your diuers capacities, you will finde
> enough, both to draw, and hold you: for his wit can no more lie
> hid, then ['than'] it could be lost. Reade him, therefore; and againe,
> and againe: And if then you doe not like him, surely you are in
> some manifest danger, not to vnderstand him.

Through delight, perhaps even through bewilderment, they seem
to suggest, the reader is led on to reach a deeper perception. And
in the end, the text will make its point. For what Shakespeare
could not but create, the 'wit' in him that was bound to flash out
into the uniqueness of living language, cannot fail at last to be
apprehended afresh: it is there on the printed page. No one,
however, should expect a first or second reading to suffice; we
must go back again and again to the detail of what Shakespeare
wrote. That the labour is worth the gain is abundantly assumed,
for not to understand his language is to miss something of
his art.

To read too much into the editors' words would be dangerous,
and indeed, in thus expanding what they say, I may be held to
have reshaped it to suit my own thesis. What is noteworthy,
however, is that Heminge and Condell take it for granted that
much is required, even of Shakespeare's contemporaries, if they
are fully to understand Shakespeare's language. And those who
make this assumption are experienced actors, men of some power
and substance in the theatrical world. In that world also it may
have been an acknowledged truth that for producer and actor,
as well as for the later reader, each repetition of a Shakespearean
play was an enriching experience, bringing always some enhanced
awareness, some new detail of apprehension.

It is clear at all events that to understand the uniqueness, the
once-only liveliness of the language that Shakespeare made, it
was not enough simply to be an Elizabethan, habituated to think
and feel within the patterns of language that Shakespeare found;

even then one might be 'in some manifest danger, not to vnder-
stand him'. What factors might make his writing difficult to
understand Heminge and Condell do not state; the remedy that
they suggest, if it does prove so, is to give it time, to submit oneself
again and again to the experience. And this prompts the speculation
that some of the difficulties which they expect the new reader to
encounter arise from precisely this, that Shakespeare was writing
for a trained public, or, perhaps I should say, for an audience-in-
training, used to his idiom and capable of becoming the more
sharply sensitive to his increasing speed and compression. Let
us suppose that he was able to teach his audience within the
theatre to receive his metaphors more and more quickly, to feel
the full weight of the briefest allusion, to accept and enjoy all
the devices of prismatic meaning; confident that he could take
with him some part at least of such an audience, a dramatist,
although writing for the public stage and with an eye to business,
could yet engage in energetic experiment. He might sometimes
risk more intractable subject-matter, might find success in an
effort to express what would hardly go into words at all, rather
than in an achieved perfection at some apparently simpler level.
As Dr. Johnson found:

> It is incident to him to be now and then entangled with an un-
> wieldy sentiment, which he cannot well express, and will not
> reject; he struggles with it for a while, and if it continues stubborn,
> comprises it in words such as occur, and leaves it to be disentangled
> and evolved by those who have more leisure to bestow upon it.

And perhaps we should have in mind also that with an audience
trained to strenuous listening and quick response it might even
be useful to the playwright occasionally to hold up the speed of
that response. He might choose to write what would be, momentarily, unintelligible; might, of deliberate intent, block the way
forward, compel the hearer to pause before taking-in. Both in
comedy and tragedy there could be profit for the playwright in
an emphasis so achieved.

I have suggested here, by reference to Shakespeare's contemporaries, that if we are to be fully alert to the language which Shakespeare made, we need something more than a knowledge of the language which Shakespeare found. It is, I believe, an important point. For we are sometimes apt to suppose that the main barrier between ourselves and the Shakespearean experience is an ignorance of linguistic fact, whereas, of course, the final difficulty for the non-contemporary is to achieve a creative interplay of—contemporary—fact and fantasy. Language, in the streets and on the stage, does not stand still while someone from the outside examines it. And if we are to understand something of what was there, within the given text, for Shakespeare's first audience and first readers, we need at once their linguistic background, and, arising from that background, their kind, not our kind of linguistic inventiveness, their way of reacting to what was new in the detail of Shakespeare's language. We need, as it were, to move smoothly in their linguistic grooves before we can feel how Shakespeare occasionally jolted them out of these grooves. And it follows from this that we must discard knowledge as well as acquire it. Observation shows that as we learn a foreign language we hear sound-distinctions which to a native speaker are non-meaningful, while at the same time our ear fails to record significant distinctions which, in our own tongue, would mean nothing. Shakespeare's English is foreign to us by ten or so generations, three and a half centuries of changing vocabulary and idiom, pronunciation and syntax. Sometimes too his eighteenth-century editors have introduced, as it were, other 'dialect' forms; they may have embedded in his text chippings of a later stratum. It must be admitted that, ideally speaking, there is virtually no limit to the amount of information that we need from external sources: by patient accumulation of such evidence as has survived, both in printed books and in manuscript materials, we need to squeeze out of our memories all that has happened to the English language since, let us say, 1616 (the year of Shakespeare's death) or 1623 (when the First Folio was published), and

to soak ourselves afresh in the language that Shakespeare heard
in Stratford and in London. And the somewhat fragmentary
information we can obtain by laborious fact-finding is a basis only,
a necessary precondition of an imaginative perception, an intuitive understanding of a poet's art.

3

In exploring the language of Shakespeare's England as evidenced
in the printed books of his time, editors have long been prodigal
of labour. As Malone points out:

> The meanest books have been carefully examined, only because
> they were of the age in which he lived, and might happily throw
> light on some forgotten custom, or obsolete phraseology.

It has never been supposed that, because one might look long and
find little, one should not, or need not, look at all. Pope may
laugh at Theobald, one of the greatest of the early editors, for
giving us in his edition of Shakespeare a sample of 'all such
reading as was never read', but Steevens, himself a scholar of
tireless energy, offers a fitting answer:

> If Shakespeare is worth reading, he is worth explaining; and the re-
> searches used for so valuable and elegant a purpose, merit the thanks
> of genius and candour, not the satire of prejudice and ignorance.

And there is Malone's famous and modest affirmation:

> I scarcely remember ever to have looked into a book of the age
> of Queen Elizabeth, in which I did not find somewhat that tended
> to throw a light on these plays.

Any notion that Shakespeare might be 'buried under his Commentators', Malone sets aside:

> While our object is, to support and establish what the poet wrote,
> to illustrate his phraseology by comparing it with that of his

contemporaries, and to explain his fugitive allusions to customs long since discussed and forgotten, while this object is kept steadily in view, if even every line of his plays were accompanied with a comment, every intelligent reader would be indebted to the industry of him who produced it.

Johnson does not envisage any end to this gradual and piecemeal discovery of relevant information: no complete and systematic explanation of Shakespeare's meaning can be expected from any single scholiast. The common colloquial language, which is necessarily Shakespeare's medium, admits 'many phrases allusive, elliptical and proverbial'; many details concerning modes, customs, formalities

> which naturally find places in familiar dialogue, are so fugitive and unsubstantial, that they are not easily retained or recovered. What can be known will be collected by chance, from the recesses of obscure and obsolete papers, perused commonly with some other view. Of this knowledge every man has some, and none has much; but when an author has engaged the publick attention, those who can add any thing to his illustration communicate their discoveries, and time produces what had eluded diligence.

My own small contribution to linguistic information comes from just such recesses as Johnson speaks of, from manuscript local records, mainly of the sixteenth and seventeenth centuries, which I began to read for quite other purposes than the light they might throw on Shakespeare's language. Some of the evidence they provide—evidence consciously sought—is directly relevant to the interpretation of his text; what is not directly relevant is, I think, no less important, in that it brings us back to the working principle of the great editors of earlier centuries—that, whatever we may know of the spoken language of Shakespeare's time, there is always more that we may, by chance, discover. This realistic postulate has, not unnaturally, been somewhat lost sight of at the present time, since the completion of the *New English Dictionary* has made available so much that can be known of the language of printed books of earlier periods. For although it is generally accepted that many details of this 'printed book' language may yet be added to our greatest of dictionaries, it is not always realised that manuscript records also, unsearched by any lexicographer, exist in considerable numbers. Local records especially, preserved by chance, and, for the most part, uncalendared, not always readily accessible, and perhaps, even at the present time, not very well cared for, may offer much that is of value to the language student. One cannot know in advance what one is likely to find, but the experienced searcher, lucky enough and persistent enough to come upon the right kind of documents, can count on getting new information on meaning and usage, spelling and pronunciation, and even, although this less frequently, on grammar and syntax. The student whose attention has been thus concentrated for some few years on whatever is unexpected within the non-literary language of sixteenth and seventeenth century archives will be conditioned to make a rather unusual approach to the problems of lexical meaning which yet remain in the Shakespearean text. From my own practice the following principles emerge: In any passage which appears to have normal Elizabethan or Shakespearean structure (e.g. 'the base (though bitter) disposition of Beatrice', *Much Ado*, II i 214; 'In my defunct, and proper satisfaction', *Othello*, I iii 265; 'Let him be made an Ouerture for th' Warres', *Coriolanus*, I ix 46; 'Or of a most select and generous, chiefe in that', *Hamlet*, Quarto 2, I iii 74) words or phrases which are at present considered as unintelligible (and perhaps as textual corruptions) are accepted by the linguist as if they are genuine forms which may perhaps be shown as meaningful (*a*) somewhere within the wide range of Elizabethan spoken English patterns and (*b*) within the tightly controlled artistic unity of the Shakespearean play. Until the coincidence of meaning in areas (*a*) and (*b*) can be clearly demonstrated, problems of lexical definition are held 'pending', in the hope that a chance discovery of new external evidence in printed or manuscript language may one day suggest some better means of understanding the 'as if genuine' Shakespearean text. It is in this way that the 'perhaps' of the linguist differs from that of the textual critic.

To those who are trained, as I am not, in the ever finer intricacies of bibliographic and textual criticism, it will be clear from the start that this experiment of trusting to the genuineness of Folio or Quarto text cannot always be successful: such an act of faith takes no account, for instance, of the provable fallibility of the Elizabethan compositor. Even in itself such an experiment is by no means new. For while it has ever been the claim of the Shakespearean editor that he has altered nothing 'but what by the clearest Reasoning can be proved a Corruption of the true Text' (Theobald, 1733), it has long been his employment also 'to *restore*, in the true sense of the word; to eject the arbitrary and capricious innovations made by our predecessors from ignorance of the phraseology and customs of the age in which Shakespeare lived' (Malone, 1790). And still, after two and a half centuries of editing and re-editing, with the problems of textual criticism more specialised than ever before, it is 'astonishing to contemplate how little of a basic nature has been done' to establish Shakespeare's text, and 'how much remains to do' (Fredson Bowers, 1954).[1] It is still necessary for the Shakespearean editor to remind himself and his fellows 'to beware of eighteenth-century contamination of the text':

> Many a reading survives, even in recent editions, unperceived, unquestioned, in silence, as a legacy of the labours of an eighteenth century editor. (Sisson, 1956).[2]

And the danger remains that these brilliant emendations of the past may have become so much a part of our Shakespearean habit that the effort to look again at what was puzzling in Folio or Quarto text may seem at once unnecessary and ungrateful. For

---

[1] 'Shakespeare's Text and the Bibliographical Method', *Studies in Bibliography* VI, Charlottesville, Virginia, 1954, p. 81.
[2] *New Readings*, Vol. I, p. 3.

we see what we expect to see, and the editorial style of the Augustan age is not without its charms; what is clear and elegant stamps itself deeply on the memory. It is taken for granted, for example, following Pope and Johnson, that 'Our poesy is as a gum, which oozes . . .' rather than 'as a Gowne, which vses' (*Timon of Athens*, I i 21); Hanmer's 'spaniel'd me at heels' (*Antony and Cleopatra*, IV xii 21), for the Folio's 'pannelled me at heeles', seems to fit perfectly into the pattern of Shakespearean imagery as modern research has conceived it. It is difficult to envisage—as I shall later argue—that Shakespeare's lines may have more meaning if these and other widely applauded emendations are set aside. Yet, as modern editorial practice increasingly makes clear, there may be a certain profit in the assumption that what is in the original texts is there by Shakespeare's own design; it can sometimes be useful to free ourselves from the eighteenth-century certainties, and take again, as a new and proper starting-point, an *Elizabethan* perplexity. The advice which Heminge and Condell gave to readers of their day may still hold good:

> Reade him, therefore; and againe, and againe: And if then you doe not like him, surely you are in some manifest danger, not to vnderstand him.

The usefulness of maintaining this initial bewilderment I have yet to demonstrate and it may well seem that I exaggerate the advantages of such an approach. But I hope we may agree that, in some cases at least, it is precisely those clues which are left over after all is explained which may be of most value: the passage which is unintelligible may serve as a pointer to the artist's intention. Warburton comments that 'in clearing the obscurity, you frequently discover some latent conceit not unworthy of his genius'; in trying to understand an apparently unimportant detail we may appreciate more finely Shakespeare's meaning and style.

4

It has to be accepted in this kind of investigation that an extreme untidiness is an essential part of the day-to-day procedure: a small and apparently trivial problem may prompt new questions of wider significance; a single fragment of evidence may have several values; only after much persistent niggling does one find the broad paths forward. I have tried however to set out the results in some order, giving importance in the several chapters to different types of evidence and different methods of working. In practice, of course, the various kinds of evidence are not kept separate; linguistic principles are not hammered out in sequence; any lineal order of presentation which is subsequently adopted is necessarily rather artificial. Partly because of this, it seemed useful to have, as a beginning, a short sample chapter, bringing together a few instances which would otherwise have their place in separate sections of the book, so as to illustrate quite simply the range of evidence on which I have drawn; the argument in this chapter is set out more slowly than in the later sections.

I have worked throughout in the belief that in this type of exploration there can be no firm line dividing 'language' and 'literature', but I am very ready to accept that more people will be interested in 'literature'—the language that Shakespeare 'made', than in the general currency of Elizabethan speech and writing—the language that Shakespeare 'found'. I have tried, therefore, in dealing with more purely linguistic questions, as, for example, in Chapter VI on Shakespearean pronunciation and spelling, to set out the argument in a somewhat relaxed way and with the minimum of technicalities: I ask in return that I may be forgiven some ignorance of the techniques and terminology of the present-day literary critic.

It is well perhaps to make clear that in using the pronoun 'we' I rely on the active participation of my readers. So as to keep the exposition as uncluttered as the material will allow, I leave undiscussed and unmentioned a number of meaning factors known to and accepted by the present-day Shakespearean student which happen not to be relevant in proving or disproving whatever 'new' interpretation I am suggesting. When, for instance, I speak of 'the Candied tongue' (*Hamlet*, III ii 65) as 'sugar-candeyed' this does not mean that I reject the 'candid' sense which some editors have noticed as potentially present; in understanding Macbeth's 'Banke and Schoole of time' (*Macbeth*, I vii 6) as 'bank' and 'shoal' I have no wish to exclude from that phrase other powerful image values; in 'guessing' the Elizabethan meaning of the proverb 'Three tailors make a man' I leave it to the reader to notice or not when the bell-ringing sense of the 'nine tailors' began to be heard. Occasionally too my exposition of 'new' Shakespearean senses is implicit rather than explicit: when there is a great deal of meaning to bring out, it seems best to trust to the evidence itself (and to my arrangement of that evidence) to draw attention to some of the finer detail of what I believe to be the Shakespearean design.

I have tried to write as simply as possible and it may perhaps appear in consequence that the pronoun 'I' is over-frequently employed: a passive periphrasis, however, even if grammatically less strident, would seem to claim more authority than can properly belong to the individual student. In statements of method, in bringing forward external evidence from my own collections, and, above all, in seeking the textual origin and testing the linguistic value of my personal intuitions about Shakespearean meaning, the necessary 'I' form is imperfect rather than didactic or prescriptive. What is lacking in the evidence is freely admitted; my interest in the rigour of the game precludes any conscious cheating. From specialists in related fields I ask throughout for more evidence and more information; I am aware also that there must be many accidental and avoidable gaps in my own knowledge which it will need no specialist to point out.

One last caveat: it is not easy to argue about Shakespeare's meaning without being excited by it; one cannot preserve towards language a wholly dispassionate objectivity. But I want the reader to be on his guard against my attempts to persuade ; the principles here set out, however positively, are working tools only; any statements made about the meaning of the single line need to be tested against the larger unit, the scene, the act, the play. In every instance it is for the individual reader to decide what levels of certainty we may reach. I would request only that those who are convinced by some few of the interpretations put forward should ask themselves what evidence they have admitted as 'proof', by what arguments they, in their turn, would seek to convince others who deny the sufficiency of that proof.

CHAPTER II

Illustration of problems and methods

I

I offer in this chapter six sample instances from Shakespeare's
dramatic text where, I suggest, we can in various ways add something to our knowledge of his word-meaning. And in this sample
chapter only, I group together some instances from a single act
of a single play which would, properly speaking, have their
separate places in later sections. The reader will appreciate that it
is not normally convenient to make a play-by-play grouping;
one needs the whole range of Shakespeare's dramatic language
for each particular exploration or experimental foray. Perhaps I
should also make clear that this sample chapter should not be
considered as presenting in miniature the argument of the whole.
It may serve, however, to show the tentativeness of my approach;
about the difficulty of proof and the necessary empiricism of
method I can talk here at greater length than will later be possible.
I can indicate also, but without setting them in any order of
importance, the different assumptions which I shall later try to
justify, in isolation, chapter by chapter, but which require to be
made throughout the whole study.

I shall be emphasising throughout the obvious truth that not all
the *spoken* language of Shakespeare's England gets itself included
in the printed books of that time. It follows from this, I shall
argue, that since the great *New English Dictionary*, in so
far as it relates to the language of the sixteenth and seventeenth
centuries, was compiled in the main from printed sources, we
cannot with safety use the authority of the Dictionary to test
at any point the authenticity of Shakespeare's dramatic text.

This is not to deny that where the speaking-character uses a word or expression of which we do not know the meaning and which has not been found elsewhere, it is always possible that we are dealing with 'ghost' language, not with something that Shakespeare intended to be spoken, but merely the result of a mistake in the copying or printing of some real word in his original draft; the *editor's* task will then consist in trying to discover what the scribe or compositor misread. But for the very limited purposes of this present study I shall try to understand the puzzling words, 'ghost' or not, as if they are genuine and I shall discuss only those words for which I can suggest an explanation. I shall, as a linguist, expect to find, and indeed be pleased to find, an occasional word or phrase in the Shakespearean text, which, on NED's evidence, is not elsewhere recorded. For there is always a chance that this 'unique' Shakespearean expression may be found again, either in literary English, or to use my own research experience, in manuscript local records hitherto unsearched by the lexicographer.

I take as my first example one such quite lucky find in an undated Stratford presentment (Misc. I 160, ?1627), the phrase *arent the wich*, quoted by 'goodie bromlie' when she complains of how she has been abused and slandered by the wife of Anthrim:

> Itm the wife of Anthrim holds or sayth goodie bromlie is an ill looked wooman

(then going on without a break into the direct speech of the complainant)

> an I woold over looke her & herne as I had over looke others and bid me arent the wich & sayde I was a whore & my bastards mayntayne me & bid me get me hone howe ['one who'] wolld brushe the motes forth of my durtie gowne.

> her witnes: patiens ford: prudence wright: & good wiffe asson

'Aroint thee, witch' is twice used by Shakespeare: in *Macbeth* (I iii 6) when the first witch describes how the sailor's wife refused to give her chestnuts:

> Aroynt thee, Witch, the rumpe-fed Ronyon cryes

and in *Lear* (III iv 129) when Edgar, as poor Tom, chants the exorcism of Saint Withold against the nightmare:

> He met the Night-Mare, and her nine-fold;
> Bid her a-light, and her troth-plight,
> And aroynt thee Witch, aroynt thee (Q arint).

The phrase is not elsewhere recorded until it is found, in obvious imitation of Shakespeare, in Scott's novels and other modern writings. And it is perhaps worth making the point, in passing, that if this *aroynt* had occurred once only in Shakespeare's text, it might well have been regarded by later editors as a mistake of scribe or printer. So, for instance, with the *prenzie* Angelo . . . in '*prenzie* gardes' (*Measure for Measure*, III i 94, 97): 'In the present state of our knowledge' writes C. J. Sisson[1] '*prenzie* is meaningless and demands emendation'.

Most of my readers, I believe, will accept as I do, that the three different spellings—*arent* of the Stratford document, and *aroynt*, *arint* of the Shakespearean printed texts—stand for the same word, perhaps in slightly varying pronunciations. It is useful to realise how much we rely on context when we make this judgment. First of all, the forms are not identical in *spelling*: although they have what I shall call the same consonant shape, the vowel or diphthong of the one stressed syllable is in each instance differently spelt, *e*, *oi* or *i*, and such a distinction, to illustrate by modern approximation, could be of the first importance, as with *rater*, *Reuter*, *writer* or *later*, *loiter*, *lighter*. Secondly, we do not know the *pronunciation*, and thirdly we do not know the precise *meaning*. We may feel satisfied, however, that we are dealing with three instances of one word, rather than with three words, because the form in question belongs to the same narrow linguistic context ('aroint thee, witch!') and is used in a very similar dramatic situation. To the significance of the vowel/diphthong variants I

---

[1] *New Readings*, Vol. I, p. 83.

shall return later (p. 213). And in looking for the meaning of the Shakespearean *aroynt* I shall suggest that it may be derived from the Anglo-French *aloyner* (from *à* to + *loin* far); an English verb *aloyn*, with this derivation, is shown by NED in the appropriate sense 'to remove far off' (with three citations from the fourteenth and fifteenth centuries). It is known that an original *l* may change to *r* under certain conditions within the early French language; the same substitution can be heard occasionally in some types of present-day English. I do not want to dwell too long here on a single point, but it is useful perhaps to notice how one detail of discovery (the Stratford *arent*), one detail of procedure, leads on to further questions. If we feel that *arent* is the same word as *aroynt* (because it fits into the same contexts), it is reasonable to ask further, for the same reason, if *aroynt* may not be another form of *aloyn*. And if an awareness of an *r/l* variation within the spoken language helps with the meaning of *aroynt*, the linguistic and dramatic context of the puzzling *prenzie* of *Measure for Measure* must also be re-examined; perhaps this form might represent a pronunciation of *pollency*, of which NED shows two citations, with the sense 'power', in seventeenth-century English (p. 217). This indicates well enough how the various tiny problems branch out and re-connect.

Coming back for a moment to the complaint of 'goodie bromlie' we see further that the *overlook* of the Stratford record, in the sense 'to look upon with the "evil eye"; to bewitch' is first cited by NED from *The Merchant of Venice* (III ii 15) and from *Merry Wives* (v v 87), with the next citation not until 1697. Portia, before Bassanio makes his choice of the caskets, hints to him that her love does not depend on the fortune of his choice:

> Beshrow your eyes,
> They haue ore-lookt me and deuided me. . . .

And Pistol, as 'Hob-goblyn', attacks the mortal Falstaff in Windsor Park:

> Vilde worme, thou wast ore-look'd euen in thy birth.

This does not mean, I think, that Shakespeare is using what was in his time a characteristically Stratford dialect word. Rather it offers another instance of speech-usage insufficiently evidenced in the printed record, and first registered by NED through the accident that it forms part of the text of a much-studied dramatist. So too, *ill-looked* of the Stratford record seems to mean 'having the power to look on with the evil eye' (p. 287), a sense not shown in Shakespeare's writing, or presumably in other literary sources, and hence not included by NED.

To sum up: this first sample, the complaint of 'goodie bromlie', gives a fair idea of the kind of external evidence which I shall be using. Linguistically there will be nothing more difficult, and most of the examples will be a good deal more rewarding. It may perhaps be objected that the instance shows rather the range of our ignorance than the range of our knowledge of the spoken English of Shakespeare's time. But I shall, in general, be concerned to answer questions rather than ask them only. And if the Stratford *arent* tells us nothing of dramatic importance about the speech of the First Witch in *Macbeth*, there are other snippets to be found in the Stratford records of more relevance to Shakespeare's dramatic meaning. Meanwhile the incompleteness of the dictionary material and related collections has been demonstrated and I have suggested that we should not frown in suspicion at the occasional word (or other unit of meaning) which is to be met with in Shakespeare's plays and, apparently, nowhere else; we should be prepared to postulate, although we know that it cannot be wholly true, that Shakespeare himself intended what is in the original text(s).

2

Our second postulate must be that what Shakespeare wrote, he wrote with point; we should be positive that, when he is writing at his best, every word in the text is there to tell. If therefore any particular word seems somehow meagre, muted, inartistic, contributing only an ordinary degree of sense or feeling, the evidence for its meaning should be scrutinised again—both the internal evidence, the evidence within the text, and the external evidence, the information available from other sources. And I take as my second sample the word *trammel* in Macbeth's soliloquy (I vii 3), when, while Duncan is at supper, Macbeth contemplates murder and calculates the reckoning:

> If it were done, when 'tis done, then 'twer well,
> It were done quickly: If th'Assassination
> Could trammell vp the Consequence, and catch
> With his surcease, Successe: that but this blow
> Might be the be all, and the end all. Heere,
> But heere, vpon this Banke and Schoole of time, . . .

It has long been known that a *trammell* in sixteenth- and seventeenth-century England was a fishing or fowling-net, a hobble for a horse or a device for hanging kettles or pots over a fire and it has usually been supposed that Macbeth's image has reference to the first of these. By the assassination of Duncan, Macbeth hopes to entangle as if in a net, and so to prevent, all evil consequence for himself. The *New English Dictionary* cites Macbeth's speech as the first known instance of this figurative sense; the literal sense is well established: a Stratford inventory of 1627, for instance, includes 'an olde draughtnett & an old trammell'. Yet, although in the sequence of Macbeth's images this 'fishing-net' sense may be called forth, as a secondary association, by the words 'catch', 'Banke' and 'Schoole' ('shoal')[1] which follow, such a sense may well strike the reader as insufficiently powerful at this point. Why it seems so can be asked later; if meanwhile we follow up this intuition and turn again to the NED, another sense is there available, 'to bind up (a corpse) within the shroud'. The

---

[1] Not, of course, the only sense of *Schoole*, but the only sense which is relevant to this portion of my argument.

Dictionary shows three instances of this, for the funerals of Queen
Katherine, of King Henry VIII and of Queen Mary:

> 1536 . . . (Funeral Q. Kath.) The Corps must be sered, tramayled,
> leded and chested. 1546-7 . . . (Funeral K. Hen. VIII) Surely bound
> and trammel'd with cords of silk. c. 1558 . . . Whoo [Q. Mary]
> after her Departuer was . . . cered, and tramelled in this Manner.

How would this square with the evidence in the rest of the speech,
the scene, the play? Could it be the sense in Macbeth's mind or
in the mind of dramatist and audience? If in Macbeth's it would
show in him an underlying awareness of the fear which he denies.
He admits that he is afraid of the 'euen-handed Iustice' of this
world and of the universal pity which Duncan's death will
rouse; he wishes to wear 'in their newest glosse' the golden
opinions he has so lately won; he does not yet admit the knowledge
he has of his own nature, his fear that as a murderer he will
'sleepe no more'. But the word 'trammell' would betray in him
an underlying awareness of that 'strange infirmity' which he
shares with all men: it would show how his human fear of mortal
guilt expresses itself in the most primitive and terrible symbolism,
the apparition of his murdered king, untrammelled by the silken
cords that bind the waxen shroud, 'come out on's graue'. He
would know now, before the murder of Duncan, as he is to know
again after the murder of Banquo, that the time has never been

> That when the Braines were out, the man would dye,
> And there an end. . . .

This is to give weight to the fact that it is Macbeth who speaks
the word 'trammell'; those students, on the other hand, who have
come to distrust the exclusive preoccupation with 'character' of
the nineteenth-century critics may prefer to concentrate less on
Macbeth's mind than on the playwright's; they would see in the
'trammell' image a kind of dramatic irony, Shakespeare's fore-
warning of his audience, his shaping hand rather than Macbeth's
latent self-knowledge. It may however be generally agreed that

'to bind within the shroud' is at once more poetic and more precise than the earlier sense accepted. It is useful next to examine the immediate context of the verb in Macbeth's speech and to ask what linguistic factors led to this expectancy of some stronger meaning. We see first that at the beginning of his speech, which opens the scene, Macbeth's language is controlled, 'hooded' as it were, but what the 'it' stands for, the deed he dares not name, he and the audience well know; the compulsion towards it is so strong that, although the noun may not be spoken, the verb 'done' is three times repeated.

> If it were done, when 'tis done, then 'twer well,
> It were done quickly. . . .

And when Macbeth gives to his projected action its plain term—assassination—that which must be its consequence for his kinsman, king and guest, he can only say in other words; the word 'death' he cannot plainly say. Only Lady Macbeth can say this word, as her last word in this scene, and even she speaks of how, for their own purposes, they will, as they must, make lamentation 'Vpon his Death'. The emotion that Macbeth has kept out of his first statement, that he is trying to drive underground, may be expected to present itself in his first image, the first 'charged' verb of the speech and of the scene; between this verb and its hideous subject some extra-grammatical connection may well be looked for. This is admittedly to come upon the solution first and to see the significance of the clues afterwards. And it is also, in this particular instance, to 'psychologise', to allow a character in a play which is, as some will argue, an unreal abstraction, made only out of words—to have levels of thought and consciousness lying below the surface of speech. 'What else does Shakespeare direct us to, in this particular play?' must be my answer; how many times do the characters say that they are afraid to think or see? Lady Macbeth comments immediately after the murder:

> These deeds must not be thought
> After these wayes: so, it will make vs mad.

And Macbeth himself who, at the time of his battle against the Norwegians is described as nothing afeared of what he himself has made 'Strange Images of death' finds soon enough that a 'horrid Image', 'horrible Imaginings' have entered his heart; when he says

> Let not Light see my black and deepe desires:
> The Eye winke at the Hand

it is not only of the light of day, of the eyes of others that he speaks. Whether or not it is accepted that Shakespeare intends the trammel image to show something of the less conscious mind of his created 'character', I hope it may be agreed that the text itself gives evidence that such a meaning of 'trammel' as I have suggested was known to the dramatist and to some of his audience: it is unnecessary to offer additional evidence that the sense continued in currency after 1558, the last date shown by NED, or that Shakespeare came upon the word when, for instance, he was apprenticed to an undertaker. What he writes can serve as sufficient evidence for what he knew. But it should be noted also that I cannot *prove* either Shakespeare's knowledge or his purpose; I can only show that the external dictionary evidence ties in neatly enough with the internal contextual evidence.

3

It will be argued in Chapter III that a knowledge of contemporary proverbial idiom may help at the same time to establish and to interpret Shakespeare's text; accordingly, I take as my third sample a somewhat obvious instance from *Macbeth*, I iii 97, when Ross, bringing to Macbeth the title of Cawdor, describes how Duncan has received the news of his triumphs in battle:

> as thick as Tale
> Can post with post, and euery one did beare
> Thy prayses in his Kingdomes great defence,
> And powr'd them downe before him.

This is usually emended, following Rowe, to 'as thick as hail Came post with post'. 'Can' seems clearly enough to have the meaning 'came'. And to the 'thick as hail' version we are so accustomed, from our schooldays onwards, that *thick as Tale* seems merely comic—only a 'tail' is 'thick' in present-day English—and we fail to notice the strangely hostile flavour of the emended comparison; what comes thick as hail we would like to find shelter against. The position of a subordinate who is more successful than his principal is potentially one of danger; and if the details of Macbeth's victories were known to have come to Duncan 'thick as *hail*', one might argue, facetiously, that Macbeth did well to murder Duncan before Duncan had him disposed of! In Shakespeare's text, of course, there is no word of this. And the authentic 'thick as Tale' meaning 'as fast as the *spoken* word (rather than a sequence of written messages)' would be well within the normal language patterns of this time. *Tale* can mean 'talk' (as in *Romeo and Juliet*, II iv 99, 'Thou desir'st me to stop in my tale against the haire', with the obvious accompanying pun); 'talk' can be *thick* in the sense 'quickly spoken, the words coming in rapid succession' (as in Fuller, 1642, 'Great talkers discharge too thick to take always true aim'), and 'to talk fast' is, proverbially, 'to talk *post*'; Tilley[1] shows two instances (T 61):

> 1630 Some haue the agility to ride Poast, some the facility to runne Poast; some the dexterity to write Post, and some the ability to speake, poast; 1632 'Twere no good manners to speak hastily to a gentlewoman, to talk post (as they say) to his mistress.

To comment briefly on my procedure in this instance: I have looked, but without success, for an Elizabethan *can* spelling with the 'came' sense which this *Macbeth* context seems to require, and I agree, provisionally, that this may well be an instance of necessary emendation. I have not shown the actual Shakespearean phrase 'thick as Tale' in use among Shakespeare's contemporaries,

---

[1] *A Dictionary of the Proverbs in England in the Sixteenth and Seventeenth Centuries*, by M. P. Tilley, Ann Arbor, 1950.

but I claim to have shown that the ingredients out of which such a phrase could have been improvised were readily available. The reader will note my assumption that what was in the written language in 1642, 1630, 1632, could have been heard in the spoken language forty or fifty years earlier. And, lastly, I agree that I have in this detail, if my evidence is accepted, done no more than clear away from the accepted text a slight and unnoticed error. All students are pressed for time and those who are interested in 'literature' rather than 'language', in Shakespeare's art rather than in the general currency of Elizabethan English, may fairly object that the labour involved in this particular instance is hardly worth the gain: I need three pieces of information only to understand a single word in Shakespeare's text and that, too, a word of no dramatic import. And it must, of course, be freely admitted that my method is extravagant; one cannot know in advance which intuitions are most worth following; one can only hold firm to the postulate that every 'full'[1] word in the Shakespearean text has its quota of meaning.

4

I shall suggest in Chapter V some of the ways in which we might better understand the detail of Shakespeare's word-meaning if we were able to share with him that 'small Latine and lesse Greek' which was so important a part of the language context of his time. And I take as my next sample the *Strange Images of death* in this same line of Ross's speech (I iii 97):

The King hath happily receiu'd, Macbeth,
The newes of thy successe: and when he reades
Thy personall Venture in the Rebels fight,

---

[1] See *A New English Grammar* by H. Sweet, Part I, Oxford (1891), 1950. § 58: 'In such a sentence as *the earth is round*, we have no difficulty in recognising *earth* and *round* as ultimate independent sense units' (full words); *the* and *is* are 'form words'.

His Wonders and his Prayses doe contend,
Which should be thine, or his: silenc'd with that,
In viewing o're the rest o'th'selfe-same day,
He findes thee in the stout Norweyan Rankes,
Nothing afeard of what thy selfe didst make
Strange Images of death . . . .

If we had to translate this passage, rather than take the gist of it, we might perhaps be puzzled as to the precise significance of the 'Strange Images': since, it may be asked, a dead or dying soldier is, properly enough, an image of death which might remind the victorious enemy of his own peril, why then should these Norwegian soldiers be called 'Strange Images'; is there any earlier reference to something unusual in the way these men have died. The Captain, we find, has described to Duncan how, when the Norweyan lord began a fresh assault, Macbeth and Banquo 'doubly redoubled stroakes vpon the Foe'. And a line quoted in Withals' Dictionarie[1]—which, as Baldwin makes clear, was the regular grammar school dictionary for memorisation in Shakespeare's time—shows, I suggest, the kind of connection that would exist for Shakespeare and his audience between these 'redoubled stroakes' and the 'Strange Images of death':

Aspera pugna novas varia sub imagine Lœthi, dat formas,
Cruell buffeting giueth new formes of death under a diuers image.

The quoted line, given in Withals' Dictionarie without a reference, is from the Punica of Silius Italicus (Book XVII, l.481), where Scipio is described at the battle of Zama.[2]

---

[1] 1616 ed., p. 289.

[2] Parte alia, ceu sola forent discrimina campo,
qua misceret agens truculentum Scipio Martem,
aspera pugna novas varia sub imagine leti
dat formas. hic ense iacet prostratus adacto;
hic saxo perfracta gemit lacrimabilis ossa;
ast hos, turpe, pavor fusos proiecit in ora;

Elsewhere, as if there were no fighting on the field except where Scipio drove the rout before him in furious warfare, the fierce battle displayed strange and

Other questions which arise—how common was this figure in other Latin authors read in the Elizabethan grammar schools, and whether Shakespeare uses other images found in the *Punica* but not included in Withals' *Dictionarie* are beyond my present range. Baldwin[1] knows 'of but one very feeble parallel to Silius Italicus in Shakespeare, and that in a play of doubtful authorship'.[2]

Whether or not Shakespeare remembered this particular figure from having seen it in Withals' *Dictionarie*, the fact of its quotation there makes clear beyond doubt that such a Latin usage was part of the language background of Shakespeare's contemporaries; knowing this usage we may better understand the meaning of '*Strange* Images of death' as the speaking character intends it, with its reference back to the 'doubly redoubled stroakes' of which the Captaine has told. As Shakespeare intends it and as the reader or hearer perceives it, some additional meaning of the phrase may lie ahead, in the contrast between what Macbeth appears to be and what he is and will be, between the soldier's courage as he looks on those he has slain and the murderer's terror as he sees his imagined victims. For if Macbeth is 'Nothing afeard' of these 'Strange Images', the 'horrid Image' of his dead king is already present in his mind and makes his 'seated Heart' knock at his ribs 'Against the vse of Nature' (I iii 137). And if Macbeth and Banquo have struck down their enemies in battle with extravagant force, Banquo is later to lie safe

> With twenty trenched gashes on his head;
> The least a Death to Nature (III iv 28)

while Macbeth, confronted by his 'horrible shadow', is to become 'quite vnmann'd in folly' (III iv 73).

---

diverse forms of death. One man lies prostrate, pierced by the sword; another whose bones have been shattered by a stone, groans pitifully; some whom fear laid low lie prone in dishonour (*Silius Italicus, Punica*, Loeb Classical Library, with an English translation by J. D. Duff, 1934, Vol. II, p. 475).

[1] *William Shakspere's Small Latine and Lesse Greeke*, by T. W. Baldwin, Univ. of Illinois Press, Urbana, 1944, Vol. II, p. 551.

[2] I *Henry VI*, I ii 133-5; see Malone, 1790, Vol. VI, pp. 16, 17.

Readers who accept the explanation so far offered will allow that the Shakespearean phrase has meaning in two areas of context. I shall suggest that it may have some further significance from the fact that *sleep* is the usual 'image of death' in Elizabethan poetic language; this third and slighter meaning it will be more convenient to mention later (p. 183) when considering some of the connotations of 'sleep' which could have come from classical literature into Elizabethan thought and imagery.

5

These four examples from the first act of *Macbeth* will, I hope, show something of the difficulty of proof and the necessary empiricism of method. For in trying to establish meaning-within-the-text, no two problems are quite the same. And one's way of working is, first of all, intuitive; only afterwards does one analyse how the suggested solution was arrived at, discover the hypotheses—useful this time—that might be useful again. I have supposed that, when Shakespeare is writing at his best, no word in his text is meaningless or muted—put in to fill up a space. And if then we stop to question the meaning of a single word, it may be useful to be so halted: we may otherwise miss some part of the sense of several lines. With every problem the first step is to deduce meaning from the internal evidence—both from the narrower linguistic context, and from the wider dramatic situation. The second stage is to match the alleged Shakespearean usage with similar instances in external sources—perhaps elsewhere in Shakespeare's plays or poems, in other literature of the time, in the spoken language, which will include memorised grammar-school Latin, or in manuscript records. Any 'proving' that I can do will consist in this kind of 'matching'. And what I should like the reader to do is to take the instances slowly, to be conscious of our instinctive preference for the generally emended text or for the more limited meanings to which we may have grown accustomed. It is necessary to give the new evidence time to settle.

The *aroynt* example shows how patchy is the evidence with which we have to work; for the three others, *trammel*, *tale*, *strange*, I have been able to adduce external evidence near enough contemporary. For my fifth sample I take an instance from *Hamlet* where the external evidence is presumptive rather than actual; the point of entry is the word *relative* (II ii 633). Hamlet has seen the player change colour, 'Teares in his eyes' for Hecuba, and asks himself

> What would he doe,
> Had he the Motiue and the Cue for passion
> That I haue? He would drowne the Stage with teares,
> And cleaue the generall eare with horrid speech. . . .

He himself, by contrast, is a 'Rogue and Pesant slaue', who does no more than 'peake Like Iohn a-dreames' and 'can say nothing'. The scene ends with the resolution he has taken:

> Ile haue these Players,
> Play something like the murder of my Father,
> Before mine Vnkle. Ile obserue his lookes,
> Ile tent him to the quicke: If he but blench
> I know my course. The Spirit that I haue seene
> May be the Diuell, and the Diuel hath power
> T'assume a pleasing shape, yea and perhaps
> Out of my Weaknesse, and my Melancholly,
> As he is very potent with such Spirits,
> Abuses me to damne me. Ile haue grounds
> More Relatiue then this: The Play's the thing,
> Wherein Ile catch the Conscience of the King.

'Relative' as used here by Hamlet, is cited by the *New English Dictionary* as the earliest known instance of the sense 'pertinent, relevant'. It seems to me that unless it is part of Hamlet's character to use language imprecisely this gloss is unsatisfactory; there is no question of a gradation of relevance. If the ghost is a true ghost, no one in Hamlet's situation could have grounds more pertinent;

if the ghost is a devil, Hamlet has no grounds at all. Some different meaning of *Relative* seems to be required; 'definitive', 'decisive', 'conclusive' have been suggested. But *relative* does not, at the present time, mean 'offering *decisive* proof'; on the contrary. And although the adjective is commonly used in Shakespeare's time (NED shows it from 1530) there is no evidence that it was ever used to mean 'conclusive'. It is necessary then to ask, in trying to find some other meaning, whether it is possible to break down the word and recompose it; what might the *-ive* suffix mean elsewhere in Shakespeare's writings. In the Forest of Arden Orlando hangs verses on the trees: 'O Rosalind, these Trees shall be my Bookes'. He bids himself

> Run, run Orlando, carue on every Tree,
> The faire, the chaste, and vnexpress*iue* shee.
>
> > (*As You Like It*, III ii 10)

In the Grecian camp outside the walls of Troy Ulysses tells Achilles that his reason for refusing to fight against the Trojans is known:

> 'Tis knowne Achilles, that you are in loue
> With one of Priams daughters.

He counters the affront and amazement of Achilles that his secret is no secret:

> Is that a wonder?
> The prouidence that's in a watchfull State,
> Knowes almost euery graine of Plutoes gold;
> Findes bottom in th' vncomprehens*iue* deepes;
> Keepes place with thought; and almost like the gods,
> Doe thoughts vnuaile in their dumbe cradles. . . .
>
> > (*Troilus and Cressida*, III iii 198)

We can see that Orlando's *unexpressive* means 'inexpressible', Ulysses' *uncomprehensive* means 'incomprehensible, deep beyond all sounding'. Hamlet's *relative* means, I suggest, 'able to be related, having some chance of being believed'. The story that he had seen his father's ghost might well be received with scepticism; only those would believe who themselves could see. Horatio declares, when he has seen the vision:

> I might not this beleeue
> Without the sensible and true auouch
> Of mine owne eyes. (I i 58)

Until he has found 'each word made true and good' his ears are fortified against the sentries' story. And when the ghost appears to Hamlet in her room, the Queen, not seeing, says to her son as the world would say:

> This is the very coynage of your Braine,
> This bodilesse Creation extasie is very cunning in. (III iv 138)

Hamlet hopes for evidence against his uncle which can be seen, which proclaims itself to all:

> I haue heard, that guilty Creatures sitting at a Play,
> Haue by the very cunning of the Scœne,
> Bene strooke so to the soule, that presently
> They haue proclaim'd their Malefactions.
> For Murther, though it haue no tongue, will speake
> With most myraculous Organ. (II ii 623)

If it is agreed that the sense of *relative* here suggested is in accord with the demonstrable pattern of Shakespearean word-formation and that such a sense is here 'in context', what would be the dramatic value of this new meaning? I must make here the rather obvious point that the major characters of Shakespeare's tragedies do not see themselves, and are not seen by others, as static; in Hamlet's character different motivations operate simultaneously; neither hope nor despair predominate. But his wish for public justification would show at this point of the play a hope based on reality, an expectation that he might, in seeking public support against his uncle, gain the throne of Denmark for himself. He is not yet guilty of the death of Polonius; vengeance might yet be justice and no more. In regaining an inner security he might yet establish the stability of his kingdom. We see that this theme of public justification is in the mind of the king also. He explains to Laertes why he cannot proceed against Hamlet:

> The other Motiue,
> Why to a publike count I might not go,
> Is the great loue the generall gender beare him. . . . (IV vii 18)

And Hamlet, on his return from England, seeks private reassurance from Horatio:

> Does it not, thinkst thee, stand me now vpon
> He that hath kil'd my King, and whor'd my Mother,
> Popt in betweene th'election and my hopes,
> Throwne out his Angle for my proper life,
> And with such coozenage; is't not perfect conscience,
> To quit him with this arme ?   (v ii 68)

Even as he dies he asks Horatio to live on, 'report me and my causes right',

> Oh good Horatio, what a wounded name
> (Things standing thus vnknowne) shall liue behind me.
>
> (v ii 356)

To understand *relative* correctly is, I suggest, to accept the reality of Hamlet's ambition for kingship and his hope, however impermanent, of attaining it.

6

It is my purpose in this present chapter to illustrate both the degree of awareness that Shakespeare demands of all his readers, and also the kinds of certainty about his word-meaning which we, as twentieth-century readers, can expect to reach. In rating the probability of the interpretations so far offered I would put *trammel* at the higher end of the bracket; *relative* may seem to deserve a lower placing, since I cannot offer another instance of its use in the sense I suggest, although if the interpretation is correct, we should expect that such instances might be found. I want now, for my sixth and last sample, to give an instance of the invented language of comedy, wherein by the dramatist's precontrivance, a word or phrase is given unique meaning through what will appear on the stage as the momentary improvisation of speaking-character. The dramatist, that is to say, contrives to have us consent that, in a given dramatic situation, a word or phrase shall take on a sense that it has not been known to have before and may never have again. In any example of this kind I suspect that the wit will be a surface ripple only; the dramatist will not entrust to 'new' or nonce-language what is of importance to our under-standing of the persons or action of the play; 'old' language is the only safe kind for the conveying of information. Yet the un-completed jest, the joke that depends on audience-participation, is of value also. By arranging that the wit is not there unless we come halfway to meet it, the dramatist brings us, as it were, into the scene. We agree with the players that the rules of language can sometimes be broken, and in so doing add something of our own to the living quality of the stage dialogue.

In the instance now offered—one tiny splinter of a joke—the speaker compresses into a single phrase some four or five meanings; two of these are new meanings, offered and accepted as if they are genuinely existent; as fanciful extensions of an incomplete pattern they have the stamp of potential reality. I shall digress for a moment to illustrate in terms of modern English what I mean by this last statement. And it may be well to make the point also that I ask throughout this book for the freedom of a certain incon-sistency: we shall need to look at language now in this way, now in that; to isolate artificially first one factor and then another. For the moment I shall suggest that we may regard any given language structure as a series of patterns, all of them incomplete; it is this incompleteness which I am stressing here. So, for instance, the English language, from its earliest origin to the present day, has had a pronoun system, capable, but only partly so, of registering sex distinction: *he* and *she* include in their meaning an indication of sex; *I*, *we* and *you* and *they* do not; *it*, so runs the grammarian's joke, deliberately abstains. Again, the English language of today allows us to say that we have *nowhere* to sit; if however we want to say that we have no time to sit down even for a minute we cannot, as the Russians can, speak of having *nowhen*. Any number of examples of this incompleteness could be given: *do up*, *dress up*, *touch up*, *wash up* all belong to the same formal pattern but the objects to which each can apply are variously limited; substitute *down* for *up* and the range of meaning of each takes at once an unexpected limitation and a new precision. The trained observer, looking at a language from the outside, can see which pieces of pattern are not there; the users of language, those inside the given boundaries, historic or geographic, do not usually feel that their language is defective. We suppose, in fact, that our patterns are endlessly logical, capable of being repeated in any direction, until it may suddenly happen that some verbal Charlie Chaplin, some Touchstone of our number, draws our attention to what we cannot say by himself saying it. So long as he gives us the necessary clue, *nowhere*-ness, the actual, preceding *nowhen*-ness, the invented, we shall laugh and understand; the existence of the first presupposes the possible existence of the second. But when Shakespeare's Touchstone makes this kind of joke, instantaneous perception is not always possible for the non-contemporary. We have to inform ourselves of the language that was actual for dramatist, actor and audience before we can imagine the language that Touchstone, or Shakespeare for him, was in process of inventing. We have to discover what was general before we can appreciate what was unique.

In listening to Shakespeare's Touchstone for one split second, as he speaks a sentence end—'not with bagge and baggage, yet with scrip and scrippage' (*As You Like It*, III ii 171), we expect his exit line to be effective and look therefore for the point of *scrippage*, his invented word, and of *scrip and scrippage*, his last phrase as he leaves the stage. The situation is this: After philosophic discussion with the shepherd Corin on the country *versus* court theme, Touchstone has poured forth mockery on the love-verses found by Rosalind. Celia enters 'with a writing' and reads the verse she has. The text is as follows:

> Celia. How now backe friends: Shepheard, go off a little: go with him sirrah.
> Clowne. Come Shepheard, let vs make an honorable retreit, though not with bagge and baggage, yet with scrip and scrippage.

I consider first the generally available meanings of *scrip* and the senses of Touchstone's invented noun *scrippage* which would obviously derive from these.

1. The clown Touchstone and the shepherd Corin have each their *scrip and scrippage*, the countryman's 'wallet' or satchel and its contents. 2. It is probable also that Touchstone steals forward from his position as a back-friend to possess himself of 'a writing'. His *scrip* then is also 'script', as in Bottom's directions to Quince: 'You were best to call them generally, man by man, according to the scrip' (*Midsummer Night's Dream*, I ii 3). Touchstone's *scrippage* is in this case the love-verse. 3. The 'wallet' and the 'writing' the audience can see, and the third sense of *scrip*, 'a scornful grimace, mock or jeer' could be made no less plain. For this suggested sense there is what I regard as good external evidence. NED cites the noun once only, in a Scottish poem of 1470, but the verb is shown, also in Scottish writings, meaning 'to mock, deride, scoff, jeer' from *c.* 1450 until 1658. (About the propriety of using Scottish meanings to interpret Shakespeare's English I shall be arguing in a later chapter.) If *scrip* is a grimace or a single gibe, *scrippage* would be Touchstone's whole stock-in-trade.

Coming now to the point of this inquiry, meanings 4 and 5, which, I suggest, Touchstone himself invents—tiny and unimportant extensions of the Elizabethan language patterns—I note first that he himself draws attention to the fact that *scrip and scrippage* has meaning in 'opposition'[1] to *bagge and baggage:* 'though not with . . . yet with. . . .' And since *bag* can have in seventeenth-century English the sense of our present-day *sack*, 'dismissal',[2] Touchstone's *scrip* we can well imagine is intended as a diminutive of this, 'dismissal for a time' (often the jester's portion while the business of the play proceeds).

So too 'to go with bag and baggage' was in fact 'to make an honourable retreat'; the phrase is used from the early fifteenth-century to the credit of an army or general. NED shows, for instance,

> 1544 The kynge gave them alle there lyffes and pardynd them to goo with bagge and bagges; 1667 Upon honorable conditions, marching off with Bag and Baggage, Drums beating, Colors flying.

In claiming something less than the full honours, and coining another naive dimunitive, *with scrip and scrippage*, Touchstone adds further to his score.

It has been suggested, then, that Touchstone's *scrip* has four senses: 'wallet', 'writing' and 'scornful jest' are 'old' meanings; 'dismissal for a time' is a new coinage, a momentary improvisation which has not acquired general currency. *Scrippage*, which seems itself to be an invented word, has three senses: 'contents of wallet', 'what is written' and 'mockery', while a third unit of meaning, the phrase *with scrip and scrippage*, also a new formation, has the sense 'with some modicum of honour'.

It may seem that I have spent too long in explaining what is neither very difficult nor very important; I hope, however, that the instance will illustrate some points of my procedure. I assume

---

[1] So, for instance, to explain the technical term 'opposition' through an actual example, a young foreign student, arriving late at a Youth Hostel and creeping after lights-out into the allotted dormitory was puzzled by a whispered interrogative 'Mile?', which became comprehensible only by 'opposition', when, after a pause, the questioner continued 'Or femile?'

[2] See *Oxford Dictionary of English Proverbs*. The idiom 'to give someone the bag' with the sense 'dismiss' is first registered in a sermon of 1629.

that there can be an overlap of meaning units and that the non-contemporary who is trying to understand the meaning of Shakespeare's dramatic text in terms of such an overlap may count on the actor's having used all resources of intonation, pause and pantomine to emphasise first one sense and then another. It seems to me that I have 'proved' as far as proof is possible the new meanings which I suggest; I cannot, that is to say, allow for the existence in Shakespeare's texts of 'old' jokes or word-play only; there will be in the dramatic dialogue momentary mutations, both comic and non-comic, which, in the written record at least, are not repeated. As for the number of meanings that can be picked up from the single word or phrase, that is a matter for the individual reader or 'auditor'. The commentator can only demonstrate what senses might be available. Those of my readers who think I demonstrate too many are invited to grade my suggestions in order of probability and take the number they prefer. But I hope that they will not for the present make a general rule as to the optimum Shakespearean number for the average Shakespearean audience.

CHAPTER III

Proverb and proverb-idiom

The previous chapter dealt with sample instances and I come now to the various areas of reconnaissance. The next four chapters emphasise the obvious truth that a dramatic text is primarily something spoken and something heard. The value of approaching Shakespeare's text as something spoken—in accepting, that is to say, that the identity of his words may lie in their sound rather than in their spelling—will be discussed in Chapter VI; I want meanwhile to concentrate attention on the dramatic dialogue as something heard—'conceived in the mind for an actor's voice and published to the world on an actor's lips'[1]—in which dramatist and speaking-character could count on their audience to hear in full what was spoken only in part. The material to be examined here falls readily into three quite separate sections: proverb and proverb-idiom in Shakespeare's language, the vocabulary of the sex joke as Shakespeare uses it, and the Latin meanings to be heard in Shakespeare's English words. I do not of course suggest that these brief headings would suffice for a full investigation into the aural aspects of Shakespeare's language, but I have found them useful for my sample explorations.

To students of Shakespeare's language trying to discover the meaning of some of those words and phrases within the plays which are as yet unexplained, Shakespeare's use of proverb and proverb-idiom offers an area of investigation of special interest, where the validity of our methods is most directly challenged. From a close analysis of what Shakespeare has written we have

---

[1] 'Shakespeare and Elizabethan English' by G. D. Willcock, *Shakespeare Survey* 7, 1954, p. 12.

to find a way of entering into the particular kind of proverb-games which characterised the speech community in which he lived. And the key, it seems, will consist in a disciplined imagination: specialised knowledge and linguistic fantasy are equally necessary. With the sober ant-like industry of the professional scholar we have to assemble what external evidence is available to us; with the grasshopper swiftness of the crossword puzzle addict (as well as the relaxed alertness of the confidence trickster) we have to imagine, to construct, a good deal of the evidence that we can never hope to find. The practical difficulties are formidable: we are attempting, by reference to a demonstrably insufficient amount of written English, to recognise proverb quotation and allusion within a society which is, in material objects and mental furniture, in its reality and its metaphor, very different from our own. And a further obstacle comes from the fact that the ordinary speaker who applies a proverb, in Shakespeare's day as in any other, is likely to attempt, in some minor way, a kind of literary art; he will only too seldom quote the proverb in full and use it 'straight'. He may re-arrange or re-word, he may deliberately extend or limit the usual range of meaning, he may try to give a new turn to an old joke. The more wittily the speaker can apply what he has borrowed from the common stock, the less easy it will be to discover what was in the common stock. Obviously also, Shakespeare's characters are no ordinary speakers: theirs is not the spoken language of actuality; we can expect in their proverb usage an economy, speed and compression of an unusual kind.

It may be agreed at once that complete understanding of the *spoken* idiom of any past age is impossible of attainment, even if every scrap of writing had survived and been searched through. For we know from present-day experience (and excluding from consideration the more obvious linguistic taboos) that the English idiom which finds its way into writing and into print is something less than the whole of the spoken language. One is never too old to hear a 'new' catch phrase or proverb fragment of an

earlier generation. A Staffordshire grandmother, for instance, sees
to the upbringing of 'me daughter's misfortune'; a Shropshire
woman, as an explanation of an adult's secretiveness and suspicion,
uses the gentler phrase 'She came down the rainbow'. Each of
these I have heard on one occasion only and I assume, perhaps
wrongly, that neither idiom is widely current.[1] But I suppose, too,
that *hearing* them, for the first time, in genuine use, an observer
could gloss them correctly enough without the help of any
accompanying situation. The kind of voice, the tone of voice,
would, as it were, supply a context. Where the Shakespearean
proverb-idiom is concerned, we are cut off from this immediacy
of presentation; in trying to imagine the kind of voice, the tone
of voice, we must look for direction to the tiniest contextual
indications. *Seeing* my sample 'new' idioms, in single instance,
in some printed text of a past age, it would be possible to manage,
I think, with no more situation than I have supplied: for the first
we should require enough to make the misfortune a person and to
show the sex of the one who is deemed unlucky; for the second
we need only enough to imply some permanent disadvantage.[2]

The 'misfortune' idiom, it will be seen, is likely to be accompanied by the linguistic clues which are necessary for its understanding; for 'down the rainbow', should it happen to be recorded
once only, in isolation, the hearer has a one-in-three chance of
postulating a correct definition. Neither idiom, it may be
supposed, would appear to the outsider as completely 'arbitrary';
from the given form, from the literal meaning of the given
words, there is a possibility of guessing the range of appropriateness of the whole.

It is not easy in practice to draw a hard and fast line between
those proverb-idioms which are non-arbitrary, which carry

---

[1] The first is registered by NED from nineteenth-century dialect (1801-81);
the second I have not come upon in the usual proverb dictionaries.

[2] Sufficient, that is to say, to eliminate two linguistic possibilities, first that
the subject has 'a heart of gold', such gold as is found at the rainbow's end, and
second, that the subject, having been 'up in the clouds' has just 'come down to
earth', has suffered some temporary disappointment.

within themselves sufficient linguistic clues, and those which have meaning only because one happens to live in a society which knows their secret. In theory, however, the distinction can be made and some proverbs belong clearly on this or that side of the dividing line. 'A stitch in time saves nine' is non-arbitrary; it is quite clear why it means what it means. So too with the proverb 'to sow beans in the wind'; it is no great disadvantage if such a proverb is registered once only (c 1579); knowing the literal meaning of the words we are likely, without much context, to deduce that it means 'to labour in vain'. Similarly those who have ever worked a pump handle will know the sense of 'the cow with the iron tail' (cited by the *Oxford Dictionary of English Proverbs* once only, in 1896), although 'cow' is admittedly something of a false clue, so that it might be necessary to have the text dated before the era of milk from slot-machines. In the arbitrary group could be classed such phrases as 'dog in the manger', 'dead as a door-nail'; it is worth noting also that while the meaning of the first rests on a knowledge of fable which is still current, the 'dead as a door-nail' phrase belongs to the group about which we know 'how' but not 'why'; present-day society remembers the kind of situation for which the comparison is appropriate without remembering why it was first considered so. Among the semi-arbitrary proverbs of Shakespeare's time we might place 'to water one's plants' which has the sense 'to shed *tears*' and 'to dine with Duke Humphrey' which is 'to go *without* one's dinner'.[1] 'The Welsh ambassador' meaning 'the cuckoo'[2] and 'to fell oaks' for 'to be seasick'[3] seem to me wholly arbitrary.

A few further points should perhaps be made before we come to the end of these preliminary exercises. The non-arbitrary proverb may remain meaningful even if it is cut in half; the positive value of 'A stitch in time' proclaims itself and it would be easy enough for the outsider to understand the negative capabilities

---

[1] Tilley, P 391, D 637.   [2] Tilley, A 233.
[3] Withals' *Dictionarie* (1616 ed.), p. 51.

of 'Too many cooks' or to appreciate the qualities common to
'bachelors' wives and old maids' children'; for the Russian
proverb 'When with the wolves' it would be possible to invent
an ending not unlike 'howl like the wolves'. In other instances
the proverb fragment might be capable of several implications.
Only the insider would know that whereas 'While the sun shines'
gives the command 'Make hay', 'While the grass grows' deprec-
ates the fact that 'the silly horse starves'; the outsider, it has been
pointed out, might well suppose that 'The rolling stone' gets its
corners rubbed off. In trying then to invent a beginning or
an end for the truncated Shakespearean proverb, we must be
ready to let the cat jump in several directions. It will be apparent
also that a slight difference between the wording of an earlier
proverb-idiom and the wording as we know it today may present
a very great obstacle to our understanding. As has been shown
earlier (p. 37), 'to be given the bag' in seventeenth-century
England would be 'to get the sack' at the present time. Enough
instances are on record to make clear the meaning of the earlier
form; otherwise, I must admit, I should have found it very
difficult to reason backwards to invent it. For it seems that to change
one's language habits by a small fraction requires a more painful
effort than to adjust to something quite new; it needs great
dexterity to give a *slight* shake to the kaleidoscope. In other
instances the apparently slight difference in form between the
Elizabethan proverb and our own may conceal a great difference
in meaning. The merit of 'helping lame dogs over a stile' is
readily conceded by a nation of dog-lovers; Withals' *Dictionarie*
cites the English proverb 'To helpe a dogge ouer a stile' with the
gloss 'spoken of helpe where is no neede' and the Latin translation
'Cani navare operam' (sic)[1]. And it seems very possible that the
lame dog came in as a lame excuse.[2]

My last suggestion is that, if we have to deduce the meaning of

---

[1] 1616 ed. p. 62.
[2] Tilley, D 479, quotes from Thomas Draxe, 1616. 'He helpeth a lame dogge
ouer a stile' under the heading 'Excuse'.

an Elizabethan proverb from only one or two examples of its use, we must be careful not to generalise too firmly about the kind of situation to which the proverb is applicable. A speaker or writer may take pleasure in using current idiom in a quite unusual manner; one proverb may serve as the foundation of a number of quite different images. The 'fire in the flint',[1] for instance, does not for Shakespeare represent one thing only: the flint may be a symbol of the chastity of Lucrece:

> As from this cold flint I enforst this fire,
> So Lvcrece must I force to my desire. (*Lucrece*, l. 181)

of the calmness of Brutus' temperament:

> O Cassius, you are yoaked with a Lambe
> That carries Anger, as the Flint beares fire
> Who much inforced, shewes a hastie Sparke,
> And straite is cold agen. (*Julius Caesar*, IV iii 111)

of the mechanical skill of the mercenary artist:

> the fire i'th' Flint
> Shewes not, till it be strooke.... (*Timon of Athens*, I i 22)

twice it represents 'boneheadedness'—which is perhaps the nearest to the 'normal' Elizabethan meaning, as when a clown is commended for his wit

> a good luster of conceit in a turph of Earth, Fire enough for a Flint, Pearle enough for a Swine.... (*Love's Labour's Lost*, IV ii 90)

and when the foolish Ajax is dispraised

> bites his lip with a politique regard, as who should say, there were wit in his head and twoo'd out; and so there is: but it lyes as coldly in him, as fire in a flint, which will not shew without knocking.
> (*Troilus and Cressida*, III iii 257)

---

[1] The exact form of the proverb from which Shakespeare quotes is not on record. Tilley cites 'In the coldest flint there is hot fire' (F 371) and 'Out of two flints smitten together there comes out fire' (F 374).

2

I come now to a consideration of some of the proverbs in Shakespeare's text which, as far as I know, need still to be recognised and explained. No reader who has participated in the problems of the preceding section will expect me to advocate any fixed method of approach; we have to meet the difficulties as they come, to improvise, to cast about. I would suggest only that we must be alert for the briefest reference to proverb usage within the dramatic dialogue. The smallest splinter may be a sharply pointed 'quotation' within the charged language of an Elizabethan playwright. My first ten or so instances are taken from the comic dialogue of the plays, and I shall hope to indicate through these less important examples how the non-contemporary may recognise and understand the wit and humour which Shakespeare has intended: after some consideration as to the amount of evidence that may reasonably be required I proceed in later sections to instances of more dramatic significance.

That the written record of the Elizabethan language is incomplete we shall be often enough reminded. Sometimes, for instance, in the language of the plays we come upon an allusion to incident or story—as in the 'dog in the manger' type of reference—some fifty years or so before we get the clue to the background 'fable' or narrative which the speakers take for granted. The verb *sauce* is used, meaning 'to overcharge', in *Merry Wives* (IV iii 11) when the Host of The Garter, asked to provide three horses for hire, agrees to do so but with this private resolve:

> They shall haue my horses, but Ile make them pay: Ile sauce them
> . . . they must come off, Ile sawce them, come.

Those who resent and yet must needs obey repeat over and over the private threats with which they ease their anger. The host's repetition sufficiently glosses this unfamiliar sauce: 'Ile make them pay . . . they must come off', for *come off* in seventeenth-century

English is also 'to pay'. But if we can know well enough *what* the verb means, we lose the richness of *how* it means it; the metaphor has no sparkle. A sharp comment of a Warwickshire man (churchwarden of Solihull, 1666) presents the proverb in fuller form. The warden has to arrange for the cutting of some timber for the church use and is trying to make a good bargain, I think perhaps by using 'non-union' labour. First he gets an estimate from the 'sawyers' and pays fourpence for the expedition's expenses:

> Thomas Palmer & my selfe went before to vew the timber & caused sawers to looke on it   0-0-4

The record continues:

> Another time I took 2 Carpenters to looke on it and to saw it & I found ye sauce worse then the meat   0-0-8

It is worth noting that such a comment, in isolation, would be puzzling to a later reader; the words of Shakespeare's host provide us with a gloss: one does not expect to pay more for the sauce than for the meat. So the wardens expect to pay less to the carpenters than to the professional woodcutters. And one wonders here if Thomas Palmer and his companion found solace for their chagrin at being thus overcharged in the deliberate 'sawers'/'sauce' pun. It is also of some interest to observe how proverbs come and go in the language. Although there is not, I think, an equivalent phrase for this in present-day English,[1] equivalent practices survive: an up-and-coming café advertises very reasonably priced meat dishes, but the accompanying vegetables, as the customer discovers too late, cost more than the main dish. Shakespeare's host may have known this type of trade trick.

The Solihull wardens in the incident quoted lost fourpence;

---

[1] Literary English contains the proverb in shortened form; NED: *Sauce sb.* 3c. *to pay sauce*, *to cost* (a person) *sauce* 1678-1718; Tilley: S 101 *to pay sauce worth* 1624, 1666.

in Madeley, Staffordshire, 1708, a much larger sum, £6 'and upwards', is in question. The record begins

> The Accts of George Perry . . . and Hugh Broomhall . . . were passed but lost . . . The Balance . . . (viz.) what was due to the Parish not known.

The writer continues with the indignant comment 'A very pritty Character for three sleeves'. The 'three sleeves' fragment is somewhat puzzling, and I wondered at first if it might be some early form of rhyming slang for 'thieves'; later I realised that, although it does imply thieving, the thieving is originally that of a tailor stealing some of his client's material:

> For it is a common prouerbe throughout all the towne,
> The Taylor he must cut three sleeues for euery womans gowne
> (1612).[1]

Macbeth's porter grants admission, at Hell Gate, to an English Taylor come hither, for stealing out of a French Hose (II iii 15), and a similar sleeve reference is made, less explicitly, in *Taming of the Shrew* (IV iii 142). Petruchio attacks the tailor who has made Kate's gown for the outrageous fashion of it

> Oh mercie God, what masking stuffe is heere?
> Whats this? a sleeue? 'tis like [a] demi cannon,
> What, vp and downe caru'd like an apple Tart?   (IV iii 89)

The tailor complains that he has made the gown as the servant Grumio gave order and Grumio grudgingly admits, piece by piece, the instructions he gave: 'I confesse *two* sleeues'. Here again, I suggest, the whole of the proverb is implied in this single-word quotation from it. Petruchio complains that the tailor is incompetent; Grumio hints that all tailors, given the chance, are something worse. The tiny joke here is one of many, so that, if we are not alerted to it, we have no sense that we are missing some intended effect. And this may perhaps prompt the question:

---

[1] Tilley: T 18.

how then can the interpreter claim to know that such an effect is intended? Have we not at this point moved away from that reality of the printed text on which we have taken so firm a stand? Does not the joke here suggested depend on the creativeness of the actor, in that it is Grumio, and not Shakespeare, who will make the point that 'two' means 'But not three'. To this kind of objection there is, I think, a proper linguistic answer: the present-day script-writer who uses the phrase 'Two cheers!' can be held to have sufficiently directed his actor to the emphasis and intonation required for the word 'two'. Once admit the general currency of the 'three' idiom, and the intended implication of the 'two' variant must be conceded.

In this particular Shakespearean instance the danger is that we may not recognise the whole of the original proverb in the slyly presented snippet. Where, on the other hand, it is made quite clear from the construction of the dialogue that the speaker has scored a palpable hit, the task of the commentator is easier. In asking what point is intended we are led to the proverb to which allusion is made. So in 2 *Henry IV* (ii iv 250), when Pistol is turned out of the tavern and Falstaff protests how valorously he has attacked him, Doll Tearsheet counters his boasting with a mixture of acquiescent flattery and pitying appraisal:

> Dol. . . . alas, poore Ape, how thou sweat'st . . . Thou art as valorous as Hector of Troy . . . tenne times better then the nine Worthies . . .
> Falstaffe. . . . I will tosse the Rogue in a Blanket.
> Dol. Doe, if thou dar'st for thy heart . . .
> Falstaffe. . . . A Rascall, bragging Slaue: the Rogue fled from me like Quick-siluer.
> Dol. And thou followd'st him like a Church . . . when wilt thou leaue fighting . . . and begin to patch vp thine old Body for Heauen?

Tilley's *Dictionary* shows the proverb 'Church work goes on slowly' in seventeenth-century English; the first recorded instance is of 1629: 'If the Overseers looke not well to the buseness, too

many will make Church-worke of it; for such loytering is now
fallen into a Prouerbe'. The term 'church work' here would
include the various tasks allocated to the parishioners by the
constables and overseers, such as road-mending, repairing bridges,
etc. Obviously such collective unpaid labour of stated duration
would be done without undue energy or haste.

This instance illustrates once more how a proverb will take root
in the spoken language before it finds a place in the printed
collections. And we shall not be surprised therefore if the single
word in Shakespeare's text seems to invite us to recognise quotation from a proverb which is only later recorded in full. Ray's
collection of 1678 shows the proverb 'I will not make my
dishclout my tablecloth'.[1] Juliet's Nurse advocates Paris' cause
with the words:

> I thinke it best you married with the Countie,
> O hee's a Louely Gentleman:
> Romeos a dish-clout to him. . . .   (*Romeo and Juliet*, III v 221)

Sometimes, too, it may be necessary to go back to an earlier
source for the explanation of a joke that Shakespeare offers
unintroduced, unelaborated, in the full confidence that his
audience will know its significance. Falstaff, in a mood of re-
pentance, laments to Bardolf

> And ['An'] I haue not forgotten what the in-side of a Church is
> made of, I am a Pepper-Corne, a Brewers Horse . . . .
>
> (1 *Henry IV*, III iii 10)

Why the *Brewers Horse* should be held in such contempt by
Falstaff is shown in Heywood's epigram (1562):[2]

> The butler and the beere horse both be like one.
> They drawe beere both: that is true to bide one.
> Bothe drawe beere in deede, but yet they differ Ione:
> The butler drawth and drinkth beere, the horse drinkth none.

---

[1] Tilley, D 380.
[2] *Proverbs and Epigrams* of John Heywood, 1562 (Spenser Society, 1867, p. 178).

This epigram, it seems, is an expansion of some briefer riddle or comparison; it shows the content rather than the form of current idiom. Later proverb usage shows the brewer's horse smiling, presumably in foolish contentment[1]—'He smiles like a brewer's horse' (1659)—and for this proverb also another of Heywood's epigrams suggests an earlier currency:

> A Tilt horse, *alias* a beere horse to bee,
> Which wouldst thou bee? a beere horse I say to thee.
> When the horse is seene cheerely to drawe the beere
> He is so praysed, that he may be proude to heere. [2]

3

Elsewhere in Shakespeare's comic dialogue the joke may be recognisable only if we know it already. So with the following passage from *Twelfth Night* (IV ii 40) when the clown, in the person of Sir Topas, the curate, visits the imprisoned Malvolio. Malvolio begs him to 'goe to my Ladie . . . do not thinke I am mad: they haue layde mee heere in hideous darknesse' and Sir Topas questions him

> sayst thou that house is darke?
> Malvolio.   As hell sir Topas.
> Clowne.   Why it hath bay Windowes transparant as baricadoes, and the cleere stores toward the South north, are as lustrous as Ebony: and yet complainest thou of obstruction?

The *bay Windowes* reference may well seem to us in the same vein of simple nonsense as the 'clerestories toward the south north'. But it is also possible that, to Shakespeare's contemporaries, just as 'sauce' might mean 'charge too much' and 'three sleeves' might

---

[1] As earlier commentators have pointed out, 'malt-horse' was a common term of reproach in Shakespeare's time; Dover Wilson notes that the 'brewer's horse' typifies stupidity in the extreme, since horses past other service were sold to brewers as dray-horses. See also Furness Variorum.

[2] Heywood, Spenser Society, p. 178

mean 'stealing', so *'bay* windows' could suggest 'imprisonment'. Again the joke is found in John Heywood's epigrams (1562):[1]

> All Newgate wyndowes bay windowes they bee.
> All lookers out there stand at bay we see.

We may need to know the current proverb so as to recognise some deliberate variation of its meaning or its form. In *Winter's Tale* (IV iii 99) Autolycus tells the clown how he has been robbed by a certain fellow ('some call him Autolicus'):

> I knew him once a seruant of the Prince: I cannot tell good sir, for which of his Vertues it was, but hee was certainely Whipt out of the Court

and the clown answers in the same vein of paradox

> His vices you would say: there's no vertue whipt out of the Court: they cherish it to make it stay there; and yet it will no more but abide.

His word *abide* is intended, I suggest, to echo the proverb 'Things well fitted abide' (first recorded 1640),[2] implying that if Virtue felt herself at home she would remain at court. But by adding the 'no more but' qualification, the clown has given 'abide' a second sense, quite opposed to that in the proverb, namely 'to stay only for a moment, to pause before going on'.[3]

The Elizabethans knew the proverb 'A pleasant prey enticeth many a thief' and Shakespeare uses it in *Venus and Adonis*: 'Rich prayes make true men theeues' (l. 724). A variant form, 'A fair booty makes many a thief' (not registered in Tilley's collection, but noted by Fuller, 1732)[4] may also have been current in Elizabethan times and may underlie Falstaff's word-play on *thieves of the day's beauty*. He asks the prince if, when he becomes king, those who take purses by night may not have finer names:

---

[1] Heywood, Spenser Society, p. 204.   [2] Tilley: T 207. 1640 Herbert.
[3] NED: *abide*, 1. To wait. *Obs.*, 1634 last cit.; 2. To wait before proceeding further . . . *Obs.*, 1535 last cit.
[4] *Gnomologia*, by Thomas Fuller, p. 4, No. 86.

> Marry then, sweet Wagge, when thou art King, let not vs that are
> Squires of the Nights bodie, bee call'd Theeues of the Dayes beautie.
> Let vs be Dianaes Forresters, Gentlemen of the Shade, Minions of
> the Moone. . . .   (1 *Henry IV*, I ii 28)

'Beauty' and 'booty' are, no doubt, near-synonyms for Falstaff,
and Kökeritz concedes the possibility of such a pun in the pronunciation of Shakespeare's time.[1]

4

Difficulties of interpretation sometimes arise because those
inside the speech community take pleasure in brevity and economy; what might serve as clues for the outsider will have been
trimmed away. To find written evidence of the earlier stages of
such a proverb joke may well be impossible; if, on the other hand,
we regard the given phrase—in its oblique, compressed, final
form—as spoken, not written, language, we may be able to guess
at how the jigsaw puzzle once fitted together. To look first at a
proverb-idiom unpointed in Shakespearean usage: the phrase
'dead as a door nail', recorded some hundred years before Shakespeare's time seems, in his day[2] as in ours, no more than a formal
unit of known contextual appropriateness. At what period of the
language, it may then be asked, did the idiom spring into life;
when, that is, did the community know at once why a door-nail
(rather than, for instance, a coffin-nail) should serve to intensify
the idea of deadness? The answer might well be, when one word,
in general use, happened to signify both concepts; the missing
piece of this jigsaw may be the word *charnel*. As a 'nail' it was
exclusively a door-nail in the sense of a hook or hinge on which
a door hangs; as a 'burial-place, charnel-house' it held more of
death than the single grave. If this conjecture is right, I hope that

---

[1] *Shakespeare's Pronunciation*, p. 70.

[2] 2 *Henry IV*, v iii 127: What, is the old King dead? As naile in doore. 2 *Henry VI*, IV x 43: if I doe not leaue you all as dead as a doore naile.

some scrap of written evidence may one day be found: perhaps a pun on 'charnel' or even a fragment of 'char-nail/door-nail' juggling in an early text. The evidence so far available shows only *ded as a dorenail* current from *c.* 1350, with the joke apparently over.[1] Whether or not my postulate is accepted, the instance will serve to show the kind of evidence with which we may have to work in trying to understand the clipped colloquialism. Present-day speech can offer examples also. Textile workers knew of 'fag-ends'[2] before they smoked 'fags'. Those who know the related sense 'fag-end of a rope' and have as children drawn lots by 'taking a bunch' cannot but derive the dialectal *Fogger*, 'My turn first' from the drawing of lots by each seizing a loop of the bunched rope, priority being given to the first to claim possession of an end as the rope is pulled out. Had Johnson been accomplished at skipping rope (my references are from N. Staffs.) I am tempted to think that such an etymology might by now be traditional.

When Johnson envied the finery of his neighbours his mother would tell him that 'Brag was a good dog, but Holdfast was a better' (*Rambler*, 197, 3). Pistol, off to the wars, uses a moiety of this proverb when counselling his wife, the tavern hostess, not to give credit (*Henry V*, II iii 54): 'The world ['word'] is, Pitch and pay: trust none: for Oathes are Strawes, mens Faiths

---

[1] ODEP shows the variant forms Dead (Deaf, Dumb) as a door-nail (door-tree), and glosses door-nail as 'A beam used for fastening the door. *Cf* OE. 'næʒl' The first citation of the proverb is *c.* 1350, *ded as dorenail*. NED shows *charnel*, 'burial place', from 1377 and *charnel*, 'hinge', from *c.* 1470. If a *charnel* pun precedes the proverbial phrase, as I suggest, it would be necessary to suppose both senses of *charnel* current in speech before these dates.

I happen to have come upon the two senses of *charnel* side by side in sixteenth-century parish accounts: the wardens of Rye, Sussex, for instance, in 1517 paid 'for a kay and the mendyng off a loke to the Charnell house'; later years show the entries 'for a paire of charnells for the said dore' (1525), 'for vi paier of Charnells for Said pew dores' (1552). I should find it difficult to believe that no pun on charnel was ever made at parish meetings of this time, even if the origin of the door-nail simile had by then been long forgotten.

[2] NED: *Fag-end*, 'The last part of a piece of cloth . . . Of a rope: An untwisted end'. I suggest that 'fag' would come to be used for the cigarette when once the metaphorical 'fag-end' had been applied to the cigarette-end. The phrase 'fag-ends of cigars' is first cited by NED in 1853.

are Wafer-Cakes, and hold-fast is the onely Dogge...' It seems to me that the inception of the proverb is the interconnection through the word *dog*, of a series of puns. *Brag* is a large nail; *dog*, a mechanical device for gripping or holding—a catch, lever, spike, etc., and *holdfast*, a staple, hook, clamp or bolt. For Johnson the proverb is a formal unit only; why Brag ever seemed doubly apt as the name of a ('brisk, lively') dog has been forgotten; to the eighteenth-century editor Pistol's 'holdfast' makes a single point. For Shakespeare and his audience, I suggest, the proverb is still doubly-significant in its separate parts so that Pistol can chip off and apply just the bit he wants. In a momentary interchange with the clown, Sir Andrew Aguecheek aims another fragment, 'I am dogge at a Catch' (*Twelfth Night*, II iii 64), picked up and re-turned at once in the complementary answer 'Byrlady sir, and some dogs will catch well'. *Dog-bolt*, applied to a man as a term of contempt,[1] and *bolt*, 'pimp, pander' come, no doubt, within the same semantic range. Once more the chief card of the commentator is the coherence of the evidence.

5

'Brag is a good dog but Holdfast is a better' offers a three-pun series firmly fixed in proverb form. I want next to suggest that a similarly formed double pun may be the centre pattern of the whole complex of meaning which was there for Shakespeare's contemporaries in Hamlet's deliberately puzzling phrase *know a Hawk from a Handsaw*, as he sums up his situation for Rosen-crantz and Guildenstern (*Hamlet*, II ii 397):

> You are welcome: but my Vnckle Father, and Aunt Mother are deceiu'd.
> Guildensterne.   In what my deere Lord?
> Hamlet.   I am but mad North, North-west: when the Winde is Southerly, I know a Hawke from a Handsaw.

---

[1] Cf NED's suggestion for *Dog-bolt* 2 : 'Perh. orig. = Mere tool to be put to any use.'

'Handsaw' is generally explained as a corruption of 'hernshaw' (= heron) so that Hamlet is hinting to his pretended friends that he can distinguish the bird of prey from its victim; he can recognise the danger in their approach. I shall try to show that a number of other implications are more in context and that both the 'hawk' and (hand) 'sore' of the falconer and the 'hawk' and 'handsaw', the workman's tools, are for Shakespeare and his audience language counters of considerable value. (The falconer's 'sore' is 'a hawk of the first year that has not moulted and still has its red plumage'.)

Looking first at Hamlet's 'meaning' as it is directed to and understood by those who hear him on the stage, we see that some of the imagery is that of falconry and some of the argument is concerned with the difference between the fully grown and the not yet grown: Hamlet comments also on the world's customary inability to distinguish that which has merit from that which has not. He first asks Rosencrantz and Guildenstern 'were you not sent for?' and so that their secrecy to the King and Queen may 'moult no feather' he himself informs them why they have been asked to come. They tell him of the approach of the players, the tragedians of the city in whom he took such delight, and who have now been obliged, because of their waning popularity, to go out as a travelling company. The overwhelming success of the boy-actors, 'an ayrie of Children, little Yases', Hamlet judges

> is not strange: for mine Vnckle is King of Denmarke, and those that would make mowes at him while my Father liued; giue twenty, forty, an hundred Ducates a peece, for his picture in Little. There is something in this more then Naturall, if Philosophie could finde it out.

As evidence of his own sanity he offers the statement that he can tell a hawk fully grown from one which is not. And Polonius who enters just at this point seems in his judgment a perfect example to the discerning eye of infancy in age, so that he whispers to Rosencrantz and Guildenstern:

that great Baby you see there, is not yet out of his swathing clouts implying, as Rosencrantz understands and glosses, that 'an old man is twice a childe'.

Thus far the internal evidence. External sources show a proverb phrase 'not to know a buzzard from a hawk' (1600).[1] There is some evidence also of the figurative use of soar-hawk in early seventeenth-century literature: 'The first yeere of her trade she [the Whore] is an eyesse, . . . the second a soare'.[2] I think, then, it may be fairly argued that 'To know a hawk from a sore', either as a new coinage or an old proverb, would present no difficulty to a Shakespearean audience; to the falconers of his day and later, the difference between a hawk and a sore would be of practical import. Symon Latham's *Falconry* (1615) gives the definition 'Sore-hawke, is from the first taking of her from the eiry, till shee haue mewed her feathers'; George Turberville (1611) shows that 'Thirdly they are called sore Hawkes, from the end of August, to the last of September, October and November. . . . those first plumes that they haue, when they forsake the Eyrie, those do they keepe one whole yeere before they cast or mew them, and that kind of feather, is called Sore-feather.'[3]

---

[1] Tilley: H 226. One instance cited.

[2] NED: *sore sb.*[2] 2. *Falconry. a* 1613, Overbury, *Characters, Whore*. Overbury uses the imagery of hawking in a long description of stages of a whore's trade: 'The first yeare of her trade she is an Eyesse, scratches and cries to draw on more affection: the second Soare: the third a Ramage whoore: the fourth and fift, shees an intermewer, preyes for her selfe and ruffles all she reaches; from thence to ten. . . .' I take this quotation from *The Overburian Characters*, ed. by W. J. Paylor (Percy Reprints XIII), Oxford, 1936, p. 28.

[3] *The Booke of Falconrie*, 1611, p. 31.

J. S. Sebright (*Observations upon Hawking*, 1826, p. 32) comments: 'The young hawks of the year are called *red* hawks, from the colour of their plumage. The older hawks are called haggards: it is these that ornithologists have mistaken for a distinct species, calling it the Peregrine Falcon. These certainly differ very much from the young birds, in the colour of their plumage. Their feathers assume a blue or slate colour, and become lighter at every succeeding moult; and what is more remarkable, the bars on the breast-feathers of the red hawk are longitudinal, and those of the haggard are transverse. The same change takes place in the feathers of many other hawks. These changes are quite notorious to falconers, who have all had occasion to see the same individual hawks, at different periods of their lives, in the two different states that I have described.'

The compound 'hand-sore' I have not found as a term of falconry. Turberville refers to hawks as 'in hand' when 'under a Falconers keeping and usage' (p. 77); they may be trained either as eyasses, as soarhawks or as full-grown birds. One stage of the training is over when your hawk 'will abide the Hoode: and to bee handled, without striking or byting at your hand' (p. 142); she is to be taught to feed and to know the call of her keeper; the keeper is to handle her 'softly with your hand about the head', to stroke 'her softly about the wings and body' (p. 142), 'vsing your voice and giuing her many bits with your hand' (Latham, p. 12); such are samples of the directions given. 'Hand-sore', then, as an image of falconry, I am inclined to regard as a compound of Hamlet's own making to be received by Shakespeare's audience as Hamlet's comment on the self-interest of his professed friends. 'Empty hands no hawks allure' is a widely current proverb of this time; and while Hamlet, as he tells them, is a beggar 'euen poore in thankes', Rosencrantz and Guildenstern have already been promised by the King and Queen 'such thankes As fits a Kings remembrance'.

On the second level of meaning, 'hawk' and 'handsaw' (and this has already been pointed out)[1] are workmen's tools. *Hawk* as the plasterer's tool is not registered by NED until 1700, but it is clear that the bird of prey/plasterer's hod pun may have been available a century earlier: Cotgrave's Dictionary (1632) shows that the French *oiseau* can translate both meanings:

> *Oiseau:* m. A Bird, a fowle; and (particularly) a Hawke; also a Hodd; the Tray wherein Masons, etc; carrie their Mortar.

It seems to me likely, although unproven, that the 'hawk' joke had its natural origin on some high-level (? Anglo-French)

---

[1] Dover Wilson in his 'New Cambridge' *Hamlet* notes that 'hawk' as a plasterer's mortar-board is still in every day use; he cites also Dowden's suggestion that 'hawk' or 'hack' is in Elizabethan English a heavy cutting tool of the mattock or pick-axe type, 'which both in weight and manner of operation would form a more appropriate contrast to the light neat-cutting "handsaw" '. For my own part I find the 'hawk' as plasterer's board more in context.

scaffolding, with the 'sore'/'saw' pun to be added later, either by Hamlet or by some earlier speaker, as wit of a more conscious kind. For Hamlet's particular purpose here, 'hawk' (= plasterer's tool) could well imply, within the speech conventions of sixteenth and seventeenth-century English, that the office of Rosencrantz and Guildenstern was to gloze over some injury, to patch, soothe or alleviate. NED shows, among others, the following citations:[1]

> With light cost of rough cast rhetorick, it may be tolerably plaistered over (1599);
> A promis'd Parliament can plaster ore This Gash (1649).

We remember how firmly the King has assured Hamlet at the beginning of the play

> You are the most immediate to our Throne,

how anxious he is to learn, through Rosencrantz and Guildenstern, the reason of Hamlet's 'transformation',

> What it should bee
> More then his Fathers death, that thus hath put him
> So much from th'vnderstanding of himselfe,

how quickly Rosencrantz has raised the question of 'Ambition' in his talk with Hamlet in this present scene. Hamlet, however, has resolved to 'haue an eye' of his good friends: a Handsaw, in proverb usage, 'is a good thing, but not to shave with' (first cited 1732). Dangerous at close quarters, the Rosencrantz-Guildenstern combination is perhaps also too clumsy a tool for the king's purpose. A further derogatory implication may be that Rosencrantz and Guildenstern are so subdued to their office that they lack all individuality and are able to work their tool—a two-handed saw—in perfect unison: 'to hand the saw with' is 'to take turns, change parts, with another in some work or function' (1674).

---

[1] *plaster* 1. c.1599 Nashe *Lenten Stuffe* (1871); 2. b.

We remember how, when they come to visit Hamlet, the words of the king

> Thankes Rosincrance, and gentle Guildensterne

are echoed by those of the queen

> Thankes Guildensterne and gentle Rosincrance.

We notice how, immediately after he speaks to them of a *Handsaw*, Hamlet invites them both, emphasising his care to make no distinction between them, to come close to him to hear his whispered description of Polonius:

> Hearke you Guildensterne, and you too: at each eare a hearer. . .[1].

The 'saw' image for Hamlet and his audience may have the additional minor connotation of 'fruitless discussion'; NED cites the phrase 'To draw the saw (of contention or controversy)' with the sense 'to keep up a fruitless dispute', as for instance 'It would be of little avail to draw the Saw any longer of Answers and Retorts' (1688).[2] And earlier in this scene, after hearing them enunciate with stereotyped eloquence that ambition is the shadow of a dream, 'but a shadowes shadow', Hamlet has closed down the exercise with the words

> shall wee to th'Court: for, by my fey I cannot reason?

At this point of my exposition the present-day reader may feel that enough is enough; but there remains, I think, a third, although less important strand. Just before his hawk-handsaw speech Hamlet goes through the action of welcoming his friends

> Gentlemen, you are welcom to Elsonower: your hands, come: The appurtenance of Welcome, is Fashion and Ceremony. Let me comply with you in the Garbe. . . .

---

[1] In this last phrase Hamlet calls attention to his double-meaning. Cotgrave, 1611, shows 'Un pot a deux anses' as 'An equivocation'. See NED: *Ansal*.

[2] NED: *Saw sb.*[1] 1b. In obsolete phrases. *To draw the saw (of contention or controversy)*: to keep up a fruitless dispute; 1659 first cit.; *To hand the saw:* 1674 only cit.

For those watching the, no doubt, over-elaborate pantomime, 'handsaw' might bring to mind yet another proverb, 'Many kiss the hand they wish to cut off' (recorded from 1599).[1]

Those of my readers who feel impatient at the elaborateness of meaning I have tried here to elucidate will decide for themselves how much they care to bear in mind of the information now presented. The painfulness of learning, from the printed page alone, the many possible implications of a spoken language I readily concede; such a process takes a long time and cannot but seem far removed from that intuitive comprehension of the whole Shakespearean design which is the final purpose of Shakespearean scholarship. But those outside Shakespearean society who want to hear his words more sharply or more fully, may agree in principle that a rigorous analysis of this kind of evidence, if not by the general reader then by the editor working for him, is a necessary preliminary to artist-audience communion.

Before leaving this instance I should like once more to draw attention to the relatedness of the evidence; the jig-saw is more than two-dimensional. For, even as we are testing whether or not Shakespeare has given to his kingpin-comment words such values as can be established for them in the English language outside his theatre, we find in the less-meaningful background verbiage of the play a new kind of order; an apparently random sequence is seen to have its own reasons; the meaning of the key words gives unity to what would otherwise be separate pieces of the dramatic design. And once more we have to recognise the incompleteness of our knowledge of this earlier spoken language: how much of Hamlet's hawk-handsaw combination was already proverbial for Shakespeare and his audience cannot now be estimated. For present-day speakers who use the 'know a hawk from a handsaw' phrase, it is the verb and preposition only which

---

[1] Tilley: H 85. And, to dot the last i, if the now dialectal (Scottish and North Country) *hawk* (a form of *hack*) with the senses, among others, of 'a cut, wound; a chap or crack in the skin of the hands . . .', was current in Shakespeare's time in more southern areas, Hamlet's 'hawk' might well suggest the resulting 'handsore'.

have weight; our society knows nothing of *hawk/soar*, *hawk/saw*, distinctions; a *hand*saw has for us no special implications. And whether Hamlet brought in the *hand*saw as a pertinent variation, or whether the Shakespearean speech community had already replaced the simpler 'saw' by this more arbitrary form (just as, I have suggested, the clue-obscuring *doornail* replaced the original *charnel*) there is, in Shakespeare's text, no indication. We can say only that the language which Shakespeare made, is deeply-rooted in the language which he found; what is available to him is richly used.

6

I want next to suggest that in Kent's *Lipsbury Pinfold* (*Lear*, II ii 9) Shakespeare is using, momentarily, an existing joke on two senses of *lip*—'to kiss' and 'to shear (a sheep)'. It seems to me that Kent's phrase is an improvised variation on a known pun, although I would agree, this time, that the available evidence cannot certainly prove the truth of my suggestion. To recognise this kind of joke, I suppose, one has to know already the materials out of which it is made. Oswald and Kent, each with letters to deliver, reach the entrance to Gloucester's house.

> Steward. Good dawning to thee Friend, art of this house?
> Kent. I. [Aye]
> Steward. Where may we set our horses?
> Kent. I'th'myre.
> Steward. Prythee, if thou lou'st me, tell me.
> Kent. I loue thee not.
> Steward. Why then I care not for thee.
> Kent. If I had thee in Lipsbury Pinfold, I would make thee care for me.

No actual *Lipsbury* having been discovered, Nares's suggestion is usually accepted: Lipsbury, he thinks, might be a coined name meaning 'the teeth, as being the pinfold within the lips', so that

Kent is wishing that he had Oswald in his jaws, in his clutches. Having no more than the few lines of dialogue in Shakespeare's text, we might well accept Nares's postulate, but if we are ready to juggle imaginatively with some few fragments of additional external evidence, we can, I think, come nearer to the language fantasy of Shakespeare and his contemporaries. I am arguing here not so much about actual jokes made—of which I have rather too few examples from literary sources—but about joke material available for use within the spoken language; I shall therefore, for clarity's sake, number my evidence sections, and I hope that if my feeling for the language patterns is correct, some readers will be able to offer further actual instances of the type of joke I am considering.[1]

1. The verb *lip* in seventeenth-century English can have the two meanings 'to kiss' (as in *Othello*, IV i 72 and *Antony and Cleopatra*, II v 30) and 'to shear (a sheep)'.[2]

2. Although I have found no instances of a pun on these senses in Shakespeare's writing, there is in the jesting love talk of Boyet

---

[1] Additional evidence of *pinfold* as an image of loving is found in George Gascoigne's 'The Reporter', included in *A Hundreth Sundrie Flowers*, *c.* 1573 (ed. by C. T. Prouty, Columbia, 1942, p. 198). The *delight* of a lover is described:

> The lingring dayes he spente in trifling toyes,
> To whette the tooles which carved his contente,
> The poasting nightes he past in pleasing joyes,
> Wearying the webbe whiche love to him had lente:
> In such a pinfolde were his pleasures pent
> That selde he coulde hir companie eschewe,
> Or leave such lookes as might his lacke renewe.

See also *Venus and Adonis*, ll. 229-34:

> Fondling, she saith, since I haue hemd thee here
> Within the circuit of this iuorie pale,
> Ile be a parke, and thou shalt be my deare:
> Feed where thou wilt, on mountaine, or in dale;
>   Graze on my lips, and if those hils be drie,
>   Stray lower, where the pleasant fountaines lie.

[2] NED: *Lip v.*[1] 1b.

> *Lip v.*[2] *Obs.* . . . 1607 Their sheepe bring foorth twice in a yeare, and are likewise twice lipped.

and Maria (*Love's Labour's Lost*, II i 220) clear evidence of a 'sheep', 'lips', 'kissing' association[1] for Shakespeare and his audience:

> Boyet.   No Sheepe (sweet Lamb) vnlesse we feed on your lips.
> Lady.   You Sheep & I pasture: shall that finish the iest?
> Boy.   So you grant pasture for me.
> La.   Not so gentle beast.
> My lips are no Common, though seuerall they be.

And in the disgusted reproach of Hamlet to his mother the same association is more obscurely suggested (III iv 66):

> Could you on this faire Mountaine leaue to feed,
> And batten on this Moore?

3. It is interesting to note that there are other words in Elizabethan English which seem, through their duality of meaning to make inevitable a 'sheep'/'embracing' joke: *clip* is 'to embrace' and 'to shear (a sheep)'; *fold*, 'to embrace' and 'to pen up (a sheep)'. A jingling compound 'lip clip', but without the possible pun being emphasised by any accompanying elaboration, is found in the play *Wily Beguiled* (1606):

> A Maid cannot loue, or catch a lip clip, or a lap clap, but heers such tittle tattle, and doe not so . . . and do not kisse, and do not loue . . .[2]

The jingling rhyme survives into the nineteenth-century; NED shows it used by Hood, a. 1845 (*What can old Men do*)

> 'Love will not clip him, Maids will not lip him'.

4. In English as in other languages, the lips and teeth are proverbially the guardians (bars, hedges, gaolers, etc.) of the tongue; we find in Shakespearean imagery:

> 'Tis a secret must bee lockt within the teeth and the lippes:
> (*Measure for Measure*, III ii 143)

---

[1] That *lip* and *sheep* may occur together in shepherd's language for yet another reason is suggested by NED's citation from Blackmore's *Lorna Doone* 1869, 'No good sheep-dog even so much as lips a sheep to turn it.'

[2] Malone Society Reprint, 1912, p. 21.

the banished Mowbray complains (*Richard II*, 1 iii 166)

> Within my mouth you haue engaol'd my tongue,
> Doubly percullist with my teeth and lippes.

And as Tarquin muffles the cries of Lucrece, her lips enclosing her cries are the sheep*fold* (*Rape of Lucrece*, 676-79):

> The wolfe hath ceazd his pray, the poor lamb cries,
> Till with her own white fleece her voice controld,
> Intombes her outcrie in her lips sweet fold.

In these instances the Shakespearean image is part of a larger complex of meaning; similarly, I suggest, Kent's 'Lipsbury pinfold' derives its unique force from the individual context of its usage. It would be possible to speak the given dialogue at the beginning of this scene in such a way that Kent's every answer is understood as a counter-check, a linguistic side-step, a refusal to speak the same language as this 'super-seruiceable' steward whose mission he had hoped to forestall. Kent has promised Lear 'I will not sleepe my Lord, till I have deliuered your Letter', but it is unfortunately during the night that he arrives at Gloucester's house. Oswald's 'Good dawning', although not a deliberate gibe, may well suggest to Kent and to the Shakespearean audience the rueful comment 'Early up and never the nearer', 'Though you rise early yet the Day comes at his time and not till then';[1] Kent's 'aye' to Oswald's 'art of this house' may be an oblique regret that he is still, unluckily, outside the house, his message un-delivered.[2] His 'I'th'myre' is, clearly, half a proverb turned to literal use: 'Dun [the name of a horse] is in the mire', a proverb in common use in the sixteenth and seventeenth centuries, has the sense 'Things are at a standstill.' To Oswald's conventional 'if thou lou'st me', Kent gives back the plain statement 'I loue thee not.' And when Oswald answers with negligent hostility 'Why

---

[1] Tilley: D 104.

[2] Abbott, *Shakespearian Grammar* §166 cites a number of instances where Shakespeare uses *Of* for 'out of', 'from', with verbs that signify, either literally or metaphorically, depriving, delivering, etc.

then I care not for thee', Kent, it would be not unreasonable to
suppose, offers at once the pretence of sugared affection and a
scornful comment on Oswald's stupidity: 'If I held you prisoner
with my kisses—as sheep may be penned in the fold for shearing,
I would make you care for me.' That Shakespeare's 'Lipsbury
pinfold' results from some such momentary improvisation might
explain why it is that we look without success for other instances
of the idiom or place-name. It would, of course, be unwise to
press this argument too far; one cannot allege that the as yet
undiscovered is for ever indiscoverable. But it is true also that
Shakespeare, like all poets and all men, was at once language-
user and language-maker; it would be unrealistic to expect to
find his every joke an unmutated repetition of some earlier form.

In *Sarum plain* and *Camelot*, later in this same scene, Kent
makes use of a second, apparently unique, place-name idiom: he
explains to Cornwall the reason for his anger against Oswald,

> That such a slaue as this should weare a Sword,
> Who weares no honesty

and turns on the 'wagtaile':

> A plague vpon your Epilepticke visage,
> Smoile you my speeches, as I were a Foole?
> Goose, if I had you vpon Sarum Plaine,
> I'ld driue ye cackling home to Camelot.   (II ii 90)

It may be that here also the geographic form is a joke of arrangement only, and that what is put out as a place-name relationship
would be, for the seventeenth-century hearer, an opposition
between the idea of 'plain-speaking' and 'specious eloquence'. It
is indeed Kent's 'occupation to be plaine', and 'Sarum Plaine',
from his lips, might be calculated to bring to mind the kind of
man who for 'his malaparte tongue' is called 'Thom trouthe, or
plain Sarisburie'.[1]

---

[1] NED: under *Tom* 7c. 1542 from Udall's translation of the *Apophthegmes* of
Erasmus, For his malaparte toungue called at home ... Parrhesiastes (as ye woulde
saye in englyshe) Thom trouthe, or plain Sarisbuirie.

'Camelot', in seventeenth-century English, has, as far as I can at present discover, only one possible meaning; if it is a common noun, and not a place-name, it is a dress material, which may, or may not, have a wavy lustrous finish; if the material has this wavy finish it is 'water camlet', as, for instance (1601) 'The waued water Chamelot was from the beginning esteemed the richest and brauest wearing.'[1] On NED's evidence *camlet* as a verb has always this 'water' sense, 'to mark as (watered) camlet; to mark with wavy veins': so in Bacon's *Sylva* (1626) 'The Turks have a pretty Art of Chamoletting of Paper.' And just as one concludes despairingly that the trail has run out, that this 'camelot' has nothing to do with Kent's 'Camelot', one finds such 'watering' registered by NED, 1646, with the sense 'To give a specious appearance to (defective or inferior goods)'.[2] What is more, the term is applied to a style of speech, as part of what is clearly a 'dress-material' image:

> The pretty Allegories and Allusions of which Discourse (but the watering of weak and worthless *stuff*) might possibly shew not unhandsomly in an Oration, but are too *airy and thin* for a Sermon (1663).

If we assume that this 'watered material' image was in currency some fifty years earlier than the dictionary evidence shows, it may well be that Kent is using 'Camelot' = 'a watered fabric', to imply Oswald's high-sounding pretence of courage. The goose is proverbially stupid, fierce in show but cowardly by nature. Ray cites the proverb phrase 'As fierce as a goose' (1670); Sidney in his *Arcadia* speaks of how

> this goose (you see) puts downe his head, before there be any thing neere to touch him (*a* 1586).[3]

'Cackling' implies 'to fry in words, freeze in deeds' (1629), 'to cackle often, but never lay an egg'.[4] Oswald is a cowardly rascal,

---

[1] NED: *Camlet, sb.* 7-8 camelot. Shakespeare has the form *Chamblet* (*Henry VIII*, v iv 93) for 'a garment made of camlet': You i'th' Chamblet, get vp o'th'raile.
[2] NED: *Water, v.* 9c. 1646, 1663.
[3] *Arcadia* III (1633) 237. As cited by NED: *Goose* l. e.   [4] ODEP: Cackle.

and just as Kent, if left to settle the quarrel between them without outside interference, would

> tread this vnboulted villaine into morter, and daube the wall of a
> Iakes with him

so too he would drive him like a goose before him; if plain-dealing would serve, the accusation of cowardice which Kent makes against Oswald should indeed be driven home. It is possible, too, that the mortar-daubing threat is connected with the cackling goose image through the secondary meanings to be heard in Kent's *Smoile* and *drive: smoiliness* is 'fylthynesse' (NED: 1530, one instance only cited), and *drive* can mean 'to spread plaster'.[1]

If my interpretation is correct, Kent's words have only a pretended syntax; the grammatical arrangement which he gives them is part of his 'place-name' joke but his audience would know that no actual goose could ever be driven to the Camelot of which he speaks. And we should, I think, expect to find a few further instances of 'camlet', chamblet', 'camelot', etc., as a derogatory term in English usage.[2] It is noteworthy that *Camelote* in the French language has still the sense 'Cheap goods, shoddy goods, trash'.[3] Littré's *Dictionnaire* (1958)[4] gives the definition

> Camelote—Ouvrage mal fait; marchandise de mauvaise qualité.
> Mot du langage populaire, ainsi dit parce que le camelot était une
> étoffe de médiocre valeur.

In considering how much a Shakespearean audience might take in of such language jokes as these, it is perhaps worth remarking

---

[1] NED: *Drive, v.* 12. To spread or beat out thin; so, 1530 Drive this playster abrode.

[2] So, in Middleton's *Anything for a Quiet Life* (*Works of Thomas Middleton*, ed. by A. H. Bullen, 1885, Vol. IV) the mercer, Water-Camlet, is described by his wife as one who cheats his customers: 'your shop-wares you vent With your deceiving lights' [i.e. in a darkened shop so as to palm off goods of an inferior quality], pp. 270-1; 'you vent ware that is not warrantable, braided ware, and you give not London measure', p. 299.

[3] *Harrap's Standard French and English Dictionary* by J. E. Mansion, 1934.

[4] *Dictionnaire de la langue francaise*, by E. Littré, Paris, 1958.

that Kent's 'cackling home to Camelot', like Hamlet's 'know a
Hawke from a Handsaw', comes at the end of a speech, and, one
might say, of a paragraph. There is a natural pause available for
the dust to settle; those listening could be given a little time to
take in what was new or special in the language.

7

Instead of there being double meaning within the detail of the
proverb, there may be, as it were, a pun in its application; the
figurative idiom may be turned back to its literal use. Such a
'pun' is of obvious value to the dramatic artist and it is interesting
to see the different ways in which Shakespeare employs it. The
joke may be deliberately unsubtle. In the proverb idiom 'By line
and level', meaning 'by measure', *line* is clearly the builder's cord,
and Trinculo accordingly makes the obvious jest 'we steale by
lyne and leauell' as they take the 'glistering apparell' from where
it hangs on a *line* outside Prospero's cell (*Tempest*, IV i 239). The
poverty of his witticism is emphasised in Stephano's praising of it:

> I thanke thee for that iest; heer's a garment for't: Wit shall not
> goe vn-rewarded, while I am King of this Country: Steale by line
> and leuell, is an excellent passe of pate: there's another garment
> for't.

Elsewhere the device is used with a simplicity that is startlingly
effective. In the scene of Lear's madness, when he wishes to see
the trial of his daughters, the Fool's words

> Cry you mercy I tooke you for a ioyne stoole (III vi 64, Q 1608)

literally reapply a current proverb. As proverb, the words imply
injury without regard for the one who is hurt—Goneril's attitude
to her father. And where Lear in his madness can see only this
Goneril who has kicked her father, the Fool in his sanity sees
nothing but the actual *ioyne stoole*. In using the proverb image

for literal statement, the Fool obliges the Shakespearean 'auditor' to make a sharp readjustment, to accept as actual what he has been accustomed to know as language symbol. And it is exactly this kind of readjustment that the cruelty of Goneril has forced upon her father; in the language of the madman what should be symbol has become reality.

The traditional and generalised proverb-metaphor can be reapplied with special emphasis to some individual re-enactment of the original proverb situation. The 'younger brother', for instance, is the subject of several proverbs in sixteenth- and seventeenth-century England. 'He has made a younger brother of him' (1597) emphasises the disadvantage of such a status, so that Orlando, as he shows himself more than a match for Oliver in physical force, at once accepts and rejects that status as he says, his hand on Oliver's throat,

> Come, come elder brother, you are too yong in this.
>
> (*As You Like It*, 1 i 57)

'We will not lose a Scot' is first noted as a proverb (Tilley, S 157) in Fuller's Worthies (1662):

> That is, we will lose nothing, how inconsiderable soever, which we can save, or recover . . . This Proverb began in the English Borders, when . . . they had little esteem of, and less affection for, a Scotch-man.

Assuming that the proverb was current in speech some sixty years earlier, it would be heard as an additional point in Hotspur's angry repetition of his resolve not to give up a single one of his Scottish prisoners to King Henry IV:

> Worcester.   Those same Noble Scottes
> That are your Prisoners.
> Hotspurre.   Ile keepe them all.
> By heauen, he shall not haue a Scot of them:
> No, if a Scot would saue his Soule, he shall not.
>
> (1 *Henry IV*, 1 iii 214)

6

In this instance, I suggest, the heard proverb has two effects. Shakespeare is able through the briefest allusion to make reference to a whole segment of already formulated experience, so setting his speaker in the real world of practical matters and generalised language. He is able also to make more individual the personal situation, to make closer the connection between the form and content of a character's words. For if the not-losing-a-Scot proverb is part of the London language of Shakespeare's day, then Shakespeare's Hotspur, refusing to give up his Scottish prisoners, can hardly escape using it; the language-groove is there, the intention-to-be-expressed runs mechanically into it. But Hotspur ignores the groove. The energy of his indignation is not to be channelled away into the humour of general idiom. He is not interested in hearing what the available language form has made out of his words. This kind of control he rejects just as he rejects the control of the king, the authority of Worcester and his father. The dramatic situation shows him 'drunke with choller'; he can 'lend no eare' to Worcester's purposes. Northumberland very properly rebukes him as an

> impatient foole . . .
> Tying thine eare to no tongue but thine owne.

The linguistic situation deepens this impression.

In such cases, where Shakespeare has his characters make literal use of some proverb now gone from our language, the outsider may fail to recognise that a proverb is being used. Elsewhere we may recognise this readily enough, but still be left with an uneasy sense that we have not caught the full point of its Shakespearean application. How, for example, are we to understand the meaning of the Fool's last utterance 'And Ile go to bed at noone' (*Lear*, III vi 92)? It comes at a very significant point of the play:

> Kent.   Now good my Lord, lye heere, and rest awhile.
> Lear.   Make no noise, make no noise, draw the Curtaines:
> so, so, wee'l go to Supper i'th'morning.

Foole.   And Ile go to bed at noone.
Gloucester. Come hither Friend:
Where is the King my Master?
Kent.   Here Sir, but trouble him not, his wits are gon.

Why, we should like to know, has the time now come for the
Fool to disappear from the stage? How has Shakespeare intended
his role? If, among other functions, he has represented some aspect
of Lear's contact with reality, why is the Fool himself aware that
his part is now played out, finished too early? 'To go to bed at
noon' seems to imply some acceptance of unreality—a purposive
pretence that things are other than they are. The tired adult by
his own choice, the tired child because of the nurse's humouring,
consents to turn day into night; the curtains are drawn so that
sleep may come; as a result of a conscious choice the normal
activities of the waking mind are suspended. This is, of course,
to *imagine* the meaning of the proverb. What would we not give
to *find* in early written sources some half dozen instances of its
use? Tilley's magnificent collection affords no more than one
clear example and two near similarities, and he does not himself
attempt a definition; it is interesting to consider how precisely
we can isolate the 'straight' meaning of the proverb from the
literary evidence which he makes available. John Heywood
(1546), like Lear's Fool, takes pleasure in turning back the metaphor to a literal use. A 'late old wydow, and than ['then'] old new
wyfe' reproaches her young husband for infidelity:

Many kysse the childe for the nurces sake.
Ye haue many godchyldren to looke upone,
And ye blesse theim all, but ye basse but one.
This half shewth, what the holle meanth, yt I meeue.
Ye fet circumquaques to make me beleeue
Or thynke, that the moone is made of a grene chese.
And whan ye haue made me a loute in all these,
It semeth ye wolde make me go to bed at noone.
Naie (quoth he) the daie of dome shall be doone
Er thou go to bed at noone, or nyght, for me,

Thou art, to be playn and not to flatter the,
As holsome a morsell for my comly cors,
As a shoulder of mutton for a sycke hors.[1]

The figurative element common to Heywood and Shakespeare would seem to lie in this reference to over-credulity, a drawing of the curtains to shut out the light of reality; we may note the fantasy of Lear's direction 'make no noise, draw the Curtaines'. A variant idiom 'bid goodnight at noon' is found in the work of the poet Grange, 1577. He concludes an epistle dedicatory 'Thus trusting to your Honors curtesie, at noone I bid good night' and writes in one of his poems of his lady who, refusing his love, 'Doth force my harte with woe to pine, and biddes my ioyes at noone good nighte'.[2] The common factor here would seem to be the reference to over-sanguine expectations, hope of achievement, in poetry and in love, unfulfilled. And although one would like to find some neater correspondence of meaning between the two variants, any arrangement to produce it would be suspect; the idioms 'go to bed at noon' and 'bid goodnight at noon' overlap, but are not coincident. As for the Fool's proverb, it may well be that, if it has hitherto been his office to voice Lear's unacknowledged sense of the harsher realities, Shakespeare intends his last words here to indicate Lear's decision—conscious or half-conscious—to withdraw from the actual world into the world of hallucination, in which, as Gloucester is later to express it,

woes, by wrong imaginations loose
The knowledge of themselues. (IV vi 290)

This is the best we can do, I think, with the evidence available. It is necessary to admit that, without more instances of usage of this five-word proverb, we cannot clearly understand in this particular instance what Shakespeare is about as a dramatist; we cannot be sure what he knew and felt about the workings of the human mind.

---

[1] From photostat facsimile of copy in Huntingdon Library, San Marino, California, leaf K.   [2] *The Golden Aphroditis*, by John Grange, 1577; N4 v, R.

8

Although it is tantalising enough to be held up by lack of evidence, there is at least some profit in knowing what kind of evidence one would like to find. In the *Lear* instance the proverb fragment is big enough to be recognisable; the outsider can try to match it. Elsewhere in Shakespeare's work the single puzzling word may itself be a quotation from one of those many expressions which, as F. P. Wilson says, 'his audience recognised as proverbial and which we do not'.[1] And it may be only by chance that one remembers the puzzle when, months later, one happens across the whole of the proverb for which the fragment stands. For the puzzles themselves one has not far to seek; the second sentence of Heminge and Condell's Address to the Readers seems to end with a little explosion;

> To the great Variety of Readers.
> From the most able, to him that can but spell: There you are number'd. We had rather you were weighd. Especially, when the fate of all Bookes depends vpon your capacities: and not of your heads alone, but of your purses.

The word *weighd* means, presumably, weighed with money, but one does not see why it means this, nor why the editors think they have scored a point. One sees their target only when one finds the proverb 'The reasons of the poor weigh not' (first cited in Herbert's collection of 1640),[2] and then can feel no doubt, in the 'judgment' (*heads*), 'money' (*purses*) context, that the single-word quotation stands for the whole.

Sometimes the Shakespearean text affords a double clue. When Oswald, obeying Goneril's instructions to serve her father with 'weary negligence', is insolent to Lear, Kent trips up this 'base Foot-ball plaier' (I iv 96) and threatens him further:

---

[1] *Shakespeare and the Diction of Common Life*, by F. P. Wilson, Annual Shakespeare Lecture of the British Academy, 1941, p. 20.

[2] Tilley: R 50.

> Lear. Do you bandy lookes with me, you Rascall?
> Steward. Ile not be strucken my Lord.
> Kent. Nor tript neither, you base *Foot-ball plaier*.
> Lear. I thanke thee fellow.
> Thou seru'st me, and Ile loue thee.
> Kent. Come sir, arise, away, Ile teach you *differences:*

Kent's phrase may be regarded as a certain reference to the proverb 'All fellows at football' which is variously glossed in the seventeenth-century dictionaries 'Never stand upon place', 'All alike, no difference, . . . without any distinction'.[1]

In instances like these, where it is only by accepting the relevance of the proverb that we see the meaning of the Shakespearean text, the would-be explicator is not open to any charge of over-subtlety. Elsewhere perhaps we should be more tentative: we can suggest that the dramatic text has a richer meaning if we have in mind a certain proverb, but it would be hard to 'prove' from definite clues within the Shakespearean dialogue that the given proverb was known to the dramatist and his audience. And the question of 'proof' is more difficult if several meanings are simultaneously in play. So in *Love's Labour's Lost*, III i 74.

> Page. A wonder Master, here's a Costard broken in a shin.
> Armado. Some enigma, some riddle, come, thy Lenuoy begin.
> Clowne. No egma, no riddle, no lenuoy, no salue, in thee male sir. Or sir, Plantan, a plaine Plantan . . . .

The modernised-spelling text is usually printed 'no salve in the mail, sir' and 'mail' has then the sense 'wallet'; there is no ointment 'in the bag' which will cure Costard's shin. But 'a broken shin', as John Crow has recently suggested, is also a slang term for a sexual disappointment. 'A merry new song how a Bruer meant to make a Cooper cuckold, and how deer the Bruer paid for the bargaine' ends with the cooper's dismissal of his frustrated rival:

'Packe away, quod he, Bruer, with your broken shin'.

---

[1] Tilley: F 182.

Costard, 'taken with the manner', 'sorted and consorted' with
Iaquenetta, has been separated from her and condemned to
imprisonment and fasting; for his broken shin there is obviously
one remedy only. 'Seek your salve where you got your sore' is a
proverb of Shakespeare's time[1] and Costard's lamentation 'No
salve in the *male*, sir' would be relevant not only to his predicament but to that of the king and his lords also. The phrase could,
in fact, serve as an 'egma' or 'riddle' appropriate to the whole
action of the play.

Sometimes the contemporary proverb may do no more than
give extra firmness to the texture of the dialogue. When Lear
(I i 131) dismisses Cordelia with the words

> Let pride, which she cals plainnesse, marry her

it is probable that the *plainnesse/marry* combination takes stronger
emphasis from the current proverb 'Plain dealing is dead and
died without issue.'[2] Sometimes, we may suspect, a number of
senses from different proverb-phrases coalesce in a single word,
as with the expression *tender-hefted* (*Lear*, II iv 174, Folio),[3] when
Lear, cursing Goneril, reassures Regan:

> Regan.   O the blest Gods!
> So will you wish on me, when the rash moode is on.
> Lear.   No Regan, thou shalt neuer haue my curse:
> Thy tender-hefted Nature shall not giue
> Thee o're to harshnesse: . . . 'Tis not in thee
> To grudge my pleasures, to cut off my Traine,
> To bandy hasty words . . . Thou better know'st
> The Offices of Nature, bond of Childhood . . .
> Thy halfe o'th'Kingdome hast thou not forgot,
> Wherein I thee endow'd.

Haft or *heft* is commonly the handle of a cutting instrument; a
verb *haft*, in the sixteenth and seventeenth centuries, is also 'to use
deceit, to haggle';[4] so Lear speaks of 'to *cut off* my Traine, To

---

[1] Tilley: S 83, 1577 first citation.   [2] Tilley: P 384, 1616 first citation.
[3] Quarto: tender hested.   [4] NED: *Haft, v.*[2] 1519 first citation.

bandy hasty words'. A third verb, found in eighteenth-century Scottish and northern English, is 'to accustom (sheep, cattle) to a pasturage, to set or fix firmly'.[1] Through this sense Lear appeals to Regan's affection; although Goneril is guilty of 'Sharpe tooth'd vnkindnesse' and he wishes the 'stor'd Vengeances of Heauen' to fall upon her, Regan is different from her sister. Her nature has been formed and fixed in tenderness, the love of child for father and father for child. So Lear says. But what has been and what is the quality of his tenderness? We see that Regan's tenderness for him is like his tenderness for Goneril; father is like daughter and sister close to sister as haft to knife; close companions are proverbially 'like heft and blade' (1884).[2] Lear trusts in vain to Regan's kindness: 'to be loose in the haft' is to be unreliable, to stagger or flinch upon a trial.[3] He is to say to his daughters 'I gaue you all'; his use of the form *hefted* may suggest that he realises the folly of having done so: Withals' *Dictionarie*[4] shows the proverb

> It is too late to spare when al is spent: An old sayd-saw, when all is gone and nothing left, what helpes the dagger with the dudgean heft?[5]

A further implication would also be in context: in this scene, every speech of Regan's has been a sharp rebuff to Lear and it is *after* she has advised him to go back and ask Goneril's forgiveness

---

[1] NED: *Haft, v.*[3] Sc. and *north. dial.* 1725 first citation. EDD: *Hefted*, accustomed, wonted.

[2] EDD: under *Haft sb.*[1] gives the phrase 'like heft and blade', close companions, Kircudbright, 1884.
The old song 'Billy Boy' (as given in *Oxford Dictionary of Nursery Rhymes* by I. and P. Opie, Oxford, 1951, p. 79) shows the comparison
'She's as fit to be my wife
As my blade is for my knife';
I think I have as a child sung the version 'As the haft is to the knife'.

[3] NED: *Loose in the haft* (*fig.*) unstable, unreliable; first cit. *c.* 1325. Cotgrave (1632): Bransler au manche. To be loose in the helue, or heft; to stagger, wauer, shake, or flinch, upon a triall . . .

[4] 1616 ed. p. 43.

[5] See NED *dudgen*, a dagger with a handle of this material being cheap and often regarded as an inferior, unreliable weapon; 1590 Greene, Loose in the haft like a dudgin dagger.

that Lear speaks to Regan of her 'tender-hefted Nature'. Can it be that he is teaching himself patience? The 'heft' image may suggest the proverb question 'If the axe were gone, is this the remedy to hurle the helue after it?' (1587).[1]

With this last example I have come perhaps to the outer edge of useful speculation: for the proverb implications of 'tender-hefted' here put forward I can cite no linguistic pointers within the text. Must it therefore follow that no one of them was in the mind of Shakespeare as he wrote? Or, to put the same question in a different form, is it worth while recording any of these proverbs in the memory-equipment we bring to the play? Memory itself will no doubt give an answer; what is worth while will find a place. For a proverb-image is a tenuous thing; often, as Tilley says, 'only a characteristic proverbial metaphor, woven into the texture of the thought, is all that remains to remind us of the original proverb'.[2] And linguistic progression is not always linear; the present-day student of Shakespeare's language may find from time to time that the complexity of his shifting meaning is only to be grasped by those who already have the proverbs of his day as part of their own feeling and thinking patterns. The non-contemporary must patiently seek out these patterns or lose the intricate exactness of the Shakespearean exposition. So, I suggest, in my next example, some fifteen lines from the opening scene of *Henry VIII*. Buckingham hears from Norfolk how the English and French kings

> Those Sunnes of Glory, those two Lights of Men
> Met in the vale of Andren . . .

and learning that the splendid pageantry

> was ordred by the good Discretion

---

[1] See Tilley, A 411 He sends the ax after the helve (1546 first cit.); H 413 To throw the helve after the hatchet.

[2] *Elizabethan Proverb Lore in Lyly's Euphues* by M. P. Tilley, New York, 1926, p. 7.

of Cardinal Wolsey he cries out in anger

> The diuell speed him: No mans Pye is freed
> From his Ambitious finger. What had he
> To do in these fierce Vanities? I wonder,
> That such a Keech can with his very bulke
> Take vp the Rayes o'th'beneficiall Sun,
> And keepe it from the Earth.

Norfolk answers him:

> Surely Sir,
> There's in him stuffe, that put's him to these ends:
> For being not propt by Auncestry, whose grace
> Chalkes Successors their way; nor call'd vpon
> For high feats done to'th'Crowne; neither Allied
> To eminent Assistants; but Spider-like
> Out of his Self-drawing Web. O giues vs note,
> The force of his owne merit makes his way
> A guift that heauen giues for him, which buyes
> A place next to the King.[1]

To Wolsey, 'not propt by Auncestry', but believed to be the son
of a butcher, Buckingham applies in scorn his dialect term *keech*,
'the fat of a slaughtered animal rolled into a lump' (a word in
frequent use in the Stratford kitchens of Shakespeare's day;
see p. 321). And the 'Sun' of England, whose warmth this keech
engrosses, is obviously the king, the king's favour and the power
derived therefrom. It is an image to be used again when Wolsey
speaks of his fall from power (III ii 410):

> No Sun, shall euer vsher forth mine Honors,
> Or gilde againe the Noble Troopes that waighted
> Vpon my smiles

and when he tells his loyal servant Cromwell

> Seeke the King
> (That Sun, I pray may neuer set). . . .   (III ii 415)

---

[1] Editors have been particularly puzzled by l. 63. O has been variously read
as *he* or *'a* or as an exclamation. We may note that Shakespeare uses O as a noun
some half dozen times, twice in the plural and otherwise with an article.

Buckingham here speaks of the rays of the sun as 'beneficiall'; had others been allowed to organise this great pageant they might have enjoyed the thanks and rewards of the king. But the sun is also a source of danger: 'He that walks much in the sun will be tanned at last'.[1] So Hamlet warns Polonius of Ophelia's danger, 'Let her not walke i'th'Sunne' (II ii 185). And Buckingham wonders spitefully that 'such a Keech' is not in special danger from 'these fierce Vanities': 'He that has a head of wax must not walk in the sun'.[2] Norfolk demurs at this description; surely there is better 'stuffe' than wax in Wolsey's head. As far as concerns 'Auncestry', 'high feats done to'th'Crowne', and 'eminent Assistants', certainly Wolsey is nothing; he is O, a cipher among numbers, to 'note' or fill a place, himself of no value.[3]

But whereas 'an O without a figure' is nothing (*Lear*, I iv 212), 'a Cypher (Yet standing in rich place)' can 'multiply' (*Winter's Tale*, I ii 6), and Wolsey stands in a 'place next to the King'. Another proverb comes into play here: 'A man's gift (i.e. normally his 'bribe') maketh room for him and bringeth him before great men';[4] Wolsey's own merit, a 'guift that heauen giues for him' has won him this place. 'Spider-like' implies Wolsey's self-sufficiency and also his 'Malice, and his Potency'[5] of which Norfolk is to

---

[1] Tilley: S 972, 1553 first citation.
[2] Tilley: H 249, 1640 first citation.
[3] ODEP: Like a Cipher in arithmetic.
    1399 Langland, Than satte summe, as siphre doth in awgrym,
    That noteth a place, and no thing availith.
    1547 Our presidentes . . . doo serue but as Cyphers in
    Algorisme, to fill the place.
    1598-9 Shakespeare *Henry V*, Prol. 17:
              Or may we cramme
    Within this Woodden O, the very Caskes
    That did affright the Ayre at Agincourt?
    O pardon: since a crooked Figure may
    Attest in little place a Million,
    And let vs, Cyphers to this great Accompt,
    On your imaginarie Forces worke.
[4] ODEP: A man's Gift makes room for him. 1611 Bible, Proverbs xviii. 16, as quoted above. 1732 Fuller.
[5] Tilley: B 208 Where the bee sucks honey the spider sucks poison, *a* 1542 first cit.; M 152 The great man is the spider, the poor man is the fly, 1616 first cit. See

give Buckingham explicit warning (1 i 105). His pride and self-approbation are referred to in 'giues vs note': the word *note* has, I think, three or four senses. Wolsey, the zero symbol (Latin *nota*, 'A cypher, note or abbreviation), lets them know ('to give note' is 'to inform')—and this knowledge is a reproach to those who claim other advantages of 'Auncestry' etc.—that he has nothing but the 'force' of his own merit; this *force* is 'the power or value of a symbol', as in *Henry V*, Prologue 18, 'your imaginarie Forces' (NED cites, 1741, 'An unite before a cypher has the Force of ten').[1] Wolsey's own merit is such a unit. If this explanation is accepted, the puzzling *O* of the Folio text, so far from needing emendation, gives us the key to the meaning of Norfolk's speech; we see also the close inter-relation of Norfolk's answer to Buckingham's angry outburst. And it is a measure of Shakespeare's artistry that this method of detailed linguistic analysis, applied at random because of an apparent textual difficulty, is justified in its complete success. When Shakespeare is writing at his best, every word in his text is there for at least one good reason; often for three or four at once.

9

Other instances may be offered where a knowledge of contemporary proverb-idiom helps at the same time to establish and to interpret Shakespeare's text and I end this section with a consideration of some five examples from *Timon of Athens*, a play which contains a number of detailed textual problems hitherto unsolved. 'Certainly many speeches are difficult to follow', writes Sir Walter Greg, 'and not only the text but the structure

---

also NED's citations of Spider-like: e.g. 1839 I have that within me I can live upon: Spider-like spin my place out anywhere.

[1] Cooper's *Thesaurus*, 1578 ed., *Nota*, . . . A defamation . . . A cypher, note, or abbreuiation.

NED: *Note*, *sb*[2] 10. A sign or character (other than a letter). 20c. information. 8. stigma, reproach (with *of*). Force, *sb.*[1] 9.

of the play seems incoherent.'[1] I shall argue as before that there may be profit in concentrating attention on the 'one very poor original text', as Hardin Craig describes it, and in trying to hear the unintelligible word or phrase of this original text against the wider background of contemporary spoken language.

Our Poesie is as a Gowne (I i 21).

At the beginning of the play, the poet and painter are waiting to present their work to Timon and the poet is reading over part of his dedication:

> When we for recompence haue prais'd the vild,
> It staines the glory in that happy Verse,
> Which aptly sings the good.

The painter comments

> Painter.   You are rapt sir, in some worke, some
> Dedication to the great Lord.
> Poet.   A thing slipt idlely from me.
> Our Poesie is as a Gowne, which vses
> From whence 'tis nourisht: the fire i'th'Flint
> Shewes not, till it be strooke: our gentle flame
> Prouokes it selfe, and like the currant flyes
> Each bound it chases.

The poet's first words are an acknowledgment of the painter's question, but in the next lines, I suggest, he goes on reading from the dedication of his long poem, a poem which is to warn Timon that, when Fortune 'in her shift and change of mood' withdraws her favour, those who now flatter and follow will then forsake him. From these flattering 'Dependants' the poet evidently seeks to dissociate himself; the compliments which he will pay in his dedication are sincere and deserved. It is unfortunate, however, that praise offered to a patron is always suspect; poets have been

---

[1] *The Editorial Problem in Shakespeare*, by Sir W. W. Greg, 2nd ed., Oxford, 1951, p. 149.

known to praise 'for recompence'. Now comes the puzzling
'Gowne, which vses'. To understand this the non-contemporary
needs to know that the gown 'is his that wears it'; more specifically
'The gowne is not his that maketh it, but his that enioyeth it'.[1]
The verb *use* can mean 'to eat up', 'to wear' and 'to use up or
wear out'.[2] One may say that 'clothys and other things' which are
getting old 'Weryn, or vson' (c. 1440); similarly, finely coloured
materials 'with a whiles use will soone loose theire luster' (1670).
The sense of the poet's words is then, to expand simply and somewhat tediously:

> A complimentary poem is like a gown belonging not so much to
> the poet-creator as to the patron-wearer, so that the honour
> conferred loses lustre and grows threadbare in so far as it is known
> to be purchased ('nourisht' by patronage). In contrast to fire, which
> has to be struck out of the hard flint, the noble inspiration of a poet
> ('our gentle flame') needs no external agency to call it forth; in
> fact, that inspiration finds its free flow blocked if the poet is pre-
> pared to compromise his art by chasing after wealth and patronage.
> So the free-flowing current, rippling towards the confining shore,
> flows swiftly back from what it seems to pursue ('flyes Each bound
> it chases').

If this interpretation is accepted, the modernising editor need do
no more than arrange the punctuation so that the poet reads or
recites two closely connected extracts from his verse. At present
the passage is usually emended to read:

> Our poesy is as a *gum*, which *oozes*
> From whence 'tis nourish'd: the fire i'the flint
> Shows not till it be struck; our gentle flame
> Provokes itself, and, like the current, flies
> Each bound it chafes.[3]

---

[1] Tilley: G 387, 1573 first citation.

[2] NED: 11. 'to consume by eating or drinking'; 8b. 'to wear as an article of
apparel'; 12. 'to expend or consume (a commodity, etc.) by use; to exhaust by
employment'.

[3] So the 'Old Cambridge' 1892, and so, substantially, Kittredge 1936, Alexander
1951, Craig 1951, Sisson 1954, 'New Cambridge' 1957. The words 'gum' and

these moyst Trees (IV iii 223)

Apemantus scorns Timon for his affectation of the ascetic's life; does he expect now that the creatures of nature will flatter him?

> Thou hast cast away thy selfe, being like thy self
> A Madman so long, now a Foole: what think'st
> That the bleake ayre, thy boysterous Chamberlaine
> Will put thy shirt on warme? Will these moyst Trees,
> That haue out-liu'd the Eagle, page thy heeles
> And skip when thou point'st out? Will the cold brooke
> Candied with Ice, Cawdle thy Morning taste
> To cure thy o're-nights surfet?

The 'moyst Trees' of the original were changed to 'moss'd trees' by Hanmer; Johnson praised the elegance of the reading and it is still found in some modern texts.[1] But 'moist' in Shakespeare's time can mean 'wet', and not merely 'somewhat wet' as it does today; and wet trees, in seventeenth-century proverbial idiom, were thought of as affording less than no shelter. 'He is doubly wet that shrouds himself under trees' (1611); 'Who stands under a bough, hath that which rains, and that which drops' (1666).[2] Apemantus asks Timon what service he can hope for from the 'bleake ayre', the 'moyst Trees' and the 'cold brooke'. To change 'moyst' to 'mossed' is, I believe, to weaken the dramatic sense and to destroy the argument sequence. It is worth noting also that the trees have 'out-liu'd the Eagle', and perhaps, in so

---

'issues' were first inserted by Pope, Johnson subsequently replacing 'issues' by 'oozes'. As a Shakespearean linguist who has knocked, sometimes in vain, at the gates of literary strongholds, I confess to a certain pleasure in observing from whose pen the 'gum' first issued, as if for Shakespeare's poet, just as for the infant Pope, poetry were a kind of natural secretion:

> As yet a child, nor yet a fool to fame,
> I lisped in numbers, for the numbers came.

[1] F. P. Wilson would restore the original 'moist' which he understands as 'full of sap, pithy'. *Shakespeare and the Diction of Common Life*, Annual Shakespeare Lecture of the British Academy, 1941, p. 16.
[2] Tilley: T 508.

describing them, Apemantus makes another thrust at Timon. In Withals' *Dictionarie* we find

> Aquile senectus, an Eagles age, spoken of him that hath liued so long, that hee can feed no longer, to liue any longer.
>
> (1616 ed., p. 26.)

willing misery Out-liues: incertaine pompe, is crown'd before (IV iii 243)

Apemantus continues his attack on Timon:

> If thou did'st put this sowre cold habit on
> To castigate thy pride, 'twere well: but thou
> Dost it enforcedly: Thou'dst Courtier be againe
> Wert thou not Beggar: willing misery
> Out-liues: incertaine pompe, is crown'd before:
> The one is filling still, neuer compleat:
> The other, at high wish: best state Contentlesse,
> Hath a distracted and most wretched being,
> Worse then the worst, Content.
> Thou should'st desire to dye, being miserable.

Lines 242-3 are usually arranged

> willing misery
> Outlives incertain pomp, is crowned before.

Johnson so punctuates (but with a semi-colon after 'pomp') and understands 'crowned before' to mean 'arrives sooner at . . . the completion of its wishes'; so, substantially, more recent editors (Deighton, Kittredge, Alexander, Craig, and Sisson). I suggest that the grammar of the original is more meaningful: the contrast between 'The one' and 'The other', both subjects of their sentences, is paralleled in the antithesis between 'willing misery' which lives on and endures, and 'incertain pompe', which, crowned before the end of the story, is always seeking again the moment of completion, the high flood of honour: 'Thou'dst Courtier be againe Wert thou not Beggar'. *Out-live* as an intransitive verb is found in one other instance in Shakespeare's text, in *Titus Andronicus*, II iii 132:

> But when ye haue the hony we desire,
> Let not this Waspe out-liue vs both to sting.

And 'The end crowns all' is a common proverb with Shakespeare and his contemporaries;[1] the end 'declareth all', 'is worth all', 'shall trulye try'; 'The end is crowne of euery worke well done'; Hector says 'the end crownes all, And that old common Arbitrator, Time, Will one day end it' (*Troilus and Cressida*, IV v 224). 'Crown' and 'content' are also closely linked; 'A minde content both crowne and kingdome is' is a quite common sentiment in Elizabethan literature. Henry VI, taken prisoner, is, ironically, 'a King crown'd with Content' (3 *Henry VI*, III i 66). Apemantus who delights to express himself in paradox finds the greatest content in the complete absence of content; it is at such a moment of 'high wish' that a man should 'desire to dye'.

The Common legge of People (III vi 90)

Timon, having invited his former friends to a banquet of 'Smoke & lukewarm water', says grace before the dishes are uncovered:

> The Gods require our Thankes:
>
> *You great Benefactors, sprinkle our Society with Thankefulnesse. For your owne guifts, make your selues prais'd: But reserue still to giue, least your Deities be despised. . . . Let no Assembly of Twenty, be without a score of Villaines. If there sit twelue Women at the Table, let a dozen of them bee as they are. The rest of your Fees, O Gods, the Senators of Athens, together with the common legge of People, what is amisse in them, you Gods, make suteable for destruction.*

The eighteenth-century emendations 'foes' for 'fees' and 'lag'

---

[1] Tilley: E 116, in variant forms, from *c.* 1550; Shakespeare—2 *Henry VI*, v ii 28 *La fin Corrone les eumenes [couronne les oeuvres]*; 2 *Henry IV*, II ii 50 Let the end try the man; *All's Well*, IV iv 35 All's well that ends well, still the fines the Crowne.

for 'legge' still survive in some present-day editions.[1] But NED shows that *fee* can mean 'homage rendered', or 'a tribute or offering to a superior'. Dekker uses this last sense in an epigram which seems to have the ring of a proverb (1602)

> Knees Are made for kings, they are the subjects Fees.

And Shakespeare has the same image in *Troilus and Cressida* (III iii 49):

> for supple knees,
> Feede arrogance, and are the proud mans fees.

This is of obvious relevance to Timon's speech: he believes that men praise the gods for the gifts which the gods bestow and he calls on them to punish for their sins both the Senators of Athens who pay them homage and tribute, and also the common people who kneel, or make a leg, before them. It is interesting to note that he refers to the guests at his banquet in similar terms as 'Cap and knee-Slaues'.

In the next example which is offered very tentatively, the passage I am trying to interpret seems to be unfinished but an impression is none the less conveyed of the energy and passion of the speaker. It seems likely that the dramatist has determined the content, or part of the content, of what is to be spoken, although he has not yet achieved the full compression or clarity he is seeking.

Ile locke thy heauen from thee (I ii 255)

> Timon. Nay, and you begin to raile on Societie once, I am sworne not to giue regard to you. Farewell, & come with better Musicke.   *Exit*
> Apermantus. So: Thou wilt not heare mee now, thou shalt not then.
> Ile locke thy heauen from thee:
> Oh that mens eares should be
> To Counsell deafe, but not to Flatterie.

---

[1] As, for instance, those of Kittredge and Alexander; Craig and Sisson read *'fees'* and *'lag'*.

In this passage 'heauen' is usually taken as meaning 'good advice', the only thing by which Timon could be saved. This explanation, I think, fails to take into consideration that the 'Counsell' which Apemantus now offers consists of the most bitter abuse. The word 'then' is also strongly emphasised: Timon who will not listen to Apemantus now, shall not hear him *then*, when his inevitable ruin comes upon him. 'To spit against Heaven', like 'to throw stones against the wind' is foolishly to invite great and unavoidable disaster. And a second proverb, using the same phrase, 'Who spits against Heaven, it falls in his face' carries the implication 'Curses return upon the heads of those who curse'.[1] Webster, for instance, has a variant of this:

> for your names,
> Of Whoore and Murdresse they proceed from you,
> As if a man should spit against the wind,
> The filth returne's in's face.
>
> (*The White Devil*, III ii 152)

Shakespeare, I suggest, may intend Apemantus to combine these two proverbs and to give the combined image a new application: in Timon's disaster the curses which Apemantus now speaks shall *not* fall upon Timon's head. Apemantus will *then* be silent; 'Ile locke thy heauen from thee'. If there is any comfort in hearing bitter reproaches for headstrong folly, even that comfort Timon shall not know.

Whatever may be the judgment of the individual reader on this last interpretation, I hope we may agree at least that it is proper in this study to take as a starting point the original text; it is in that text only that we shall hear those swiftly glancing allusions—comprehensible at once in Shakespeare's day—to a proverb-imagery now gone from our language. And the non-contemporary may be directed to those illuminating splinters of quotation by nothing more tangible than a feeling for how the text is to be spoken, how the emphasis is to be placed. Such an

---

[1] Tilley: H 355, H 356.

intuition, I would argue, can derive only from an acceptance of the authentic text. Only the language of 'Shakespeare' can call forth precisely that kind of creative response which his artistry demands; if we dilute that language with chippets of elegance and order appropriate to a later age, to that extent we limit and falsify our response to the energy of the original. So with *Timon*. Ideally we should come first to the Folio text, and we should come unpuzzled. If our eyes are accustomed to traditional emendations, we must try the harder to submit unfrowning to the authority of an earlier version. In this way, and with the linguistic equipment of the present century, we may expect to by-pass some of the difficulties which confronted earlier editors and scholars. And this is not to detract from what they in their time achieved; it is merely to follow the tradition they laid down.[1]

---

[1] So Dr. Johnson: 'the history of our language, and the true force of our words can only be preserved, by keeping the text of authors free from adulteration.'

CHAPTER IV

The less decent language of the time

I

In the last chapter I have tried to show that the non-contemporary seeking to establish the meaning of some of the words and phrases in Shakespeare's plays which are as yet unexplained may sometimes need to regard such words as code signs, highly significant snippets of larger language groupings. Such quotation fragments bring with them, as it were, their own context and are stamped with the meaning of the larger phrase or sentence unit in which they habitually occur within the spoken language. The word *church*, for instance, may mean 'what goes slowly'; *sleeves* in a 'tailor' context will imply reference to a thief. And whereas Shakespeare's contemporaries would be able at once to hear in full what in Shakespeare's text was spoken only in part, the later student, confronted by the puzzling word, has patiently to investigate both the meaning-directives within the Shakespearean dialogue and the potential implications which were current within the ordinary language. The search for this external evidence may in itself be somewhat laborious. A proverb from which Shakespeare quotes only one or two words may not exist in printed literature in its full form and with its plain meaning; we may have to reconstruct this postulated simple original from different fragments variously applied by other writers of his day. And it is necessary at the same time to make clear by a detailed examination of Shakespeare's text that the implication we believe to exist in current idiom is fully relevant both to the narrower linguistic context and to the wider dramatic situation within the scene and the play.

I want next to consider what might be regarded as a special subdivision of this code language, the vocabulary of sex-innuendo as it may concern the explicator of the Shakespearean text. It may be agreed, first of all, that some skilful exploitation of this powerful and half-secret language is bound to have its place in any uncensored and highly charged dramatic language which is concerned with sex relationships. And I should like as a linguist to by-pass all question of *social* propriety, and to accept, without more ado, that what would be improper in an actual restricted-context conversation of a given society, may yet be highly proper in a dramatic presentation offered within that society. Whether Shakespeare 'represented the real conversation of his time is not easy to determine' says Dr. Johnson. Perhaps we may accept that we are not concerned with 'real conversation', but with the tension between various kinds of reality which it is the business of drama to exploit. Life has its physical crudities as well as its surface decencies. And because a play is composed of spoken words the dramatist may well require to have his characters state plainly, or suggest obliquely, what in a restricted social context might remain unspoken, even though most powerfully present to thought and feeling. Many readers will be aware also that there are contexts outside literature where verbal inhibition ceases to apply. And some present-day critics would surely claim that the defiance of linguistic inhibition by writers such as Lawrence, Joyce and Beckett constitutes a rediscovery of a source of power and truth which was known to many great literary artists of the past. I hope then that readers will concede that if it is useful and interesting for the non-contemporary to try to recognise within Shakespeare's dialogue elements of proverb-idiom alive in his day but now gone from ordinary language, so too it may be necessary to be alert for elements of sexual idiom, the meaning of which has been obscured by time. Perhaps we should admit also that in this particular area of vocabulary the normal slow process of historic change is by no means the only barrier between the non-contemporary and the Shakespearean experience. Very

strong emotional sanctions of which we cannot always be aware
are in operation also. Because the 'decent language' code of any
given generation seems to those inside the system to be wholly
reasonable, the last word of good sense and of good taste, there
is always the danger that we may try to appraise the artistic
language of an earlier age by what may be a wholly local and
temporary standard. It is well to bear in mind that since the
beginning of Shakespearean scholarship in the early eighteenth
century, few, if any, of our English editors and critics have
moved freely and without constraint in their exposition of the
sex imagery and allusion of Shakespearean art.

At the beginning of the eighteenth century a new 'decent
language' code was in process of formation in educated society;
new standards of natural and modest conversation were laid
down. And there was as a result some serious undervaluing of
Shakespeare's dramatic achievement. Writing as one conscious of
this new refinement of manners, Johnson, for instance, gives somewhat faint praise to the lively dialogue of Shakespeare's comedies.

> In his comick scenes he is seldom very successful, when he engages
> his characters in reciprocations of smartness and contests of sarcasm;
> their jests are commonly gross, and their pleasantry licentious;
> neither his gentlemen nor his ladies have much delicacy, nor are
> sufficiently distinguished from his clowns by any appearance of
> refined manners. Whether he represented the real conversation of
> his time is not easy to determine; the reign of Elizabeth is com-
> monly supposed to have been a time of stateliness, formality, and
> reserve, yet perhaps the relaxations of that severity were not very
> elegant.

Condemnation of Shakespearean indelicacy is often more strongly
formulated, so that some defence of Shakespeare the artist has
to be attempted. It is assumed that he was obliged to write as he
did to suit an audience totally lacking in taste and judgment. As
Pope describes it:

> In comedy, nothing was so sure to please, as mean buffoonery, vile
> ribaldry, and unmannerly jests of fools and clowns.

Some editors thought it their duty to expurgate the impropriety; Hanmer records his conviction that

> a great deal more of that low stuff, which disgraces the works of this great author, was foisted in by the players after his death, to please the vulgar audiences by which they subsisted.

Johnson, however, as a linguist, is to that extent dispassionate. The difficulties of an editor in dealing with the 'gross' and 'licentious' vocabulary of an earlier age he frankly concedes:

> There is danger lest peculiarities should be mistaken for corruptions, and passages rejected as unintelligible, which a narrow mind happens not to understand.   (*Proposals*, 1756)

One such small mistake on Johnson's part and its subsequent correction by Malone is worth noting; we see that it is the practice of the eighteenth-century Shakespearean commentator silently to accept that *double entendre* of which that age so much disapproves. Just before the play within the play, Hamlet engages Ophelia in a conversation which Steevens designates as 'of the lowest kind', first misleading her with an apparently sexual suggestion and then pretending that the idea is in her mind, not his (see p. 119):

> Do you thinke I meant Country matters? (III ii 123)

Johnson proposed here to read 'country manners'—

> Do you imagine that I meant to sit in your lap, with such rough gallantry as clowns use to their lasses?

Malone, obliged through Johnson's mistake to offer his own interpretation of the line, takes it for granted that all readers can recognise and understand the allusion which Shakespeare intended:

> Dr. Johnson, from a casual inadvertence, proposed to read— country *manners*. The old reading is certainly right. What Shakespeare meant to allude to, must be too obvious to every reader, to require any explanation.

In this particular instance the post-Victorian student who notes the *count*ry pun will escape the charge of reading into Shakespeare's text some new obscenity, self-invented. And we realise from this somewhat obvious example that where the question of Shakespeare's intention is of greater dramatic importance, his earlier editors may well have credited him with a fullness of meaning to which they felt it unnecessary to draw attention. It is likely also that the eighteenth-century editors were aware of some implications in the Shakespearean text which, because of the narrower code of verbal decency imposed in Victorian times, no longer have a place in the ordinary language of protected academic life.

Thomas Bowdler in his *Family Shakespeare* (1818) gives us indirectly some information as to those elements in Shakespeare's vocabulary which were recognised as 'vulgar' and 'indelicate' in early nineteenth-century society. Among the instances to be considered in this chapter, the comment of Escalus, for example (*Measure for Measure*, II i 38):

Some rise by sinne, and some by vertue fall

seems still to be understood as having some crude physical reference; as a general comment on the uneven justice of this world it would scarcely require emendation. The words 'erection' and 'yearn', on the other hand, set down side by side in Mistress Quickly's speech (*Merry Wives*, III v 41, 45) are not reckoned among such expressions as cannot with propriety be read in a family; no improper connotation lingers about the word 'tailor' in Puck's *And tailour cries* (*Midsummer Night's Dream*, II i 54); the meaning of the old lady's cry is innocently obscure. How much of the English sex-implication vocabulary which was used by Shakespeare and understood by his eighteenth-century editors, went underground in nineteenth-century society it is difficult to judge, and perhaps indeed it is not very important to consider. But we tend, I think, to overestimate the degree of our emancipation from Victorian rules of language decency. We forget how large a step forward has had to be taken. At the beginning of the present century, for instance, a woman doctor who had been asked to give a course of lectures to the students of a Domestic Science training college, found herself obliged to stipulate for a revision of syllabus before she could accept appointment: 'Physiology from the waist up'—to give its informal title—had previously been the scope of the course. In the field of Shakespearean scholarship the agreed syllabus is still somewhat restricted; interpretation of Shakespearean innuendo, even when that innuendo is similarly organic, is not always acceptable. The occasional critic may testify, but without giving examples, to his pleasure in the 'ingenious obscenity' and no editor would wish to deny that

> Victorian propriety is thought to have gone to too great lengths in deciding what Shakespeare did or did not write in his plays.[1]

There are many, however, who would think it best not to give too much attention to this particular area of artistic language; we are perhaps not yet ready to give to it that degree of attention which Shakespeare gave. And the editor, of course, as distinct from the linguistic commentator, can restore what he perceives to be the original Shakespearean implication in a quite unobtrusive way. The 'New Cambridge' editors (1923) who give as their text in *Love's Labour's Lost*, IV iii 59,

> O, rhymes are guards on wanton Cupid's hose—
> Disfigure not his shop

note simply that Theobald and most editors read 'slop', adding a reference to their glossary entry:

> 'Shop, the organ of generation (see NED *sb*. 3*c*)'.

The commentator, by contrast, who may need to give evidence at greater length, will seem, on the one hand, over-naive to such

---

[1] 'Trend of Shakespeare Scholarship', by Hardin Craig, *Shakespeare Survey* 2, 1949, p. 109.

readers as are accustomed to understand Shakespeare in an eighteenth-century manner. And those who bring to Shakespearean interpretation a more restricted vocabulary will, no doubt, suspect of 'perverse ingenuity' that student of language who, seeking laboriously to explore the meaning of a problem passage, finds a new solution in some below the surface indecency. The highest poetry is still the most moral. In the words of an American scholar (1953) for whose work I have the highest respect,

> No writer is more moral than Shakespeare in fundamentals. His jests are often as bawdy as any, and he can hunt with a perverse pertinacity for off-color implications in familiar language. But these are on the surface of the man and of his theater. As so many critics have pointed out, there are, in his major characters, no stopping places between virtue and vice, no half tones between the white of purity and the black of sin.[1]

Shakespeare's contemporary, Sir John Harington, concludes a short Epistle to the readers of his *Epigrams:*

> But though I wish Readers, with stomacks full,
> Yet fast or come not, if your wits be dull.
>   For I had liefe you did sit downe and whistle,
>   As reading, not to reede. So ends th'Epistle.[2]

And I hope it may be conceded by the present-day Shakespearean student that in this particular language area we are not concerned with moral standards; where levity is necessary we shall not refuse to be lightminded.

2

I offer first two simple examples where context of situation and the tone of the speaker might well suggest that there lies

---

[1] *Shakespeare's Use of Learning* by V. K. Whitaker, Huntingdon Library, San Marino, California, 1953, p. 41.
[2] *Letters and Epigrams of Sir John Harington*, ed. by N. E. McClure, Philadelphia, 1930, p. 147.

a joke for our enjoying. In the second scene of *Troilus and Cressida* (I ii 92), Pandarus, having already opened the subject to Cressida on the previous day, visits Cressida again to recommend Troilus for her lover. As he enters, Cressida happens to be praising Hector, so that Pandarus (who would claim for Cressida more beauty than Helen has) is led on now to claim that Troilus will prove a better man than Hector. Hector, he will grant, is elder:

> Th'others not come too't, you shall tell me another tale when th' others come too't: Hector shall not haue his will this yeare.

Editors from the time of Rowe onwards[1] have thought the word *will* here, although it is found in both quarto and folio texts, to be a mistake for 'wit'. But it is as a man that Pandarus recommends Troilus—'do you know a man if you see him?'—and it is not primarily with his wit that Cressida will be concerned. *Will* in the appropriate sense of sexual energy ('Carnal desire or appetite')[2] is shown by NED with two Shakespearean citations: Tarquin

>   holds... disputation,
> Tweene frozen conscience and hot burning will.   (*Lucrece*, 247)

and Angelo giving to his 'sensuall race, the reine' advises Isabella (*Measure for Measure*, II iv 164)

> Fit thy consent to my sharpe appetite . . . .
>   Redeeme thy brother,
> By yeelding vp thy bodie to my will. . . .

'Will' in these situations is a force of evil; in the interchange between Pandarus and Cressida it makes a joke to be enjoyed and elaborated: 'Is he so young a man, and so old a lifter?' So too the one 'white haire' on Troilus' 'clouen chin' is made the matter of a jest sequence in exactly the same style. Those who are ready to enjoy the second cannot really doubt that Shakespeare intends them to enjoy the first.

---

[1] e.g. Malone, 'Old Cambridge', Alexander, Craig, Kittredge, Sisson, Dover Wilson.   [2] *Will,sb.*[1] 2.

The joke of the unconsummated marriage is used with great dramatic relevance at the end of *The Taming of the Shrew* (v ii 185), when Petruchio, having won the wager on his wife's obedience and gained his hundred crowns apiece from the discomfited husbands, winds up the play with the words:

> Come Kate, weee'le [sic] to bed,
> We three are married, but you two are sped.

We remember how Petruchio, like a falconer in his early days of training a hawk, has kept Kate 'giddie for lacke of sleepe'; he has told how 'Last night she slept not, nor to night she shall not' and is described in the 'Bridall chamber' as 'making a sermon of continencie to her'. And Kate herself—if, as I suggest, her marriage has been as yet no marriage—seems to understand why Petruchio has so valued their union that he has preferred to postpone it: in her last speech of the play she tells the disobedient wives

> A woman mou'd, is like a fountaine troubled,
> Muddie, ill seeming, thicke, bereft of beautie,
> And while it is so, none so dry or thirstie
> Will daigne to sip, or touch one drop of it.

Bianca and the widow, by contrast, whether or not in stage-time their marriages are newly accomplished—and the play is not concerned to be clear on this point—give the impression, in this last scene, of women who have been married for some little time. In her brief verbal encounter with the widow, Kate suggests that if *she* is to be accused of shrewishness, she is at least more chaste than the widow, 'And I am meane indeede, respecting you'.[1] And Bianca, roused to reply to a joke made by Gremio, is, metaphorically, 'Mistris Bride, . . . awakened, . . . but not frighted, therefore Ile sleep againe'. Kate's obedience they regard as 'foolish' and 'sillie'; their role is to show a wifely duty of the every-day kind.

---

[1] See p. 249 for this sense of *mean*, 'chaste'.

Editors have usually understood Petruchio's *sped* in the context of the single line 'We three are married, but you two are sped', *sped* having reference to the lost wager and meaning 'done for': 'the fate of you both is decided; for you have wives who exhibit early proofs of disobedience' (Steevens); NED glosses 'In . . . an evil plight'. But although this might be part of the meaning, Petruchio's victory over Kate is the real theme. And *sped* can also mean 'brought to the end desired, finished, dispatched'. There is no doubt of its implication in Shakespeare's *Merry Wives* (III v 67), in the bluntness of Ford's question when Falstaff is reporting how he has been with Ford's wife: 'And sped you Sir?' If we slightly extend the context in which we consider Petruchio's meaning—'Come Kate weee'l (sic) to bed', the short line ending with the emphasised rhyme—then 'sped' must take its meaning from the whole dramatic situation. It is the obvious climax to this comedy, and has some relevance also to the Christopher Sly framework. We recall how he agrees to see the play, although he 'may hardly tarry so long' for his 'Madame wife'.

It may be thought indeed that I labour upon a cobweb to 'prove' so obvious a joke by serious and detailed analysis; readers may feel that, editors and NED notwithstanding, some part of any audience would catch Petruchio's meaning. It must be admitted, however, that the joke which I think Pandarus is making could be heard only in the original text of *Troilus and Cressida*, not in the emended version. And the two instances will serve well enough to illustrate the accidental difficulties which hamper linguistic exploration in this particular semantic area; necessary evidence of word-meaning tends to be smoothed over. NED's brief citations illustrate single meaning only; Bartlett's *Concordance* works with a Shakespearean text as it was at the end of the nineteenth century (1875, 1891) before the NED's collections were available.

3

There are intrinsic difficulties also. The vocabulary with which we are here concerned is usually not that of the unwritten yet apparently indestructible taboo monosyllables, but with the more transient euphemisms which substitute for them, and that not formally in written English, but freely, amusingly, in the spoken language. And there are different levels, shifting levels of respectability. A word which remains at a lower level may pass out of use; Puck's *tailour* (*Midsummer Night's Dream*, II i 54) is, I suggest, one of these. Another, rising slightly to gain dictionary status, may attract to itself a respectable etymology which is henceforward to give it a new shade of meaning. Such, I think, is the Shakespearean *panel*.

To find the meaning of the indecent sixteenth- and seventeenth-century *tailour* adds little to our appreciation of Shakespeare's text, but the fact that we *can* find some part, at least, of its significance is itself of interest; it is made clear once more that no piece of language knowledge is an isolate; with this new bit of information one or two other questions are answered. The word occurs as Puck describes his mischief:

> The wisest Aunt telling the saddest tale,
> Sometime for three-foot stoole, mistaketh me,
> Then slip I from her bum, downe topples she,
> And tailour cries, and fals into a coffe.
> And then the whole quire hold their hips, and loffe,
> And waxen in their mirth, and neeze, and sweare,
> A merrier houre was neuer wasted there.

There is evidence available that 'tailor' to Shakespeare's contemporaries could have the sense 'penis' or 'pudendum'; in Puck's speech the sense 'posterior' seems to be required. The earlier eighteenth-century editors (Rowe, Pope and Theobald) offer no definition. Johnson notes:

> The custom of crying *tailor* at a sudden fall backwards, I think I remember to have observed. He that slips beside his chair falls as a tailor squats upon his board.

Halliwell (1856) would regard the word as a corruption of a Middle English *taillard*, which means, from its context, 'one with a tail'; Schmidt's *Lexicon* and Onions's *Glossary* can give no help.[1]

Although it is quite possible that Halliwell's derivation is correct, the ME *taylard* which he cites is a term of scorn applied to foreign soldiers, while the Shakespearean *tailour* carries with it no sense of physical abnormality. The main sixteenth and seventeenth-century meanings we can, I believe, sufficiently establish from Shakespeare's text, and if an etymology is needed we may postulate it, with some confidence, within the humour of spoken English. 'A word is known by the company it keeps', to quote J. R. Firth. *Yard* can mean 'penis' (as in *Love's Labour's Lost*, v ii 676); it can also mean 'a tailor's yard' (as in *The Taming of the Shrew*, iv iii 113, and *Romeo and Juliet*, i ii 40). Once these two meanings of *yard* were jestingly confused, the word *tailor* in isolation could, I suggest, take on the 'penis' sense. This we find in Shakespeare's text when Stephano sings of how Kate

> Would cry to a Sailor goe hang:
> She lou'd not the sauour of Tar nor of Pitch,
> Yet a Tailor might scratch her where ere she did itch. . . .
>
> (*The Tempest*, ii ii 55)

Next, since the tailor proper may specialise as a man's tailor or woman's tailor, I suppose that the same distinction would be made for the noun in its improper sense. So in 2 *Henry IV*, iii ii 161:

> Shallow.   What trade art thou Feeble?
> Feeble.   A Womans Taylor sir.

---

[1] Relatively few emendations have been put forward: 'rails or cries' (Hanmer and Warburton), 'tail-sore cries' and 'traitor cries' are among those proposed. For *taillard*, see Richard Coer de Lion in *Metrical Romances* ed. by H. Weber, Edinburgh 1810, ll. 724, 1766, 1820, 1876, 1950, 1996, 2112, 2146. Halliwell glosses the word as 'thief'; NED shows *tailard*, more precisely, as 'one with a tail'.

Shallow. Shall I pricke him, sir?

Falstaffe. You may:

But if he had beene a man's Taylor, he would haue prick'd you. Fine clothes may make a man; the 'tailor' in the sexual sense is also concerned. Some suggestion of this might, I think, be picked up by the audience when Cornwall questions Kent on his satirical comment against Oswald: 'a Taylor made thee' (*Lear*, II ii 60). The third stage of the joke is reached in the contemporary proverb 'Three tailors make a man' (as in Dekker, 1607. See also Tilley: T 23).[1]

The fact that *tailors* is an invariable in this proverb-form seems to me to preclude the possibility of any innocent single meaning: if the original reference were merely to a certain kind of trades-man, proverbially cowardly or unmanly, then some other trade would occasionally be named. It is true that later versions of the proverb do refer to such a lack of manliness: 'three taylers are one man', 'the Manhood of nine Taylors'; even so, when the ambiguous verb 'make' is discarded, the 'tailor' subject remains. Some form of the obscene joke seems to have survived until the beginning of the present century. J. S. Farmer's *Slang and Its Analogues* (1890-1904) includes *To do a bit of tailoring*, 'to get with child'; *sewed up* he glosses as 'pregnant'.

Returning now to Shakespeare's text, it is not difficult to see why Puck's old lady, as she topples backwards, cries out 'Tailor': as *tail* in earlier English has the three senses, 'posterior', 'penis' and 'pudendum', so *tailor* may well include the 'posterior' sense. Johnson's recollection suggests that such a cry was customary, and if we suppose that the word would attract to itself an addi-tional, more modest meaning, it could well be associated with the posture of the tailor seated at his work. The proverb 'That's as much use as a sore bottom to a tailor' was still current, so I am informed, in South Wales some twenty years ago.

---

[1] Tilley: T 23 (*a.* 1600) 1611 For two tailors goe to a man. 1607 (Dekker and Webster) They say three Taylors go to the makyng vp of a man. (The *'nine* tailors' joke is cited by Tilley from 1640.)

Before leaving Puck's speech, it is necessary to ask also if his subsequent phrase 'and fals into a coffe' serves only to link on to the sneezing which follows or if it implies some association between falling to the ground and falling into a cough. Any such proverbial usage would require to be strongly established in the spoken language since Shakespeare gives only half a line to the joke. I suggest that a proverb recorded by Ray in 1678 may have been current in Shakespeare's time: 'His tail will catch the kin-cough (= chin-cough). Spoken of one that sits on the ground'.[1] Here the antithesis of 'tail' and 'chin' gives the proverb its point in seventeenth-century polite English, although the actual meaning of *chincough* is 'whooping-cough'. Other dialect variants of this word are *kincough* and *kinkcough* and I suppose that in less genteel circles *tail* and *kin* might be recognised as synonymous (see NED: *kin sb.*[2]).

4

With this *tailour* example it is the method of discovery more than the result, which is of interest. We follow step by step the moves which are made in the language game of Shakespeare's contemporaries; it is they who are witty, rather than Puck's old lady. In my next instance, when I ask if there could be any meaning in the verb *pannelled* of the original text of *Antony and Cleopatra* (IV xii 21), a different procedure is necessary since the problem concerns not so much the language of society as what the artist has made of that language; because the inquiry is more complex the results are more significant. It may appear at first a waste of time even to raise the issue, for among those eighteenth-century emendations which are now so generally accepted that they have become, as it were, part of the Shakespear-ean context, Hanmer's 'spaniel'd' for the Folio's 'pannelled' has a high place; it seems to qualify as an inspired reconstruction, an

---

[1] *Collection of English Proverbs*, by John Ray, 1678, p. 82.

inevitable restoration of the true text. Johnson describes it as 'an emendation, with which it was reasonable to expect that even rival commentators would be satisfied', and in 1950 Dover Wilson finds it still 'A brilliant emendation, better confirmed by the context than Hanmer knew'. It is well, however, that even the most certain of emendations be sometimes questioned; other instances have shown that through the experiment of trusting firmly to the authenticity of the original text it is possible sometimes to reach a fuller understanding both of Shakespeare's meaning and of Shakespeare's art. I shall suggest here that in its compression and economy 'pannelled' may be considered genuinely Shakespearean and I shall argue my way from clue to clue, showing the stages of the linguist's procedure. Readers who prefer to appraise the worth of the evidence knowing in advance for what purpose it is adduced may look first at the end of this section for a brief statement of the interpretation I shall propose.

Contextual evidence seems strongly to support the eighteenth-century emendation of the 1623 Folio reading:

> All is lost:
> This fowle Egyptian hath betrayed me:
> My Fleete hath yeelded to the Foe, and yonder
> They cast their Caps vp, and Carowse together
> Like Friends long lost. Triple-turn'd Whore, 'tis thou
> Hast sold me to this Nouice, and my heart
> Makes onely Warres on thee . . .
> Fortune, and Anthony part heere, euen heere
> Do we shake hands? All come to this? The hearts
> That pannelled me at heeles, to whom I gaue
> Their wishes, do dis-Candie, melt their sweets
> On blossoming Caesar:

The study of Shakespeare's imagery has shown how strongly linked in his language are the fawning dog and the melting sweets; the image-cluster of this passage as Hanmer intuitively reconstructs it: 'spaniel'd me at heels', 'discandy', 'melt their sweets', seems demonstrably to belong to the Shakespearean pattern. As Caroline Spurgeon has pointed out:

> whenever the idea . . . of false friends or flatterers occurs, we find a rather curious set of images which play around it. These are: a dog or spaniel, fawning and licking; candy, sugar or sweets, thawing or melting. So strong is the association of these ideas in Shakespeare's mind that it does not matter which of these items he starts with— dog or sugar or melting—it almost invariably, when used in this particular application, gives rise to the whole series.[1]

So in the speeches of Caesar, Hotspur, Hamlet, and of Antony. In the face of such apparently convincing evidence it requires an unusual obstinacy even to suspend disbelief; and to look again at the 'pannelled' of the original asks a certain imaginative effort.

The first clue comes when, remembering the 'shrunke pannell' of Jacques's reproach to Touchstone (*As You Like It*, III iii 89), which Bartlett's *Concordance* shows as the only occurrence of 'panel' in Shakespeare's writing, we ask if the noun alone might not, for Shakespeare's first audience, imply unfaithfulness, or worse. Touchstone intends to be married to Audrey by Sir Oliver Mar-Text, and Jacques rebukes him:

> And wil you (being a man of your breeding) be married vnder a bush like a begger? Get you to church, and haue a good Priest that can tel you what marriage is, this fellow wil but ioyne you together, as they ioyne Wainscot, then one of you wil proue a shrunke pannell, and like greene timber, warpe, warpe.

In the idyllic green-wood setting, the image of 'greene timber' has an ironic appropriateness; 'shrunke' and 'warpe' may echo, faintly and incongruously, the earlier romantic affirmations of the Duke and of Amiens: 'Euen till I shrinke with cold' (II i 9) and 'Though thou the waters warpe' (II vii 187). But should we not suspect further that in the compression of Shakespeare's wit,

---

[1] *Shakespeare's Imagery and what it tells us*, Cambridge, 1935, p. 195.

'pannell' is more than a part of the warped wainscot simile? Behind the 'Wainscot' itself there could be a less respectable meaning: NED's citations show the possibility of an underlying falseness; I quote three instances:

> His face is made of seasoned wainscot, and will lie as fast as a dog can trot (1588),
> How does thy Mistriss that sits in a Wainscot Gown, like a Citizens Lure to draw the Customers (1626),
> This lost Companion [a quack], hauing a Foxes Head and an whorish and wainscotted Face (1602).

'A word is known by the company it keeps': the word *parnel, pernel*, 'a priest's concubine; a harlot', is cited by NED from 1362 onwards;[1] the spelling *panel* is first registered in an Old Lincolnshire Ballad *a*. 1800:

> Panels march by two and three, Saying, Sweetheart, come with me.

The wider currency of the word in American English would suggest however that this *panel* form was not, in *spoken* English, confined to so narrow a dialect area. In J. R. Bartlett's *Dictionary of Americanisms* (1860 ed.), *Panel-house* is a 'house of prostitution and theft combined'; it is interesting to see that by this time the 'secret panel' sense has attached itself and the *Panel-thief* enters, somewhat extravagantly, 'by a secret opening' to abstract the victim's money, watch, etc. Of what may be called 'loss of *r*' in Shakespeare's time, in such words as have originally ME *er, ar*, there is some further evidence: Kökeritz includes the spelling *tashan*, 'tertian' and shows that the rhyme *earth: death* in Shakespeare's text is found occasionally in other Elizabethan sources.[2] The above evidence I would regard as sufficient to 'prove' a pun in Jacques's 'pannell'; if I am right I must expect to find further instances of 'panel' word-play in other sixteenth- and

---

[1] Adopted, according to NED, from Old French *Peronele, Pernele*, representing the Latin *Petronilla* a woman's name, a saint so named; popularly viewed as a feminine derivative of *Petrus*, Peter.

[2] *Shakespeare's Pronunciation*, pp. 250, 252.

seventeenth-century literature which uses colloquial language.[1]
So in Dekker's *Satiromastix* (1602) Mistress Miniuer abuses Tucca
(III i 172):

> Hang thee, patch-pannell, I am none a thy Charing-crosse.[2]

Returning now to the 'pannelled' of Antony's speech it is
clear that the 'prostitute' sense would be in context in relation to
what precedes: Antony knows, even as he attacks 'The hear*ts*
That pannelled' that it is against Cleopatra only, Cleopatra,
triple-turned, that his heart makes its wars. But how would
'pannelled' lead on to the words which follow: 'at heeles', 'dis-
Candie', 'melt their sweets'? Is there some additional sense on
which the word might pivot, some language groove along
which composing-dramatist and speaking-character might move
easily to the new image? Can any clue be got from the 'spaniel,
dog, sugar' cluster elsewhere in Shakespeare's text? The 'spaniel'
image of *Midsummer Night's Dream* (II i 203) is simply presented—
'I am your spaniell'—and it has single meaning, representing
the extreme subservience of the faithful lover: 'The more you
beat me, I will fawne on you'; but as the image recurs in later
plays it becomes more complex. There is a noteworthy economy
in the king's rebuke of Gardiner's 'flattery':

> You play the Spaniell,
> And thinke with wagging of your tongue to win me
>   (*Henry VIII*, v iii 126)

when the dog-like characteristics of 'licking *tongue*' and '*wagging
tail*' are condensed into current proverb idiom of the human's
wagging tongue. And in Caesar's words when he denies in
himself

---

[1] It is worth noting that the noun *panel* can have also the sense 'saddle' and
this would increase the range of available *double-entendre;* according to the Hostesse
(2 *Henry IV*, II i 29) Falstaff 'comes continuantly to Pye-Corner (sauing your
manhoods) to buy a saddle'. The possibility of a blended panel-saddle joke might
provide a reason for the speaker to choose the -*a*- rather than the -*ar*- variant
in the *panel, parnel*, 'prostitute' option.

[2] *Dramatic Works* ed. by F. Bowers, Cambridge 1953, Vol. I, p. 342.

> such Rebell blood
> That will be thaw'd from the true quality
> With that which melteth Fooles, I meane sweet words,
> Low-crooked-curtsies, and base Spaniell fawning
>
> (*Julius Caesar*, III i 43)

the linkage of the associated images is not simply effected; the
meltable sweets are not there, as might be expected, to reward
the spaniel's fawning. Caesar, we know, is most flattered when
told that he hates flattery; for him, as for others like him, the
sweets and the fawning are equated. In Hotspur's description
of Bolingbroke's one-time affability this equation is made
explicit:

> what a caudie [candie] deale of curtesie,
> This fawning Grey-hound then did proffer me.
>
> (1 *Henry IV*, I iii 251)

Here, certainly, it is the dog which brings the sugar. So too I
would suggest in Hamlet's words to Horatio (*Hamlet*, III ii 65—
I quote the Folio text):

> let the Candied tongue, like ['lick'] absurd pompe,
> And crooke the pregnant Hindges of the knee,
> Where thrift may follow faining (Q fauning). . . .

The tongue, candied with the flattery that it brings, pretends to
take pleasure in licking a pomp which has no savour, no sweetness
(*ab-surdus*). This last interpretation I discuss in detail later (p. 160);
meanwhile I would ask the critic to note that although it would
support my present thesis it is not essential to it. What is beyond
dispute is that in Hamlet's imagery the dog is there only in action;
it is present, as any poet's dog might be, by virtue of its licking,
in its fawning attitude ('crooke', Folio) or in its actual 'fauning'
(Quarto 2), and in its having candy. Antony's dogs, I would
then argue, have their place in his image 'at heeles'; if in the verb
'panel' they carry out some action, the structure of Shakespearean
imagery directs us first to test the hypothesis that, like Hotspur's

greyhound, they bring the sugar. And NED shows plainly the
noun *panele* (1562 onwards) meaning 'Brown unpurified sugar
from the Antilles'!

I would argue then that in the one verb 'pannelled' Shakespeare
combines two meanings: the noun 'panel' (a form of earlier
'parnel') has the sense 'prostitute'; a second noun 'panele' has the
meaning 'sugar'. And I would not deny—what Hanmer recognised—that it may be part of the function of Shakespeare's
'pannelled', through the shape and sound of the word, to bring
to mind also, in this context, the 'spaniel' image. If my argument
is correct—and I suppose that, as far as it goes, it must be so, since
the available bits of evidence fit so well together—the usefulness
of being alert to the *double entendre* of 'panel' in Jacques's speech to
Touchstone is fully demonstrated. Hanmer's emendation, we
perceive, is nothing more than a watering-down of the original;
it takes too little account of that economy of expression, that
complexity of image-content which is characteristic of Shakespeare's later language.[1]

5

The 'tailour', 'pannelled' examples show something of the
game we have to play: meaning is more important than grammatical form; what might be regarded as an adolescent alertness

---

[1] Perhaps in general we should be more wary of how we 'complete' the
Shakespearean image. When Timon, for instance, contrasting the honour
accorded to 'Twin'd Brothers', says briefly (IV iii 12):

It is the Pastour ['pasture'] Lards, the Brothers sides,
The want that makes him leaue [leane]:

the highly skilful emendation 'rother's' for *Brothers* has still its adherents. Yet
Shakespeare's image is sufficiently conveyed by the noun 'pasture' and the
'lards/lean' antithesis; whereas 'rother's' would be functionless, *Brother's* relates
argument and image. Empson illustrates this editorial 'bringing back the first
draft' citing Johnson's 'May of life' for Macbeth's

my way of life
Is falne into the Seare, the yellow Leafe.... (v iii 23)

Seven Types of Ambiguity by W. Empson, 3rd ed. 1953, pp. 82-3.

to sex innuendo is more valuable than a high academic seriousness
For to understand the ingredients in the less decent imagery of
Shakespeare's time it is necessary to be aware of the joke connections, to imagine how one joke might blend into or be
answered by another; at the same time, in collecting instances of
usage to follow out the possible joke progressions, we have to
avoid being diverted from the particular track required by the
many side-branching ramifications of meaning. And what
Shakespeare may make of these ingredients is another matter.
He may make almost nothing, as with 'tailour'. He may make
something quite simple, as with the *double hen'd sparrow* of
Troilus and Cressida, extending a known image and giving it
particular application through a newly but quite normally
formed adjectival compound. He may run together several
implications into what appears to be a unique dramatic paradox
as in the *brakes of ice* passage in *Measure for Measure*.

In the battle between Greeks and Trojans at the end of *Troilus
and Cressida*, Thersites, watching the encounter of Menelaus and
Paris, eggs on cuckold and cuckold-maker (v vii 11):

> now bull, now dogge, lowe; Paris lowe;
> now my double hen'd sparrow; lowe Paris, lowe;
> the bull has the game: ware hornes ho?

Where the First Folio has *sparrow*, the Quarto (1609) has *spartan*,
and more recent editors, weighing the relative merits of these
variants, have been puzzled also by the *double hen'd;* the emendation 'double horn'd' has been proposed and is sometimes accepted.[1] Detailed study of the folio/quarto variants in this play

---

[1] Schmidt (1874) glosses *double hen'd:* 'perhaps = sparrow with a double-hen,
i.e. with a female married to two cocks, and hence false to both'; similarly
Hardin Craig (1951) thinks that the allusion is 'to Helen's belonging to two men;
she "doubles" as wife to both'. Hillebrand (New Variorum, 1953) tentatively
suggests a minor emendation: 'should we read "double-henned sparrows",
i.e. sparrows that are doubled to one hen?' Alexander (1952, 'Restoring Shakespeare: The Modern Editor's Task', *Shakespeare Survey* 5, p. 6) would follow
Kellner and make sense of the quarto text by the emendation 'double horn'd':
'This fits the context admirably. Menelaus the Spartan is fighting with Paris,

has not, however, established the general and overriding superiority of either; in this instance, I would suggest, the folio text is meaningful without emendation and should therefore be preferred. For to Shakespeare's contemporaries, as to Chaucer's, the sparrow was proverbially lecherous. Lucio, finding Angelo something 'too crabbed' wishes for the return of the Duke (*Measure for Measure*, III ii 185)

> this vngenitur'd Agent will vn-people the Prouince with Continencie. Sparrowes must not build in his house-eeues, because they are lecherous. . . .

John Davies of Hereford includes among his epigrams (*c.* 1610):

> Albertus Magnus saith that sparrows liue
> Scarce three yeares out (we needes beleeue him must)
> And for this same this naturall reason giues,
> Because so oft they doe the act of lust.[1]

Cotgrave's *Dictionarie* (1632 ed.) defines Passereau:

> 'A Sparrow; (especially the cock; whence the Prouerbe;) Passereaux, & moineaux sont de faux oiseaux. Cocke Sparrowes and (young) Monkes are (much of a disposition) shrewd lechers.'

And modern observation confirms, so I am informed, that a particularly vigorous sparrow might well keep two nests. Paris is the husband of Œnone and of Helen, so that Thersites, as he watches Paris beaten in this skirmish with the cuckolded Menelaus, may well consider this *double-hen'd sparrow* an appropriate gibe to encourage one not vigorous enough in battle.

The *brakes of ice* passage (*Measure for Measure*, II i 39) is less simple; the double meanings employed seem to be part of the play's comment on the double standards which are its theme.

---

and, as Paris has seduced Helen, her first husband is given the cuckold's horns by that scurvy commentator Thersites.' Eighteenth-century editors appear to have had no difficulty in understanding the folio text; the quarto's *spartan* they ignore, although Pope notes the variant as found 'in the old edition'.

[1] *Complete Works of John Davies of Hereford*, ed. by A. B. Grosart, 1878. Vol. II, *The Scourge of Folly*, Epigram 84, p. 17.

Claudio is condemned to death because he has 'got his friend with childe' and Escalus, having appealed in vain to Angelo for his life, speaks with some resignation of the unevenness of this world's justice:

Well: heauen forgiue him; and forgiue vs all:
Some rise by sinne, and some by vertue fall:
Some run from brakes of Ice, and answere none,
And some condemned for a fault alone.

The second line, italicised in the original text, is evidently regarded as a 'sententia', in the same group, on a decent level, as 'Vertue findes no friendes' (*Henry VIII*, III i 126) and 'Vertue it selfe, of Vice must pardon begge' (*Hamlet*, III iv 152). In Googe's translation of Palingenius's *Zodiacus Vitae* (a much used school book of Shakespeare's time) a similar sentiment is expressed:[1]

Then many filthy things I sawe, there done, and full of shame,
And nothing else of iustice left but vaine and ydle name.
Th'unguilty to be punished, the guilty scaping free,
The *Vertue hydde in vice*, and *Vice in vertue hid* to bee . . .

Another version, which seems to be half obscene,[2] refers to 'the rough Brake That Vertue must goe through'[3] (*Henry VIII*, I ii 76), so giving us one reason why 'vertue' and 'brakes' connect with each other in the speech of Escalus. And having quoted one

---

[1] Googe, p. 194.
[2] i.e. in origin, although not necessarily in subsequent application.
[3] See also *Venus and Adonis*, ll. 233-8:

> Graze on my lips, and if those hils be drie,
> Stray lower, where the pleasant fountaines lie.
> Within this limit is reliefe inough,
> Sweet bottome grasse, and high delightfull plaine,
> Round rising hillocks, *brakes obscure, and rough*,
> To shelter thee from tempest, and from raine:

Thomas Nash (*The Choise of Valentines* ? 1593) in physical description of Mistris Francis speaks of 'uglie bryers' (ed. by J. S. Farmer, 1899, p. 11). Compare also the imagery of folk-songs, as shown, for instance, in *The Everlasting Circle* by James Reeves, 1960:

> I have got a furze field, my own dearest jewel,
> Where all my fine pheasants do fly.   ('The Furze Field', p. 117.)

aphorism Escalus seems to be trying to coin another, this time one which is to be valid on two levels, 'brakes' and 'fault' being contrasted in two ways. As opposed to the very dangerous break in the ice, a *fault* would be a small flaw or crack.[1] But the word can also mean a mistake, a misdeed, a failing, a sin, an act of intercourse; Shakespeare's text shows a number of instances of word-play on these variants. Kent, meeting Gloucester's son Edmond, comments

> I cannot wish the fault vndone, the issue of it, being so proper.
>
> (*King Lear*, I i 16)

Falstaff calls for the help of Iupiter (*Merry Wives*, v v 9)

> Remember Ioue, thou was't a Bull for thy Europa . . . a Swan, for the loue of Leda . . . a fault done first in the forme of a beast, (O Ioue, a beastly fault:) and then another fault, in the semblance of a Fowle, thinke on't (Ioue) a fowle-fault.[2]

The 'Ice' may itself suggest 'sinne' through some such proverb as 'Vice is slippery like ice',[3] but it is associated also with chastity; Celia says of Orlando's kisses 'the very yce of chastity is in them' (*As You Like It*, III iv 18); Hamlet gives Ophelia

> this Plague for thy Dowrie. Be thou as chast as Ice, as pure as Snow, thou shalt not escape Calumny.   (III i 140)

Lucio says of Angelo 'his Vrine is congeal'd ice' (*Measure for Measure*, III ii 118). The recalcitrant Marina is described as 'able to freze the god Priapus' (*Pericles*, IV vi 3); Lysimachus she sends away from the brothel 'as colde as a Snoweball' (IV vi 149). And as Boult is ordered to

> crack the glasse of her virginitie, and make the rest maliable

---

[1] This sense is found in *King John*, IV ii 33:

> As patches set vpon a little breach,
> Discredite more in hiding of the fault,
> Then did the fault before it was so patch'd.

[2] See also *As You Like It*, IV i 177; I *Henry IV*, III i 245; *Henry V*, III ii 148; Sonnet 151 4.

[3] Cited by Tilley, v 44, from 1639; it may well have been current in the spoken language some thirty or forty years earlier.

so, using a similar image although less crudely, Angelo and Isabella agree, as they argue, that 'women are fraile' . . . 'as the glasses where they view themselues' and as 'easie broke' (II iv 125). So too in *The Taming of the Shrew* (I ii 267) Petruchio is to

> breake the ice . . .
> Atchieue the elder: set the yonger free. . . .

That this phrase 'to break the ice' (having the general sense 'to make a beginning') could have also this specialised sexual implication is further evidenced by a passage in Tourneur's *The Revenger's Tragedie* (1607):

> Vindice. . . . shee first begins with one,
>   Who afterward to thousands prooues a whore:
>   ,, Breake Ice in one place, it will crack in more.
> Mother.   Most certainly applyed.[1]

I suggest then that in his new aphorism, if new it is, Escalus has achieved that economy of comment which is so marked a characteristic of Shakespeare's dramatic imagery. And if we look again at the simplicity of his old proverb

> Some rise by sinne, and some by vertue fall

it begins to have other facets. Later in the play, by the virtue of Isabella, Angelo is to fall, and through that same virtue of Isabella —virtue in a rather different sense—Claudio is condemned. What has put him in peril is the fact of his getting Juliet with child: 'vertue' in the words of Escalus might here imply 'manly energy'. And if that sense is in play, those who enjoy the bawdy realism of *Measure for Measure* may find another joke in the 'rise', 'fall' antithesis. The comic generalisation would serve as an apt commentary on what all the play's pother is about. Whether or not my last suggestion is accepted, it is clear, I think, that for the composing dramatist the language here is all of a piece. It is the commentator only who finds difficulty in handling at one time the several oppositions.

---

[1] *Works of Cyril Tourneur*, ed. by Allardyce Nicoll, 1930. Act IV Sc. iv, p. 141.

6

To 'prove' the existence of an indecent joke which the dramatic context seems strongly to suggest is not always easy. Evidence which is available in the minor sources of Elizabethan and Jacobean English may not be noted in dictionary collections; readers who come upon such evidence may not be concerned with its relevance to Shakespeare's text. I cite here two such instances, where a knowledge of the grosser kind of spoken English is useful to the Shakespearean commentator. First the meaning of *poupt* (*Pericles*, IV ii 25). In the brothel at Mytilene, Pandor and Boult speak of their need to provide fresh wenches:

> Pandor.   ... the poore Transiluanian is dead that laye with the little baggadge.
> Boult.   I, shee quickly poupt him, she made him roast-meate for wormes.

As Boult leaves no doubt as to the fate of the Transylvanian, so it might be argued, Shakespeare has left no real doubt as to the meaning of the word 'pooped'. Yet the word has come to be shown in Shakespearean glossaries with a certain Bowdlerised imprecision; the present-day reader gets the impression that such a verb was current with the single and unambiguous sense 'to deceive, cheat' in the spoken English of Shakespeare's time.[1] What meaning might attach to the noun *poop* in seventeenth-century spoken English is shown clearly enough in a scurrilous epigram by John Davies of Hereford:

> Phrina (hot whoore) 'takes pepper in the nose'[2]
> Because her nose pimples some call poxes;
> Wherewith she peppers both her friends and foes,
> So makes her nose and poope, two pepper-boxes.[3]

---

[1] So in NED, Onions's *Glossary*, and Maxwell's 'New Cambridge' ed. (1956).
[2] i.e. ' takes offence.'
[3] Works, ed. by A. B. Grossart, 1878. Vol. II p. 41, 'Vpon English Proverbes' *c.* 1610, No. 7. See also No. 229. The verse suggests that Davies may have known

And if we derive the verb in Boult's speech from this noun we reach a sense more fully in context than NED's definition.

My next example (*Timon of Athens*, IV iii 143–5) is less easy to argue; the difficult line seems to be incomplete, but the whole passage is more interesting for the image-complex which it suggests. As Timon offers gold to the noble Alcibiades, the 'brace of Harlots' who are with the general ask for gold in their turn. Timon gives it, in the confidence that they will be true to their natural 'Conditions':

> . . . be whores still.
> And he whose pious breath seekes to conuert you,
> Be strong in Whore, allure him, burne him vp,
> Let your close fire predominate his smoke,
> And be no turne-coats: yet may your paines six months
> Be quite contrary, And Thatch
> Your poore thin Roofes with burthens of the dead,
> (Some that were hang'd) no matter:
> Weare them, betray with them; Whore still,
> Paint till a horse may myre vpon your face:
> A pox of wrinkles.

The chief problem here is what is meant by 'paines' being 'contrary' and why Timon wishes this to happen for 'six months'. Is the number of any real significance? It has been suggested that Timon wishes the harlots to spend six months of the year undergoing the harsh discipline of a cure (Warburton), or suffering punishment in a house of correction (Steevens), or simply having their menstrual pains abnormal (H. J. Oliver, 'New Arden', 1959); none of these interpretations, however, seems to arise inevitably from the given text. Once again, I suggest, the most difficult word may be the clue; the 'six' could be an essential directive to the meaning of the whole passage. In conjunction with 'the dead',

---

the form *pooper* as a dialect variant of 'pepper'; EDD shows *pupper* in Suffolk dialect (1823).

'six' months might bring to mind the fate of Proserpine, who spent six months of each year as Pluto's queen; six months is the longest time that life can cohabit with death. Moreover, the word 'contrary' in conjunction with 'six months' may itself imply the equal forces of the life-death opposition. A passage from Palingenius's *Zodiake of Life*, for instance, shows that if two contrary forces are equal, neither is destroyed.

> Two springs of nature chiefe there be, *Materia* and *Forma* namde:
> Of these same twaine all kinde of things, that here we see, are framde,
> Of these the earth, the Seas, the ayre, and flaming fyre springs:
> Wherefore they lye, that matter none, admit in Heauenly things.
> For contraries should then in them, be found (thus they do say)
> And by this meanes corrupted quite, they should in time decay.
> But as me seemes, this reason here, doth from the truth decline,
> For neither matter is in fault, if that in tract of time,
> The bodies fade: nor contraries, themselves will thus undo,
> If that their forces equall be, and stronger none of two:
> For when the strength and power is like, then equall is the fight,
> And victory on neither part, and neither syde doth light.[1]

If this postulate is accepted, Timon's speech is seen to have coherence of thought and feeling. He knows that he has gold

> Enough to make a Whore forsweare her Trade. . . .

But these whores are to continue, so that their 'Actiuity may defeate and quell The sourse of all Erection'. Neither Timon's gift, nor the 'pious breath' of would-be converter is to make them 'turne-coats'; 'yet' they too are not to escape Timon's curse, and in spite of what he has said about continuing, their way of trade *is* to be changed by his commands. For 'six months' long, let the 'paines' they take be with the dead and not with the living; let their activity be death-directed, 'quite contrary', their intercourse with the dead, even with those hanged on the gallows.

---

[1] Googe, p. 211.

'Thatch', the next important word, is, I think, a 'hinge' word, having relevance to this death-intercourse idea which precedes and also to the 'Weare', 'betray', 'Paint' theme which follows. This second theme I shall not take space to prove, since it is generally accepted as the total meaning of the next three lines: their hair, thinned by disease, is to be replaced by false hair from dead bodies. I would suggest, however, that this represents only half the sense. For if 'Thatch' is the hair of the head it might also stand for the 'pubic hair' of the intercourse theme. Such an implication is quite clearly present in a Scottish proverb of Shakespeare's time:

> To an old suter ane yong maid answeired Good schir
> Yow shal not thatch my new hous with old straw.[1]

Further evidence of this 'thatch' sense is available in Elizabethan and later English, but so as not to clutter the main *Timon* argument I give it in an appendix to this chapter (p. 149). The word 'burthen' in Shakespearean usage can have an obvious sexual implication, as when Juliet's nurse tells her

> I am the drudge, and toile in your delight:
> But you shall beare the burthen soone at night.
>
> > (*Romeo and Juliet*, II v 78)

Similarly 'Weare' can mean 'to possess and enjoy' as when Iachimo sneers at Posthumus' belief in the loyalty of his lady:

> Yow may weare her in title yours: but you know strange
> Fowle light vpon neighbouring Ponds. (*Cymbeline*, I iv 96)

Timon wishes the harlots, then, to earn a wretched living in commerce with the dead, surely the most apt image for prostitution. The adjectives 'poore' and 'thin' suggest poverty; the

---

[1] *Fergusson's Scottish Proverbs* ('gathered together' in the latter half of the sixteenth century, ed. by E. Beveridge, 1924, Scottish Text Society, New Series, No. 15, p. 123. The quoted saying is from a manuscript collection of the early seventeenth century.

9

verb 'thatch' is not only to 'get a roof over your heads' but also
to 'cover' in the sexual sense; 'Weare' is 'earn your finery' as well
as 'possess'. Obviously much of the dramatic force is lost when
it is necessary, for the interpretation of Timon's speech, to
examine the evidence piece-meal and at length. But if the separate
bits of evidence are accepted, then it is in the power of Timon's
irony that my interpretation is justified. It is against the whole
of this scene that the attempted explanation should be judged.

7

If, as outsiders, we fail to pick up one of the many improper
jokes in the wholly-comic wit of Shakespeare's dialogue, there
will be enough and to spare of the jokes that *are* comprehensible
to keep us still on the right wave-length: it will be obvious what
the dramatist is about. If, on the other hand, the implication-
word is made part of the material of the tragic or bitterly ironic
expression, as with Antony's 'pannelled' or Timon's 'Thatch',
then, in missing that implication, we shall lose much more than
the single word; we may even conclude that there has been a
fault in the transmission of the text. The net result is, as far as this
investigation is concerned, that the suggested allusion is more
easily 'proved' if it lies, as we suspect, at the heart of the uncomic
passage. And the more intricate the jig-saw, the more firmly the
pieces will lock together; the more certain we can feel about the
solution of the puzzle. Where we are, patently, not intended to
feel certain is with the wholly-comic *double-entendre* of Shakespeare's text. The more skilfully the improper sense is suggested,
the less likely it is that we can prove that such a sense is present.
The art of the speaker and of the dramatist will be shown, so to
say, by concealment, in the exactness with which the innocent
and less innocent meanings can counterchange, the preciseness
with which one sense fits the space taken by the other. And the
present-day reader who knows only the innocent Shakespearean

sense will not always realise which of the given counters in this particular language-game has the significant obverse side.

I take, first, two examples where, for reasons within the dramatic situation, presentation of double meaning is intended to be rather clumsy or slow, and where, as a result, the attention of the present-day reader may be directed to the accompanying improper sense. When the play within the play is about to be shown, Hamlet deliberately misleads Ophelia (III ii 121), and then pretends to have been misunderstood by her:

> Hamlet. Ladie, shall I lye in your Lap?
> Ophelia. No my Lord.
> Hamlet. I meane, my Head vpon your Lap?
> Ophelia. I my Lord.
> Hamlet. Do you thinke I meant Country matters?
> Ophelia. I thinke nothing, my Lord.
> Hamlet. That's a faire thought to ly between Maids legs. . . .

The passage leaves no doubt as to the obscene meaning of *lap*, and NED clearly confirms the now obsolete physical (non-figurative) sense,[1] which, incidentally, is not shown as relevant to this *Hamlet* passage and not noted by Shakespearean editors or glossarists. I cite this as an example where the obscene meaning can exactly replace the innocent sense; for the purpose of this demonstration it may be agreed that effectively the innocent *lap* and the obscene *lap* say the same thing, but the obscene *lap* says it more firmly and more grossly.

My next instance is from the Clown's speech to Olivia (*Twelfth Night*, I v 53). His style of formal clowning is that of relatively slow argument; Viola comments later that his 'practice' is 'As full of labour as a Wise-mans Art', and the clown himself, with

---

[1] The latest instance shown is from Crooke's *Body of Man* (1615):

> The *Clitoris* is a small body, not continuated at all with the bladder, but placed in the height of the lap.

I suppose that this sense must have survived in some regional English; in my own spoken language (N. Staffs.) the word *lap* is quite inadmissible, although I had never realised for what reason.

humorous anxiety, braces himself to meet Olivia after his truancy:

> Wit, and't be thy will, put me into good fooling: those wits that thinke they haue thee, doe very oft proue fooles: and I that am sure I lacke thee, may passe for a wise man.

He excuses himself for his absence with the 'simple Sillogisme' that 'good counsell' can mend him and that there is but little difference between the virtuous and the sinful:

> any thing that's mended, is but patch'd: vertu that transgresses, is but patcht with sinne, and sin that amends, is but patcht with vertue.

In this step-by-step argument we are given time, I suggest, to take in and think about the 'patch' repetition; we are directed to expect that, of these three counters offered in series, one at least will have a meaning other than its face value. The first, the patch mending, and the third, the patch amending, are of some moral worth; it is then the middle patch, *patcht with sinne*, that is to be suspected of impropriety. And so it proves. In two lines of John Heywood's *Dialogue* (1546) the young man who has married the rich old widow is heard lamenting his lot:

> Sluggyng in bed with hir is wors then watchyng,
> I promyse you, an old sack asketh muche patchyng.[1]

The sexual implication that can evidently form part of the 'patch' meaning[2] is shown again in Staneyhurst's maxim (1582)

> Cleaue toe the sound *Castè*, flee from thee patcherye *Cautè*.

Dekker's *patch-panell* (1602) has been noted earlier (p. 106).

---

[1] Photostat facsimile of copy in Huntingdon Library, San Marino, California; G i v.

[2] NED does not draw attention to this meaning, citing Heywood's proverb in brief isolation without indicating to what sense it is turned. Staneyhurst's line is cited under *Patchery*[2], defined as 'The conduct of a "patch"; roguery, knavery'. (*Patch* = A domestic fool; . . . clown, dolt, booby.) Farmer's *Slang and its Analogues* (1890-1904) shows *patch* as one of the many euphemisms for the female *pudendum*. See *Monosyllable*.

This time it is hard to express simply what Shakespeare's clown is doing in his word-play: his second statement 'vertu that transgresses, is but patcht with sinne', is true in two senses; the obscene 'patcht with sinne' can exactly replace the innocent sense and it says virtually the same thing as the decent phrase but in indecent terms. At the same time there is a strong opposition between the innocent face value of this second 'patcht' and its concealed obverse.

I want now to illustrate what I would regard as two similarly structured instances of wholly skilful *double entendre*. For the first kind I take an instance from *As You Like It* (IV i 67). Rosalind, disguised as the shepherd-boy Ganymede, has agreed to cure Orlando of his love:

> I would cure you, if you would but call me Rosalind, and come euerie day to my Coat, and woe me.

Celia teases them both:

> It pleases him to call you so: but he hath a Rosalind of a better leere then you.

Her word *leere* has, I suggest, three senses: first the wholly innocent surface meaning, 'complexion, appearance' (from OE *hlēor* 'face'), as generally given by glossarists and commentators. The second meaning may come from this particular context of situation: Rosalind and Celia are disguised as country folk; we remember how Celia has proposed that she will 'with a kinde of vmber smirch my face, The like doe you'. And *lear*, as NED shows, can mean the colour of sheep or cattle, due to the nature of the soil.[1] So in Holland's *Pliny* 1601

---

[1] In considering the lears of sheep, some are acknowledged as better than others:
> the browne hazell leare is of all other the best, the redd leare next to it . . . (1616).

And as late as 1883 a powder for sheep is advertised as
> producing a good Lear, which every farmer must allow is a great advantage (NED's citations).

In some places there is no other thing bred or growing but brown & duskish, insomuch as not only the cattell is all of that leere, but also the corn upon the ground.

The third sense of Celia's 'leere' would have its place in the light-hearted sex-innuendo of this scene: what Ganymede would lack of Rosalind is too good a joke for Celia to miss. This *leer* can have the meaning 'flank or loin' (probably from OE *lira*, 'the fleshy part of the body'); when Chaucer, for instance, *c*. 1386, tells us of the arming of Sir Topas, he describes how

He dide next his whyte lere
Of clooth of lake fyn and clere
A breech and eek a sherte.[1]

The word survives in this sense in some south-western dialects; northern dialects have the form *lire*, 'the fleshy or muscular parts of any animal'. In the directness of this allusion, I suggest, Celia merely deepens the thrust of her innocent-sounding comment. Her 'leere' and Hamlet's 'lap' are jokes in the same form, the implication-word coincident with the modest-seeming expression, only cutting more keenly.

My next instance is from Portia's speech (*Merchant of Venice*, I ii 144) when she learns of the arrival of the first suitor who is to make his choice of the caskets, the black Prince of Morocco. Although she speaks with pleasure of the departure of the rest—

I am glad this parcell of wooers are so reasonable, for there is not one among them but I doate on his very absence

—she cannot entirely welcome the newcomer:

If I could bid the fift welcome with so good heart as I can bid the other foure farewell, I should be glad of his approach: if he haue the condition of a Saint, and the complexion of a diuell, I had rather hee should shriue me then wiue me.

---

[1] Chaucer's *Works: Canterbury Tales*, ed. by W. W. Skeat, Oxford, 1924, p. 195.

The surface meaning is sufficiently clear; even supposing he has a saint's temper she would welcome this prince, black as a devil, rather as a confessor than as a husband. But, just as the Clown's 'patch', while pretending to an identity of meaning with others in the series, includes the licentious opposition sense, so here, I think, Portia's *shrive*, pretending to an opposition with the 'wiue' which follows, includes an indelicate similarity. There is here a double paradox: to be shrived by the devil would be the reverse of holiness and, within the humour of spoken English, to be shrived at all might be the reverse of virtue. Such an implication is, no doubt, commonly found in any language community devoutly observant of its religious duties: as early as the beginning of the thirteenth century the writer of the *Ancren Riwle* comments on how 'Sum unseli, hwon heo seide þet heo schrof hire, haveþ ischriven hire al to wundre'. The joke is glanced at elsewhere in Shakespeare's text and it is worth remarking that where it is not so neatly pointed as in Portia's paradox we see it the better. While Charles the Dauphin declares himself the 'prostrate Thrall' of Joan la Pucelle the French nobles watch with hostility from a distance (1 *Henry VI*, 1 ii 119):

> Alanson.   Doubtlesse he shriues this woman to her smock,
> Else ne're could he so long protract his speech.
> Reigneir.   Shall wee disturbe him, since hee keepes no meane?[1]

And when King Edward at last resolves to ask the Lady Grey to be his wife, Richard and Clarence comment in similar terms:

> Richard.   The Ghostly Father now hath done his Shrift.
> Clarence.   When hee was made a Shriuer, 'twas for shift.
>
> (3 *Henry VI*, III ii 108)

---

[1] The 'shrive' pun here is matched by the double-pointed 'keepes no meane'; 'mean' can be both 'moderation' and 'chastity'. So in *Merchant of Venice*, III v 82, 'meane it' is 'to live chastely' (see p. 249). Similarly in the speeches preceding the shrift pun of 3 *Henry VI* 'mean' is repeated half a dozen times, never openly with this sense of 'chaste' but in a verbal combat fought for chastity.

8

In these four examples of double meaning—'lap', 'patch', 'leere', and 'shriue'—both innocent and less innocent senses are of equal importance; the joke, as the speaker in each case contrives it, lies in the tension between the two meanings. In other instances Shakespeare may intend the speaker to remain unaware of the subsidiary sense which is most powerfully to affect the audience. So, I suggest, with the following passage (*Othello*, III iii 357) when Othello wishes only that he had not known of Desdemona's 'stolne houres of Lust':

> I had beene happy, if the generall Campe,
> Pyoners and all, had tasted her sweet Body,
> So I had nothing knowne. Oh now, for euer
> Farewell the Tranquill minde; farewell Content;
> Farewell the plumed Troopes, and the bigge Warres,
> That makes Ambition, Vertue . . .
> . . . Othello's Occupation's gone.

Occupation, as Othello intends it, appears to refer to his victorious generalship, now gone for ever, as his 'Tranquill minde' is lost. But in this dramatic situation, as Iago and the rest of us understand it, the word must refer also to his loss of Desdemona; from that place where he has 'garnered vp' his heart, he counts himself discarded (IV ii 57). It is noteworthy that the verb *occupy*, 'to cohabit with' was, in Shakespeare's day, in process of being dropped from decent usage, so that the meaning of 'Occupation' which Othello himself ignores would be the more vividly present to the Shakespearean audience. Doll Tearsheet, for instance, cries out that Pistol's claim to being a captain will bring all captains into disrepute; the word 'captain' will become

> as odious as the word occupy, which was an excellent good worde before it was il sorted. (2 *Henry IV*, II iv 161, Quarto 1600)

I do not want to make too much of this tiny point, but it seems to me that there is here another indication of the dangers in Othello's position: he stands at a certain distance from the world of common men; only rarely does Shakespeare allow the audience to identify itself with him; at this point of the play we are listening to his words with ears more sensitive, less noble, than his own.

A complete contrast to this lack of linguistic alertness is found in *Merry Wives* (III v 41) where a malapropism of Mistress Quickly's has its place in the scene only for what Falstaff can make of it as he nudges the elbow of his audience. Falstaff who has been carried away with the 'fowle linnen' and, by Mistress Ford's predirection, thrown into 'the muddie ditch, close by the Thames side', is recovering himself with a quart of sack when Mistress Quickly comes to him with a message from this same Mistress Ford. Falstaff complains:

> Mist. Ford? I haue had Ford enough: I was thrown into the Ford;
> I haue my belly full of Ford.
> M. Quickly.   Alas the day, (good-heart) that was not her fault:
> she do's so take on with her men; they mistooke their erection.
> Falstaffe.   So did I mine, to build vpon a foolish Womans promise.
> M. Quickly.   Well, she laments Sir for it, that it would yern your
> heart to see it:

Although Falstaff, like Othello, has been and is being deceived, the audience is with him in his masculine predicament; it is his wit which is made the channel of the Shakespearean joke, which draws attention to the major—unstated—meaning of Mistress Quickly's words. It may be noted also how the word *yern*, 'to grieve' and 'to become erect', catches the light here. Another form of the same word is found when Pistol, speaking of Falstaff's death, mingles grief and exhortation (*Henry V*, II iii 6)

> . . . my manly heart doth erne. Bardolph, be blythe: Nim, rowse
> thy vaunting Veines: Boy, brissle thy Courage vp: for Falstaffe
> hee is dead, and wee must erne therefore.

9

Perhaps the most interesting thing we do with language is to express verbally what is not verbally present; we have all taken part in the kind of conversation where the 'unspoken' meaning is of more significance than what is actually said. I want now to consider two or three instances where, by letting the light play on a different facet, first of one word and then of another, Shakespeare is able to make new patterns of mutually-dependent meanings—meanings which are a part of the dramatic situation although not necessarily a part of the argument or the grammar of what the speaker is saying. The question of proof here is more than usually difficult. If the Shakespearean passage is firmly shaped and of sufficient content, I suppose that we shall never be able to prove that the light-catching gleam is there at all. Falstaff's 'Honour' soliloquy before the battle of Shrewsbury has enough surface meaning to engage us (1 *Henry IV*, v i 131); he says fare-well to the prince with some apprehension:

> I would it were bed time Hal, and all well.
> Prince.   Why, thou ow'st heauen a death.
> Falstaffe.   'Tis not due yet: I would bee loath to pay him before his day. What neede I bee so forward with him, that call's not on me? Well, 'tis no matter, Honor prickes me on. But how if Honour pricke me off when I come on? How then?

His 'Catechisme', it seems, is concerned only with that honour which is 'A word . . . Ayre'; and that kind of honour which might be thought most likely to *pricke* him on, a woman's honour in the concrete sense[1] remains apparently unmentioned.

Sometimes it seems that one or two lines of dialogue have a place in Shakespeare's text only for the small firework display which they contain: while the outsider is counting the individual

---

[1] NED: *Honour*, 3. . . . Chastity, purity. b. *concretely:* cf. Ger. *die scham. Obs.* 1688 first citation.

sparks, Shakespeare's contemporaries would see the single flash as interesting but not so very remarkable. So in *Henry VIII* (v iv 26), when the princess Elizabeth is to be christened, an enthusiastic crowd has forced its way into the court precincts, and the assistant door-keeper, rebuked by his master, declares that he has done his best with his 'Cudgell':

> if I spar'd any
> That had a head to hit, either young or old,
> He or shee, Cuckold or Cuckold-maker:
> Let me ne're hope to see a Chine againe,
> And that I would not for a Cow, God saue her.

Why *Chine* and *Cow* are linked together in the last two lines here has not been satisfactorily explained: the usual explanation, that 'chine' means 'a joint (e.g. of beef) cut from the spine' might be one of the reasons, but by itself it seems too small a point for so energetic an affirmation. We are to expect that other senses will be in play. In the hitting context 'Chine' may suggest the hard blows that have been given; *to chine* can be 'to break the back' (NED: 1596 to 1741); the verb is still used in some dialects meaning 'to beat'. The word may also suggest the grazes and cuts that have resulted; (NED shows *chine* meaning 'a cut', 1387, or 'a crack in the skin' in use until 1562). So as to hit more effectively the Porter has cried out for a 'dozen Crab-tree staues', and this 'stave' idea may have put his assistant in mind of another 'stave', of great value to them both, the 'chine' which is the projecting rim at the head of a cask: NED cites a regulation from the Household Ordinances (1601)

> The yeoman drawer hath for his fee all the lees of wine within fowre fingers of the chine.

Within this area of meaning 'brown cow',[1] it may be noted, is a humorous name for a barrel of beer. On what is perhaps a third tack, R. A. Foakes (New Arden ed. of *Henry VIII*) suggests that 'Not for a Cow, God save her' may be a proverbial phrase in

---

[1] NED: *Cow, sb.*[1] 2b. one citation, 1725.

common currency: he is able to cite one further instance. And
from 'chine' as a disease of cattle, a cow might well need saving.[1]
The last and probably the most important part of the joke is
in the connection which the porter's man is able to make between
'chine' and 'cow' within the less decent vocabulary of the time.
He warns his hearers to be ready for this by his 'He or shee,
Cuckold or Cuckold-maker'; the words 'Chine' and 'Cow',
this arrangement indicates, are to be in similar opposition.
'Cow' as the woman, the Cuckold-maker, is obvious enough:
there is the common proverb 'He that bulls the cow must keep
the calf' (which Tilley shows, extant in variant forms, from
1550). 'Chine' is less obvious but not without parallel; while it
is not, I think, a quite new joke, this moment sparked-off, it puts
forward an old joke in a newer guise. The word will, I suggest,
represent 'He' (actually both 'Cuckold' and 'Cuckold-maker') in
that 'chine', 'the backbone', containing the spinal marrow, may
be thereby the 'marrow-bone'. And *marrow-bone*, cited by
Farmer (1904) as one of the many euphemisms for 'penis', is still
used in spoken English of the present time and may well have
been current in earlier speech. No instances are found in Shakespearean usage, but 'marrow' itself has the expected sexual
connotation, as for instance when Parolles (*All's Well*, II iii 298)
urges Bertram to set off for the wars:

> He weares his honor in a box vnseene,
> That hugges his kickiewickie heare at home,
> Spending his manlie marrow in her armes. . . .

Of the 'marrow-bone' implication in early seventeenth-century
English, there is clear evidence when a jealous husband, seeking
to guard his wife's virtue, conveys away

> all her wanton Pamphlets, as Hero and Leander, Venus and
> Adonis, oh two lushious mary-bone pies for a yong married wife
> (1608, Middleton, *Mad World*, Bi v).

---

[1] E.g. NED: 1607 The iuice of the black Chamæleon killeth young kie like the
chine.

My own postulation—the 'chine', 'penis' equation—Shakespeare's porter, for one, seems to understand. He answers his assistant on the same wavelength:

> What should you doe,
> But knock 'em downe by th'dozens? Is this More fields to muster
> in? Or haue wee some strange Indian with the great Toole, come
> to Court, the women so besiege vs? Blesse me, what a fry of
> Fornication is at dore? On my Christian Conscience this one
> Christening will beget a thousand. . . .

A similar joke is found in non-Shakespearean sources (*a.* 1625, *The Custom of the Country*, III iii) when Sulpitia, mistress of the male stews of Lisbon, numbers over with her servant the men who have seen service and foundered:

> Sulpitia. Where's the Frenchman?
> Jaques. Alas, he's all to fitters,
> And lies, taking the height of his fortune with a syringe!
> He's chin'd, he's chin'd, good man; he is a mourner.
> Sulpitia. What's become of the Dane?
> Jaques. Who, goldy-locks?
> He's foul i'the touch-hole, and recoils again;
> The main-spring's weaken'd that holds up his cock;
> He lies at the sign of the Sun, to be new-breech'd.[1]

In this context there is an obvious overlap between *chine*, 'penis' and *mourn of the chine*, 'to suffer from the glanders' (a disease of horses).

In this last Shakespearean example it is the sheer difficulty of understanding the text that makes it necessary to explore the several meanings with which the speaker simultaneously makes play. And even Shakespeare's contemporaries, who would have at their tongue's end the individual bits of language knowledge which later readers must laboriously acquire, may have felt some momentary bewilderment. I do not think however that the

---

[1] NED: *chined* 3. I quote from *Works of Beaumont and Fletcher*, ed. by A. Dyce, 1844, Vol. IV, p. 441.

interpretation here suggested can be considered the less credible because of its complexity. The moment of silence before the wave of laughter is often a testimony to the skill of the script-writer.

A similar example where the apparent textual difficulty lies at the heart of the meaning is found in *All's Well*, v ii 20, where Parolles, in disgrace, hopes that he may be received and helped by the Lord Lafew, and asks the clown to give him a letter. In the puzzling word *pur* of the Clown's speech are to be found a variety of meanings. He and Lafew, it seems, are accomplished jugglers, tossing several senses into the air at once and changing the ranges of meaning within the interweaving patterns; the audience too must have been quite skilful.

> Parrolles. Pray you sir deliuer me this paper.
> Clowne. Foh, prethee stand away: a paper from fortunes close-stoole, to giue to a Nobleman. Looke heere he comes himselfe.
> *Enter Lafew*
> Clowne. Heere is a purre of Fortunes sir, or of Fortunes Cat, but not a Muscat, that ha's falne into the vncleane fishpond of her displeasure, and as he sayes is muddied withall. Pray you sir, vse the Carpe as you may, for he lookes like a poore decayed, ingenious, foolish, rascally knaue. . . .
> Parrolles. My Lord I am a man whom fortune hath cruelly scratch'd.
> Lafew. And what would you haue me to doe? 'Tis too late to paire her nailes now. Wherein haue you played the knaue with fortune that she should scratch you, who of her selfe is a good Lady, and would not haue knaues thriue long vnder? There's a Cardecue for you:

Conjectural emendation would change 'purre' to 'puss' here, omitting the second 'of' before 'Fortune'. Some who keep the original text have confessed to ignorance of the sense; others interpret *purre* as 'a murmur' or 'grumble' or 'like the purring of sycophant cat, . . . calculated to procure favour and protection'. Schmidt glosses with this reference, 'the low murmuring sound of a cat'; NED cites this passage as the first instance of that sense. But the clown is a thoroughly competent wit-snapper, and the opposition 'a purre of Fortunes sir, or of Fortunes Cat' (with the pun on the homophone developed in his 'muscat' quibble and returned to by Parolles and Lafew in 'scratch'd' and 'scratch') suggests strongly that whatever the first 'pur' is, it is not simply the usual purr of a cat. The 'Carpe' and 'fish-pond' imagery, with 'Fish of Fortunes butt'ring' a few lines earlier, would make appropriate, as a secondary signification, the name of a fish, and we find in EDD *purr*, 'a small codlin' (Shetlands, 1866). More intensive collecting of material might show this word-sense in an earlier record nearer home. Further, the fish-pond image proceeds from and is part of the close-stool imagery of this and the immediately preceding passage:

> Fortunes displeasure is but sluttish if it smell so strongly as thou speak'st of: I will hencefoorth eate no Fish of Fortunes butt'ring. Pre thee alow the winde.

Within the conventions of Elizabethan clownery it should therefore perhaps be anticipated that 'purre' would also bear a meaning or group of meanings having reference to this larger image; the sense 'excrement' would be contextually proper. How much of colloquial or vulgar vocabulary in this specialised field of sex and bodily function existed in speech only, even in less linguistically inhibited ages, we can only conjecture. Paucity of dictionary evidence is to be expected, and it may well be that such forms as get into the written language of more recent times have taken on respectability through false etymology, analogical spelling, or restricted application. What evidence is available here, from NED and EDD, suggests that a word of the shape of 'pur', with the sense 'dung' was dying out in the mid-nineteenth century.[1] Further ripples and cross currents of allusion may

---

[1] NED: *Pure sb.* 5. . . . *Tanning.* Dogs' dung or other substance used as an alkaline lye for steeping hides. Also in *comb.* as *pure-collector, -finder, finding.* (Also spelt *pewer, puer*) 1851, 1858. EDD: under *Poor* shows *poor-luck*, cat's dung, Lincs. 1866.

proceed, as the clown is speaking, from *pure*, 'a kept mistress' (NED: 1688 to 1725), from *cat*, 'a prostitute' (NED: 1535 to 1708), and from *cat* suggesting *pussy* = 'cunnus' (surviving into present-day spoken English, but not shown in the written sources of NED; there are cognates in other Germanic languages). It is possible too that Lafew's words 'played the knaue with fortune' (cf. *Merchant of Venice*, II iii 12, and *All's Well*, IV v 24) throw back to 'pur' additional senses complementary on the male side to the first and third of these.[1] 'Playing the knave' also links on to the third and main significance in which the clown uses the word, 'the knave or jack in the game of post and pair.' Evidence for this main sense, clear but not extensive, is found, once more, in NED.[2] To Professor Dover Wilson belongs, it seems, the credit of first noting its relevance here. The fact that this 'pur' might be associated with 'pur-dog' may have led to the emphasised opposition 'or of Fortunes Cat', and Lafew's 'paire' may be another minor reference within the same card-game range. If my suggestions are correct, the clown's *purre* has significance in each of three concentric fields of imagery and Lafew picks up and plays back within the third range, that of 'knave'. And in this range the significance is not verbal only, but situational, dramatic. Parolles in an earlier scene (II iv) has addressed the clown as 'my knave' and the clown was then at some pains to exchange the term with him. Now the whirligig of time has brought its revenge, the clown may refer to Parolles as the knave of Fortune—if he is under the imputation of playing the knave with her, she has certainly played the knave with him; from the ambiguous 'pur' the clown passes to the plain 'knave', echoed and re-echoed by Lafew as the scene continues.

---

[1] NED: *Pur*[1] *dial.* . . . [OE, in *pur lamb*, of uncertain origin].

a. A ram or wether lamb; also *pur-lamb, pur-hog*.

b. *transf.* A male child, a boy. To 1888.

[2] *Pur*[2], *purr. Cards. Obs.* [Origin unascertained.] A name given to the knave or Jack in the game of post and pair. . . . Also *attrib.* pur-chop, pur-dog, ? a card which would take the knave.

Once again it is the difficulty of understanding the given text that opens our eyes to this display of virtuosity; the words of Heminge and Condell, Shakespeare's fellow-actors and first editors are once more justified:

> Reade him, therefore; and againe, and againe: And if then you doe not like him, surely you are in some manifest danger, not to vnderstand him.

Some of my readers may inwardly answer, although few, I think, will be so unfashionable as openly to admit that they find no great pleasure in understanding the kind of joke which is here expounded. Others may advance the practical objection that in these last examples the labour involved in understanding outweighs the aesthetic gain. And certainly it is for the individual reader to decide what industry and energy he can spare for such detailed exploration into the less edifying spoken English of three and a half centuries ago. For my present purpose, however, it is useful to illustrate what an amount of patient unravelling may be necessary if we are to understand the single word in such brief but highly compressed 'divertissements' before I come to my last example in this section—a problem of greater artistic significance.

10

Critical attention has recently been redirected to that most famous of emendations, 'his nose was as sharp as a pen, and a' babled of green fields' (Theobald, 1733), which everyone knows as the Hostesse's description of the dying Falstaff (*Henry V*, II iii 17). In the Folio the passage reads:

> Nay sure, hee's not in Hell: hee's in Arthurs Bosome, if euer man went to Arthurs Bosome: a made a finer end, and went away and it had beene any Christome Child: a parted eu'n iust betweene Twelue and One, eu'n at the turning o'th'Tyde: for after I saw

him fumble with the Sheets, and play with Flowers, and smile vpon his fingers end, I knew there was but one way: for his Nose was as sharpe as a Pen, and a Table of greene fields.

I shall try to argue that the description as given in the folio—'our only relevant authority' in the words of Sir Walter Greg—is meaningful, and that to allow Theobald to alter the original text is merely to prefer the unambiguous sentiment of a most skilful eighteenth-century editor to the complex artistry of the greatest Elizabethan dramatist. In the interpretation now put forward I shall seek to 'prove' from elsewhere in Shakespeare's text the glosses I regard as appropriate in this scene, and I claim the right also to draw upon the record of spoken English before and after Shakespeare's time.

First, what can be learned from the given text about the type of English which the Hostesse speaks? It is certainly colloquial and, we are directed to infer, socially sub-standard. She is heard, for instance, comforting Doll Tearsheet (2 *Henry IV*, II iv 25):

> Sweet-heart, me thinkes now you are in an excellent good temperalitie: your Pulsidge beates as extraordinarily, as heart would desire. . . .

In the short scene where Falstaff's death is described there is the evidence of 'bid', 'bad' ('bade'), and of 'Carnation' as a wrong or muddled response to 'incarnate'. This means that by no more than modernisation of spelling, the 'Pen' can be either 'on' or 'in' the 'Table': the 'intrusive' *d*, after 'final' *n*, was common enough in various kinds of sixteenth- and seventeenth-century colloquial and sub-standard speech, so that there occur such spellings as *wind*, 'wine', *gownd* 'gown', *frang & sense*, 'frankincense'; similarly the spelling *a* in this same speech of the Hostesse represents the unstressed indeterminate vowel: '*a* made a finer end', 'be *a* good cheare'. Further, it is usual for the scenes in which the Hostesse plays to contain bawdy allusion; what she has to say may be proper enough on one level, but its main dramatic value may consist in underlying impropriety. And we cannot always know whether it is she who intends the joke or Shakespeare: the wit may lie in the oblique applicability of a sexual meaning which is explicitly denied. When Pistoll, now her husband, says proudly (*Henry V*, II i 33)

> nor shall my Nel keep Lodgers

and she answers

> No by my troth, not long: For we cannot lodge and board a dozen or fourteene Gentlewomen that liue honestly by the pricke of their Needles, but it will bee thought we keepe a Bawdy-house straight

it is her own word 'pricke' which explodes the bubble. It must be remembered also that dictionary evidence may not exist to 'prove' that the funniest bit of her joke is there at all, as when she describes Mistris Dol as 'Sick of a Calme' (2 *Henry IV*, II iv 40), a lucky hit which Falstaff more elaborately reiterates.[1] I suggest that such considerations are relevant here, and that, in the sentence of the original text, 'his Nose was as sharp as a Pen, and (= on) a Table of greene fields', the words 'Nose', 'Pen', 'Table' and 'greene' had underlying sexual connotations to an Elizabethan audience. I contend that these meanings can be sufficiently established from elsewhere in Tudor English and in Shakespeare's text; present-day references are added for completeness but there is, I think, enough evidence without them.

In a literature which includes *Tristram Shandy* it is hardly necessary to illustrate what might be represented by 'nose'. Although I have noted no such explicit obscene comic reference in Elizabethan English, there is the obvious linguistic symbolism as when Othello (IV i 146) as he watches Cassio miming Bianca's embraces, cries out 'I see that nose of yours, but not that dogge, I shall throw it to'; Farmer's *Slang and its Analogues* (1890-1904) cites the old, half-obscene proverb 'A long nose is a lady's liking'. The obscene sense of pen is very clearly established: Gratiano

---

[1] 'So is all her Sect: if they be once in a Calme, they are sick'.

answers Nerissa's threat that, left alone, she will have as her
bedfellow that same judge's clerk to whom her husband has
given her ring:

> Well, doe you so: let me not take him then,
> For if I doe, ile mar the yong Clarks pen.   (v i 237)

Such a sense is also required, I suggest, in the pert boy's claim to
have purchased experience 'By my penne of obseruation' (*Love's
Labour's Lost*, III i 28, emended to 'penny' by Hanmer and a
number of modern editors). There is further unambiguous
evidence in the idiom 'ink in the pen' (as in *Lusty Juventus*, c. 1540),[1]
with its more modern counterpart 'lead in the pencil'.[2]

And the pen 'writes',[3] as in Tourneur's *The Revenger's Tragedy*
(1607)

> This vicious Old Duke's worthily abusde—
> The pen of his bastard writes him Cuckold!

That on which the pen writes, the actual memorandum-book or
writing tablet, is often found in Shakespearean and earlier English
in the plural form 'tables'; my Tudor and Shakespearean citations
of this word in the figurative and obscene sense are of the plural

---

[1] And, when there is no more ink in the pen,
I will make a shift, as well as other men.
Dodsley's Old Plays, 1874, ii 92.

[2] as in 'The Journal of an Old Gent', *New Yorker*, 18 Feb. 1956, p. 48.

[3] *Works of Cyril Tourneur*, ed. by A. Nicholl, 1929; II ii 120-1, p. 107. If more
evidence is required, see also George Gascoigne's *A Hundreth Sundrie Flowers*,
c. 1573. I quote from C. T. Prouty's edition, Univ. of Missouri, Columbia 1942:

> Shee had in the same house a friend, a servaunt, a Secretary: what should I
> name him (p. 58);

> he [F.J.] thought good now to smyte while the yron was hotte, and to lend
> his Mistresse such a penne in hir Secretaries absence, as he should never be
> able at his returne to amende the well writing thereof (p. 58);

> And in very deed, it fell out that the Secretary having bin of long time absent,
> & therby his quils & pennes not worn so neer as they were wont to be, did
> now prick such faire large notes, yt his Mistres liked better to sing faburden
> under him, than to descant any longer uppon F. J. playne song (p. 93).

Thomas Nash in *The Choise of Valentines* writes of the 'Eunuke dilldo' as 'this
womans secretarie', (? 1593). I quote from J. S. Farmer's ed., 1899, p. 20.

form only. A double-meaning[1] of the word is the basis of John Heywood's epigram 'Of Table-Play' (1562):

> Wife, I will no more play at tables with thee:
> When wee come to bearyng, thou begylest mee,
> In bearyng of thy men, while thou hast any,
> Eche other caste thou bearest a man to many.[2]

This may be compared with Shakespeare's use of 'tables' in Ulysses' comment on Cressida (*Troilus and Cressida*, IV v 60):

> Oh these encounterers so glib of tongue,
> That giue a coasting welcome ere it comes;
> And wide vnclaspe the tables of their thoughts,
> To euery tickling reader: set them downe,
> For sluttish spoyles of opportunitie;
> And daughters of the game.

There is also Poinz's reference to the Hostesse, now dispossessed by Doll and in conversation not with Falstaff but with Bardolph (2 *Henry IV*, II iv 289):

> And looke whether . . . his Man, be not lisping to his Masters old Tables, his Note-Booke, his Councell-keeper?

The relevant sense of 'green', with the association 'green fields' has achieved inclusion in NED: 'to give a woman a green gown' is 'to roll her, in sport, on the grass so that her dress is stained with green' (*a.* 1586-1880). It is probable that such a sense is implied in *Merry Wives*, V v 221, in *As You Like It*, V iii 19 and in *Love's Labour's Lost*, IV iii 75:

> This is the liuer veine, which makes flesh a deity.
> A greene Goose, a Coddesse, pure pure Idolatry.

If each of these words separately can have the sense I allege, it is unlikely that Shakespeare set them side by side without

---

[1] The decent reference is to the game of backgammon in which 'to bear' is to remove a piece at the end of a game. Sir John Harington has a closely similar epigram 'Of Leda that plaid at Tables with her Husband'. *Letters and Epigrams*, ed. by N. E. McClure, Philadelphia, 1930, p. 178.

[2] (Heywood, Spenser Society, p. 109.)

purpose. How then are they relevant to the dramatic situation in this scene where Falstaff's death is described? Nim and Bardolph show that there has been discussion about what Falstaff cried out of in his last moments: 'They say he cryed out of Sack' [1] . . . 'And of Women.' The Hostesse admits the first and attempts to deny the second. Her way of presenting the facts, like Theobald's, is that 'a made a finer end, and went away and it had beene any Christome Child'. Shakespeare, I think, is partly on their side: his words evoke pity for the dying Falstaff but they suggest also that death can be the climax of life's comedy. I take Bardolph's question to imply 'Was the ruling passion strong in death?' and I believe that, for some members of the Elizabethan audience, that question is answered in the Hostesse's description 'his Nose was as sharpe as a Pen, and ('on') a Table of greene fields'; other phrases here, 'eu'n at the turning o'th' Tyde'[2] etc., may come within the same sense range. No detail in the account of Falstaff's physical condition as given by the Hostesse would, so I am informed, invalidate the interpretation proposed: erection in a dying man, while not usual, is not, apparently, abnormal.[3] In any case, Shakespeare's medical knowledge and the 'reality' of Falstaff's death are not here in question; the reality with which we have to deal is that of language and of art. And the language, I claim,

---

[1] *of* here may mean 'about' (NED: *of* 26a.) as well as 'complaining against' (NED: *cry v* 21b.)

[2] If it is necessary to 'prove' that *tide* for Shakespeare's contemporaries could have other reference than to the poetic death symbolism of 'Crossing the Bar' and 'Barkiss is willin' ' ('And, it being low water, he went out with the tide', *David Copperfield*, Vol. II, Chapter 1), I cite from the end of Nash's *Choice of Valentines* (?1593, ed. by J. S. Farmer, 1899, p. 23):

> What can be added more to my renowne?
> She lyeth breathlesse; I am taken doune;
> The waves doe swell, the tydes climbe or'e the banks;
> Judge, gentlemen! if I deserue not thanks?

[3] James Joyce speaks of it as an inevitable accompaniment of judicial hanging (*Ulysses*, p. 289 in ed. of 1947). Compare also *Timon of Athens* (IV iii 145)

> (Some that were hang'd) no matter:
> Weare them, betray with them; Whore still. . . .

But it is not, in medical fact or medical mythology, confined to this kind of death.

directs us to suppose that Shakespeare is making play with the sex-death linkage for such of his audience as would perceive and relish it.

When I ask next if there is other detail within the scene which would support or refute this interpretation my attention is caught at once by the opening lines:

> Hostesse.   'Prythee honey sweet Husband, let me bring thee to Staines.
> Pistoll.   No: for my manly heart doth erne. Bardolph, be blythe: Nim, rowse thy vaunting Veines: Boy, brissle thy Courage vp: for Falstaffe hee is dead, and wee must erne therefore.

In the honesty of linguistic method I am bound to admit that if in the later part of the scene there are these implications I have suggested, then they cannot be absent from the 'rowse', 'vaunting Veines', 'brissle . . . vp' of the first part; Pistol's words to Nim and the boy must relate to the same 'erection' theme. The whole configuration of linguistic evidence would require his speech to mean 'Falstaff is dead; my heart grieves for him' and also 'Falstaff is dead; we must serve his turn'. In other words, if the Pen sentence is to have, as part of its meaning (however slightly stressed) the interpretation here proposed, then the verb *erne* should clearly bear the double sense 'to grieve', which is the accepted gloss, and also 'to become erect'. I am fortunate here in being thus able to reduce the larger problem of subjective evaluation to one precise point of demonstrable evidence, and I count myself luckier still when I am able to find such external evidence, near enough contemporary, for this postulated second meaning. The English-into-French supplement to Cotgrave's *Dictionarie* (1632) gives a cross reference from *earne* to *Yearne* and translates this latter: 's'herisser, s'herissonner, frissonne'. From the French side *Herisson* is 'An Vrchin, or Hedgehog'; *Herisser* is 'To set up his bristles; to make his hair to stare', with *Herissé* defined as 'Set, staring, or standing up, like bristles, or the hair of an affrighted creature'. . . . Present-day dictionaries show *Herisser*, to erect.

Only after finding this external evidence do I recall the 'erection', 'yern' joke in Shakespeare's *Merry Wives* (III v 41-45), of which I have already spoken (p. 125).

Once more we are reminded that when Shakespeare is writing at the height of his powers it is well to scrutinise closely the 'full'[1] words of his text. If Pistol's first words have seemed hitherto little more than bombastic patter, we become aware, in recognising Shakespeare's dramatic purpose within this scene, why his words to Nim and the boy are as they are.[2] Perhaps also it is worth while to look more keenly at his exhortation to Bardolph: 'for my manly heart doth erne. Bardolph, be blythe. . . . ' At first glance the meaning of 'blythe' seems startlingly opposed to that of 'erne': is this perhaps to call attention to some concealed congruity? There is evidence that *blithe* can have the sense 'yielding milk' (NED: 1656, 1669), and, as Farmer[3] shows, the verb *milk* may be used to mean 'to cause ejaculation', as in Ben Johnson's *Alchemist* (1612): 'For shee must milke his Epididimis'.[4]

To the bawdy in Pistol's speech the Hostesse makes no direct answer but it is possible that she responds indirectly by dissociating herself from it, through her phrase 'to *Arthurs* Bosome', instead of the expected 'Abraham's'; this particular substitution may be one more tiny detail in Shakespeare's effortless artistry. Any argument on negative evidence is necessarily tentative; on the other hand, we cannot disregard what appears to be unique dramatic usage if we want to understand dramatic wit. If this phrase 'Arthurs Bosome' is indeed a nonce-creation, as it seems,

---

[1] See p. 26.

[2] The word *vaunting* is found in a context of questionable propriety in Gascoigne's poem beginning 'Divorce me now good death, from love and lingring life':

> First love my concubine, whome I have kept so trimme,
> . . . She cast me off long since, and holds me in disdaine,
> I cannot pranke to please hir now, my vaunting is but vaine.
> . . . The boxe of oile is wasted well, which once did feede my lampe . . .

(*A Hundreth Sundrie Flowers*, ed. C. T. Prouty, Univ of Missouri 1942 p. 148.)

[3] *Slang and its Analogues.*

[4] *Works*, ed. by C. H. Herford and P. Simpson, Oxford 1937, Vol. V, p. 348.

a joke may lie in this substitution of the legendary and the harmless for the expected Scriptural and blasphemous. In Shakespearean usage 'In Abraham's bosom' is certainly 'in the abode of the blessed dead', but the word 'bosom' can have other connotations. Regan speaking to Edmund of her love for him and her suspicion that he and Goneril have been lovers, says

> I am doubtfull that you haue beene coniunct and bosom'd with hir, as far as we call hirs. (*Lear*, v i 13, Q 1608)

And the phrase 'In Abraham's bosom' may well have had in the spoken language of Shakespeare's time that reversed sense, in blasphemous antithesis to its primary meaning, which is shown by Farmer when he includes 'Abraham's bosom' under English synonyms for the female *pudendum*.[1] Other readers may be able to give Elizabethan citations for this obscene sense. Meanwhile I assume[2] that this line was intended to be spoken with a pause, for internal censorship, before 'Arthur's', and was expected to arouse in the audience some disappointed laughter.

It seems to me then that Shakespeare intends the less explicit sense of the Hostesse's words to move between the opposite poles of religion and bawdry, of sentimental piety about man's soul and realistic acceptance of man's bodily nature. The religious implications are not themselves made explicit. The word 'Bosome' in conjunction with 'any Christome Child' suggests the security and all-embracing love to be found in God the Father, and the word 'Table' in conjunction with 'greene fields' cannot but evoke in English hearers of Christian upbringing the comfort of the twenty-third Psalm. Yet the comfort which is actually offered to the dying man is not of Scriptural kind, but is based rather on the assumption that there is a time for living and a time for dying and that meanwhile it is important to keep warm in bed:

---

[1] Slang and its Analogues. See *Monosyllable*.
[2] I am aware that I am working here with insufficient contemporary evidence and I would therefore ask critics to note that no part of my main argument rests on the assumptions in this paragraph.

so a cryed out, God, God, God, three or foure times: now I, to comfort him, bid him a should not thinke of God; I hop'd there was no neede to trouble himselfe with any such thoughts yet; so a bad me lay more Clothes on his feet. . . .

Having considered the underlying implications of the words of the Hostesse I have still to ask if there is any reason, within the current idiom of the day, for the particular form in which those words are arranged. The 'sharp nose' idiom is known elsewhere in Tudor English: 'If the pacient haue . . . the typ of his nose sharpe, . . . it sygnfyeth soone death' (*Boke of Knowledge, c.* 1535; the sixth token of death); 'that is a very deadlye signe specially when the nosethrilles open and close fearcely and the nose waxeth sharpe' (*Homish Apothecary*, trans. by John Hollybush, 1561, p. 22). 'Sharp as a pen' I have not, so far, come upon in proverb or idiom, and I assume therefore (perhaps wrongly) that it is not generally current in Elizabethan London but merely an inconsequential elaboration by the Hostesse. It may be that she sees the pen lying on the 'green fields' of the counting-house table;[1] its sharpness would then be in context, for the pen of the clerk can be a cruel enemy to the illiterate: Cade's men hang the Clearke Emanuell 'with his Pen and Inkehorne about his necke' (2 *Henry VI*, IV ii 117). Another possibility is that she sees the pen as a device on a coat of arms, the field vert translated into green fields, and that she expected her hearers to pick up some topical reference to an actual coat of arms or inn sign.[2] A diligent but necessarily random search for some such well-known object brought me to the sign of the golden pen, set up outside his house in the Old Bailey, by Peter Bales, the celebrated calligraphist, to mark his triumph over a younger rival in the autumn of 1595.

I shall consider in some detail, in the first appendix to this chapter, the possibility that Shakespeare's Hostesse intends some decent reference to this 'pen' sign. And I do so not because I

---

[1] See NED: *Field sb.* 14.

[2] *Table* is found as a 'surface on which a picture is painted', Sonnet 24, 2; *field*, common enough in its heraldic sense from *c.* 1400, has this meaning in *Lucrece* 58.

regard this particular part of my case as in any way proven, but
because an experimental reconnoitre into this kind of material
is the best way to illustrate my last point in this section: that we
set ourselves a task of almost insuperable difficulty when we try
to hear and speak of those many nine days' wonders which must
have given both themes and forms of conversation to the men
of Shakespeare's London. In this particular foray some small
details of linguistic interest are discovered, but what is still
lacking in background evidence it is unlikely that the linguist
alone can supply. If I am on the right track, specialists in other
fields may already have come upon some of the other facts that
are needed.

APPENDIX I

If we are to catch some topical reference in the 'Pen, and a
Table of green fields' we need first to date the text of this part
of the play. When Shakespeare wrote the second act of *Henry V*
is not precisely known, but a short passage (perhaps an interpola-
tion) in the Chorus of Act V (ll. 29-32) affords some evidence that
the play was completed in 1599.[1] If this dating is correct the next
step is to establish that by 1599 'a pen on a green table' had some
special significance and that the allusion, since it survives in the
printed text of the play, continued to be understood for some
years thereafter.

---

[1] As by a lower, but by louing likelyhood,
  Were now the Generall of our gracious Empresse,
  As in good time he may, from Ireland comming,
  Bringing Rebellion broached on his Sword;

A number of editors accept this evidence as conclusive; Professor Sisson, for
instance, writes:

  For once, we can date the play precisely, from the Chorus to Act v which
  refers to Essex in Ireland, that is, to a period from 27 March, 1599, when
  Essex left London, to 28 September when he returned. Meres lists *Henry IV*
  in *Palladis Tamia* in 1598, but not *Henry V*.

  (*William Shakespeare: The Complete Works*, p. 549)

It is beyond doubt that Bales had considerable flair for publicity as well as unusual dexterity in penmanship. Holinshed describes how, in 1575, he

> contriued and writ within the compasse of a penie in Latine, the Lords praier, the creed, the ten commandements, a praier to God, a praier for the queene, his posie, his name, the daie of the moneth, the yeare of our Lord, and the reigne of the queene.

This Bales presented to the queen 'in the head of a ring of gold, couered with a christall' giving her also 'an excellent spectacle' through which to read it. The queen wore the ring many times upon her finger, says Holinshed. In 1587 Bales is commended for a more extensive feat:

> A most strange and rare peece of worke brought to passe by Peter Bales an Englishman a Clerke of ye Chancery of the proofe & demonstracon of the whole Bible to be written by hym everie word at length within an English Wallnut no bigger then a hennes egge, seene and viewd of many thousands wth wonderfull admiracon   (Harl. MS. 530, art. 2, f. 14).

In 1590 he published *The Writing Schoolemaster*[1] 'to be solde at the Authors house in the vpper ende of the *Old Bayly*, where he teacheth the said Artes'. The book is divided into three sections: Brachygraphie, Orthographie and Calygraphie,

> Deliuering in the first, Rules for short and swift writing:
> In the second, for true writing: In the last for faire writing.

The last section includes some practical advice, as for instance, 'for the choyce of your penknife, a right Sheffield knife is best' and

> The best and easiest writing is uppon a Deske and for comforting of the sight it is verie good to couer their deske with greene, & to use all other helpes that may be procured, for the preseruation of your eyes.

This is the nearest I can get for the present to the 'Table of green fields'. I take it as fair evidence that if Bales at any time hung out a

---

[1] Quotations are from the copy in the Lambeth Palace Library.

sign-board having a pen painted on it, the pen might be shown on a green background; if his sign showed a pen lying on a writing-table, that table would have a green surface.

Bales's short account of his *Winning of a Golden Pen* (Harl. 675) in 1595 is interesting for itself and as offering some fragments of linguistic evidence unregistered by NED. It is just worth remarking that one or two senses and word-groupings ('collocations') which in NED's collections are noted first in Shakespeare's text, appear here also. The little manuscript book, beautifully penned, is entitled 'The golden Pen of twentie pounde: Wonne by Peter Bales . . . Maister in writing, generall Chalenger[1] for the same'. It is addressed to the reader in these words:

> I esteeme most of excellent faire Writing, a qualitie worthie of a serious love; and so of a serious defence; especiallie synce under the same Shielde fightes my Reputation: Others perhaps will thinke I labor upon a Cobwebbe; But what none can amend, Lett none reprove.

Bales explains how one Daniel Johnson made and set up a challenge for one whole year together, both for writing and teaching. No one answered or accepted, so that Johnson got more scholars than before 'and procured more doings in the exercise of his penne', while Bales's own 'forbearance turned to his hinderance, for that his doings[2] in Writing & teaching were thereby verie much lessened'. Yet when Bales in his turn set up a challenge, Johnson 'within one houre after, verie arrogantly accepted thereof, in most despightfull & disgracefull[3] manner'. Bales challenged

---

[1] So in Orlando's reply to Rosalind (*As You Like It*, I ii 180):

Rosalind.   Young man, haue you challeng'd Charles the Wrastler?
Orlando.   No faire Princesse: he is the generall challenger, I come but in as others do, to try with him the strength of my youth.

This Shakespearean instance (1600) is the only illustration of the phrase *general challenger* I have noticed in NED; see under *Challenger*.

[2] NED: Doing, *vbl. sb.* 2 . . . transaction, . . . piece of business. Bales uses the word in a slightly different sense.

[3] NED: 3. Inflicting disgrace . . . contumelious. Bales's usage slightly antedates NED's citation.

any opponent: 'ffirst, to write most kinds of hands usuall . . . a full, a meane, a small: with lynes, & without lynes, or anye other help: In a slowe sett hand; in a meane facile hand; and a fast running hand'; second, 'to teach best and speediest', and third 'to write . . . from a mans mouth'.[1] Johnson not only accepted this challenge, but meeting Bales four days later 'did shewe forth a piece of writing of Secretarie hande, wch he had verie much laboured in fine abortive parchment' and challenged Bales to equal it.

It was agreed that the decision on the whole contest should be given on Michaelmas Day by five chosen judges. On the day before, Johnson circulated a printed denial that he and Bales were acting in concert, saying further that he had not dared accept Bales's offer to increase the stake to £1,000 because Bales had not so much as a thousand groats. As he describes this incident Bales vigorously attacks this 'obsolete'[2] defendant, asking 'who so bold as blinde Bayard, that hath not a Word of Latine, to cast at a dogge; or saye Bo to a goose'.[3]

On Michaelmas day some of the judges suggested that they should not give their verdict in open audience; their reason was, according to Bales, 'that the defendant was a yong man, & might not be utterlie disgraced to the world'. When they met the day after, Bales was judged the better in most sections (including that for the 'Romayne'[4] hand) and was named the winner.

Charges of unfairness were made by both sides. Bales was said to have brought many people to the trial 'as unto a Stage Play' and Johnson claimed that he was put off by the noise. Bales answered that he did not take money in the afternoon, there were not above a hundred people there at the most, and the 'unrulye

---

[1] Bales's usage here antedates NED's citations in some particulars and affords instances of some hitherto unregistered 'collocations'.

[2] NED gives no instance of *obsolete* as a term of personal abuse.

[3] 'Say bo to a goose': Tilley's first citations (B 481) 1588, 1607.

[4] NED: *Roman*, 5b. Of handwriting. First cit. 1601 *Twelfth Night*, III iv 31, I thinke we doe know the sweet Romane hand. But an earlier instance (1571) is given under *Secretary*.

fellowes' were brought in by the defendant himself. However, Johnson said openly and privately that he was the victor and Bales had to set out a bill in answer; Johnson replied with notices on posts throughout the city. It was alleged against Bales that he had got possession of the golden pen by a trick, asking permission to take it to show to his wife who was very ill; that he promptly pawned it and the next day sold it. As a result of this, his enemies said, all that Bales got out of this contest was five marks 'to make hym a paynted Signe of a golden Pen'. This painted sign, it appears, continued in position, but the pen which was the competition prize was more often in pawn than on show. John Davies of Hereford speaks of

> The hand and golden-pen Clophonian,
> Sets on his signe to shew (O proud poore soule!)
> Both where he wonnes ['lives'], and how the saume he wan
> From writers faire, though he writ euer foule:
> But by that hand that pen so borne hath beene
> From place to place, that for the last halfe yeare
> It scarce a sennight at a place is seene;
> That hand so plies that pen though nere the neere:
> For when men seeke it, els-where it is sent,
> Or there shut vp (as for the plague) for rent.
> Without which stay it neuer still could stand,
> Because the pen is for a running hand.[1]

How this 'painted signe' was made we are not told: it would be of great interest to know whether it was modelled or on a flat surface, and, more especially, if the pen was lying on the green writing table.[2]

The next piece of the puzzle needs a historian rather than a linguist. If it is accepted that Bales's golden pen was much talked of in the autumn and winter of 1595 it is necessary also to find

---

[1] Epigram 215 in *The Scourge of Folly* (c. 1610). Included in *Complete Works* ed. by A. B. Grosart, 1878, Vol. II, pp. 32, 33.

[2] I hoped that commendatory verses prefixed to subsequent editions of *The Writing Schoolemaster* might refer to this emblem of triumph, but have, so far, no information from this source.

what kept the allusion sharp, both for the dramatist and his audience, in 1599. Bales's pen had previously been sharp enough in government service: in deciphering and copying secret correspondence and in adding forged material to intercepted letters so as to provoke suspected traitors to disastrous action.[1]

It is known also that when, in 1599, the Earl of Essex, after his return from Ireland, was committed to the custody of the Lord Keeper, Bales was privately employed by a certain John Daniel to make copies of some letters written by the Earl to his Countess before and after their marriage—letters which the Countess thought prudent to entrust for a time for secret keeping to Jane, Daniel's wife. When the casket of letters was returned to the Countess, Daniel kept back some and asked for £3,000 before he would restore them. By the sale of her jewels the Countess raised £1,720 and the original letters were given back to her, Daniel taking an oath that he had delivered all he had, and that no man had seen them. For Daniel the affair ended disastrously: brought before the Star Chamber he was fined £3,000 and imprisoned in the Fleet. Bales' himself kept out of trouble. He seems to have been in touch with the friends of Essex, was brought to see the Countess on several occasions and gave her a written statement of Daniel's proceedings. His subsequent declaration is as follows:

> Daniell came to me in Lent, 1599, and for three weeks afterwards, to read and write letters from the Earl to his Lady . . . I meant to charge a constable if I found treason in them. I suspected it from one sentence in a letter written the August before he left Ireland. "The Queen's commandment may break my neck, but my enemies at home shall never break my heart." I wrote above a dozen copies of that letter . . . Daniell said the Countess had ordered him to have frequent copies made that he might better gull somebody. Being perplexed with these words, and that he did not return, I went to the Countess three times before she would be satisfied. At last, at her request, I wrote, in April 1600, a declaration fit for her

---

[1] See *Dictionary of National Biography*.

purpose. . . . The Countess promised me good recompense when her Lord was received into the Queens favour.[1]

It is clear enough that Bales was fishing in troubled waters and it seems possible that a detailed account of his activities in 1599 and 1600 might link him yet more closely with the friends and followers of Essex, perhaps with Southampton and perhaps with Shakespeare.

APPENDIX II

Evidence for the implications of *thatch* in Elizabethan and later English:

1. In *Every Woman in her Humour* (1609), a character who has been robbed of his clothes and is carried on to the stage in a barrel is invited to come out:

> Bos, will ye not forsake your Cabbin?

He answers with what seems to be a suggestive application of a decent proverb:

> Oh sir, he that has not a tilde house must bee glad of a thatch house.[2]

2. The euphemism 'Beneath the thatched house', noted by J. S. Farmer (*Slang and its Analogues*, 1904-11), as used in the following song needs no definition. The song 'The Sentiment Song' is included in *Songs, Comic, and Satyricall*, collected by G. A. Stevens, 1772, p. 125. I quote five verses to illustrate the vocabulary of this kind of imagery:

I

> Dinner o'er, and Grace said, we'll for Business prepare,
> Arrang'd right and left in support of the Chair,
> We'll Chorus our song as the circling Toast passes,
> And manage our Bumpers as Musical Glasses.

---

[1] *Calendar of State Papers, Domestic Series, 1601-1603*, p. 78.
[2] *A Collection of Old English Plays*, ed. by A. H. Bullen, 1885, Vol. IV, p. 367.

VII

Fair befall ev'ry Lass, fair may fine Ladies fall,
No colour I'll fix on, but drink to them all;
The black, the brunette, and the golden-lock'd Dame—
The Lock of all Locks, and unlocking the same.

IX

Lads pour out Libations from Bottles and Bowls,
The *Mother of All-Saints* is drank by *All-Souls.*
Here's the *Down Bed of Beauty* which upraises Man,
And *beneath the Thatch'd House* the *miraculous Can.*

X

The *Dock-Yard which furnishes Great Britain's Fleets,*
The *Bookbinders Wifes* manufact'ring in Sheets,
The *Brown Female-Reaper,* who dares undertake her?
And the Wife of Will Wattle—*The neat Basket-Maker.*

XI

Here's *Bathsheba's Cockpit where David stood Centry;*
Eve's Custom-house, where Adam made the First Entry;
The pleasant plac'd Water-fall 'midst Bushy Park;
The Nick makes the Tail stand, the Farrier's Wife's Mark.

3. Even from the 'thatched' of Shakespeare's text such an
implication is not excluded by any factor of language or situation.
If it is not for Hero to say, it may be for some of the audience to
hear, in the interchange between Pedro and Hero in the masking
scene of *Much Ado* (II i 102):

> Pedro. My visor is Philemons roofe, within the house is Loue
> [Joue].
> Hero. Why then your visor should be thatcht.

Jacques, listening to the talk of Touchstone and Audrey and hear-
ing Touchstone compare himself to 'honest Ouid . . . among the
Gothes's comments on his 'knowledge ill inhabited, worse then
Ioue in a thatch'd house' (*As You Like It,* III iii 11). What the word
Jove suggests to people like Falstaff and which aspect of the god's
activities comes first to mind has already been shown (p. 112).

CHAPTER V

'Latin' reference in Shakespearean English

I

Our imagined aim in this present section has been to listen to the Shakespearean text with ears which have been trained for ten, twenty, thirty years to understand immediately all that there was of sound and language in the Elizabethan air. In considering therefore what the later reader can know, and not know, of Elizabethan proverb idiom and of the less decent vocabulary of Shakespeare's time, it has seemed sensible to use—experimentally, but as if with full confidence—that ordinary linguistic ingenuity through which child and adult are accustomed, intuitively and consciously, to analyse the unnumbered intricacies of native and foreign tongue. In my next subsection such ingenuity is in itself of less importance: it is not simply by an effort of the imagination that the outsider can become responsive to those Latin-English language patterns which the grammar schooling of Elizabethan England fixed for life in the average memory. And I can hope merely to sketch out a few ways in which a non-classicist's tentative suppositions about that knowledge content may show us a little more of what was in the Shakespearean text for the eyes and ears of his contemporaries.

T. W. Baldwin in his *William Shakspere's Small Latine and Lesse Greeke* (1944) has very thoroughly demonstrated that, even though there is 'no direct evidence that he ever attended grammar school a single day', Shakespeare's writing itself makes clear that he 'had such knowledge and techniques as grammar school was calculated to give'.[1] The fragments of information here put

---

[1] Vol. II, p. 662.

forward support Baldwin's argument 'that Shakespeare did have a ... grammar school training': in trying to discover the 'meaning' of some sample words in his dramatic text, the present-day student is reminded afresh that for Shakespeare, as for his educated contemporaries, a knowledge of Latin was in grain, part of the material of mental growth.

Baldwin has shown that it was 'a cardinal pedagogical principle of the time' that all lessons were to be committed to memory and that whatever classical knowledge Shakespeare and his audience got in their grammar schooling they ' would have so long as memory did last'.[1] And Professor Willcock has emphasised that the more scholarly their grammar school, the more humanist their master, the more these young students would be 'encouraged, not only to write, but to think in Latin, and to find in "the Ancients" a complete code for the ordering of life, literature and language'.[2] 'Not only to write, but to think in Latin' is beyond the range of the average twentieth-century reader of Shakespeare's plays; what there is of Latin origin in the creativeness of Shakespeare's language few of us can hope to apprehend in the easy, effortless manner of his first audience; the slowly acquired sensitivity of his contemporaries we cannot pretend to attain. But in thus admitting the deficiencies in our knowledge of classical Latin we may have in mind also that whereas this same classical Latin, in any educational system, admits of no modern innovation, the 'English-Latin' of Shakespeare's time had something of the flexibility of a living language. Where there is in Shakespeare's text some problem word of Latin shape, it may be possible to understand it as an Elizabethan rather than as a classical compound.

---

[1] Vol. I, p. 197.
[2] 'Shakespeare and Elizabethan English', by G. D. Willcock, in *A Companion to Shakespeare Studies*, ed. by H. Granville-Barker and G. B. Harrison (1934), p. 123.

2

Classical Latin alone may solve the problem of Othello's *defunct, and proper satisfaction* (1 iii 265). Desdemona asks that she may be allowed to go to Cyprus with her husband and Othello seconds her request:

> Desdemona. . . . Let me go with him.
> Othello. Let her haue your voice.
> Vouch with me Heauen, I therefore beg it not
> To please the pallate of my Appetite:
> Nor to comply with heat the yong affects
> In my defunct, and proper satisfaction.
> But to be free, and bounteous to her minde:

Theobald believed the penultimate line, as printed and stopped in the original, a period of stubborn nonsense obtruded by earlier editions upon poor Shakespeare: 'What a preposterous creature is this *Othello* made, to fall in Love with, and marry, a fine young Lady, when *appetite* and *heat*, and *proper satisfaction* are *dead* and *defunct* in him! (For *defunct* signifies nothing else, that I know of, either primitively or metaphorically).' Subsequent editors have been similarly puzzled. Emendations proposed have taken two main forms: in the first, 'defunct' is replaced by an adjective or noun of similar consonantal structure (distinct, defect, defenc't, default, disjunct); in the second group, 'defunct' is retained through the grammatical change of *my* to 'me' with consequent repunctuation:

> Nor to comply with heat—the young affects
> In me defunct—and proper satisfaction.[1]

---

[1] This grammatical change is found in more recent editions, as for instance, those of Aldis Wright (1892), Kittredge (1939), Alexander (1951), Hardin Craig (1951) and Sisson (1954). H. C. Hart, 'Old Arden' (1903) retains the original reading; he judges the signification 'dead' for 'defunct' quite intolerable, and rightly asserts that the primary sense of *defunctus* is 'discharged from'; this, however, he sees as referring to Othello's 'laid aside' marriage rites. M. R. Ridley, 'New Arden' (1958), also retains *defunct* and notes the possibility 'that Shakespeare was for once using it in some such sense as "normal", "part of a natural function", a sense which it bears nowhere else whether in Shakespeare or any other writer'. Alice Walker, 'New Cambridge' (1957), emends to 'distinct'.

The grammatical emendation has won the day, I think, by the apparent economy of the change proposed: a single letter only is altered; on the other hand the passage when emended *sounds* very different in syntax and intonation from the original. Since this original rests on the combined authority of Folio and Quarto, it is worth inquiring whether for Shakespeare's first audience, as perhaps for his first printers, 'defunct' might bear a sense in some way akin to 'proper', its 'collateral Epithet', even though such a sense has not been found elsewhere in literary use. Where, it may be asked, could Shakespeare and some at least of his contemporaries have heard this sense often enough for it to become part of their linguistic background? In the Elizabethan schoolroom is perhaps the answer. Baldwin describes Cooper's *Thesaurus* as 'the standard dictionary of Shakespeare's youth' and shows that a copy of it was bequeathed in 1565 to the school of Stratford. *Defungor* is there glossed 'To be deliuered, ridde, and no more troubled or chargeth with a thing: to be dispatched of a matter', with these citations among others: 'Defunctus fato. Liu. Past the daunger of that was prophecied to come. . . . Periculis defunctum esse. Cic. To be past daunger. . . . Oportet omnes defungi vnius poena. Liu. All the rest must be quit and dispatched with the punishment of one.'[1] 'Defunct' in Shakespeare's text might then mean 'free—of danger, punishment, penalty incurred', a sense which now begins to appear of great significance in this context: the propriety and legality of Othello's marriage to Desdemona is the central theme of the first scenes. Brabantio's power to invoke legal penalty is shown at once in his rebuke of Roderigo's uproar (I i 103); he gathers great forces against Othello. Iago warns Othello of Brabantio's 'voice potentiall':

> He will diuorce you.
> Or put vpon you, what restraint or greeuance,
> The Law (with all his might, to enforce it on)
> Will giue him Cable.

---

[1] I quote from an edition of 1578.

The Duke acknowledges the right of the injured father,

> the bloodie Booke of Law,
> You shall your selfe read, in the bitter letter,
> After your owne sense. . . .

As 'an abuser of the World, a practiser Of Arts inhibited, and out of warrant', Othello faces the ultimate penalty. And it is noteworthy that not until this charge is, by implication, withdrawn ('If she confesse that she was halfe the wooer', 1 iii 176) does Othello speak with pride and dignity of 'my Wife'.

3

In the above example the classical Latin which could be heard in the Elizabethan grammar school has been treated as an 'augmentacion' of the spoken English of Shakespeare's time; it has been supposed that Shakespeare's first audience, hearing Othello's 'defunct', would sufficiently recall the context of language and situation in which Cicero and Livy might use the word. Through this supposition, I suggest, a better understanding may be reached of Shakespeare's dramatic purpose. My next example goes a little further: the Latin which we need to hear seems this time to be schoolmaster's Latin rather than classical Latin. The problem word here is *Overture* (*Coriolanus*, 1 ix 46) and the passage in which it occurs has long been a source of difficulty.[1] After the battle for Corioli, Cominius gives thanks to Caius Martius:

A long flourish. They all cry, Martius, Martius, cast vp their Caps and Launces: Cominius and Lartius stand bare.

Martius.   May these same Instruments, which you prophane,
Neuer sound more: when Drums and Trumpets shall
I'th'field proue flatterers, let Courts and Cities be
Made all of false-fac'd soothing:

---

[1] In the Furness Variorum edition the footnote in which the passage is discussed extends to over eight thousand words.

When Steele growes soft, as the Parasites Silke,
Let him be made an Ouerture for th'Warres:
No more I say, for that I haue not wash'd
My Nose that bled, or foyl'd some debile Wretch,
Which without note, here's many else haue done,
You shoot me forth in acclamations hyperbolicall,
As if I lou'd my little should be dieted
In prayses, sawc'st with Lyes.

So as to consider the problem word in relation to the accompanying action it is necessary to quote the passage at some length.
To summarise some of the commentary as briefly as possible:
in the line in question emendations have been proposed for 'him'
(hymns, pipes, smiles, this, them, 'em) and for 'Ouerture' (coverture, armature, creature). 'Coverture' has been most widely
accepted and has survived longest, but more recently editors have
preferred to print the line as it stands in the folio.[1] Even so, there
is no general agreement as to the meaning of 'Overture' in this
context: 'opening', 'disclosure', 'offer' and 'sudden change' are
the possible senses shown by NED. There is difficulty also over
'him'; it seems as if it should refer to 'Steele', but, to get sense out
of the line, it is usually taken as referring to 'Parasites'. Two
interpretations have found strong support, although neither
would seem to derive inevitably from the dramatic context:
'When steel grows soft . . ., then let the parasite be made the
herald of war'; alternatively 'let the parasite be made an offer
to fight'. It seems to me, however, that if the two lines meant
no more than this, they could be omitted from the passage without
much loss of argument or passion; the order of ideas would be
arbitrary and unorganised. If, on the other hand, the Folio's
'Ouerture' represents what, in modernised spelling, would be
written 'ovator', such a meaning is central to the passage. Rider's
Dictionarie (I quote from the edition of 1626) cites the form
'Ouator, m. trix f. Hee or she that triumpheth'. Martius hopes

---

[1] 'Coverture' is given in 'Old Cambridge' (1892) and by Kittredge (1936).
Alexander (1951), Hardin Craig (1951) and Sisson (1954) read *overture*.

that these very drums and trumpets of war, so misused
in unnecessary praise of his success, shall never sound again.
Courts and cities may well be hypocritical when, on the
field of battle, the flourish of trumpets sounds in flattery. Only
when the man of steel grows soft should he be made 'ovator'
for what he has done in the wars. Why, Martius asks, is he offered
such exaggerated praise when he has done nothing significant,
nothing unusual. Cominius, in answer, describes him as 'Too
modest', gives him 'this Warres Garland' and the title *Coriolanus*.

For this interpretation it is necessary to show that the Folio's
'Ouerture' and Rider's 'ovator' could be sounded alike by many
speakers in London and the south of England in Shakespeare's
time. No-one, I suppose, will dispute that the unstressed medial
syllable might well be written *er* or *a*, and for evidence that the
ending *-ture* was in Shakespeare's language pronounced with a
simple *t-* I am glad to have the authority of Kökeritz.[1] The
evidence consists of two rhymes, *departure: shorter* and *venture:
enter*, three puns *departure-departer*, *features-faitors*, *pasture-
pastor* and the following spellings: (I cite, from the list which
Kökeritz gives, some of the spellings which illustrate *-or/-ure*
sound-identity) *lectors* (lectures), *tenure* (tenor), *tuture* (tutor),
valure (valor).

It is necessary also to ask how well the form 'ovator' was known
to Shakespeare's audience. Of 'ovator' as an English word, in the
special sense in Roman history 'One who receives an ovation',
NED cites one instance only, of 1661; the word 'ovation' in its
special sense is registered from 1553. And 'ovator' as a Latin
word belongs, it seems, to the Elizabethan schoolroom rather
than to the Rome of Cicero and Livy. No present-day dictionary
which I have consulted gives any citation of its use in Latin
authors. Cooper's *Thesaurus* (1578 ed.) cites *ouo, ouans, ouatus*
('The crie or shout of triumphers . . .'), together with the abstract
noun *ouatio* but not the agent-noun *ouator*. The noun *ouatio* is

---

[1] He finds in Shakespeare's plays and poems 'no trace of the modern spelling-
pronunciation [tʃɚ'. *Shakespeare's Pronunciation*, p. 271.

glossed by Cooper 'A small triumph of a prince or capitayne for a victorie without slaughter of men . . .'; Rider's *ouator* is given without reference to a Latin text. I would suggest, however, that just as the limited sense of Cooper's *ouatio* would not be appropriate to the generous triumph which Cominius accords to Martius, so we are not limited to the reality of Latin texts for the understanding of 'Latin' words in English speech and Elizabethan drama. The reality of the Elizabethan schoolroom is more important. Supposing the word no more than a schoolmaster's invention to serve in schoolboys' 'themes', it is likely that the speeches of Cominius and Martius would be recognised as variants on just such a theme; those of Shakespeare's audience who had had some years of schooling would readily understand how Martius, the 'ovator', tries to set aside the praises bestowed upon him for his triumph.

4

In the last two instances I have argued for the authenticity of the original Shakespearean texts: 'defunct' and 'Ouerture' have more dramatic meaning than the emendations hitherto proposed. So also I suggest with the form *commune* (*Henry V*, III i 7), which later editors, following Rowe, have usually corrected to 'summon'.[1] King Henry, attacking the town of Harfleur, calls on his men to 'bend vp euery Spirit':

> In Peace, there's nothing so becomes a man,
> As modest stillnesse, and humilitie:
> But when the blast of Warre blowes in our eares,
> Then imitate the action of the Tyger:
> Stiffen the sinewes, commune vp the blood,
> Disguise faire Nature with hard-fauour'd Rage. . . .

---

[1] J. H. Walter, 'New Arden' 1954, does not see how 'summon' can be justified on paleographical grounds and himself proposes *coniure*, which 'offers a satisfactory meaning in view of the current Galenist doctrines of vital spirits contained in the blood'.

Cooper's *Thesaurus* shows a Latin verb *Communio* with the sense 'To fortifie: to make strong: to fense on all partes'. NED shows the English *munite* and *munition*, regularly formed from the Latin *munio*, together with such forms as *munifience* (Spenser, 1596), *munify* (1603-35), and the verb *muniate* (1657), all of which are noted as irregularly or badly formed; *communition*, 'A fortifying or making strong on all parts', is cited by NED once only, from a dictionary of 'hard words' (1656). The irregular formations presuppose in Shakespeare's contemporaries a certain feeling for 'basic Latin'; it may be argued, therefore, that Shakespeare's audience would have no difficulty with the simple root formation 'commune' of this passage.

A similar example is found in *Pericles* (v i 72) when the king 'for this three moneths hath not spoken to anie one' and it is hoped that Marina 'with her sweet harmonie, and other chosen attractions' may 'make a battrie through his defend parts, which now are midway stopt'. Lysimachus tells her

> Expect euen here, where is a kingly patient,
> If that thy prosperous and artificiall fate,
> Can draw him but to answere thee in ought,
> Thy sacred Physicke shall receiue such pay,
> As thy desires can wish.

We should be justified, I think, in supposing that Shakespeare's audience would understand *artificiall* here, in this 'patient', 'Physicke' context, as having for part of its meaning the sense 'healing'—since Marina is to use her 'vtmost skill' for the king's 'recouerie'—even though it seems that the Latin *artificialis* does not have this sense: Cooper and later dictionaries show the Latin word only in Quintilian and with the less specialised sense 'Cunningly wrought'. But the Latin *ars*, as Cooper's penultimate citation illustrates, may mean a *physician's* cunning: 'Victa ars malo. Celsus. When the phisitions cunning cannot take away the disease'; the English 'artist' may be 'a medical practitioner'

(NED: 1592-1761), as in *All's Well* (II iii 10), when the King of France is saved by Helena after he has been 'relinquisht of the Artists . . . both of Galen and Paracelsus'. And if 'artificiall' represents a blending of two senses, in that Marina is to restore the king by her arts of song and speech, the word *fate* also may imply that Marina is to achieve her destiny through what she speaks: as NED notes 'that which has been spoken' is the literal sense of Latin *fātum* (neuter past participle of *fārī*, to speak).

5

I want next to argue for the 'basic Latin' meaning of *absurd* in Hamlet's speech to Horatio (*Hamlet*, III ii 65):

> Nay, doe not thinke I flatter,
> . . . why should the poore be flatterd?
> No, let the candied tongue licke absurd pompe,
> And crooke the pregnant hindges of the knee
> Where thrift may follow fauning. . . .

I quote here from Quarto 2, which, although not uniformly superior, is accepted as the better text; the Folio, however, 'though farther from Shakespeare's autograph . . . has somewhere behind it a good manuscript and . . . can serve to correct some of Q 2's many errors'.[1] I suggest that the meaning of *absurd* is 'tasteless' and that, because of this, we ought in this passage to accept as more meaningful the Folio variant *faining*, 'feigning', rather than the *fauning*, 'fawning' of Quarto 2.[2]

---

[1] 'The Relation between the Second Quarto and the Folio text of *Hamlet*', Harold Jenkins, *Studies in Bibliography*, Vol. VII (1955), p. 69.

[2] Hitherto 'fawning' has been so generally preferred (as by the 'Old Cambridge', Variorum and 'Old Arden' editors and, more recently, by Dover Wilson, Kittredge, Alexander, Hardin Craig and Sisson) that Caroline Spurgeon in her discussion of the image cluster (*Shakespearean Imagery*, Cambridge, 1935, p. 196) deals with this reading only, and does not comment on the paradox-compression in the *Hamlet* and 1 *Henry IV* instances. Dover Wilson's annotation on Hamlet's lines, 'The image is that of a spaniel at table, its tongue "candied" with sweet-meats, yet "fawning" for more', shows the sense in which the passage has been understood.

I note first that whereas 'absurd' meaning 'ridiculous' would be outside the range of Hamlet's imagery, 'absurd' meaning 'tasteless' (i.e. affording no sensation, no pleasure to the palate) would be in the centre of it. And the paradox in which it is the begging dog which itself proffers the candy is found elsewhere in Shakespeare's text, in Hotspur's denunciation of the smiling flattery of Bolingbroke

> Why what a caudie [candie] deale of curtesie,
> This fawning Grey-hound then did proffer me.
>
> (1. *Henry IV*, 1 iii 251)

In Hotspur's speech the image would be incomplete without the word 'fawning'; in Hamlet's lines *fauning* is already implied in 'licke' and 'crooke'; because the word adds nothing to the image or the argument, its authenticity may well be questioned. The Folio's 'faining', on the other hand, would refer back to the 'candied : absurd' antithesis: for pretending that pomp tastes sweet, the tongue, which itself brings the sugar of flattery, may hope for reward, profit, 'thrift'. If it be objected that this argument is circular, I would answer that the linguist is accustomed to rely on the relatedness of the evidence. Internal evidence, I contend, sufficiently indicates the likelihood of the gloss which I have proposed for Hamlet's 'absurd', and there is independent external evidence to confirm it. Etymologically *ab-* is an intensive; *surdus* can mean 'That which hath no sauour' (Cooper's *Thesaurus*, 1578 ed.). That these two Latin elements coalesce in the English word 'absurd' is proved, I believe, by relevant entries in Cotgrave's Dictionary. He translates the English 'absurd' *Absurde, saugrenu, sans sel ni saulge* (1632), and his French-English Dictionaries (1611, 1632)—including under *Saulge* ('The hearbe Sage') this last idiom *Sans sel ny saulge*—translate it into English 'Vnsauorie, insulse, absurd'. Such evidence as I have been able to collect suggests that it is the English 'absurd' only, and not its French or Latin equivalent which has, non-figuratively, this sense 'tasteless'. Cotgrave glosses the French *absurde:* Absurd, sottish, grosse,

foolish, unlike, abrupt, without reason, out of order. Cooper's
Thesaurus translates the Latin *absurdus:* Absurde: inconuenient:
foolish: discording: dishonest: abhorring: odious: against all
ryme and reason. The Latin *insulsus* is there translated: Without
smacke of salt: unsauourie: foolish: without wysedome . . . and
it is noteworthy that English-Latin lexicons of the nineteenth
century can still translate one of the senses of the English 'absurd'
by this *insulsus*.

6

It is when we are puzzled about the meaning of such words as
'defunct' and 'absurd'—words obviously formed on Latin roots—
that we are likely to seek for Shakespearean meaning in the
grammar-school Latin of Shakespeare's time. Other 'Latin'
meanings in Shakespeare's text are less simply to be apprehended
by the non-contemporary. The Latin reference may appear in
English form as when in *Cymbeline* (III iv 52) Imogen, reading
the letter which Posthumus has sent to Pisanio, cries out
against him:

> Some Iay of Italy
> (Whose mother was her painting) hath betraid him:
> Poore I am stale, a Garment out of fashion. . . .

In the attempt to give full dramatic meaning to the clause *Whose
mother was her painting*, a number of emendations have been
proposed but most editors of the present time are content to
give the Folio reading with Johnson's interpretation: 'made by
art, the creature not of nature, but of painting'. It has, however,
been pointed out that the Italian word *puta* means both 'jay' and
'wanton', and earlier editors have noted what may be a parallel
passage in Middleton's *A Mad World My Masters* (1608):

> see here she comes,
> The close Curtizan, whose mother is her bawde   (A 3 v.)

Cooper's *Thesaurus* shows the painting-bawd equation in the dictionary Latin of Shakespeare's day: the verb *Mangonizo* is

> . . . To polish, paint, or trimme up a thing to make it to be the better solde;

and the noun *Mango* has the specific sense

> A baude that paynteth and pampereth up boyes, women or seru-auntes to make them seeme the trimmer, therby to sell them the deerer.

Elsewhere the dramatic meaning may be contrived through the use of Latin and English side by side and there may be no difficulty of understanding to make us pause and ponder. In *As You Like It* (I ii 91) as Touchstone speaks disparagingly of the honour of a knight, one 'that old Fredericke your Father loues', Celia cuts him short with the rebuke

> My Fathers loue is enough to honour him enough; speake no more of him, you'l be whipt for taxation one of these daies.

'Taxation' can mean, as NED illustrates, citing this instance among others, 'accusation, censure'.[1] Some of Shakespeare's audience would hear, I suggest, a second sense: the Latin *tax* is 'ye sound of a stroke with a whip' (Cooper's *Thesaurus*, 1578 ed.). By placing side by side the two words 'whipt' and 'taxation' Celia has given to the noun an additional sense, momentary and perhaps unique. The joke may have been sparked off in passing to take the sting out of her own rebuke of Touchstone; it may, on the other hand, have been a pedagogue's pun of a certain grim currency in the Elizabethan grammar school.[2]

---

[1] *Taxation*, 3. A charging with a fault or offence; accusation; censure, reproof, blame. *Obs.*

[2] *Taxator* in Cooper's *Thesaurus* is 'He that rebuketh or taxeth an other'. *Taxo* is 'To reproue' and also 'To touch often'. Could this be the scholastic origin of *Touch up*, 'To stimulate by striking lightly or sharply, as with a whip' (NED, *Touch v.* 34 b.)?

Sometimes the Latin senses may have their part in quite significant dramatic imagery. Debts in Shakespeare's Stratford and elsewhere were reckoned 'sperate' or 'desperate', having some hope of being paid or else irrecoverable. Hortensius, a servant of one of Timon's creditors, leaves no doubt that he is punning on this *desperate:* 'these debts may well be call'd desperate ones, for a madman owes 'em' (*Timon of Athens*, III iv 103). And for an audience accustomed to this meaning Bolingbroke's words on his 'vnthriftie Sonne' may carry a debt-payment image:

> As *dissolute* as desp'rate, yet through both,
> I see some sparkes of better hope: which elder dayes
> May happily bring forth.   (*Richard II*, v iii 20)

His *dissolute* is a repetition from 'So dissolute a crew' a few lines earlier, with perhaps the additional implication 'unpaid': 'solution' can mean payment in Elizabethan English. Such an image is found again in Prince Hal's calculation of how, when men least expect it, he will redeem the time:

> So when this loose behauiour I throw off,
> And pay the debt I neuer promised;
> By how much better then my word I am,
> By so much shall I falsifie mens hopes. . . .   (I *Henry IV*, I ii 233)

And if, at the end of *Richard II*, the new king Henry IV has reason to complain of his 'vnthriftie Sonne', York also, in complaining of his son Aumerle, uses a similar image in deadly earnest. He fears that Aumerle, if pardoned for his complicity in the plot against Henry IV

> shall spend mine Honour, with his Shame;
> As thriftlesse Sonnes, their scraping Fathers Gold.

It is possible also that when Bolingbroke tells Aumerle (*Richard II*, v iii 81)

> My *dangerous* Cosin, let your Mother in,
> I know she's come, to pray for your foule sin,

his word 'dangerous' has a secondary meaning within this debt-payment image range: 'to be in danger' can mean 'to be in debt', as when Portia asks Antonio in the court scene (*Merchant of Venice*, IV i 180)

You stand within his danger, do you not?

'Dissolute' and 'desperate' in the Latin senses here adduced are part of the English language habit of the Elizabethan period so that no one in Shakespeare's time need miss this particular strand of meaning for want of Latin schooling. How much we miss of Shakespeare's meaning for want of Latin it is difficult to estimate; moreover, there may not always be agreement among present-day readers as to the Latin meaning that was heard by Shakespeare's contemporaries. When Claudio in *Measure for Measure* hopes that Isabella may intercede for him with Angelo

　　　　　for in her youth
There is a prone and speechlesse dialect,
Such as moue men　(I ii 188),

it may be reasonable to suppose that the English *prone* in this 'hearing' context has some of its meaning from the *aures pronas* of which Cooper's *Thesaurus* gives several citations, as for example, '*auribus pronis aliquid accipere.* Tacit. Willingly to hear.' And when Sir Toby (*Twelfth Night*, III iv 270), in delivering Sir Andrew's challenge to the disguised Viola, assures her that Sir Andrew has not purposely put on the quarrel merely to 'taste' his valour,

Sir, no : his indignation deriues it selfe out of a very *computent iniurie*,

it may be more than coincidence that Cooper shows '*Computationem expostulare.* Plin. To aske an account: to require a reckening'; in the usual modernisation to 'competent', some fine thread of Sir Toby's meaning may be lost.

7

So far I have relied mainly on Cooper's *Thesaurus;* the search for some of the less tangible Latin-English meanings in Shakespeare's text brought me next to Withals' *Dictionarie.* Baldwin has demonstrated that this *Little Dictionarie* of Withals was the regular grammar school dictionary for memorization in Shakespeare's time, while Cooper's *Thesaurus* was the standard for reference.[1] First produced in 1553, Withals' vocabulary 'had attained at least a fifteenth, possibly a sixteenth, known edition by 1634', and had been several times revised and augmented by named and unnamed editors.[2] I use here the edition of 1616 and shall not concern myself as to the exact amount of Latin and English idiom and proverb which would have been available to Shakespeare at the various stages of the work's revision. As Baldwin makes clear

> it appears at least that Withals is highly illustrative of Shakespeare's plays. Either or both Shakespeare used the dictionary, or he and the 'little dictionarie' grew up together in the same environmental background.[3]

Baldwin believes that both hypotheses are true, but for the purposes of this brief reconnaissance the truth of the second would be sufficient.

Withals' vocabulary is arranged by subjects and because 'it leadeth not, as doe the rest, by the way of Alphabet' the latter-day student of Shakespeare's language cannot rapidly consult it to resolve some definite question of word-meaning in Shakespeare's time. In this disadvantage there is perhaps some profit: the reader is obliged to hear something of the Latin-English that was current in the Elizabethan schoolroom before trying to determine the relevance of that school language to the understanding of

---

[1] Vol. I, p. 151.   [2] Vol. I, p. 709.   [3] Vol. I, p. 713.

Shakespeare's text. The *Dictionarie* is 'deuised for the capacity of
Children and young Beginners ... for the ease, profit and delight
of those that desire Instruction', and the Latin phrases and proverb-
idioms which it includes are sometimes translated literally, perhaps
with an accompanying explanation; sometimes they are replaced
by an English equivalent. The language to which the memory is
thus exposed is lively and entertaining and cannot but make great
appeal to the imagination and the associative faculty. It is obvious
that Withals and his successors intended the users of this vocabulary
to understand the Latin language in terms of contemporary
(Elizabethan) reality and to be capable of forming all kinds of
patterns of Latin-Latin, English-Latin language connections.
That there is no dead language in this Latin dictionary may be
best illustrated by two or three examples. Few readers of the
present century finding 'Zonam perdidit, Hee hath left his
purse in his other hose' (p. 584) would be able to forbear a
further modernising. And any reader finding under 'The Names
of Corne' (p. 103) 'The blacke in the end of the beane, Hilum ...'
with an accompanying note that 'The word Hilum ... dooth
also signifie a nothing, a trifle' is thereby invited to see in the
Latin idiom the origin of our own phrase 'I haven't a bean' or
of its earlier form 'Not worth a bean' (first recorded by Tilley
from *c.*1527). In the section headed 'The field and land abroad in
the country, with that belonging to it' one and the same column
(p. 74) contains the following entries:

> A greene or grassy banke, that they cal by London, Primrose hill,
> Agger gramineus ...
>
> That waxeth greene againe, like the woods, as they call him, an old
> colt, Reviresces,
>
> A greene gowne, a dangerous garment for Damsels and maydes to
> weare, oftentimes it marreth their marriages, Torus viridans,
> vestitus riparum.

Would some of Shakespeare's contemporaries, we may ask,
catch a reference to Withals' 'Primrose hill' in Ophelia's 'Primrose

path of dalliance' from which she warns Laertes (*Hamlet*, 1 iii 50)? She herself, in her father's opinion, speaks 'like a greene Girle' of the tenders of his affection which the prince Hamlet has made to her.

Throughout this little 'Dictionarie' language is offered, not as a finished product, but as a delightful raw material; it is taken for granted that the human memory works creatively, that the speaker seeks always a new image for an old reality. That Shakespeare and the 'Dictionarie' grew up together there is much evidence. *Sententiae* found alike in Withals and other sources are used in various forms in the language of the plays. As Whitaker, who considers it 'certain that Shakespeare did attend grammar school', has rightly said:

> Shakespeare abounds in quotable sentences simply because he learned to think in *sententiae* as he sweated over translation from Latin to English or from English to Latin, trying in each exercise to achieve maximum brevity and maximum point.[1]

'Hope doth sustain a banished man', 'Speech doth cure sorrow', 'What is done cannot be undone', 'Means cannot last when the charge exceeds the gain', 'Nature hath given a defect to every thing created'; these and many others would come the way of the Elizabethan schoolboy.[2] And part of the meaning of Shakespeare's language for his contemporaries would lie in the pleasure of recognising ideas and phrases which they long had known. When the fool, for instance, jests with King Lear (*Lear*, 1 iv 170) his egg-shell image is part of grammar school language.

> Foole. Nunckle, giue me an egge, and Ile giue thee two Crownes.
> Lear.   What two Crownes shall they be?
> Foole.   Why after I haue cut the egge i'th'middle and eate vp the meate, the two Crownes of the egge: when thou clouest thy

---

[1] *Shakespeare's Use of Learning*, by Virgil K. Whitaker, Huntingdon Library, San Marino, California, 1953, pp. 14, 25.

[2] I quote here from *Sententiae Pueriles*, Sentences for Children, English and Latin, Collected out of sundry Authors long since by Leonard Culman And now translated into English by Charles Hoole. London, 1744.

Crownes i'th'middle, and gau'st away both parts, thou boar'st
thine Asse on thy backe o're the durt, thou had'st little wit in thy
bald crowne, when thou gau'st thy golden one away:

Withals has the verse (p. 233)

> Sicut ego novi, plus testa, pars valet ovi,
> As I know and understand very well
> A peece of an Egge is better then all the shell.

So too with the Fool's pun on 'crowne' and his rebuttal of the
presumption that wit might be expected to go with baldness.
Under 'Cloathing, or apparrell for men' Withals includes (p. 252)

> To crowne, Corono.
> Crowned, or that hath a balde crowne, Coronatus.
> Quisque coronatus non presbyter est vocitatus
> Euery one that hath a balde crowne is not called a Priest.[1]

Withals' Latin expression 'Hæsitantia cantoris tussis' is in English
'When the singer hath forgot his note. Hee makes as though a
crum stucke in his throat' (p. 558). Shakespeare's audience may
have been reminded of some form of this as Rosalind says to
Orlando 'verie good Orators when they are out, they will spit'
(*As You Like It*, IV i 76), with the further outrageous parallel 'and
for louers, lacking (God warne vs) matter, the cleanliest shift is to
kisse'. 'Counterfeite colour and constrayned loue' are linked
together as things which 'doe fade and decay': 'Decrescit factus
color, ac amor ipse coactus' found in the section 'Colours of
cloth' (Withals, p. 168); on the same page in the preceding column
is the phrase 'Dyers weede, or graine of scarlet'. Such an association may have been in the mind of Shakespeare and some of his
audience as Olivia speaks with Cesario of a beauty which is fast-
coloured—'in graine', and of a love which cannot be constrained.
Just before she tells Cesario

> Your Lord does know my mind, I cannot loue him

---

[1] Apperson cites a proverb of similar sense: The head grey, and no brains yet.
Fuller, 1732.

she has drawn her veil aside to allow Cesario to 'negotiate' with her face

> Looke you sir, such a one I was this present: Ist not well done?
> Viola.   Excellently done, if God did all.
> Olivia.   'Tis in graine sir, 'twill endure winde and weather.
>
> (*Twelfth Night*, I v 255)

A knowledge of Latin idiom may reinforce the Shakespearean meaning, as when Portia, disguised as the young doctor Balthasar, rebukes Bassanio for refusing her his ring (*Merchant of Venice*, IV i 440):

> I see sir you are liberall in offers,
> You taught me first to beg, and now me thinkes
> You teach me how a beggar should be answer'd.

Although the young doctor does not say to Bassanio that his refusal is 'shamelesse', the unspoken word may have been vividly present to those onlookers who knew the proverb 'Multa petentibus desunt multa: A shamelesse beggar would haue a shamelesse deniall' (p. 549). Elsewhere the background Latinism may mitigate an apparent harshness in the dramatic narrative. At the end of *Love's Labour's Lost* the service which Rosalind imposes upon Biron seems out of tune with the lightheartedness of the earlier scenes:

> You shall this tweluemonth terme from day to day,
> Visite the speechlesse sicke, and still converse
> With groaning wretches: and your taske shall be,
> With all the fierce endeuour of your wit,
> To enforce the pained impotent to smile.

Withals shows the proverb 'In audaces non est audacia tuta' which is translated 'It is not good iesting with those that are desperate' (p. 547). It is likely that a student set to write on such a theme would, for one of his variant sections, take 'desperate' in the limited sense 'desperately *sick*'; those of Shakespeare's audience who had been through such a training might perhaps understand Biron's reply to Rosalind as an amplification of this:

To moue wilde laughter in the throate of death?
It cannot be, it is impossible. (v ii 865).

If so they would appreciate Rosalind's device rather as a variation on a *sententia*, providing a formal ending for a formalised play, than as a piece of dramatic realism.

It will be apparent that in this section I am trying to expound meaning in quite other ways than by dictionary definition; only occasionally is it appropriate to offer a simple gloss of the single word. Sometimes indeed I am explaining meaning in the sense of suggesting why two words are found side by side in the dramatic text. So in *Troilus and Cressida* (i iii 65) when Nestor is described as 'venerable Nestor (hatch'd in Siluer)' the words *hatch'd* and *Siluer* standing together might be understood as a reference to the Latin adage 'In magno pretio ruga senilis erat: The wrinckles of olde men shall bee in great account' (p. 333). In literal use the word 'hatch'd' can mean, as NED shows, 'engraved, inlaid with narrow strips of silver'; if my suggestion is correct this sense has been combined with the Latin image. A similar image is found in *Julius Caesar* (II i 144) when Metellus wishes Cicero to be included in the conspiracy

> O let vs haue him, for his Siluer haires
> Will purchase vs a good opinion. . . .

Sometimes the single Shakespearean word may seem to carry the Latin allusion. In *Love's Labour's Lost* (IV i 141) the courtier Boyet, after a brisk interchange of wit with the ladies and the clown Costard, retires from the scene:

> Clowne. She's too hard for you at pricks, sir challenge her to boule.
> Boyet. I feare too much rubbing: good night my good Oule.
> Clowne. By my soule a Swaine, a most simple Clowne.
> Lord, Lord, how the Ladies and I haue put him downe.
> O my troth most sweete iests, most inconie vulgar wit,
> When it comes so smoothly off, so obscenely, as it were, so fit.

Withals cites the idiom 'The Owle singeth, Bubo canit, a Proverbe used when ignorant persons will reason of matters beyond theyr learning and skill' (p. 31). This particular shade of meaning is in keeping with Boyet's good-natured acceptance of the ignorant Costard as an opponent on his own intellectual level; in wit, although not in learning, they prove well enough matched. For Costard is no Dogberry; he is not the 'wiseacre or *solemn dullard*' which, according to NED's definition is the sense implied in the English owl.

In the opening scene of *Merchant of Venice* Gratiano warns Antonio not to be like those men who cultivate a deliberate silence, 'a wilfull stilnesse', such men who 'therefore onely are reputed wise, For saying nothing.' We understand one of the reasons for his next image

> *fish* not with this melancholly baite
> For this foole Gudgin, this opinion   (I i 101)

if we know that, whereas the silent man in English proverb 'hath not a word to cast at a dog, no more words then the poast', he is in Latin 'Magis mutus quam *piscis*' (Withals, p. 564).

Elsewhere we may better appreciate some touch of subtlety in the Shakespearean phrase if we have its Latin background. At the beginning of *Taming of the Shrew* (Ind. 1 6), Christopher Sly defends himself against the abuse of the Hostesse:

> Y'are a baggage, the Slies are no Rogues. Looke in the Chronicles, we came in with Richard Conqueror: therefore *Paucas pallabris*, let the world slide: Sessa.

Withals includes the idiom 'To passe ouer time, to let the world slide, Traducere tempus' (p. 5), and, for any of Shakespeare's audience who would remember together all three phrases, the single phrase of the tinker 'let the world slide', which seems by itself not to refer specifically to the passage of *time*, might suggest the trick that is to be practised against him. He is to be persuaded that he has been in a dream 'These fifteene yeeres'; a long space of time has been passed over.

The single word in the Shakespearean text may bring with it from the English-Latin school language an implicit allusion of precise relevance to the dramatic situation. In *Much Ado* (III iii 107) Borachio meets Conrade, only, it seems, so that he may tell him, and be overheard by the watch, how he has 'to night wooed Margaret the Lady Heroes gentlewoman, by the name of Hero'. The incident begins

Borachio.   Conrade I say.
Conrade.   Here man, I am at thy elbow.
Borachio.   Mas and my elbow itcht, I thought there would a scabbe follow.
Conrade.   I will owe thee an answere for that, and now forward with thy tale.
Borachio.   Stand thee close . . . and I will, like a true drunkard, vtter all to thee.

Borachio who abuses his friend as a *scabbe* may, as one who is ready to *vtter all*, himself deserve the same reproach. Conrade might give him as 'an answere' the proverb saying 'Commissa tacere qui nequit, hic niger est: He that is a blab, is a scab', which Withals includes (p. 550). The genuineness of the English 'blab-scab' idiom is further suggested by the fact that a 'blab' may be a 'scab' in a second, literal, sense; as a by-form of *blob* and of the still current *bleb*, it can mean 'a blister, a swelling'.[1] Such a pun within the English proverb[2] would help both to fix its form, and because of the available joke, to increase its currency; the connection between 'scab' and 'blab' would be doubly pointed.

I want next to suggest that the *wallet* in Ulysses' speech to Achilles, 'Time hath (my Lord) a wallet at his backe' (*Troilus and Cressida*, III iii 145), includes as part of its meaning a reference to

---

[1] NED: *Blob* 2. A pimple, pustule. *north dial.* 1597 first cit.
Bleb 1. A blister or small swelling . . . 1607 first cit.
Blab sb.[2] A bubble; a blister, a swelling. 1656 first cit.

[2] Tilley B 434, cites the English proverb as first found in Withals' *Dictionarie* of 1616; no doubt it was of earlier currency in the spoken language.

the situation in an earlier scene when the Greeks, under Ulysses, have overwhelmed Ajax with ironic praise of his own humility in contrast to Achilles' pride:

> Nestor.   What a vice were it in Aiax now—
> Ulisses.   If he were proud.
> Diomedes. Or couetous of praise.
> Ulisses.   I, or surley borne.
> Diomedes. Or strange, or selfe affected.   (II iii 250)

When Achilles' pride is hurt by the Greeks' neglect he asks Ulysses 'What are my deedes forgot?' and Ulysses answers:

> Time hath (my Lord) a wallet at his backe,
> Wherein he puts almes for obliuion:
> A great siz'd monster of ingratitudes:
> Those scraps are good deedes past,
> Which are deuour'd as fast as they are made,
> Forgot as soone as done:

In his vocabulary section on the horses' stable Withals includes 'A trusse or packe, Sarcina . . .' and gives a long explanation:

> It is a double poake, bagged at both the ends, and hangeth behind and before on his shoulders that doth weare it, and thereof is our prouerb, *non videmus manticæ quod in tergo est*. Wee see not that wallet that hangeth behind. It is spoken of reprehension in other mens faultes by such as can not see their owne, who bee supposed to put other mens faultes in the wallet before them, and their owne in that behinde them (p. 189).

Neither Ajax nor Achilles is capable of seeing his own faults, but Ulysses has judged both men aright. Achilles he has described as

> so plaguy proud, that the death tokens of it,
> Cry no recouery   (II iii 187).

And when Ajax attacks Achilles as 'A paultry insolent fellow' Ulysses comments on his self-deception:

> The Rauen chides blacknesse.

In this context the 'wallet' allusion in Ulysses' speech to Achilles would imply his own awareness of the situation he is seeking to control. The word serves to point the contrast between the grave and distant respect offered by him to Achilles and the gross flattery which Ajax, in the earlier scene, 'drinckes vp'.

In the last example of the way in which Shakespearean meaning may exist more richly for those trained in the schoolroom language of his time it is assumed that an allusion which is presented explicitly for one purpose may, because of the dramatic situation have a second—implicit—connotation. My next instances postulate that, through an English word which has logically one meaning, simple and unambiguous, a kind of pun may be present, half consciously, for those who have this school Latin in memory's grain. Lear disinherits Cordelia with these words (*Lear*, 1 i 113):

> Let it be so, thy truth then be thy dowre:
> For by the sacred radience of the Sunne,
> The miseries ['mysteries'] of Heccat and the night:
> By all the operation of the Orbes,
> From whom we do exist, and cease to be,
> Heere I disclaime all my Paternall care,
> Propinquity and property of blood,
> And as a stranger to my heart and me,
> Hold thee from this for euer.

Heilman points out that

> Even in the midst of this tumultuous injustice Lear calls on the 'orbs'—the ordered universe, the Nature to which later he will appeal directly.[1]

I suggest also that, to some of Shakespeare's first audience, this word *orb* may, for a secondary underlying reason, have conveyed a strong sense of order and of retribution. 'The mayde that is fatherlesse, bereaued of her father' is in the Latin 'Orba patre

---

[1] *This Great Stage*, by R. B. Heilman, Louisiana State Univ. Press, Baton Rouge, 1948, p. 266.

Virgo'; and 'One being violently depriued of their sight, is called Orbus' (Withals, p. 97); a similar association may have existed between 'the wheel' and 'blindness'. So as not to appear to 'prove' a case by careful selection of the evidence, I quote in full (except for grammatical detail) the relevant extract (Withals, p. 96-7):

> The utter part of the wheele, called the trade, Orbis.
> The word is also used for the World, The round world, so sayd of old, viz.
> Est Orbis Mundus, apparens esse rotundus.
> The tracke, or Cart-wheele Rut, Orbita, . . . ab orbe, & rota dicta, of that resemblance of the world, which the wheele hath, so round it is, and so inconstant it is, Et dicitur orbata, quasi orbis iter, vel via, And so they wheele about that haue lost their eye-sight, or bee depriued otherwise of Wife, Children, Substance, &c. so neare and deare unto them. Orbus . . . that do so wheele about.

The 'wheel' image and the 'blindness' of Gloucester are very closely interconnected in the passage in which Edgar declares his identity to the dying Edmund:

> My name is Edgar and thy Fathers Sonne,
> The gods are iust, and of our pleasant vices
> Make instruments to plague vs:
> The darke and vitious place where thee he got,
> Cost him his eyes.
> Bastard.   Th'hast spoken right, 'tis true,
> The Wheele is come full circle, I am heere.   (v iii 174)

In these last examples the 'meanings' I adduce are tenuous and insubstantial. I suppose, however, that even though all readers of Shakespeare might not agree that these particular significances are there in the text, the instances themselves will sufficiently illustrate the ways in which poetic meaning, not easily available for a later audience, might be obliquely present for the dramatist and his contemporaries.

In my next instance also I cannot 'prove' the meaning proposed; once again my case depends on linguistic background, on the

kind of thing that Shakespeare's contemporaries were accustomed
to hear outside the theatre, outside the piece of text discussed.
The problem word here is *Charg-house* from the passage in
Love's Labour's Lost (v i 87) where the schoolmaster Holofernes
and the Spanish gentleman Armado walk apart for private talk;
the commentator's task on this occasion is somewhat easier in
that the stage characters, at least, understand each other. As outsiders we can recognise that some meaning was communicated.

> Bragart. *Arts-man preambulat*, wee will bee singled from the
> barbarous. Do you not educate youth at the Charg-house on the
> top of the Mountaine?
> Pedant. Or *Mons* the hill.
> Bragart. At your sweet pleasure, for the Mountaine.
> Pedant. I doe *sans question*.
> Bragart. Sir, it is the Kings most sweet pleasure and affection,
> to congratulate the Princesse at her Pauilion, in the *posteriors* of this
> day, which the rude multitude call the after-noone.

The emendation 'church-house', tentatively suggested by Theobald, has found some support, but present-day editors usually
agree in retaining the 'charge-house' of the original texts, even
though that form is not elsewhere recorded. NED glosses 'a house
for the charge of youth, a (boarding) school'; Dover Wilson
(1923) and others believe 'that the allusion, which no one has been
able to explain, is a topical one'. It may be, however, that the
word has not been found elsewhere because it has come 'fire-new'
from the mint of Armado's brain; this once-only Shakespearean
joke is perhaps to be understood, with *Arts-man preambulat* and
posteriors of this day, by reference to the Latin background of the
speakers and their audience. In Withals' 'little Dictionarie' (p. 282)
'A Maister' is 'Preceptor' and the English 'A Precept, a lesson,
a commandement, a charge' is the Latin 'Preceptum'; from
Armado's lips, the 'Charg-house' would be readily recognisable as
the building in which the master gives lessons; it would be a
generic term, not an allusion to some individual school. Similarly
the 'top of the Mountaine' might be, as it were, allegorical. To

refer to a school as so sited could constitute a compliment to the school's master. Learning has long been considered among the higher things of life; in Cooper's *Thesaurus* 'Profounde learning' is 'Altiores literae'; on Parnassus 'the nyne Muses did inhabite or dwell'. Palingenius's *Zodiacus Vitae*, prescribed as a textbook in many grammar schools, opens with the lines:

> My minde with fury ferce inflamd of late I know not how,
> Doth burne Parnassus hils to see, adournd wt Laurel bow, . . .[1]

And if in this phrase 'top of the Mountaine' Armado is paying Holofernes the highest of compliments, we have then the reason for the next two lines of dialogue. *Mons* is 'A mountayne or hill' (Cooper's *Thesaurus*); Holofernes, translating Armado's English into Latin and out again, disclaims the mountain top but accepts some lower eminence. And Armado, while not wishing in courtesy to disagree with him, speaks for a second time the word of compliment.

8

As a collection of both Latin and English idiom current in Shakespeare's time, Withals' *Dictionary* is of great interest to the present-day student, even though it cannot of course be regarded as the certain source of any of the words, phrases or ideas in Shakespeare's text. But, as Whitaker points out

> It is more important, fortunately, to recognise when Shakespeare shared and reproduced the ideas of his age . . . than it is to determine exactly where he derived them.[2]

And it is likely, as Kenneth Muir has said, that often enough 'Shakespeare himself could not have told us the precise source'[3]

---

[1] Googe, p. 1.
[2] *Shakespeare's Use of Learning*, by V. K. Whitaker, Huntington Library, San Marino, California, 1953, p. 9.
[3] 'Shakespeare Among the Commonplaces', *Review of English Studies*, Vol. X, No. 39 (1959), p. 288.

of those borrowed phrases and ideas which he was to make so
memorably his own. One or two simple instances will illustrate
this problem. But first a word about my next source of material,
the *Apophthegmes of Erasmus* as translated by Nicolas Udall in
1542.[1] Baldwin has shown that the *Apophthegmes of Erasmus* (or the
adaptation of that collection by Lycosthenes) was regularly used
in the sixteenth-century grammar schools, and he has given the
interesting detail that John Bretchgirdle, Vicar of Stratford-on-
Avon, in his will of 20 June 1565 left 'Apothegmata in laten' to a
certain 'William Smith, who was probably round about twelve
years old, doubtless with an eye to his needs in Stratford grammar
school'.[2] Erasmus made his collection of 'notable good & brief
saiyngs' from 'the best allowed, and thesame the most auncient
writers, bothe in Greke and Latine' and hoped that his book might
be used by teachers 'as often as vacaunte tyme is geuen, or the
case reqireth hilaritee and mirthe' and that it would provide the
pupils 'with themes, or argumentes to write on' which might, 'so
that the schoolemaister dooe open and declare the rewles and
waies, . . . bee delated and sette out more at large'. 'The principall
beste sorte of Apophthegmes' he defines as

> that saiyng, whiche in fewe woordes, doeth rather by a colour
> signifie, then plainly expresse a sense, not comen for euery witte
> to picke out, and soche a saiyng, as no manne could lightely feigne
> by studie, and whiche the longer ye doe consider it in your mynde,
> the more and more it dooeth still delite you.

He believed that we remember best when we learn with pleasure:

> And these writynges, as thei be learned with pleasure and delite,
> and do lightly sinke and settle in the mynde, so doe thei conteine
> more good knowledge and learnyng, in the depe botome or
> secrete priuetee, then thei shewe at the first vieue   (p. xxii).

In 1542 Nicholas Udall, late of Eton, published a translation of

---

[1] My quotations are taken from the ed. of 1564 as literally reprinted by R.
Roberts, Boston, Lincolnshire, 1877.
[2] Vol. I, p. 490; Vol. II, p. 342.

two of the eight books of the *Apophthegmes*, so as to give his readers 'a taste of this, bothe delectable and fruitefull recreacion', not wishing to wait 'vntill the whole werke might be perfectly absolued and finished'. My references in this section will be to these two books only.

Erasmus himself, speaking of the difficulty of ascribing a certain saying to a precise source, dismisses the problem as of relatively small importance.

> For it forceth not so greatly, of what persone a thyng is spoken, as it doeth, what is spoken: albeit in deede a famous speaker, and one that hath the fauour and hartes of menne, geueth to the saiynges moche weighte and grace also (p. xix).

So too I am concerned here rather with the 'weighte and grace' which Shakespeare gave to 'what is spoken' than to the precise source from which his saying is originally derived. As with Withals' *Dictionarie* I take Udall's translation as no more than a specific example of what was generally available to the linguistic consciousness of Shakespeare's contemporaries. And in suggesting some passages in Shakespeare's dialogue which seem to echo the wit and wisdom of the Greeks and Romans as set out in these *Apophthegmes*, I shall, for my first instance only, make reference to other sources which would be equally available.

When Bolingbroke is banished (*Richard II*, 1 iii 279, Quarto 1597), Gaunt tries to offer him philosophic comfort:

> All places that the eie of heauen visits,
> Are to a wise man portes and happie hauens:
> Teach thy necessity to reason thus,
> There is no vertue like necessity,
> Thinke not the King did banish thee,
> But thou the King.

A passage in Lyly's *Euphues* has been recognised[1] to contain closely similar ideas:

---

[1] See *Shakespeare's Books*, by H. R. D. Anders, Berlin, 1904, pp. 105-6.

Euphues advises Botonio, to take his exile patiently.

. . . though thy exile seeme grieuous to thee, yet guiding thy selfe with the rules of Philosophie it shal bee more tollerable . . . Plato would neuer accompt him banished yat had ye Sun, Fire, Aire, Water and Earth, that he had before, where he felt the Winters blast and the Summers blaze, where ye same Sun and the same Moone shined, whereby he noted that euery place was a country to a wise man, and al parts a pallace to a quiet mind . . . when it was cast in Diogenes teeth, yat the Sinopetes had banished him Pontus, yea said he, I them of Diogenes.[1]

This same incident of Diogenes' banishment is described in the *Apophthegmes* when Erasmus tells of Diogenes:

To a certaine persone in the waye of reproche obiecting vnto him that he was a man banished his countrie: Thou sely creature, saied he, for this verie cause did I at the first become a Philosophier.

Udall notes: Either for that banishment had enforced & driuen Diogenes to enter the studie of philosophie, or els because he had purposely learned philosophie, to thende that he might be able with a pacient & contentfull mind to endure banishment & other semblable chances.

Vnto an other feloe saiyng to him in despite, Nay, the Sinopians haue condemned thee with banishing thee, neuer to come more in that countrie, And I theim, quoth he, to abide there and neuer to come thence.

Udall notes: . . . A Philosophier, who indifferently taketh euery grounde & euery land vnder the cope of heauen (which so euer it be) for his owne natiue countrie, if he be commaunded to departe any whence by banishement, is a man exiled out of some one particular Citee or nacion onely. But he that can not liue in an other place besides his owne countrie, where he was borne & breden, is a man banished out of regions almost innumerable. As touching Diogenes, in deede he was banished his countrie for counterfaitinge or coyning of money, as men thinke . . . (p. 125-6).

---

[1] *Euphues*, Arber's Reprints, 1923, pp. 187-8.

Withals' *Dictionarie* (p. 540) includes a saying which is of relevance:
'Omne solum forti patria est: A valiant man accounteth euery
place his owne Countrey' and the little collection *Sententiae
Pueriles* has the adage 'Hope doth sustain banished men, Spes alit
exules' (p. 9).

It seems clear from this one instance that whatever Shakespeare
had taken of idea and language from classical story had entered
living into 'the quick Forge and working-House' of his thought.
His memory diversifies and recomposes. Diogenes is believed to
have been banished for the coining of money; Lear in his madness
defends himself against arrest (*Lear*, IV vi 83, Q 1608):

> No they cannot touch mee for *coyning* I am the king himselfe
>
> > (F: *crying*).

Diogenes, when 'banyshed or exiled from a place by enforcement
and compulsion' (Udall) turns philosopher; Gaunt advises
Bolingbroke

> Teach thy necessity to reason thus . . .

Diogenes claims that he has banished the Sinopians; Bolingbroke
is urged to think that he has banished the king. Plato speaks of
the same sun shining (*Euphues*); Bolingbroke, sentenced by King
Richard, at once replies:

> Your will be done: This must my comfort be,
> That Sun that warmes you heere, shall shine on me. . . .

Udall, in his gloss on Diogenes' words, explains that the man who
'can not liue in an other place besides his owne countrie, where
he was borne & breden, is a man banished out of regions almost
innumerable'; Shakespeare's Mowbray, who must forgo his
'natiue English' and is now 'too old to fawne vpon a Nurse',
uses negatively this same sun image; he has to leave his country's
light

> To dwell in solemne shades of endlesse night.

Udall speaks of 'euery ground & euery land vnder the cope of heauen'; Gaunt has the phrase

All places that the eie of heauen visits;

again the sun image is implied. And where Gaunt uses the literal-image 'portes and happie hauens', Withals, for example, in his section on 'The Sea with that which belongeth to it', includes the image 'From the Maine to the Hauen, spoken of him that is deliuered from a Sea of troubles' (p. 45).

I have argued earlier (p. 27) that we shall better understand the 'strangeness' in the phrase 'Strange Images of death' (*Macbeth*, I iii 97) if a certain line cited in Withals' *Dictionarie* is already stamped into our memories:

Aspera pugna novas varia sub imagine Loethi dat formas
Cruell buffeting giueth new formes of death under a divers image.

It is possible that Macbeth's phrase would have further significance—especially to those who already knew the play—from the fact that in poetic and classical convention the usual 'image of death' is 'sleep'; sleep and death are brothers. So, for instance, Erasmus quotes a jest of Diogenes:

When he was awaked out of his mortall slepe, that is to saye, the laste that euer he had before his death, and the Phisitian demaunded, howe it was with him? Right well (quoth he) for one brother embraceth the other.

Udall notes: Alluding vnto the Poete Homere, who feigneth ... death and ... slepe to be brothers germaine. For that slepe is a certain Image and representacion of death (p. 173).

The figure is common enough in Elizabethan poetry: as Christopher Sly, the drunken tinker, is discovered sleeping, the Lord who stumbles upon him exclaims (*Taming of the Shrew*, Ind. I 35):

Oh monstrous beast, how like a swine he lyes.
Grim death, how foule and loathsome is thine image. . . .

In the later scenes of *Macbeth* the image is powerfully employed;
it is the sleeping and not the dead who are to show the usual
'Images of death'. Paradox heightens the effect: from an innocent
sleep the sleeper may be awakened again to life and its duties,
as when Macduff cries out to Malcolm:

> Shake off this Downey sleepe, Deaths counterfeit,
> And looke on Death it selfe   (ɪɪ iii 81);

those on the other hand who are alleged to have neglected their
duty to watch over the sleeping king—

> when in Swinish sleepe,
> Their drenched Natures lyes as in a Death   (ɪ vii 68)—

struggle back from sleep only to die.

In yet another way sleep is a reminder of man's mortal nature.
Erasmus tells of Alexander:

> Where he was by the commune talking of many one reported to be
> a God, he saied that by twoo thinges especially, he did well perceiue
> him selfe to be a man or creature mortall, that is to wete, by slepe,
> and by compaigniyng with women.
>
> > Udall notes: For that these two thinges did principally aboue
> > all others discrie the feblenesse of mannes bodie. As touching
> > all thinges els, he was inuincible. For slepe is an Image and
> > representacion of death, and the acte of venerous copulacion
> > a playne spiece of the falling euil   (p. 229).

And, like Alexander, Macbeth and his queen are mortal also in
their need for sleep, their horror of 'terrible Dreames'. Instead
of Duncan asking of Macbeth, the victorious general, 'Which
should be thine, or his', it is Macbeth, who, once become king,
would choose Duncan's part: 'Better be with the dead . . . After
Lifes fitfull Feuer, he sleepes well' (ɪɪɪ ii 23). This last sleep-death
equation which Shakespeare has built so strongly into the structure
of his play might well be reckoned, in its simplest form, a 'natural'
image; in all societies and all languages we are likely to find that
the dead lie sleeping, the sleeping look like the dead. I would

argue nonetheless that the complex meaning of this Shakespearean image may be better understood in the Elizabethan context; the wise sayings of the Greeks and Romans, as Erasmus has collected them, are a relevant part of that context.

Other 'natural' images are found alike in Erasmus' *Apophthegmes* and in Shakespeare's dialogue. That 'Blushing is virtues's colour' (Bashfulness . . . a sign of grace) must be a truth that is widely known. Tilley shows the proverb in English from 1562; Erasmus credits Diogenes with the wit of this observation:

> To a certain young ladde blushing, & by reason of the same blushing sore dismayed: Take a good heart my sonne (quoth he) that same hewe or coloure is of vertuous diyng, or doth the dieuat of vertue geue (p. 140-1).

Shakespeare uses a form of this proverb as the basis of a pun at the end of *Two Gentlemen* (v iv 165) when Julia's disguise is made known:

> Valentine. What thinke you of this Page (my Lord)?
> Duke. I think the Boy hath grace in him, he blushes.
> Valentine. I warrant you (my Lord) more grace, then Boy.

The observation is made with serious purpose in *Much Ado*, first by Claudio in scorn of Hero's hypocrisy (IV i 35) and then by the Friar in sober confirmation of Hero's innocence (IV i 163). And in contrast to Diogenes' reassurance of the virtuous young lad, Poinz attacks Falstaff's page with vigorous elaboration:

> Come you pernitious Asse, you bashfull Foole, must you be blushing? Wherefore blush you now? what a Maidenly man at Armes are you become? Is it such a matter to get a Pottle-pots Maiden-head? (2 *Henry IV*, II ii 81).

The capacity of the sponge to absorb, may constitute another of these 'natural' images such as might have arisen independently but which probably came into Elizabethan English from classical sources. Erasmus tells how

Demosthenes had been one of the tenne whom the Atheniens had sente ambassodors vnto Philippus kyng of Macedonie. So after that Aeschines and Philocrates (which two Philippus had especially aboue the residue, familiarely embraced, and made of) being come home again from the said ambassade, gaue the king moche high praise, partly for many other thinges, and especially for these three folowyng, that he was full of fauour and beautie, that he had a goodly eloquent toung, and that he could drink lustily. Demosthenes made this cauillacion that he auouched in all those praises, to be not so moche as one poincte comelie for a king. For the first, he said, belonged to women, the seconde to Sophistes and Rhetoricians, and the thirde to spounges (pp. 371-2).

Portia uses the same image in a dramatic situation of similar structure; she describes the qualities of her various suitors so as to dispose of any claim that might show them worthy of praise. The young German she likes

> Very vildely in the morning when hee is sober, and most vildely in the afternoone when hee is drunke

and she bids Nerissa

> set a deepe glasse of Reinish-wine on the contrary Casket, for if the diuell be within, and that temptation without, I know he will choose it. I will doe any thing Nerrissa ere I will be married to a spunge (I ii 108).

Demosthenes ends his 'cauillacion' on the word 'spounges'; Portia's description of her several suitors ends also on 'spunge'. NED cites Portia's image as the first use of 'sponge' meaning an immoderate drinker (1596) but other figurative uses are registered for a few years later. Hamlet, having spoken of Rosencrantz as a 'Spundge . . . that sokes vp the Kings Countenance, his Rewards, his Authorities', makes the natural image extension as he tells him that when the king needs once more what his officer has gleaned,

> it is but squeezing you, and Spundge you shall be dry againe.
>
> (Hamlet, IV ii 12, 22)

Those of Shakespeare's audience who knew the apophthegm of Demosthenes might recognise and appreciate Portia's application of it to what is, linguistically, the same situation; in my next instance the great soldier of the ancient world and the Shakespearean character who may seem to echo his words, are in the same basic situation but react very differently. Erasmus recounts of Alexander:

> At what time he had the doughters of Darius prisoners with him, he would bid theim good morrowe, good euen, or good spede, not casting his iye on theim, but looking downe to the grounde, and that but seldome neither, standing in feare of himselfe to be rauished with their excellent beautie. And emonges his familiares these words folowing wer much in his mouth: The damiselles of Persia maken sore iyes.

Udall notes that 'in all the time that they wer with Alexander' they never heard 'come out of his mouthe so muche as one wanton word' (pp. 221-2). In Shakespeare's *Richard III* (I ii 150), Gloucester encountering Anne, widow of the murdered Prince Edward, refuses to let her attendants pass, bearing King Henry's coffin, and Anne is forced to listen to his words. In answer to her abuse

> Out of my sight, thou dost infect mine eyes

he professes to have been injured by looking on her:

> Thine eyes (sweet Lady) haue infected mine.

Shakespeare has fused several images in this one line of Gloucester's reply. 'The sore eye infects the sound' is an English proverb (registered by Tilley from 1561): 'It is seene in a sore eye, that beholding steadily a sound one, giueth him his disease.' If Anne's eyes are infected through looking on a toad, Gloucester's eyes are infected as they look on hers; they are injured also by her basilisk hatred; and, more important, her beauty has made his eyes 'blinde with weeping'; her beauty has provoked him to kill King Henry and to stab young Edward.

A story told of Philip concerns the unique skill of the minstrel in the 'twangyng of harpestryngs':

> Like as himself was mery conceipted and full of pretie tauntes, so did he muche delite in the saiynges of others, if thesame had any quickeness or grace in theim. Wherefore, when he was disposed on a time, as he sate at his supper, to comtrolle a minstrelle plaiyng at that present before him, and talked his phansie of fingreing & striking the stringes of the instrumente: God forfende sir king (quoth the minstrelle) that ye should haue more sight and knowledge in this geare, then I (p. 199).

In a reversed situation Hamlet uses the 'recorder' image against Rosencrantz and Guildenstern (III ii 371-89):

> Guildenstern.   I know no touch of it, my Lord.
> Hamlet.   'Tis as easie as lying: gouerne these Ventiges with your finger and thumbe, . . . Looke you, these are the stoppes.
> Guildenstern.   But these cannot I command to any vtterance of hermony, I haue not the skill.
> Hamlet.   Why looke you now, how vnworthy a thing you make of me: you would play vpon mee; you would seeme to know my stops: . . . Why do you thinke, that I am easier to bee plaid on, then a Pipe? Call me what Instrument you will, though you can fret me, you cannot play vpon me.

Again, I would suggest, the minstrel's reply to Philip comes near enough what Shakespeare has given to Hamlet; the 'meaning' of Hamlet's words might well include, for those who knew it, a reference to this Grecian story.

Of Socrates it is related that

> When Aristippus, the disciple of Socrates, . . . of his gaines, of setting vp the teaching Philosophie for money . . . had sent .20. poundes vnto his maister: Socrates sent the money backe again vnto hym forthwith, alleging that his familiar good Aungell would in no wise suffer him, to take it.

> > Udall notes: For Socrates saied, that he had a familiare ghost or Aungell peculiare and proper to himselfe, of whom he was

by a priuie token forbidden, if he attempted, or went about to dooe any vnhonest thyng. Verely, that familiare good Aungell, I suppose, was reason (p. 36).

A 'good angel' appears in a 'sending back the money' context when after the Gadshill robbery, Falstaff asks

Now Hal, to the newes at Court for the Robbery, Lad?
How is that answered?
Prince. O my sweet Beefe:
I must still be good Angell to thee.
The Monie is paid backe againe. (1 *Henry IV*, III iii 200).

Falstaff does not like 'that paying backe'; since Hal is now good friends with his father and may do anything, he asks

Rob me the Exchequer the first thing thou do'st

and continues unrepentantly

Where shal I finde one that can steale well? O, for a fine theefe of two and twentie, or thereabout: I am heynously vnprovided.

The talking bird which has been trained to speak the name of the enemy is the theme of one of Erasmus' anecdotes of Augustus Caesar:

When he returned to Roome, with all pompe and ioilitee, from the victorie gotten at Actium, emong a greate multitude meetyng hym for to welcome him home, a certain persone bearing on his fist a crowe hauyng been taught to speake these woordes: All haile Cæsar Emperor moste victorious: Augustus being moche delited with this salutacion, bought the crowe, and gaue sixe thousand pieces of gold for hym. The partener of him that had doen this feact, because no porcion of that liberal reward had come to his snapshare, did Cæsar to weete, that the self same felooe had yet an other crowe to, which he besought of Cæsar, that the feloe might bee compelled to bryng before him. When she was brought, she souned out plainly soche woordes, as she had learned, which were these: All haile Antonius most redoubted conqueror. Augustus

being nothing stiered to anger, onely commaunded the reward
afore giuen to be egually parted with the feloe that was the pro-
moter of the later crowe (p. 279).

If Shakespeare has this idea in mind, he uses it less subtly than in
the original story; Hotspur wishes simply to enrage Bolingbroke
(1 *Henry IV*, 1 iii 224):

> He said, he would not ransome Mortimer:
> Forbad my tongue to speake of Mortimer.
> But I will finde him when he lyes asleepe,
> And in his eare, Ile holla Mortimer.
> Nay, Ile haue a Starling shall be taught to speake
> Nothing but Mortimer, and giue it him,
> To keepe his anger still in motion.

A slight link between the two incidents may be the word 'popin-
jay'.

> Augustus being semblably hailed or saluted by a Popiniaie, com-
> maunded her to be bought to (p. 280).

Hotspur explains to Bolingbroke how, immediately after his
victory at Holmedon, 'a certaine Lord . . . Fresh as a Bride-
groome'

> Among the rest, demanded
> My Prisoners, in your Maiesties behalfe.
> I then, all-smarting, with my wounds being cold,
> (To be so pestered with a Popingay) . . .
> Answer'd (neglectingly) I know not what. . . .   (1 iii 50)

The philosopher Diogenes who, 'renouncyng and forsakyng
the worlde . . . had neuer a little hous, or corner of his owne,
where he might quietly eate his meat', found even so that he had
superfluous possessions.

> When he had espied on a time a ladde drinkyng out of the palme
> of his hande, he saied: This lad is in frugalitie a degree aboue me,
> that dooe carrie about me superfluous furniture of houshold, &

forthewith toke oute of his scrippe a litte treen tankard or dishe
that he vsed for his cuppe to drynk on, & thesame cast awaie from
him, saiyng I knewe not that nature hadde in this behalfe also made
prouision for vs. When he had seen an other boie, for asmuch as
his treen saucer was broken, to take vp peason oute of the potte
with a crust of breade made holowe for that purpose, he cast awaie
from him his treen potagedishe too, as a thynge superfluous (p. 101).

Lear, asked by his daughters why he should need even one
knight to attend on him, answers

> O reason not the need: our basest Beggers
> Are in the poorest thing superfluous,
> Allow not Nature, more then Nartue [Nature] needs:
> Mans life is cheape as Beastes.   (II iv 268)

Udall hopes that 'The frugalitee of Diogenes may shame our
superfluitees and excesses' (p. 101); Lear, in the tyranny of the
storm, pities 'houselesse pouertie':

> Take Physicke, Pompe,
> Expose thy selfe to feele what wretches feele,
> That thou maist shake the superflux to them,
> And shew the Heauens more iust.   (III iv 35)

And immediately after this, meeting with poor Tom in the hovel,
Lear asks

> Is man no more then this? Consider him well. Thou ow'st the
> Worme no Silke; the Beast, no Hide; the Sheepe, no Wooll;
> the Cat, no perfume. Ha? Here's three on's are sophisticated.
> Thou art the thing it selfe; vnaccommodated man, is no more
> but such a poore, bare, forked Animall as thou art.   (III iv 113)

The 'bare, forked Animall' may perhaps echo another story of
Diogenes, 'bare' recalling 'having no feathers' and 'forked'
representing 'with two feet'.

> This also goeth in a tale, albeit vneth beleuable. Plato had thus
> diffined a man: A man is a liue thyng with twoo feete, hauyng no
> fethers. And when the scholares of Plato hadde made signes and

tokens of well allowyng thesame diffinicion, Diogenes brought
forth into the schole, a cocke pulled naked oute of all his fethers,
bothe great and small, saiyng: Loe, here is Plato his manne[1] (p. 110).

Edgar in his role of poor Tom, 'vnaccommodated man', is
regarded by Lear as a 'Philosopher', 'Noble Philosopher', 'good
Athenian'; and since learning and lack of possessions are thought
of here as synonymous, he is also 'this same lerned Theban'
(III iv 162). Of the extreme poverty of the Thebans Erasmus gives
an instance when he tells 'How Alexander vsed the Grekes which
toke wages of his enemies to fight against him':

> When the Grekes, that tooke waiges to fight againste Alexander,
> vnder the baners of his enemies, were come vnder his power and
> iurisdiccion, as for the Atheniens, he commaunded to be laied fast
> in shaccles and fetters, because that, where thei might haue had
> waiges competent, at home at the publique charges of their own
> citee, thei had for all that become souldiers with his enemies.
> Of the Thessalians also, he commaunded thesame . . . but the
> Thebanes he demised and let go at their libertee, saiyng: These
> poore soules are by vs put out of all together, nor haue any thyng
> at all left vnto them, neither citee to dwel in, nor lande to tille
> (pp. 214-15).

In the next scene with poor Tom, Lear takes him into his service:

> You sir, I entertaine for one of my hundred; only, I do not like
> the fashion of your garments. You will say they are Persian; but
> let them bee chang'd (III vi 85).

The unacceptable excuse that a certain fashion is Persian is found
in a story told of Socrates and Aristippus:

> When Socrates spake sore against soche persones as were perfumed
> with swete sauours, and Charondas . . . demaunded what feloe it
> was, so perfumed with swete oiles and sauours, Aristippus saied,
> Euen I it is miserable & wretched creature that I am, and a more

---

[1] Udall notes: Whereupon it was added to the diffinicion, hauyng brode
nailles, for that no byrdes haue anie suche.

miser then I, the kyng of the Persians. But marke, said he, that like as he is in this behalfe nothyng superiour to any other liuyng creature, so is he not a iote better then any other man.

Udall's note here is of some relevance to the Shakespearean king-beggar juxtaposition:

His meanyng was, that manne by externall or outward gooddes is made not a whitte the better. Bothe an horse all be smered with oile of balme or spike, should haue the self same sauor, that shuld a king: & a sely poore begger, being anointed or perfumed with the like kinde of oile or sauor, smelleth euen as well as doeth the highest prelate of them all (pp. 75-6).

I have spoken earlier of 'natural' images such as are likely to occur in all languages; certain jokes also, I suppose, would be found in many communities, as, for instance, that of the letters big enough for a blind man's eyes. Erasmus tells of Antigonus

Thesame Antigonus when he had taken vp in his hande an instrument, written in greate letters of texte hande: Yea Marie (quoth he) these letters are big enough to se, euen for a blinde mannes iyes.

Udall notes: Jestyng at the bleamishe and impediment of his own iyes. For he had no more but one iye to see withall. But those same words, an other bodie should not haue spoken without ieopardie (p. 251).

When Lear asks Gloucester

Reade thou this challenge, marke but the penning of it

Gloucester answers, carrying the image to its farthest limit,

Were all thy Letters Sunnes, I could not see.   (IV vi 143)

Many societies would recognise as true the comment of Diogenes:

When he sawe a feloe going to prison that had embesled and conueied awaye a cup of golde out of the treasurie or chaumbre of the citie. . . . See, see (quoth Diogenes) the graund theues leden the petie theef to ward (p. 117).

Lear assures Gloucester

> A man may see how this world goes, with no eyes. Looke with thine eares: See how yond Iustice railes vpon yond simple theefe. Hearke in thine eare: Change places, and handy-dandy, which is the Iustice, which is the theefe: (IV vi 158).

Udall's note on Diogenes' saying is of interest also:

> Would God this same word might not be without a lye saide of some publique officers of Christentee, by whome sometimes is trussed vp, and hanged on the galoes a poore sely soule, that hath percase pielfed away tenne grotes, where theimselfes by great pielage, brybrie, or extorcion, yea and for a faire touch, by deceiuing & beguiling their prince or the commen weale, do growe daily and encrease in welth and richesse no manne saying blacke is their eyen.

It is perhaps just possible that his last phrase here, 'blacke is their eyen', is the connecting link in Shakespeare's mind between the eyelessness of Gloucester and the example which Lear elects to give of what may be seen without eyes.

Such a paradox as 'The better . . . the worse . . .' is unlikely to be confined to any one language. Erasmus quotes Diogenes as saying

> To an other young man feactely and trickely representing at the baines, a certaine lasciuious playe . . .: Sirrha, young manne, quoth Diogenes, the better ye doe, the worse it is.
>
> > Udall notes: Utterly disalowing & condemning the feate which of it self was vnhonest and naught . . .

The game was 'a foolishe game that louers had . . . by the bobleyng that the drinke made, whiche remained in the cuppe after they had dronken, for the drinke that was left, they would cast vp on high, and by the clocking, plashing, or soune that it gaue in the fall, they would take a signification whether their louers were true to them or not' (p. 121). Some of Shakespeare's audience may have been reminded of Diogenes' comment on this 'loves me, loves me not' device when Ophelia uses a briefer version of

the phrase in her rebuke of Hamlet's jests as they are watching
the play:

Ophelia.   You are a good Chorus, my Lord.
Hamlet.   I could interpret betweene you and your loue: if I
could see the Puppets dallying.
Ophelia.   You are keene my Lord, you are keene.
Hamlet.   It would cost you a groaning, to take off my edge.
Ophelia.   Still better and worse.   (iii ii 261).

That 'Action' in its classical sense 'is eloquence' is also an
obvious enough idea. The story is told of Demosthenes

To a certain persone demaunding what was the principall poincte
in eloquence, he made aunswere, hypocrisis, that is, action or
pronunciation. To thesame persone eftsones asking, what was the
next poinct and what the thirde, he still made none other aunswer
but action, action.

Udall notes: Referring so moche to pronunciation, that he
thought altogether to consiste in thesame. And in deede the
action or pronunciation comprehendeth many things mo then
one, that is to weete, the tempering and qualifying of the voice,
the earnest loke of the yies, the porte of the countenaunce, and
the gesturing or conveighaunce of all the whole body (p. 381).

Those who knew this saying of Demosthenes might appreciate the
shift of meaning in Volumnia's application of it, when she urges
Coriolanus to humble himself to the citizens:

I pry thee now, my Sonne,
Goe to them, with this Bonnet in thy hand,
And thus farre hauing stretcht it (here be with them)
Thy Knee bussing the stones: for in such businesse
Action is eloquence, and the eyes of th'ignorant
More learned then the eares. . . .   (*Coriolanus*, iii ii 76).

In this last example Shakespeare may be consciously employing
a phrase of classic currency; it is possible too that his image of a
wound as a mouth which speaks, derives from classic story.
Erasmus tells of Alexander:

At the siege of a certain citee, whyle he serched for the weakest places of the walles, he was striken with an arrowe, but yet he would not leaue of his purpose. Within a whyle after that, the bloud being staunched, the anguishe of the drie wounde encreaced more and more, and his legge flagging down by the horses syde, by litle and litle was all aslepe, and in maner sterke stife, he being of force constreigned to geue ouer that he had begonne, and to call for his Surgeon, saied to soche as were present: Euery body reporteth me to be the sonne of Iupiter, but this wounde saieth with an open mouth, that I am a mortall manne (pp. 234-5).

Antony, as he prophesies over the dead Caesar's wounds, uses a rather more complex image: Caesar's wounds, as mouths, beg for Antony's voice and tongue.

Ouer thy wounds, now do I Prophesie,
(Which like dumbe mouthes do ope their Ruby lips,
To begge the voyce and vtterance of my Tongue). . . .   (III i 261)

And when he speaks to the crowd of his own lack of eloquence he can only, as he says,

Shew you sweet Cæsars wounds, poor poor dum mouths
And bid them speake for me: But were I Brutus,
And Brutus Antony, there were an Antony
Would . . . put a Tongue
In euery wound of Caesar, that should moue
The stones of Rome, to rise and Mutiny.   (III ii 232)

When in *Coriolanus* the citizens discuss whether they can withold their votes from Coriolanus, the image is further compressed. The word 'mouth' is not mentioned; the 'tongues' within the wounds of Coriolanus are the *voyces* of those who will elect him. Although the citizens have power to deny him, they recognise that

it is a power that we haue no power to do: For, if hee shew vs his wounds, and tell vs his deeds, we are to put our tongues into those wounds, and speake for them. . . .   (II iii 7)

Occasionally the English of Udall's annotation affords an instance of an image which is to be found again in Shakespeare's dialogue. The assemblies of people swarming about the orators and advocates of Athens Diogenes called 'pimples'; Udall glosses his Greek word

> little pimples or pushes, soche as of cholere and false flegme, budden out in the noses and faces of many persones, & are called the Saphires & Rubies of the Tauerne (p. 79).

Falstaff uses such an image in his 'discord' with Doll Tearsheet (2 *Henry IV*, II iv 53):

> Falstaffe. If the Cooke make the Gluttonie, you helpe to make the Diseases (Dol) we catch of you (Dol) we catch of you: Grant that, my poore Vertue, grant that.
> Dol. I marry, our Chaynes, and our Iewels.
> Falstaffe. Your Brooches, Pearles, and Owches: For to serue brauely, is to come halting off. . . .

Udall describes Lais as

> an harlot of Corinthe of excellent beautie, but so dere and costly, that she was no morsell for mowyers. She was for none but lordes and gentlemen that might well paie for it. Whereof came vp a prouerbe, that it was not for euery man to go vnto Corinthe (p. 379).

Cleopatra describes herself as she once was

> Broad-fronted Cæsar,
> When thou was't heere aboue the ground, I was
> A morsell for a Monarke. . . . (*Antony and Cleopatra*, I v 31)

Udall's 'no morsell for mowyers' has the ring of current idiom, and Shakespeare's 'morsell for a Monarke' may be an individual variant on a known phrase.

When Malvolio, because of the 'catterwalling', threatens to report Maria to Olivia, she answers him with contempt:

> Malvolio. Mistris Mary, if you priz'd my Ladies fauour at any thing more then contempt, you would not giue meanes for this vnciuill rule; she shall know of it by this hand. *Exit.*
> Maria. Go shake your eares. (*Twelfth Night*, II iii 134)

14

Udall tells how

> when men doe mocke any body, thei wagge their handes vp and
> doune by their eares at the sides of their hed and doe counterfeact
> the facion of an Asses eares. So then the Asse also appereth by
> waggyng his eares vp and doun, to mocke & skorne folkes yet
> is there no bodie therwith displeased, or greued (p. 149).

Maria describes Malvolio as 'an affection'd Asse', and the ears
which he is to shake are, no doubt, the ears, not of a dog (as
NED suggests for other instances of this idiom[1]), but of an ass.
Withals' *Dictionarie* includes the sentence

> Ex verbis fatuos, ex aure tenemus asellos, By their wordes wee
> know fooles, and Asses by their eares (p. 84).

9

This chapter might best be concluded with the words of
Wolsey's sad admission: I have, these many pages, 'ventur'd . . .
in a Sea of Glory' but 'farre beyond my depth' (*Henry VIII*,
III ii 358). My defence must be that I came of necessity to
Cooper's *Thesaurus* and was tempted on by the interest of the
subject first to Withals' half-English, half-Latin vocabulary, and
then to Udall's wholly English text. I can claim only to have shown
the usefulness of exposing the memory of an average twentieth-
century student (little Latin and no Greek) to some very limited
areas of the school Latin of Shakespeare's time. It will be clear that,
for such a sample reconnaissance, other texts might have served
equally well and I end accordingly with a mention of one of
these, the *Zodiacus Vitae* of Palingenius, prescribed as a textbook in many schools, and translated by Barnabe Googe (1560-
1565). This compendium, in the words of Rosemond Tuve, is

---

[1] NED: To shake one's ears: (? as a dog when wet); also, ? to make the best of
a bad bargain; also, to show contempt or displeasure.

a mine of Renaissance commonplaces, most of them with a long history in mediaeval or classical literature. . . . Many conventional images which we know best in Sidney, Shakespeare, Chapman, Spenser, are here in more abbreviated or more diluted form.[1]

J. E. Hankins has pointed to many 'parallels of subject matter' between Shakespeare's works and the *Zodiake* for which Shakespeare 'could be indebted to either the English or the Latin' text; the verbal parallels, however, he judges as 'clearly reminiscent of Googe's lines'.[2] One instance will show how Shakespeare uses what may have come to him from this source. Palingenius, to illustrate 'the cares and bitter strife Wherwith this mortall life abounds', speaks of the anxious merchant's deep and groaning sighs:

> So depe with groning winde
> The Merchant sighes, and feares as oft as he doth call to minde
> The perils great that ships are in, the force of Pirats hand,
> The boystrous winds, & raging Seas, with rocks & drenching sand.[3]

Salanio, trying to diagnose the cause of Antonio's 'sadnesse' (*Merchant of Venice*, I i 22) uses the sigh/wind image with far greater economy and immediacy:

> My winde cooling my broth,
> Would blow me to an Ague, when I thought
> What harme a winde too great might doe at sea. . . .

Palingenius uses a heard image; Salanio *feels* himself both blowing and blown upon. In Palingenius's lines it is the adverb clause of time 'as oft as he doth call to minde' which is the causal linkage between the 'groning winde' of the merchant's sighs and the 'boystrous winds' of shipwreck. In Shakespeare's lines, three winds are one wind. Salanio's broth he sees as the ocean, so that the

---

[1] *The Zodiake of Life* by Marcellus Palingenius, trans. by Barnabe Googe, Introd. by R. Tuve, New York 1947, p. xii.
[2] *Shakespeare's Derived Imagery*, by J. E. Hankins, Univ. of Kansas Press, Lawrence, 1953, p. 15.
[3] Googe, p. 100.

cheerful and measured blowing of hearty appetite changes to an ague fit of fear at the thought of a wind too great at sea.

Elsewhere the reference may be less explicit; the image-commonplace found in Palingenius may be recognised as present in the Shakespearean situation without there being an exact verbal correspondence between the parallel passages. Palingenius' fourth book begins:

> O Sunne that with perpetuall course about the world doest flye:
> The Parent chief of euery thing, and Dyamonde of the skye.
> The Prince of all the Starres, and spring of euer lasting light:
> Beholding euery thing abroade, whyle as wyth colour bright
> Of crimson hew, thou leaust aloofe the brinkes of Persian lande
> With rysing face, and passing forth doest *hyde* thy fierie brand
> Amydde the westerne fluddes, and laste of all, doest burne the hyll
> Of Calpe great, and eke that course, frequentest alwayes styll.
> By thee, doe all things plaine appeare, whose colour late the night
> Bereft, *hir darknesse by no meanes, abyding once thy lyght.*
> The *syght and eye* of all the worlde . . .
> Disperse the cloudes from hence, and let the day be bright and cleare:
> Let Seas lay down their roring lookes, strait, when thou dost appeare....
> Let pleasaunt aires on us be blown, from fiery Pyros vail,
> And make all thinges by thy *returne*, in quite rest remayne.[1]

Richard II, on his *return* from Ireland, speaks to Aumerle of his confidence in his kingly power:

> Discomfortable Cousin, knowest thou not,
> That when the *searching Eye* of Heauen is *hid*
> Behind the Globe, that lights the lower World,
> Then Theeues and Robbers raunge abroad vnseene,
> In Murthers and in Out-rage bloody here:
> But when from vnder this Terrestriall Ball
> He fires the prowd tops of the Easterne Pines,
> And darts his Lightning through eu'ry guiltie hole,
> Then Murthers, Treasons, and detested sinnes
> (The Cloake of Night being pluckt from off their backs)

---

[1] Googe, pp. 40, 41.

Stand bare and naked, trembling at themselues.
So when this Theefe, this Traytor Bullingbrooke,
Who all this while hath reuell'd in the Night,
Shall see vs rising in our Throne, the East,
His Treasons will sit blushing in his face,
Not able to endure the sight of Day. . . . . (*Richard II*, III ii 36-52)

Sometimes as with *contrary* (*Timon*, IV iii 144; p. 116) and *the still-peering aire* (*All's Well*, III ii 113; p. 263) a knowledge of Palingenius may be of direct help for the interpreting of the puzzling word or phrase of the Shakespearean text.

CHAPTER VI

Spelling habits and pronunciation variants

At the beginning of this investigation I accepted as a working principle that all of Shakespeare's meaning which is available to the non-contemporary is that which is contained on the printed page of Folio and Quarto texts. This word 'contained' should now perhaps be modified: 'indicated' might seem more accurate. For in so far as Shakespeare's language is a 'code' language its fuller meaning must be sought outside the Shakespearean page. Where the dramatist uses for his individual purpose some short-hand symbol of quotation or allusion, it is against the background of the general talk of his contemporaries that we can, if at all, expand that symbol. Yet even so, although this imagined background of spoken language is a reality which we can very properly postulate, the fragment of written evidence is the only reality with which we can safely work in the detail of linguistic argument. It is useful once more to emphasise this point before coming to this last subdivision of the 'spoken language' section, where I consider some of the ways in which Shakespearean spelling may cloud our understanding of Shakespearean meaning.

For the purpose of this present limited reconnaissance it will not be necessary to attempt any comprehensive account of the sound system within the developing standard language of Shakespeare's time. Such an account has already been given by Kökeritz in his illuminating and detailed study of *Shakespeare's Pronunciation* (1953); his work and that of E. J. Dobson on *English Pronunciation 1500-1700* (1957) offer a rich storehouse of material for the student of historical phonology. And since also the specialists in this field —Dobson, Kökeritz, Daniel Jones and the earlier scholars—do not always agree in their final evaluation of the very intricate

pronunciation evidence, I shall try to argue my proposed Shakespearean interpretations on the simpler evidence of demonstrable
spelling-convention groupings. If it can be shown, for instance,
that two words, not now identical in sound, could sometimes have
the same spelling in sixteenth- and seventeenth-century English,
the fact may be of relevance to the study of Shakespeare's meaning
even though it cannot be certainly established what pronunciation,
or range of pronunciations, such a spelling would represent.

There is general agreement that the developing standard
language of the early modern English period admitted a much
greater variety of pronunciation than is heard in the different
types of present-day educated English. Kökeritz speaks (p. 6) of
'the amazing diversity of usage that prevailed, particularly in
pronunciation' during the period in which Shakespeare lived.
Dobson's central theme is that there were 'many variant pronunciations, many levels and styles of speech, co-existing at any
time'.[1] In London especially many varieties of regional dialect
must have been heard. As Stow indicates in his *Survay of London*
(1603), people of all regions and social classes, 'by birth for the
most part a mixture of all countries of the [Realme], by bloud
Gentlemen, Yeomen and of the basest sort, without distinction',
were attracted to the capital:

> Retaylers and Artificers, at the least of such thinges as pertaine to
> the backe or belly, do leaue the Countrie townes, where there is no
> vent, and do flie to London, where they be sure to finde ready and
> quicke market . . . for not onely the Court, which is now a dayes
> much greater & more gallant then in former times . . . is now for
> the most part either abiding at London, or else . . . neare unto it . . .
> but also by occasion thereof, the Gentlemen of all shires do flie,
> and flocke to this Citty, the yonger sort of them to see and shew
> vanity, and the elder to saue the cost and charge of Hospitality,
> and housekeeping.[2]

For Stow, as for many others, London was a symbol of the nation's
unity, its 'estate . . . in the persons of the Citizens . . . friendly

---

[1] Vol. I, p. v.   [2] Stow's *Survay of London*, 1603, pp. 558, 563.

enterlaced and knit in league with the rest of the Realme' (p. 559). In such a society, relatively quickly formed and re-forming, yet compact and conscious of unity, the speakers would be more than usually aware of the linguistic differences within their common language and more than usually alert to the varying social and regional ways of pronouncing.[1]

What is of importance to the later student is that the single word (or sound-group) in the English of Shakespeare's London, must often have been capable of more than one value. The listener, that is to say, would judge the meaning of the sounds he heard—whether for instance he was to understand 'bitter' or 'better', 'brine' or 'brain'—both against the background of the speaker's particular kind of pronunciation and against the general context of what was said. We are accustomed well enough to make this adjustment in listening to present-day speech. Professor Daniel Jones has shown that this 'overlapping of diaphones', as he names it, is of common occurrence:

> a particular sound may be the one used in one set of words by one speaker, but in another set of words by another speaker.[2]

To quote briefly from his examples and observations: sounds which at the present time mean *high* and *bite* to some mean *hay* and *bait* to others;

> a high variety of *a* . . . may be the sound used by one speaker in words like *bad, back, jam*, but the same sound may be a diaphonic variant of *e* and may be heard from some speakers (chiefly Northern) in *bed, beck, gem*.

What in the speech of an American would mean *possible* 'is much the same as the southern English pronunciation of *passable*'. And so on. And whereas the single word in isolation might be ambiguous to the listener, the necessary allowances are instinctively made in ordinary connected conversation. To illustrate this point

---

[1] Hence in World War II the overwhelming success of the 'Itma' programmes.
[2] *The Phoneme: Its Nature and Use*, Cambridge, 1950, p. 198.

Daniel Jones gives the instance of a child evacuated from London in 1940 and sent to live with a family in the country.

> When asked his name by the children of the family, he gave it as "dʒaimz". The children took this to be a name they had never heard of before—a name that they would naturally have spelt *Jimes* if they had been asked to write it. It had to be explained to them that what the boy said was the London way of pronouncing *James*. But when this London boy carried on a connected conversation, he was understood without any difficulty.[1]

I remember being helped to fill in a ticket for a book in the British Museum reading room, a kindly attendant dictating what I was to write. Told to write 'I', I mistakenly did so, but when the instruction was corrected to 'No, not *I*; *I* for epple' I knew what letter was required.

As present-day students of Shakespeare's language, seeking to make the necessary allowances for Elizabethan pronunciation variants reflected in the spelling of the early printed texts, we cannot so easily proceed. One obstacle is that the *Jimes* spelling, as it were, may be met with in isolation; it may be necessary to understand the *I* without the 'epple'. If it is clear that the character's part is intended to be spoken as social or regional dialect the unusual spellings present no difficulty. 'Exion' is recognised as 'action' when Mistress Quickly, the tavern hostess, warns the officers not to let Falstaff escape:

> I warrant he is an infinitiue thing vpon my score . . . I pra'ye, since my Exion is enter'd . . . let him be brought in to his answer.
>
> (2 *Henry IV*, ii i 32)

Fluellen's indignation is seen to have good reason when the French 'Kill the poyes and the luggage'; his question 'What call you the Townes name where Alexander the pig was borne?' sets the audience the easiest of translation problems (*Henry V*, iv vii). The spelling 'Ouerture', on the other hand, in a speech of

---

[1] *The Phoneme*, pp. 199-200.

Coriolanus, a non-dialect speaker, seems very puzzling; it is not easy to appreciate that the given form must represent what in modern spelling would be 'ovator':[1]

> When Steele growes soft, as the Parasites Silke,
> Let him be made an Ouerture for th'Warres:
>
> (Coriolanus, I ix 46)

To understand this we need the information, as given by Kökeritz, that -*ture* in Shakespeare's English was pronounced in the same way as -*ter*, -*tor;* in Shakespeare's text *departure* rhymes with *shorter*, *venture* with *enter;* spellings such as *lectors* 'lectures', *tenure* 'tenor', *valure* 'valor' are found.[2] The difficulty here is that the present-day standard English way of saying the -*ture* ending has developed from some other type of pronunciation than that in use in the normal London language of Shakespeare's time.[3]

We must bear in mind also that it is far more difficult to adjust to the unexpected form when we meet it in written or printed language; for the present-day reader the identity of the printed word is rigidly established. As Mossé has so aptly illustrated:

> we respond in great strength to orthographic variation. . . . Alteration of the spelling disturbs us deeplee nd wee reegahrd such chanjz az chanjz in the langgwij.[4]

Others have noted that in so far as we are wholly habituated to a standard spelling system, our eyes may see what they expect to see rather than what is there: even when proof-reading, we may automatically see the correct form rather than the single misprint. But when, on the other hand, we are confronted with some passage of ordinary modern English on which an unusual and perhaps less arbitrary spelling has been consistently imposed, we have to read much more slowly and perhaps even to read aloud.

---

[1] The Latin evidence for this interpretation is given earlier, p. 156.

[2] *Shakespeare's Pronunciation*, p. 271.

[3] Kökeritz notes (p. 271) 'The only St. E. survivor of the older pronunciation I know of, besides *figure*, is *fritter* < fr *friture;* cf. dialectal and vulgar *critter* < *creature*'.

[4] *A Handbook of Middle English*, by F. Mossé; trans. by J. A. Walker, Baltimore, 1952, p. ix.

In any such attempt to understand-by-pronouncing the unusual form of the Shakespearean text it is the consonant shape of the puzzling word which is likely to be most significant for the present-day student; what pronunciation we should give to the stressed vowels and diphthongs cannot be certainly established. This is because in the study of vowel sounds and vowel change it is possible to pass by almost imperceptible degrees from one sound to another so that the exact point of development which has been reached at any given period can never be precisely expressed in the few available letters of the written language. Most consonant sounds, on the other hand, 'fall naturally into well-defined classes. . . . As a rule it is not possible to pass by almost imperceptible degrees from one consonant to another'.[1] And obviously also there are many more letters available in the written language to express these consonant sounds.

One further difficulty remains to be noted. The non-contemporary who has first to meet the Shakespearean text as something seen rather than as something heard may, on occasion, too easily understand the Elizabethan variant in terms of modern spelling. When the Shakespearean spelling seems to represent a word that looks right without modernisation and that, as far as meaning is concerned, could fit quite well into grammar, syntax and dramatic situation, it is possible sometimes not to notice that there is, contextually, a better option. If the Elizabethan spelling is unlike our own, we are safe enough: 'chist' we know to mean 'chest'; grammar and context may give clear indications that 'since' represents 'sense'. But when in *As You Like It* (II vii 13) Jacques describes excitedly how he has met Touchstone and himself become 'ambitious for a motley coat', it is easy to misunderstand the 'world' spelling of his speech:

A Foole, a foole: I met a foole i'th Forrest,
A motley Foole (a miserable world:)

---

[1] *An Outline of English Phonetics*, by Daniel Jones, Cambridge, 1950, p. 41. I shall not complicate the argument here by naming the exceptions to this general rule.

His phrase *a miserable world* is usually taken,[1] following Dr. Johnson, as

> a parenthetical exclamation, frequent among melancholy men, and natural to Jaques at the sight of a fool, or at the hearing of reflections on the fragility of life.

But, as Jacques describes himself, he has been laughing for an hour *sans intermission*, and he is full of exuberant plans for himself taking on the role of the wise and worthy fool. Touchstone has answered his greeting 'Good morrow foole' with the words

> Call me not foole, till heauen hath sent me fortune,

and 'fool' itself is a miserable term for such a one as Touchstone is and Jacques wishes to be. 'Word' can have the meaning 'name, title, appellation' in Elizabethan England: NED quotes the ending of a letter (1571)

> Your assured loving friend, William Cecill. I forgot my new word, William Burleigh.[2]

The spelling 'word' for 'world' is noted by NED from the thirteenth to the sixteenth centuries. And elsewhere in Shakespeare's text the 'world' spelling has the 'word' sense, when Pistol, bidding farewell to his wife, the tavern hostess, counsels her not to give credit during his absence:

> Let Sences rule: The world is, Pitch and pay: trust none: for Oathes are Strawes, mens Faiths are Wafer-Cakes, and hold-fast is the onely Dogge. . . .   (*Henry V*, II iii 51)

The evidence indicates that for some speakers of Shakespeare's time 'world' (with silent *l*) and 'word' had the same sound; either spelling might thus be found for either word and actor and reader would know from the context which word was intended.

Even the single letter *a*, simplest of spelling forms, may require

---

[1] Emendations suggested include 'varlet' and 'ort', meaning 'remnant'.
[2] *Word*, 12 b. (*a*) As designating a thing or person.

to be interpreted in terms of pronunciation and context. Claudio maintains that Benedicke is 'in loue with some woman':

> a brushes his hat a mornings.
> What should that bode?   (*Much Ado*, III ii 41)

In *Love's Labour's Lost* Rosalind teases Katherine, saying that she will 'nere be friends' with Cupid, 'a kild your sister', and Katherine admits that her sister indeed died 'sad, and heauy' for love, but countercharges briskly

> had she beene Light like you . . . she might a bin a Grandam ere she died.   (v ii 17)

The English nobles newly returned from France have learned to look and move in stately fashion:

> They haue all new legs,
> And lame ones; one would take it,
> That neuer see 'em pace before, the Spauen
> A ['Or'] Spring-halt rain'd among 'em.   (*Henry VIII*, I iii 13)

Autolycus assures the shepherd and his son that he is indeed a courtier

> Think'st thou, for that I insinuate, at toaze ['or toaze'] from thee thy Businesse, I am therefore no Courtier?
>
> (*Winter's Tale*, IV iv 760)

Guiderius and Arviragus regret that they 'haue seene nothing' of the life of courts; when Belarius judges that their hunters' life is 'Nobler' Guiderius answers:

> Out of your proofe you speak . . .
> . . . Hap'ly this life is best,
> (If quiet life be best) sweeter to you
> That haue a sharper knowne. Well corresponding
> With your stiffe Age; but vnto vs, it is
> A Cell of Ignorance: trauailing *a* bed,
> *A* Prison, or *a* Debtor, that not dares
> To stride a limit.   (*Cymbeline*, III iii 34)

In Guiderius's image list, *trauailing a bed, A Prison, or a Debtor*, the first *a* represents an earlier 'on' while the third is clearly the indefinite article. The second is probably part of a 'hinge' phrase on which the changing syntax pivots from the adverbial 'a bed' to the elliptic noun-in-apposition 'a Debtor'. The phrase 'A Prison' that is to say, in conjunction with 'a bed' would represent adverbial 'in prison', while in conjunction with 'a Debtor' it might well represent also the noun 'a prisoner'. (NED shows prison in this now obsolete sense, with the last citation registered in 1494.)

2

A number of similar instances are found where, it may be argued, context rather than spelling will better direct the later reader to the intended meaning of the apparently puzzling word. In *Julius Caesar* (III i 39) as Metellus kneels before him to present his petition, Caesar protests the constancy of his justice:

> I must preuent thee Cymber:
> These couchings, and these lowly courtesies
> Might fire the blood of ordinary men,
> And turne pre-Ordinance, and first Decree
> Into the lane of Children.

'Lane' has not hitherto been satisfactorily explained and Johnson's emendation 'law' has been generally accepted. It is likely, however, that no emendation is necessary and that *lane* represents a variant pronunciation of the noun 'line' in its now obsolete sense 'rule, canon, precept'.[1] 'Line' in this sense would be known to Shakespeare's audience in a 'justice' context from its Biblical use, as in Psalm xix:

> The heavens declare the glory of God . . . Their line is gone out through all the earth . . . The law of the Lord is perfect . . .

---

[1] NED: *Line, sb.*² 5. 1340 to 1611.

And in Isaiah (xxviii, 5-10), true justice is spoken of as coming from God while those who err in judgment are compared, by implication, to infant children:

> In that day shall the Lord of hosts be . . . for a spirit of judgment to him that sitteth in judgment . . . But . . . the priest and the prophet have erred . . . they err in vision, they stumble in judgment . . . Whom shall he teach knowledge? and whom shall he make to understand doctrine? them that are weaned from the milk, and drawn from the breasts. For precept must be upon precept . . . line upon line.

Of this 'lane' type of pronunciation and spelling (*a* + Consonant + *e*) in the sixteenth and seventeenth centuries for words which have *i* (*i* + Consonant + *e*) in modern English there is some external evidence. Kökeritz refers to 'the once fashionable pronunciation of *china* as *chaney*' and instances the clown in the play *Respublica* (1553) who puns on the words *respublica* and *rice-puddingcake*.[1]

Stratford spellings I have noted are *Layneing*, 'lining' (for a coat) 1605; *one paire of holland sheets Laned and one paire pillow beers laned* 1625. Other Midland records show such spelling as *wayne* 'wine', *layme* 'lime', *saited* 'cited', *hayde* 'hide', *layninge* 'lining', *bay* 'buy', *bey* 'buy', *teyling* 'tiling', *teill* 'tile'. The *English Dialect Dictionary* registers the *ei* diphthong (as heard in literary English *fate*, *say*, *eight*) in such words as *wide*, *wife*, *drive* in some Midland dialects of the present time.

Those who say 'lane' for 'line' may on occasion write the reversed spelling *i* for *a*; it is possible therefore that the form *despised* has the sense 'dispaced' in *Richard II* (ii iii 95) as the Duke of York, regent in Richard's absence, angrily questions the banished Bolingbroke:[2]

---

[1] *Shakespeare's Pronunciation*, p. 216.
[2] This is to explain in the simplest terms. But it is possible that *despised* represents a genuine pronunciation of 'dispased'. W. Matthews, in *Cockney Past and Present*:

> Why haue these banish'd, and forbidden Legges,
> Dar'd once to touch a Dust of Englands Ground?
> But more then why, why haue they dar'd to march
> So many miles vpon her peacefull Bosome,
> Frighting her pale-fac'd Villages with Warre,
> And ostentation of despised Armes?

Various emendations for 'despised' have been proposed, including despightful, disposed, despited, despoiling. Present-day editors who keep the original text, understand 'despised' as 'able to be despised' and hence 'despicable'; such a meaning, however, seems to me out of context. As Warburton comments: 'But sure the ostentation of *despised* arms would not *fright* anyone.' And York makes a very realistic appraisal of the situation; he admits the weakness of his power to oppose Bolingbroke's forces:

> Well, well, I see the issue of these Armes,
> I cannot mend it, I must needes confesse,
> Because my power is weake, and all ill left. . . .

Bolingbroke has come from Ravenspurgh on the Humber to Berkley in Gloucestershire and has no doubt been gathering support in his march of so many miles across country. I suggest that 'dispaced' in the sense 'moving, on the march' would support the sense of 'ostentation' and 'So many miles' in York's complaint against him. NED shows an obsolete verb *Dispace*, of doubtful derivation (perhaps formed on *dis* + *pace* or else on Latin *di* + *spatiari*, Italian *spaziare* 'to walk') used by Spenser (1588, 1591) and by Giles Fletcher the younger (1610), in the sense 'To walk or move about'. In the instances cited by the Dictionary a free, wide movement is suggested: a serpent 'long time . . . did himselfe

---

A Short History of the Dialect of London (1938) cites similar spelling evidence from Machyn's diary (1550-63) and from London parish records of Shakespeare's time:

> In a fair number of spellings, long *a* and *ai* are replaced by *i* or *y*: *chynes* (chains), *obtyninge, ordined, Byes* (bays), *Rile* (rail), *strynge, nighbower*, etc. On the face of it these spellings reflect a pronunciation which is regarded as the most characteristic of Cockney variants at the present time (pp. 20-1).

dispace'; a butterfly is seen 'dispacing too and fro'; allegorical ships, 'dispasing wide, Through windy thoughts, that would their sails misguide' come safe at last to harbour. Such a movement of his forces, unopposed and unconstricted, Bolingbroke has been able to carry out.

I want next to consider the possibility (already mentioned in the 'sample' chapter, p. 19) that the verb 'aroint' (*aroynt, arint, arent*) found in the Shakespearean and Stratford phrase 'Aroint thee, witch!' represents a pronunciation variant of the English *aloyn* (Old French *aloigner*) and that the noun or adjective *prenzie*, found only in Shakespeare's *Much Ado* (III i 94, 97), may similarly represent a mishearing or mispronunciation of the seventeenth-century English noun *pollency*, 'power' (Latin *pollēntia*, strength). For ease of reference I number the stages of the argument.

1. The *t* of *aroynt* is no obstacle to the *aroynt/*'aloin' identification; in Shakespeare's text, as Kökeritz shows (p. 301), an 'excrescent *t* appears frequently at the end of words, particularly after *n*' and I shall therefore not take space to offer examples of this. The *oy, i, e* variants are, I think, to be regarded as instances of that diaphonic overlap which results in such Shakespearean spellings as *Smoile*, 'smile' (see p. 65) and *lane*, 'line' (see p. 210).

2. For the *prenzie/*'pollency' identification I need to postulate a Shakespearean *polléncy*, having the stress on the second syllable instead of on the first. Abbot notes (§ 490) that many words in Shakespeare's text 'such as "edict", "outrage", "contract", &c. are accented in a varying manner' and cites, among other examples, the noun *effigies* which keeps the Latin stress unaltered:

> And as mine eye doth his effigies witnesse,
> Most truly limn'd, and liuing in your face. . . .
>
> (*As You Like It*, II vii 193)

3. It is necessary to show that the *r* of *prenzie* might be syllabic: spellings in the Shakespearean text which give evidence of this, *Garace*, 'grace' (*Titus Andronicus*, II iii 182) and *thereat*, 'threat'

(*Lear*, iv ii 57, Q 1608) are noted in Chapter X (p. 317), with similar spellings from local records.

4. A number of present-day languages afford evidence of an *r*/*l* confusion or interchange.[1] Present-day English is tolerant of the *l*-like *r* as a personal uncorrected speech-deficiency; even in the speech of a B.B.C. news announcer 'light' may be acceptable as an opposition to 'left'.

The earlier history of French and English gives some evidence of *l*/*r* interchange in certain special conditions. Old French has a number of instances where *l* > *r* and *r* > *l* by dissimilation:[2]

> Si deux consonnes homophones se suivent à courte distance, l'une d'elles peut changer; ordinairement c'est la première qui se dissimile, moins souvent la dernière. *R — R > L — R ou R — L; Bertherot* (dér. de *Berthier*) > *Berthelot; contrarier > contralier* (forme fréquente au moyen âge); *ensorcerer > ensorceler* . . . *frigorosus > frileux;* peregrinus > pèlerin;
>
> L — L > R — L *umbilicum > *nombril*.[3]

Zachrisson has shown that there was interchange of *l*, *n* and *r* in English place-names at a time when these names were virtually loan-words in Anglo-French. To cite the two best known examples of *l*/*r* interchange, the Anglo-French form prevails in *Salisbury* as against English *Sarum* and in *Salop*, English *Shropshire*. Zachrisson notes further that a similar interchange of *l*, *n*, *r* is found in several English dialects, although, on his evidence,

---

[1] To mention two examples: Daniel Jones remarks that Japanese students of English 'are generally unable to make any kind of *l* with certainty. They confuse it with *r*, and use varieties of *l* and *r* indiscriminately . . .' (*An Outline of English Phonetics*, 1950, p. 163.) It has been observed that in certain dialects of Igbo (Nigeria) 'a sound intermediate between *l* and *r*' occurs before certain of the vowels while 'an ordinary single flap *r*' occurs before the others. (*The Phoneme*, by Daniel Jones, 1950, p. 21.)

[2] A similar change is found in the history of the Russian language. See *Russian Historical Grammar* by W. K. Matthews, 1960: 'Dissimilation, especially of adjacent liquids, whose beginning we noted in the thirteenth century, continues to be illustrated sporadically till the sixteenth and early seventeenth.'

[3] *Grammaire Historique de la Langue Francaise*, by Kr. Nyrop, Copenhagen, 1935, Vol. I, p. 481.

this 'is mainly confined to foreign words in the vernacular. Cf. *calavan* for *caravan*, *paltridge* for *partridge*, *synable* for *syllable*'.[1] The interchange of unstressed *le*, *re*, *ne*, which is usual in French, was transferred to many early forms of English place-names: Sydenham occurs in Domesday Book as *Sidreham*, *Sidelham*.[2] P. H. Reaney in a later place-name study finds that, in the dialect of Essex as illustrated in its place-names, interchange of the liquids *l*, *n* and *r* is very common; *l* has replaced an *r* in *Crockleford* ('The potter's ford', OE *croccere*, 'potter'), *Malyons* and *Skillet Hill*, while *r* has replaced *l* in *Forest Hall* (earlier Folyat(te)s Hall, Folyathall).[3] In these last English examples, the *n* variation is of particular interest: *n* follows *r* in both *aroynt* and *prenzie*.

The *English Dialect Dictionary*, in its registration of eighteenth- and nineteenth-century dialect, notes a dissimilation of *l* to *r* (§ 252) in the single word *frail* meaning 'flail; the whip part of the old-fashioned flail'; this is found in Scotland and in some of the northern, midland and southern counties of England.

What is evidently another instance of this same sound change crops up in Laurie Lee's account of his Gloucestershire childhood (*Cider with Rosie*, 1960, p. 270), when a certain Mrs. Clissold habitually refers to herself as Mrs. Crissole. Occasional instances of *l* for *r* are also found: NED shows *obstropalous*, *obstrapalous*, etc. as illiterate or humorous pronunciation variants of the eighteenth and nineteenth centuries; in present-day midland speech there can be heard such forms as *scholary* for 'scholarly'.

In the local record material of the midland counties in the sixteenth and seventeenth centuries I have noted two instances where *l* > *n*: *leveninge*, 'levelling', St. Mary's, Shrewsbury, 1581; *whorne*, 'whorl', Bilston, Staffs. 1698. Evidence of *l/r* variation is found in Oswestry, Shropsh. where the word 'surplice' occurs in the following forms:

---

[1] *Introduction to the Survey of English Place-Names*, Part I, ed. by A Mawer and F. M. Stenton, Cambridge, 1924; Chapter V, 'The French Element' by R. E. Zachrisson, p. 106.   [2] Zachrisson, p. 107.
[3] *The Place-Names of Essex*, by P. H. Reaney, Cambridge, 1935, p. xxxviii.

sirples and *shirples c.* 1590, but also *silpres* 1584, 1597, 1599, 1602, 1603, 1605; *silpris c.* 1590, 1599, 1607; *shilpres* 1599; *silpis, silpes* 1593; *silypris, slipers, shiliprs, sylpris* 1596.

NED shows many variant forms of this noun (as adoptions of Anglo-French *surpliz*, Old French *sourpeliz*, also *supelis, souplis*): two fifteenth-century forms have the *-lpr-* consonant combination: *solepers, sullipers*.

The Shakespearean printed text has one instance of what may be *l, n, r* variation in the speech of the King of France (*Henry V*, v ii 77):

> I haue but with a curselarie eye
> O're-glanc't the Articles. . . .

Where F1 has *curselarie* and later folios *curselary*, the form *cursenary* is found in Quartos 1 and 2 and *cursorary* in Q 3 ('1608'). In *Macbeth* (I ii 13) *r* is found for *l* in *Gallowgrosses*, 'gallowglasses', a spelling which is corrected in later folios. It is possible that this 'error' derives from the existence of an *l/r* pronunciation-variant in the language of dramatist, scribe or compositor, which remained uncorrected in the First Folio for the reason that *gallowgrass* (as a slang name for hemp, from its use for ropes and halters) was itself a genuine word.

This concludes for the present the pronunciation evidence— evidence which although somewhat fragmentary seems to me to suggest a consistent pattern. If I am right in my interpretation of the Shakespearean forms it is to be expected that further evidence of *l, r* interchange will be found. I should of course be particularly interested to have written evidence of *l* changing to *r* in words or sound-groups where *n* follows.

5. The quasi-proverbial 'Aroint thee, witch' is found in fixed phrasal form, twice in the Shakespearean text and once in an undated, early seventeenth-century Stratford record. I can offer no instances of Old French *aloigner*, Anglo-French *aloyner*, either with an *r* for *l*, or used reflexively in the imperative, or in a 'witch' context and I have come upon no instances of the English

verb *aloyne* other than those registered by NED with the sense
'To remove far off, to carry away' (1303, *c.* 1325, 1464). It seems
to me, however, that this sense 'to remove far off' is entirely in
keeping with the 'aroint' context.

6. *Pollency* is cited by NED in the sense 'power, strength' in two
instances only, the first in 1623 from Cockeram's *English Dictionarie, or an interpreter of hard English words*, the second from Royal
Society Trans. 1665-6: To determine readily what Pollency the
Buble hath. The meaning-units -*pollent*, -*pollence* are, however, in
frequent use from the beginning of the fifteenth century as part
of the adjective *equipollent* and the noun *equipollence*. So, for
instance

> Ther may no gretter Perill growe to a Prince, than to have a
> Subgett equipolent to himself *c.* 1460;
> That in his equipollence He judgeth him equivalent With God
> Omnipotent   *a.* 1528 Skelton

The noun *equipollency* is first registered by NED in 1623 but
equipolences as a plural of *equipolence* (from which a '-pollency'
singular might be adduced) is cited from *c.* 1400.

Cooper's *Thesaurus*, the standard reference dictionary of the
Elizabethan grammar school, gives the definitions

> Polleo . . . To may, or can: to be of power or puisance: to be of
> vertue or strength: to beare rule, stroke, or authoritie.
> Pollens . . . He that can doe much and is of great power.

7. Internal evidence shows that Isabella visiting her brother in
prison fears his reaction to the 'diuellish mercie in the Iudge';
before letting him know 'the point' on which he might 'be freed'
she asks him 'Dar'st thou die?' so prompting him to speak of the
resolution with which he will, if he must, 'encounter darknesse':

> Isabella.   There spake my brother: there my fathers graue
> Did vtter forth a voice. Yes, thou must die:
> Thou art too noble, to conserue a life
> In base appliances. This outward sainted Deputie,

Whose setled visage, and deliberate word
Nips youth i'th head, and follies doth emmew
As Falcon doth the Fowle, is yet a diuell:
His filth within being cast, he would appeare
A pond, as deepe as hell.
Claudio.   The prenzie, Angelo?
Isabella.   Oh 'tis the cunning Liuerie of hell,
The damnest body to inuest, and couer
In prenzie gardes . . .

To Claudio at this point of the play, 'The prenzie, Angelo' is essentially 'He that can do much and is of great power'. The comma which follows 'prenzie' makes clear that Angelo = Angelo's function; no emotional judgment of Angelo the man is in question; as far as Claudio knows, no relationship exists between the two men other than that between Angelo by law condemning and Claudio by law condemned. So, at the time of his arrest when, before being taken to prison, he is shown to the world by Lord Angelo's 'speciall charge', Claudio acknowledges the justice of what the law commands:

Thus can the demy-god (Authority)
Make vs pay downe, for our offence, by waight
The words of heauen; on whom it will, it will,
On whom it will not (soe) yet still 'tis iust.   (I ii 127)

At this time also he speaks of Angelo as 'the new Deputie', 'this new Gouernor', the 'strict deputie'; the fault that he imputes to him is 'the fault and glimpse of newnes'. In asking

Whether the Tirrany be in his place,
Or in his Eminence that fills it vp. . . .   (I ii 168)

he judges that Angelo 'puts the drowsie and neglected Act' upon him 'for a name, . . . 'tis surely for a name'. Even when on the eve of his execution he learns from his sister of Angelo's falseness it is still with Angelo as law-enforcer that he is primarily concerned: his surprise that Angelo the man should scorn the law is expressed in one brief sentence:

> Has he affections in him,
> That thus can make him bite the Law by th' nose,
> When he would force it?   (III i 110)

In contrast to the neutrality of Claudio's 'prenzie', Isabella's phrase 'In prenzie gardes' expresses in dramatic form that over-harsh evaluation of worldly power and authority which it is some part of the play's business to examine and modify; 'prenzie gardes', I would argue, are here the trappings of power. So, for instance, in Philemon Holland's translation of Pliny's *Historie of the World* (1601)

> A Senatour was distinguisht from the Gentlemen . . . by his coat embrodered with broad gards and studs of purple.[1]

The play is largely concerned with power, the symbols of power and the false-seeming of the powerful. Isabella, urged by Lucio to 'Assay the powre' she has (I iv 76), speaks to Angelo of the 'ceremony that to great ones longs', the 'Kings Crowne', the 'deputed sword', and the 'Iudges Robe'. She wishes that she had the 'potencie' of Angelo (II ii 67). Proud man is 'Drest in a little brief authoritie'. And when like others, great men also sin, the power which they have 'skins the vice o' th top' (II ii 136). Angelo comes bitterly to realise that the authority of which fools are in awe is a 'case' and 'habit' of place and form, 'false seeming' only (II iv 15). The Duke wonders at the sins which a man, 'Though Angel on the outward side', may hide within (III ii 286). When the Duke returns to take up his authority Isabella conjures him to believe that a wicked man may 'seeme' just, as Angelo 'In all his dressings, caracts, titles' may be an arch-villain (v i 56). And even Lucio, as he avows Frier Lodowick to be a dishonest person, uses a proverb and image of dress: '*Cucullus non facit Monachum*, honest in nothing but in his Clothes' (v i 263).

Returning now to the 'prenzie' passage, I suggest that Isabella, in her linkage of the dress image with the 'outward sainted'/

---

[1] NED: *Guard* 11 a.

'diuell . . . within' contrast, expresses one side only of the power/ seeming proposition: the 'damnest body' is invested in 'prenzie gardes' as the devil's 'Liuery'. Angelo, in his 'case', 'habit', 'false seeming', 'Angell'-devil linkage of an earlier and closely parallel passage, acknowledges in addition the power of the body, the force of the body's desires:

> Blood, thou art blood,
> Let's write good Angell on the Deuills horne
> 'Tis not the Deuills Crest. . . . . (II iv 17)

I have tried in this brief analysis to indicate that 'prenzie' in the sense 'pollency' would have full dramatic significance as argument and image. It is an important part of my case that as the word is repeated in the dramatic text after a two-line interval a new facet of its meaning is presented.

A smaller textual difficulty occurs in *King John* (III iv 2), *A whole Armado of conuicted saile*. I suggest here that the Folio's 'conuicted' should be printed 'convected' in a modern-spelling text, and that the word has the meaning 'assembled'. Philip of France, with the English prince Arthur, has met his ally, the Emperor of Austria, before the town of Angiers which they are jointly to attack. In the ensuing battle, Angiers is lost, Arthur taken prisoner and the Emperor slain:

> And bloudy England into England gone,
> Ore-bearing interruption spight of France.

Those who had hoped that they might in the end win England itself for Prince Arthur have encountered 'vnlook'd for' opposition and have suffered shameful defeat at the very beginning of their campaign. The scene which follows this battle begins with these words of King Philip:

> So by a roaring Tempest on the flood,
> A whole Armado of conuicted saile
> Is scattered and dis-ioyn'd from fellowship.

Editors who take 'conuicted' at its face value are bound to regard it as meaning 'vanquished, defeated'.[1] For this sense there is external evidence near enough contemporary: Minsheu's Dictionary (1617) shows 'To convict, or convince, à Latin convictus, overcome'. And the reference to an armada scattered by the tempest seems conclusive: Shakespeare's countrymen had given thanks to God for the storms which had helped to destroy the Spanish fleet. It may be argued, however, that this sense, although in keeping with the general dramatic situation, is not appropriate to the immediate linguistic context: as long as an 'Armado' is 'whole', no part of it is 'conuicted' in the sense of 'vanquished'. Shakespeare's audience knew the naval tactics employed against the Armada of 1588: not until Howard's fireships had broken the enemy formation and the Spanish ships were scattered was the decisive battle fought. 'A whole Armado', not yet 'scattered and dis-ioyned from fellowship' was a formidable threat; so King Philip, in this play, had hoped that the combined forces of France and Austria might prove invincible. The 'roaring Tempest' of which he speaks was the unforeseen disaster, the unlooked for expedition of the English voluntaries (II i 79). Linguistic context leads one to expect for the folio's 'conuicted' the sense 'assembled', implying also movement in formation; many of the emendations proposed by earlier editors[2] clearly derive from this expectancy. But no emendation is necessary if we have in mind how the word might be pronounced: many spellings of *i* for *e* are found in the language of Shakespeare's time.[3] And *con-vectus*, 'sailing together' would be well within the Latin-English language patterns of Shakespeare's contemporaries. Rider's *Dictionarie* (1626 ed.) shows

---

[1] NED gives this Shakespearean instance as the first of two citations (1595, 1607) to illustrate this obsolete sense. Similarly Schmidt (1874); so also Malone, and, more recently, Dover Wilson (1954). Honigmann ('New Arden', 1954) prefers the Cowden Clarkes's 'condemned, doomed to perdition'.

[2] Collected, convented, consorted, connected, convoyed, convexed, compacted, combined, conjointed.

[3] Kökeritz notes in Shakespeare's text numerous cases of *i* for ME ĕ, evidenced by spellings, rhymes and puns (p. 186).

con, 'With, together, a preposition . . . that is never used but in composition . . .';

Cooper's *Thesaurus* includes under *Vectus*

Multa per æquora vectus. Catul. Sayling ouer.

No very satisfactory explanation has been offered of the form *cheff* (Folio), *chiefe* (Quarto 2) in the precepts of Polonius to Laertes (*Hamlet*, i iii 74):

Costly thy habit as thy purse can buy;
But not exprest in fancie; rich, not gawdie:
For the Apparell oft proclaimes the man.
And they in France of the best ranck and station,
Are of a most select and generous cheff in that.   (Folio)

Or of a most select and generous, chiefe in that: (Quarto 2)

I suggest that the line is to be understood as in Quarto 2 and that *chiefe* is a verb denoting some reaction of the best in France to the man-proclaiming apparel; its spelling then represents a variant pronunciation of the now obsolete *chave* with the sense 'to separate (corn, etc.) from chaff'. To deal first with the spelling/pronunciation evidence: NED registers no variation of vowel or diphthong for the particular form of this verb which has initial *ch*, but for the comparable verb *cave*, in use from *c*. 1420, the modern dialect forms *keave*, *keeave* are included.[1] EDD shows a verb *cave* with a variant *keeave* and also a verb *chave* with the associated noun *cheevings* as the 'bits of broken straw, dust, refuse'.[2] No form of the verb is registered with final *f*, but I assume that, by analogy with the noun *chaff*, *f* instead of *v* might be heard in the verb.

---

[1] NED: *chave v*. 1. To mix or strew with chaff, *c*. 1420. 2. To free (corn, etc.). from chaff and short straw; to separate the chaff from, 1649-1726.
cave v[4] Obs. and dial. form of CHAVE, to separate chaff and empty ears from the corn.

[2] EDD: *cave v*[3]; *chave v*. Yks. Chs. Shr. Written *cheev-* Chs.

The separating of corn from chaff is an image in frequent use.
The prince of Aragon regrets that 'cleare honour' is not to be
'purchast' by 'merrit' only:

> How much low pleasantry [peasantry] would then be gleaned
> From the true seede of honor? And how much honor
> Pickt from the chaffe and ruine of the times,
> To be new varnisht. . . .

(Merchant of Venice, II ix 48)

Mowbray fears that if the rebels make their peace with the king,
no conditions of that peace can stand:

> Wee shall be winnowed with so rough a winde,
> That euen our Corne shall seeme as light as Chaffe,
> And good from bad finde no partition.

(2 Henry IV, IV i 195)

As Coriolanus leads the enemies of Rome against the city,
Cominius describes how he has tried to 'awaken his regard' for
his 'priuate Friends':

> His answer to me was
> He could not stay to picke them, in a pile
> Of noysome musty Chaffe.   (Coriolanus, V i 26)

This interpretation of chiefe as 'chave' rests on the assumption
that Polonius can express the image-action 'separate corn from
chaff' in a single word. In support of this assumption one may
note, for instance, his rebuke of Ophelia later in the same scene:

> Affection, puh. You speake like a greene Girle,
> Vnsifted in such perillous Circumstance   (I iii 102)

and Henry V's reproach against Lord Scroop who with other
English lords had plotted his death:

> Such and so finely boulted didst thou seeme. . . .   (II ii 137)

Polonius' phrase 'in that' would mean then 'by observing a man's
dress': NED illustrates the use of the preposition in 'Of means and
instrumentality' (13). It is possible also that the word 'select' in his

speech may be the reason for his choice of the *chiefe* form of the
'chave' sense: in the Elizabethan language-memory both 'picked'
and 'chief' may be associated with the word 'select'. Cooper's
Thesaurus defines the Latin *Selectus* 'Chosen from among other:
piked: chiefe among other: select'.

There is difficulty in interpreting as it stands the line *And either
the deuill, or throwe him out* in Hamlet's speech to his mother
(*Hamlet*, III iv 169, Quarto 2):

> Good night, but goe not to my Vncles bed,
> Assune [Assume] a vertue if you haue it not,
> That monster custome, who all sence doth eate
> Of habits deuill, is angell yet in this
> That to the vse of actions faire and good,
> He likewise giues a frock or Liuery
> That aptly is put on to refraine night [refraine tonight]
> And that shall lend a kind of easines
> To the next abstinence, the next more easie:
> For vse almost can change the stamp of nature,
> And either the deuill, or throwe him out
> With wonderous potency:

It is generally accepted that some word has been omitted after
'either' and editors from the eighteenth century onwards have
tried, in various ways, to supply the missing verb: curb, mate,
house, usher, aid, throne, lay, lodge, quell and shame are among
the proposals made. Some have adopted 'master' from the reading
of the fourth Quarto (1611) *And Maister the;* the line has then been
given 'And master even the devil', *even* being supplied as the
necessary extra syllable.

It is possible, however, that we should accept the line as it
stands in the Second Quarto, taking 'either' as a verb meaning
'make easier', its final *r* representing the extra syllable necessary
for the rhythmic pattern of the line. This sense would be fully
in context in the quoted passage ('habits', 'vse', 'aptly', 'easines'
'more easie'). The adjective *eathe*, *iethe*, common enough in the

Old English period in the sense 'easy', survives in Scottish proverbs to the present time: EDD shows the word still known in Scotland, Ireland and the northern counties of England. Johnson included it in his Dictionary with the note 'An old word'; in Cotgrave's *Dictionarie* (1632 ed.) it is employed to translate *Facile:* 'Easie, facile, eeth, prone . . .'. From the evidence given in NED under *Eath, eith* there is no need to suppose that the word was confined to northern usage in Tudor England: it is found in the writings of Thomas More (1532).

I woulde euery other thinge wer as ethe to mend as thys is;

the comparative form *ether* is registered by NED in 1538 from Starkey's *England.*[1]

As regards the pronunciation of Hamlet's 'either', it is possible to cite a number of instances in Shakespeare's text where '*Er final* seems to have been sometimes pronounced with a kind of 'burr', which produced the effect of an additional syllable'.[2] So in *Hamlet* (III iii 38):

It hath the primall eldest curse vpon't,
A Brothers murth*er*. Pray can I not,
Though inclination be as sharpe as will. . . .

And in *Macbeth* (II iii 46) the comparative 'near' occurs in dissyllabic form:

Where we are, there's Daggers in mens Smiles;
The neere in blood, the neerer bloody. (II iii 146)[3]

---

[1] *England in the reign of King Henry the Eighth*. A Dialogue between Cardinal Pole and Thomas Lupset. Early English Text Soc., Extra Series, 12, 1871, p. 32, 1.183: Wel, then, let vs now, I pray you, retorne to our purpos, that we may the bettur (and *other* also, avoyd thys ignorance, the fountain of al yl.
It should be noted here that *ether* as cited by NED is editorial for MS. *other*.

[2] Abbott's *Shakespearian Grammar*, 1875, § 478.

[3] Alternatively it might be possible to argue that the first syllable of Hamlet's *either* was lengthened by diphthongisation: it is believed that *i:* was diphthongised in some varieties of early English and Daniel Jones has noted that at the present time 'Many English speakers use a diphthong in place of a pure i: The diphthong begins with an open variety of i and moves to a closer position.' (*An Outline of*

In *Hamlet* (I iii 109) Polonius advises Ophelia not to believe in Hamlet's 'tenders Of his affection':

> Marry Ile teach you; thinke your selfe a Baby,
> That you haue tane his tenders for true pay,
> Which are not starling. Tender your selfe more dearly;
> Or not to crack the winde of the poor Phrase,
> Roaming it thus, you'l tender me a foole.

The puzzling word *Roaming* of the Folio text (Quarto 2 *Wrong*) has been variously emended: 'wronging', 'wringing', 'ranging' have been suggested; 'running' is most commonly found in more recent editions. It may be that here also no emendation is necessary since, in some types of Elizabethan speech, 'roaming' and 'rooming' could have the same pronunciation, and 'rooming' in the sense 'extending' would be fully in context. That 'roam' and 'room' could have the same spelling there is clear evidence.[1] Kökeritz shows that Shakespeare puns on 'Rome'/'room' (*Julius Caesar*, I ii 156) and on 'Rome'/'roam' (I *Henry VI*, III i 51)[2] and it seems likely that all three words could be pronounced in Shakespeare's time with the pronunciation we now give to 'room' alone. NED shows a verb *room* with the sense (3c.) 'to give (onself) free scope':

> 1621 . . . He had a scope of a hundred and twentie miles long and a hundred and odd miles broade to runne and roome himself;

the meaning 'to extend, enlarge' is last cited in general use in *c.* 1425:

> Than Iohne bischop of Glasgw Rowmyt þe kirk of Sanct Mongw;

in the specialised sense 'extending the bottom of a bore-hole' (a term used by sinkers) it is registered in the Northumberland

---

English Phonetics, Cambridge, 1950, p.64.) Sixteenth- and seventeenth-century spellings with *ei* and *ie* in such words as *wheille*, *keiping*, *stieple*, *steipell* may indicate some variant of this kind.

[1] Among the forms of *roam* shown by NED are 4-7 rome; 4-6 rowme; 5, 7 roome; *room v.*[1] may be similarly 4-5 roume, 5-6 rowm(e).

[2] *Shakespeare's Pronunciation*, pp. 141-2. See also Dobson, Vol. II, § 154.

dialect in 1894.[1] Polonius, giving himself such scope to extend the meaning of his poor phrase 'Tender' is afraid that he may crack its wind, 'rooming' it thus.[2]

3

It is perhaps worth remarking that although this last 'crack the winde' phrase is still intelligible to the present-day reader, it is now outside the permitted usage of ordinary polite conversation, and if indeed a gloss were required to make the Shakespearean image intelligible, the present-day commentator might well encounter the objection that so crude an interpretation is stylistically improper. The serious old statesman, it might be argued, would not speak thus to his daughter. Such an objection, it should be noted, would be the harder to refute because of the easy casualness with which the image is employed. I want next to suggest that the famous *Schoole of night* phrase (*Love's Labour's Lost*, IV iii 255) is to be understood primarily as a joke of sex-innuendo—a joke which is also the harder to 'prove' in that it is unemphasised and swiftly taken. But the speakers at least are young men in love and their talk is of the black beauty of Berowne's Rosaline:

> King.   By heauen, thy Loue is blacke as Ebonie.
> Berowne.   Is Ebonie like her? O word diuine?
> A wife of such wood were felicitie.
> O who can giue an oth? Where is a booke?
> That I may sweare Beauty doth beauty lacke,
> If that she learne not of her eye to looke:
> No face is faire that is not full so blacke.
> King.   O paradoxe, Blacke is the badge of hell,
> The hue of dungeons, and the Schoole of night:
> And beauties crest becomes the heauens well.
> Berowne. Diuels soonest tempt resembling spirits of light.

---

[1] NED: *room v.*[1] Now *dial.* or *arch.* 3c. 1598, 1621; 4.

[2] It may be noted also that 'wind' and 'room' are in collocation in early seventeenth-century nautical language. See NED: *Room* adj. 2b. 1632 only citations; *Room* adv. 3. Very common from about *c.* 1580-1630.

Emendations proposed for 'Schoole' include scowl, stole, shade, suit, soil; it has also been supposed 'that there was a real "Schoole of Night" existing at this time, and that it was synonymous with the "Schoole of Atheism" of which Sir Walter Ralegh was reputed by contemporaries to be the chief patron.'[1] I shall try to show that no emendation is necessary and that the *Schoole of night* phrase has its full meaning in the punning paradox of stage dialogue; no extraneous non-dramatic allusion need be looked for.

I note first that, as the 'New Cambridge' editors comment (1923), the Quarto 'prints "The hue of dungions, and the Schoole of night" as if "hue" and "Schoole" balanced each other'. Further, the 'Schoole', 'school' form remains unemended in later Folios. I believe that the word was probably to be pronounced with initial *sh* and, as representing within Elizabethan spelling conventions what would now be *shell, scale* and *shewel*, could include within itself several very apposite meanings. NED shows that the noun *shell* occurs in the fifteenth century in the form *schull(e)*, in the seventeenth century as *shul* and in nineteenth century dialect as *shull*.[2] One meaning of this *shell* that would be fully relevant in the 'varnish', 'painting' context of the Shakespearean passage is 'a mussel-shell containing pigment'. So in Cooper's *Thesaurus* (1578 ed.) *Conchae* are 'Shelles wherein painters put theyr coulours'. 'Schoole (= shell) of night' is thus balanced against 'hue of dungions' as in the quarto text. A second meaning, I suggest, primary but not plainly stated, is *cunnus*, a sense of *shell* which has achieved inclusion in NED and which is illustrated by the *Dictionary* in sixteenth-century Scottish verse.[3]

---

[1] I quote from Richard David's note in his 'New Arden' *Love's Labour's Lost* (1951) on the suggestion made by Arthur Acheson (1903).

[2] NED: *shell, sb.*[1], OE. *sciell* . . . OTeut. **skaljo* f. **skall* for other derivatives of which see *scale sb.*[1], *sb.*[2] . . . *scale, sb.*[1], a.ON skal.

[3] *shell, sb.*[1] 2b. Used as a target. Sc., chiefly with indecent allusion (cf. L. concha = *cunnus*). So in David Lindesay's 'Answer to . . . ye kingis flyting' (1536), he warns the king:

That the word 'blacke' used of a woman's 'Beauty' might itself bring to mind this 'cunnus' sense is indicated in an epigram by Sir John Harington (1603):

> These thirty things that Hellens fame did raise,
> A Dame should haue that seeks for beuties praise:
> Three bright, three blacke, three red, 3. short, 3. tall,
> Three thick, three thin, three close, 3. wide, 3. small:
> Her skin, and teeth, must be cleare, bright, and neat,
> Her browes, eyes, priuy parts, as blacke as Ieat:[1]

The king then, in attacking the 'paradoxe' of Berowne, would be drawing attention to the underlying paradox of his own (pretended) dispraise of a beauty 'blacke as Ebonie'.[2]

Other senses may be in play in the 'Schoole of night' phrase. NED shows the noun *scale*[3] (*sb.*[1]) with the spellings *scole, scoale, skole* in the sixteenth and seventeenth centuries. This 'scale' may be a heavenly sign, the sign of Libra. There would then be a hidden significance in the third line of the king's speech

And beauties crest becomes the heauens well

> Thocht ye be now strang lyke ane Elephand,
> And in till Venus werkis maist vailyeand, . . .
>   tak tent, and your fyne powder spair . . .
> Thocht ye rin rudelie, lyke ane restles Ram,
> Schutand your bolt at mony sindrie schellis
> Beleif richt weill, it is ane bydand gam . . .
>
> I giue your counsale to the feynd of hell,
> That wald nocht of ane Princis yow prouide;
> Tholand yow rin schutand from schell to schell,
> Waistand your corps, lettand the tyme ouerslyde;
> For, lyke ane boisteous Bull, ye rin and ryde
> Royatouslie lyke ane rude Rubeator,
> Ay fukkand lyke ane furious Fornicatour.

Minor Poems, ed. by J. A. H. Murray (Early English Text Society), 1871, p. 564. (I have substituted y for 3 in the above.)

[1] Of a faire woman; translated out of Casaneus his Catalogus gloriae mundi', *Letters and Epigrams of Sir John Harington*, ed. by N. E. McClure, Philadelphia, 1930, p. 154.

[2] And Berowne, in praising ebony, 'A wife of such wood were felicitie' may glance at a second sense of 'wood'—'infatuated, mad for love'. (See citations by NED under *wood a.* 2.)

[3] NED: *Scale sb*[1] 5. 1631 Sayle By the signe Libra, that Celestiall scale.

16

which would support the preceding praise-dispraise paradox. And in Biblical language scales on the eyes typify moral blindness; NED cites[1]

> 1611 Bible Transl. Pref.: Hee remoueth the scales from our eyes, the vaile from our hearts. 1629 The skailes of darknesse which our eyes be-night.

A further sense of the 'Schoole' form may have been brought out by the reference to the frightening 'Diuell' and the 'Blacke/faire' antithesis. The King would claim that 'Blacke is the badge of hell' and when Berowne declares that he will vindicate his lady's beauty,

> Ile proue her faire, or talke till dooms-day here,

the King retorts

> No Diuell will fright thee then so much as shee.

A noun *shewell*, which NED shows (*c.* 1250–1688, then 1888) as 'a scarecrow', and as

> a Paper, clout, or any thing hanged vp to keep a Deere from entring into a place (1616)

may be figuratively a frightening bugbear.[2] And it may, presumably by its brightness, both frighten away and drive into capture. NED shows, for instance,

> 1535 Getheryng up part of the saide bowke leiffes . . . therwith to make him sewelles or blawnsherres to kepe the dere within the woode, thereby to have the better cry with his howndes

and

> 1661 He knows both with what baites to incite them, and with what shewels to drive into the Net and Toyle.

---

[1] NED: *scale sb.*[2] (for which no spellings with *oo* or *u* are shown) 4; see also *shale sb.*[1] 3. A scale (of a fish, of metal, of a scaly disease, etc.). The relevance of the scriptural 'scale' to this Shakespearean passage was noticed by A. E. Brae (1860).

[2] As in Sidney's *Arcadia* (a. 1586) So are these bug-beares of opinions brought by great Clearks into the world, to serue as shewelles to keepe them from those faults, whereto [etc.]. . . . I quote from the ed. of 1598, Bk. 3,z 2.

Additional minor senses of this 'Schoole' form (= *shell, scale*) may be glanced at in the quipping depreciations of Rosaline's dark beauty which follow immediately on the quoted passage. To Berowne's claim that the others' mistresses 'dare neuer come in raine', the King answers

> 'Twere good yours did: for sir to tell you plaine,
> Ile finde a fairer face not washt to day.

Cooper's *Thesaurus* and Rider's *Dictionarie* show 'a washing boll' as one of the senses of the Latin *concha*. And whereas Cotgrave's Dictionary (1632 ed.), which gives French *Escaille* as one of the meanings of the English *scale*, translates this *Escaille* as

> also, the crust, or upper laying, of a Pauement,

the last joke of the Shakespearean sequence has reference to street paving (iv iii 278):

> Longavile.   Looke, heer's thy loue, my foot and her face see.
> Berowne.   O if the streets were paued with thine eyes,
> Her feet were much too dainty for such tread.
> Dumane.   O vile, then as she goes what vpward lyes?
> The street should see as she walk't ouer head.

Whether there are sufficient indications in the Shakespearean text to bring into prominence these various senses of the 'Schoole' spelling which I have tried to show as potentially available to dramatist and actor, it must remain now for the individual reader to consider. I would agree that the clues are presented with a certain polished lack of insistence, but so too I would argue with a number of passages in this scene where the young men talk of love and lovers.

4

A few other instances of Shakespearean double- or multi-meaning which rest on pronunciation variants no longer heard

in standard English may be more simply dealt with. Sometimes
the recognisable single meaning may seem sufficient, as when in
Macbeth (I ii 65) Duncan condemns the treacherous Cawdor:

> Goe pronounce his present death,
> And with his former Title greet Macbeth.

Here the *greet* spelling may contain a further sense, that of the
verb 'great', as cited by NED in 1605 (the last registered usage):

> This false Politick, Plotting to Great himself, our deaths doth
> seek.[1]

There is good evidence, in Shakespeare's time and later, that
'great' in one type of speech had the pronunciation normally
given to 'greet'. The later Folios agree in the reading *great* in
this line. And greatness and degrees of greatness is a theme of
much importance in the early scenes of the play.

Elsewhere in the Shakespearean text the present-day meaning
which is commonly given to the Folio spelling may seem startlingly insufficient. So with the King's phrase *though grieu'd with
killing griefe* in *Titus Andronicus*, II iii 260. Some editors, as, for
instance, Dover Wilson (1948) would look on this as an example
of 'Careless writing' in the dramatist; others judge that ' "griev'd
by grief" is surely too careless for him to have written'.[2] It may,
however, be argued that context and spelling evidence
indicate for this 'grieu'd' form the double sense 'graved' and
'grieved'. So as not to describe the action with my own inserted
stage-directions I quote the passage at some length. Martius has
fallen into the pit in which the body of Bassianus has been thrown,
and Quintus, trying to help his brother to climb out, himself
falls in:

> Quintus.   Thy hand once more, I will not loose againe,
> Till thou art heere aloft, or I below,
> Thou can'st not come to me, I come to thee.   *Boths* [sic] *fall in*

---

[1] NED: *great, v.* 2. *trans.* To make great.
[2] As J. C. Maxwell, 'New Arden', 1953.

Enter the Emperour, Aaron the Moore.

Saturninus.   Along with me, Ile see what hole is heere,
And what he is that now is leapt into it.
Say, who art thou that lately did'st descend,
Into this gaping hollow of the earth?
Martius.   The vnhappie sonne of old Andronicus,
Brought hither in a most vnluckie houre,
To finde thy brother Bassianus dead.

. . . .

Enter Tamora, Andronicus, and Lucius

Tamora.   Where is my Lord the King?
King.   Heere Tamora, though grieu'd with killing griefe. (Q. griude)
Tamora.   Where is thy brother Bassianus?
King.   Now to the bottome dost thou search my wound,
Poore Bassianus heere lies murthered.

It seems clear from the dramatic situation that, however the scene might actually be staged, the emperor is speaking to Tamora as it were from the pit itself, earlier referred to as 'poore Bassianus graue'. He then climbs out to receive the letter which Tamora brings; Martius and Quintus remain below until he gives the order 'drag them from the pit vnto the prison'. And as NED's evidence indicates, the verb 'grave' might in the sixteenth century have the same spelling as the verb 'grieve'.[1] A dialect pronunciation of 'grave' with a high front narrow vowel is shown by EDD in parts of Lancashire, Shropshire and Gloucestershire at the present time.

If this interpretation of the spelling-pronunciation evidence is correct, the form 'grieu'd' has then three senses: 'graved', i.e. hidden from sight in the pit which is his brother's grave, and 'grieved', i.e. suffering anguish of mind so great that he seems to be suffering a physical wound.[2] 'Heere' where the King is and

---

[1] *grave, v.*[1] Forms: 6 greve; *grieve* Forms: 3-6 greve.
[2] NED: *grieved* 2. Afflicted with pain or disease. 1577-1689.

where his brother 'heere lies murthered' is at once 'the bottome' of the pit and the depth of his own almost mortal grief.

In 3 *Henry VI* (II v 119) during the civil war 'a Father that hath kill'd his Sonne' not knowing who was his foe, laments the untimely death of his only child:

> My sighing brest, shall be thy Funerall bell;
> And so obsequious will thy Father be,
> Men for the losse of thee, hauing no more,
> As Priam was for all his Valiant Sonnes,
> Ile beare thee hence, and let them fight that will,
> For I haue murthered where I should not kill.

A number of emendation for *Men* have been put forward,[1] 'E'en' or 'Even' being most generally accepted. It could, however, be argued that no emendation is necessary and that 'Men' represents what in modernised spelling would be 'Mean'.

NED shows the adjective *mean* (found in the form *men* from the fourteenth to the sixteenth century) with the very relevant sense 'intermediary; employed as an agent'.[2] A second available sense, 'moderate in degree' or 'comparatively less', is brought to mind by the linguistic context; 'Men' is in some contrast to 'more'.[3] Such a contrast, however, is suggested by the speaker only so that he may the more vigorously deny it; he will admit no proportioning of his grief to that of Priam. A third sense, 'poor, abject', may also have been heard by those accustomed to Shakespearean punning, comic and non-comic, on the various senses of 'mean'.[4] So Romeo, hearing his sentence of banishment, asks the Friar

> Had'st thou no poyson mixt, no sharpe ground knife,
> No sudden meane of death, though nere so meane,
> But banished to kill me?   (*Romeo and Juliet*, III iii 45)

---

[1] E.g. sad (Rowe), man (Steevens), son, mere, main, meet.
[2] *mean a.*[2] and *adv.*[2] 4. 1377-1615.   [3] NED: *mean a.*[2] and *adv.*[2] 6c.; B *adv.* 1.
[4] NED: *mean a*[1]. 2b. Poor, badly off, 1362-1776; 2d. Of conditions. Abject, debased; *c.* 1680 only citation.

It may also be of some relevance that a noun 'mean' (NED: *sb.*[1]) has the sense 'lament', while the related verb 'mean' (*v.*[2], found, on NED's evidence, after the fifteenth century, only in Scottish and northern dialect) can have the specific sense 'to lament for (a dead person)'. Whether or not these subsidary meanings would be brought to mind, it is for the individual reader to decide. For my main argument that the Folio spelling 'Men' represents 'mean' = 'agent' I rely on the spelling evidence of NED.[1]

The verb *liue* in *Richard II* (III iii 95) seems to have several meanings, as the king, from the walls of Flint Castle, speaks to Northumberland of the 'dangerous treason' of Bolingbroke:

> He is come to ope
> The purple Testament of bleeding Warre;
> But ere the Crowne he lookes for, liue in peace,
> Ten thousand bloody crownes of Mothers Sonnes
> Shall ill become the flower of Englands face . . .

The sequence of poetic punning suggests that 'liue' represents both 'live' and 'leaf' or 'leave'. NED registers the spelling *leve* for the verb 'live' in the sixteenth century and EDD shows *leeve* as the present tense of 'live' in parts of the south-western as well as the northern counties. The first sense of the Shakespearean 'liue', 'live—in peace', stands in opposition to 'bleeding Warre' and 'bloody crownes'; the second, 'to put forth leaves' (NED: *leave v*[2]) attaches to the subject 'the Crowne' as 'the leafy head of a tree or shrub' (NED: *crown* 25);[2] the third, following 'to ope The purple Testament' suggests both 'to turn the leaf' and 'to bequeath'.

---

[1] Kökeritz has noted the possibility of a *mean/men* pun in 1 *Henry VI*, I ii 120-1, which would provide further confirmation:

Reigneir: Shall wee disturbe him, since hee keepes no meane?
Alanson: He may meane more then we poor men do know,
These women are shrewd tempters with their tongues.

See *Shakespeare's Pronunciation*, p. 128.

[2] Compare 3 *Henry VI*, III ii 168-81, as explained by M. M. Mahood, *Shakespeare's Wordplay*, 1957, p. 27.

5

The greater fluidity of pronunciation and spelling in Shakespeare's time made it possible for the dramatist to present more meaning than can be contained in a modern-sounding modern-spelling version of his work: as well as sounding like another, a word might look like another; identities might merge on two levels. This chapter ends therefore with a *caveat*: there can be no rigid ruling that the reality of the Shakespearean text consists only in how it was *heard*. Contemporary *spelling* may sometimes indicate a double meaning which modern English cannot so simply exhibit.

When the Chief Justice alleges against Falstaff 'all the Charracters of age', asking in his catechism of antiquity 'Is not your voice broken', Falstaff answers him:

For my voice, I haue lost it with hallowing and singing of Anthemes.

(*2 Henry IV*, I ii 213)

Any modernisation of spelling which takes away the *a* and *w* from Falstaff's *hallowing* diminishes that claim to a life of sanctity which the dramatist intends him to make.

The Folio's spelling *weyward Sisters* in the earlier scenes of *Macbeth* (I iii 32, I v 8, II i 20), in conjunction with their words 'faire is foule and foule is faire' (I i 11), may give to the 'three Witches' a perverted eye and judgment which is not expressed in the normalisation 'weird', 'having the power to control the fate or destiny of men'. NED cites from Wyclif, 1382 (*Matt.* vi 23) ȝif thyn eiȝe be weyward (Vulgate *nequam*)[1]. And if the 'perverted' eye is also 'perverting', the 'three Witches' are ill-looked women in the Stratford sense (pp. 17, 20).

As the witches greet Macbeth, Banquo asks that they shall speak to him also:

---

[1] *Wayward*, a Ic.

> My Noble Partner
> You greet with present Grace, and great prediction
> Of Noble hauing, and of Royall hope,
> That he seemes wrapt withall. . . .

His word *wrapt* (I iii 57) may contain more meaning than the usual modernisation 'rapt' would suggest: as well as having relation to the imagery of 'borrowed Robes' and 'strange Garments' which follows (lines 109, 145), it may imply also Banquo's later judgment (line 124):

> oftentimes, to winne vs to our harme,
> The Instruments of Darknesse tell vs Truths. . . .

The word can mean 'entangled, caught' or 'implicated'[1] as in 1562

> How surely are the wareles wrapt by those that lye in wayte

and 1525

> wrapped with treason.

After hearing the Player speak of the deaths of Priam and Hecuba, 'Teares in his eyes, distraction in's Aspect', Hamlet attacks himself for his apparent lack of feeling:

> Oh what a Rogue and Pesant slaue am I?   (II ii 576)

His adjective *Pesant*[2] may do more than emphasise the meaning of 'slaue' which follows; in the sense 'weighed down, oppressed, as with drowsiness etc.', it would link on to the 'dull and muddy-metled Rascall' some few lines below. So in *Timon* (II ii 228) the adjectives 'dull' and 'heauy' are in collocation as Timon speaks of the ingratitude of the senators:

> These old Fellowes . . .
> Their blood is cak'd, 'tis cold, it sildome flowes . . .
> And Nature, as it growes againe toward earth,
> Is fashion'd for the iourney, dull and heauy.

---

[1] NED: *wrap* 3 b, 4.   [2] NED: *peisant, pesant*. Heavy.

Hamlet speaks in this same soliloquy of what the Player would do if he had Hamlet's 'Motiue' and 'Cue for passion':

> He would drowne the Stage with teares, . . .
> Make mad the guilty, and apale the free,
> Confound the ignorant, and amaze indeed,
> The very faculty of Eyes and Eares.

Hamlet's *apale* here (II ii 590) has the sense 'to make pale with fear'. If the spelling 'appal' is preferred we lose the reference back to the appearance of the Player in his 'dreame of Passion' when 'all his visage' wanned (Folio *warm'd*, Quarto 2 *wand*). We lose also the intensity of suspicion with which Hamlet resolves to 'obserue his lookes' as the king watches the murder-play:

> Ile tent him to the quicke: If he but blench
> I know my course.

(II ii 626)

CHAPTER VII

New external evidence: the language that Shakespeare 'found'

The non-contemporary who wishes to understand more of the detail of Shakespeare's meaning can either begin at the centre and move out or begin on the outskirts and move in. It is possible to take as a starting point some minute problem of the Shakespearean word which seems to mean too little, or even to mean nothing at all and, concentrating on internal evidence of language and situation, to try to determine what sense would be fully appropriate within the given context, hoping later to find other instances of that meaning or usage in some limited field outside the play. An alternative method of approach is to look for new information about the speaking and hearing habit-patterns of Shakespeare's contemporaries in any hitherto unsearched records, in the hope that some fragments of the information obtained may be of relevance to Shakespearean language problems. In this chapter the second method is followed.

Although both procedures have a necessary part in Shakespearean language study, initially at least they must be regarded as quite separate projects: in the larger operation of haystack searching one may not find anything like the Shakespearean needle. And both methods have serious disadvantages: while the first is insufficiently thorough in its use of external evidence, depending for its success on a kind of inspired sampling, the second is, by contrast, over-extravagant. It offers information which may have relevance to Shakespeare's text only as a by-product of more extensive research undertaken primarily for some larger purpose. Even with this second method the haystacks searched must themselves be samples somewhat arbitrarily chosen.

My researches have extended over the local records of five counties: Derbyshire, Staffordshire, Shropshire, Warwickshire and Sussex, and I began with the aim of distinguishing the regional dialect characteristics of the first three areas during the period for which records are extant. A side-result, not at first anticipated, was the finding of lexical evidence of considerable indirect importance for the interpretation of such earlier literature as is composed primarily in the spoken language. It gradually became apparent that there are still many details to be discovered about what people were able to mean and how they were able to mean it in the ordinary spoken language of sixteenth- and seventeenth-century England. The great collections of the *New English Dictionary* which are derived in the main from printed sources can be usefully supplemented from the vocabulary evidence of these manuscript local records. Such non-literary sources frequently show a word or sense in currency a hundred years (sometimes 300 years) before the first, or after the last, citation of it by NED; further, the localisations suggested by NED are to be regarded as tentative only.

About the *direct* value of contemporary local language to the Shakespearean student there will be no dispute: in the records of Stratford we may reasonably hope to come upon an occasional form or meaning not noted perhaps in the *New English Dictionary* or the *English Dialect Dictionary* which may enrich or illumine for us what Shakespeare has written; this 'local' language I deal with in my last chapter. The *indirect* value of the lexical evidence which can be obtained from the local records of any area is less generally recognised, and it will be useful therefore to turn aside for the moment from purely Shakespearean problems to give a brief description of this local language material and some instances of the detail that may be found. What is most impressive is the amount of such detail, and that I cannot illustrate.

The most valuable local records for the philologist are the detailed accounts of the parish officers showing item by item the day-to-day disbursements of churchwardens, constable and overseers of the poor. Most of the quotations which follow are taken from such records; all quotations are from manuscripts and I speak without attempting any generalising qualification of my own experience only. Such accounts may have been preserved, but very rarely, from the mid-fifteenth century; by the seventeenth century they are to be found in many parishes. But even today such papers are not always well looked after and the searcher is often enough reminded of the fortuitous nature of the surviving evidence. The wardens of All Saints, Derby, 1466, regret that they cannot give a full list of

> oder sepulcr serges sustened of charite by oder of the parishe whose names shulde lykewyse be her expressed botte that som wyked creature hath kytte ['cut'] the lefe furthe of the old boke.

This 'sepulchre cierge' is 'a wax candle burning before the sepulchre in which the reserved Sacrament (sometimes also the Cross) was buried on Good Friday'; NED happens not to show this compound although it includes 'sepulchre light' 1505, 1546.

The materials from which the accounts were compiled—bills and receipts—rarely survive, but the details may be copied year by year into the parish book and the vicar and some of the 'neighbors' sign their names or make their mark that the disbursements are allowed and the 'overplus' handed on to the succeeding officers. So at Billingshurst, Sussex, 1552, the meeting acknowledges that 'the sayd churchwardens haue made a levell accompte & stand thereby dyschargyd'. In this sense of 'level' there seems to be nothing remarkable, yet NED does not show the adjective so used; the verb 'level', meaning 'to balance or settle accounts' is illustrated only in the records of Springfield, Massachusetts, 1660.[1] The constables of Kenilworth, Warwickshire, 1683, 1684, meet other parishioners at the 'Rectifying'[2] of their accounts. NED shows this sense 'To declare right, approve of' in one instance only, 1567. The officer concerned may himself write the accounts or he may name someone else as receiving a fee 'for

---

[1] *level, v.*[1] 1 c.   [2] *rectify*, 9.

keping my boke considering I cannot write no rode' as in Rye, Sussex, 1560. The dialect phrases 'no road', 'some road' are shown by NED from 1883 onwards.[1]

On the whole the receipts make dull reading except that sometimes gifts or bequests are noted, or the church may own and let or hire out property and cattle. Billingshurst parish, 1520-8, owns 'iii ken ['kine'] a red hauked a brown hawked & a blake hauked'; another entry speaks of 'ii ken a wallow hawked & a brendyd'; the wardens receive payment 'for a whyt kow & a browen kow & a browen hawked'. The adjective *hawked* is found, on NED's evidence, in Scottish and northern dialect only, from 1500, used of cattle 'Having white spots or streaks; spotted, streaked'; so 1612-13 'A cow . . . red hawked in colour'. The noun *hawkie* 'a cow with a white face' is registered, also in Scottish and northern dialect, from 1724. *Wallow* used of the colour of cattle is not shown in NED, but EDD notes, for Westmorland only, the usage 'Wallow coo', i.e. a cow of a colour which is neither dun nor red, but between the two. So too, I am informed, in Inverary, Argyll (1955) a brownish-red cow is similarly 'a wallow cow'.[2] The meaning of the adjective *Wallow* as defined by NED is 'tasteless, insipid, sickly' while the corresponding verb has the sense 'to wither, fade'.[3]

Another item in Billingshurst accounts, 1551, shows that the officers 'receyved of to ['two'] cosers on Hole yeres Rent of ye shopes'. The noun *Cosser, coser*, 'a dealer' is registered by NED once only, in an undated fifteenth-century vocabulary, with the associated *coseri*, 'bargaining', in a text of *a*. 1400; the verb *coss*, 'to barter, exchange' found from *c*. 1470 is noted as 'chiefly Scottish'.[4]

Many payments are made for the repair and upkeep of the

---

[1] *road*, 8 c.

[2] I am indebted to a former London University student, G. A. McD. Wood, for this information.

[3] NED: *wallow a.* Now *dial.* Tasteless, insipid, sickly. [OE. *wealȝ*, . . . Norw. *valg*, tasteless.] *wallow*, *v²* To wither, fade; to waste away. See also *walsh*, *waugh*, *welk*; *v¹*; and compare *wall-eyed*, which can mean 'Having eyes of differing colour'.

[4] See also *corse, course*, 'To exchange . . . barter . . . In later use only in *to corse horses*'.

church and its property. In Walsall, Staffs., 1469 there is the entry 'for tymber to rachomode', NED has this verb *raccommode* from 1673 onwards in what seems a figurative sense 'to restore to good relations (*with* a person); to set right'. And whereas NED illustrates the form *orgle* in use until 1426, Rotherfield parish, Sussex, pays for 'certaine orgle pypes' (1607), 'certaine orgaine pypes' (1608). Technical words are found, some much earlier than NED's citations. Ecclesfield, Yorks., 1638, has the entry 'for floytes & ringes, for a Coller, ffloytes & claspes for the great Bell'. NED shows the word *flight* as the tail of the bell-clapper from 1872 (*sb.*[1] 13c.). Under the senses of the noun *blade* NED includes (10a.) 'the principal rafter of a roof' (1851, Dictionary of Architecture) and quotes from a Shropshire Glossary, 1879, the definition 'that timber in a roof which goes at an angle from the top of the "king-post" to the beam of the "principal"'. The accounts of the Abbey, Shrewsbury, 1577, show the word in use three hundred years earlier: 'a pyce of tymber to make a blode for the yle 0-5-8', 'in saying ['sawing'] the blade'.

For the noun *drug* (*sb.*[1]) NED shows two quite different senses, 'an original, simple, medicinal substance. . .' (known from 1327) and 'a commodity which is no longer in demand, and so has lost its value or become unsaleable', now usually *a drug on the market;* this second sense is found from *a.* 1661. The Dictionary questions if this second can be the same word as the first. The parish records of Oswestry have an earlier instance of this second sense in 1608 when payment is made 'for carring out of the church and churchyard the druggs and rubbes and cleansing of the same', and these Oswestry *druggs* have plainly never been on the market. The general disbursements include many small sums for *berage*, i.e. for drink for the workmen. This word is not registered by NED but is quoted by EDD in the form *barrage* from the churchwardens' accounts of Goostrey, Cheshire, 1648, with the sense 'An allowance for beer given to workmen'. The records which I have seen offer a great variety of spellings: beredge, beradge, berech, bearege, birrage, berridge, etc.

The parish officers gave charity to the poor who could prove legal settlement, paid the doctor or mountebank for attending the sick, bought winding sheets of wool and paid for affidavits that the dead had in fact been buried in wool. In Chetwynd, Shropsh., 1684, there is the entry 'for glanning ['woollen cloth'] and a arther david for the widow bround Childe'. The parish beadle of St. Werburgh's, Derby, is no doubt appropriately, 'ye bang-beger'; NED cites this compound from 1865; St. Werburgh's record is of 1670. The detailed expenses for housing, clothing and feeding the poor afford, as might be expected, a number of instances of words earlier or later than NED's limiting dates. *Crock-butter*, 'butter salted and put down in a crock for winter use' is cited by NED from a Shropshire dialect glossary of 1879; in Rotherfield, Sussex, 1732, elevenpence is paid for 1 lb. 'of Crock Butter' and 1 lb. 'of new'.[1] The parish of Wisborough Green, Sussex, lists as part of the pantry equipment of its House of Industry ('work-house') in 1830 a 'Coarser and Cleaver'. NED shows *cleaver* in its sense 'a butcher's chopper' but *causer, cawser* is cited only from two word-lists of *c.* 1450:

Incussorium, a causer, quidam malleolus est; *Incussoria*, cawser.

In the Wisborough Green linguistic context this sense, 'hammer' or 'mallet', would be appropriate.

2

The above examples show that, in the less literary non-abstract language of day-to-day life, a word or sense may be found (1) considerably earlier, or (2) later, or (3) in a quite different dialect area from that shown by NED's citations. It will scarcely need saying that this is not in any way to lessen the authority of our greatest of dictionaries but rather to extend it. For if the examples I have given are fairly representative of my own collections and if my

---

[1] See also *crock v.*[1], To put up in a crock or pot; 1594, 1859, 1887 Kentish Glossary.

estimate is correct as to the amount of such evidence that may yet be collected, then the Dictionary's limits of date and place may quite properly be regarded as useful observations deriving from the language of printed books but not so certainly applicable to the earlier spoken language or to the kind of literature composed partly in such spoken language. Within this literature we need not refuse to accept internal contextual directives to word-meaning solely on the ground that the external confirmatory evidence is of a considerably earlier or later date, or of a very different dialect area. To illustrate this first by an instance from the Dictionary itself: one sense of the noun *trash* (*sb.*[1]) is given as 'an old worn-out shoe' (dialectal) with the first instance *c.* 1360

> þen þe harlot with haste helded to þe table
> With rent cokrez at þe kne & his clutte [= clouted] trasches

and later instances of *c.* 1746, 1828, 1885. The Dictionary notes that this first quotation 'fits the sense; but its date, 150 years before any other example of the word, makes its place doubtful'. I shall argue that a number of hitherto unexplained words in Shakespeare's text can be seen to have full meaning within linguistic and dramatic context if we are prepared to accept what 'fits the sense' and is exactly confirmed by earlier or later Dictionary evidence.

The Shakespearean *skaines mates* (*Romeo and Juliet*, II iv 162) is apparently unique; NED notes that the origin and exact meaning of the word are uncertain. It is not an expression that keeps the best of company: as Juliet's nurse seeks out Romeo to give him Juliet's message, Benuolio cries out 'She will endite him to some Supper' and Mercutio pretends to have discovered 'a baud . . . something stale and hoare'. After they have left the stage the Nurse complains to Romeo and to her man Peter of Mercutio's 'roperie':

> Nurse. . . . scuruie knaue, I am none of his flurt-gils, I am none
> of his skaines mates, and thou must stand by too and suffer euery
> knaue to vse me at his pleasure.

17

Peter. I saw no man vse you at his pleasure: if I had, my weapon should quickly haue beene out.

From the build and emphasis of the Nurse's sentence—syntax, prosody, and collocation—'skaines mates' appears to be closely related in sense to 'flurt-gils',[1] a compound first found here, but attested by NED within a similar range of collocation: 1613 You heard him take me vp like a flirt Gill, and sing baudy songs upon me; 1618 As I had been a Mawkin, a flurt Gillian.

Earlier commentators have proposed interpretations based on 'skene', 'a knife or dagger' (to which Peter's 'weapon', in one sense, is, no doubt, a punning reference), or on 'skein of thread': loose companions who frequent the fencing school, cut-throat companions, swaggering fellows; milliner-girls, winders of skeins looked upon as the lowest kind of people among the weavers in Spitalfields. Of these only 'milliner-girls' is in suitable semantic relation to 'flurt-gils', and lexical evidence suggests that 'milliner' took on the necessary suggestiveness after Shakespeare's time. But if it is accepted that the single instance in the dramatic text may indicate firmly grounded colloquial usage, a better meaning can be found. NED shows the verb *skent* 'to entertain, amuse', last recorded for *a.* 1250, and cites as an instance of the verbal substantive an extract from Laȝamon's *Brut* (dated *c.* 1205):

þis iherde þe king þer he læi an skentting (1.19167),

which tells how King Uther, magically changed in appearance, is with Ygærne, wife of Gorlois, as if he is her husband, on the night when King Arthur is begotten; tidings come to Uther that Gorlois is slain and the King at once 'leop ut of bure'. If the sense of Lazamon's *skennting* is defined with unbowdlerised contextual precision, Shakespeare's 'skaines mates' can be seen as exactly parallel to 'flurt-gils', in a sense fully apposite to verbal context and dramatic situation. On the formal level of written

---

[1] See also NED: *flirt, sb.* 5. A woman of a giddy, flighty character . . . 1562-1774; b. A woman of loose character. 1600-1703.

language it may seem that there are difficulties in regarding *skaines*- as a noun-derivative of *skent* (ON. *skemta*), since the *t* is an essential part of the word. But a dramatic text is primarily something spoken, and the juxtapositional elisions of ordinary present-day speech, which give rise to such compounds as Chris'mas and blin' man, are, of course, well-evidenced also in sixteenth- and seventeenth-century spellings: *hansom*, *wensday*, *wascote*, *paseboard*, *hunsman*. The *ai* of the Shakespearean 'skaines mates' may indicate a dialectal lengthening of ME *e*.

A further instance where the Shakespearean text may provide evidence of spoken usage after the dates shown by NED is found in *Much Ado*, II iii 45, when Benedicke, hidden in the arbor, is seen by the Prince and Claudio, who are prepared to tell with how enraged an affection Beatrice dotes upon him:

Prince. See you where Benedicke hath hid himselfe?
Claudio. O very well my Lord: the musicke ended,
Wee'll fit the kid-foxe with a penny worth.

The emendation 'hid-fox', put forward by Warburton, has survived into some present-day editions; Kittredge, Alexander and Hardin Craig are among those who give the original text, presumably understanding 'kid-' in the sense 'young'. A more appropriate meaning might be 'known, discovered', from *kithe*, *kythe* (OE cȳðan), a verb which was still being used in seventeenth-century speech, although its past participle, in the form *kid*, is not recorded by NED after the sixteenth century. The Dictionary's last citation is not precisely dated: 15 ... He shall be kid conqueror, for he is kende Lord, Of all Bretaine that bounds to the broad Sea. Those editors who emend to 'hid-fox' point out that Hamlet's ironical 'hide Fox, and all after' (IV ii 33) is the cry which began the game of hide-and-seek; it has been noted also that 'hide-and-fox' is the name of the game in eighteenth- century Kent (Pegge's *Kenticisms*, 1735).[1] But Claudio's point in *Much Ado* is that the fox has been discovered: it is not unlikely that the cry of *kid*,

---

[1] English Dialect Society, Vol. IV; 1873 and 1876.

'found', signalised the end of the game. Certainly the words 'kid'/'hid' are not infrequently used together; they make an effective antithesis and a neat rhyme so that to hear one of the pair may have called up an expectation of the other. NED shows several instances where the words are in collocation.[1]

It is generally considered that the verb *meane it* in Jessica's speech (*Merchant of Venice*, III v 82) 'has not been explained satisfactorily' and Pope's emendation 'merit it' is usually substituted:[2]

> Lorenzo.　And now good sweet say thy opinion,
> How dost thou like the Lord Bassiano's wife?
> Iessica.　Past all expressing, it is very meete
> The Lord Bassanio liue an vpright life
> For hauing such a blessing in his Lady,
> He findes the ioyes of heauen heere on earth,
> And if on earth he doe not meane it, it
> Is reason he should neuer come to heauen?

For the obvious error of 1600 Quarto *meane it, it/in reason*, that of 1619 reads . . . *then In reason*, while the Folio has . . . *it Is reason*, as given above. Dover Wilson comments that both these readings are 'attempts at emendation and . . . of course mere guesses'; Sisson also considers them 'clearly editorial'.[3] Pope's reading has been thought to give good sense since, to quote Dover Wilson, it

> involves no more alteration than Q. 1619, and is palaeographically simple, 'merryt' being taken for 'mean yt'.

It could, however, be argued that it is better to accept either the correction of 1619 or of the Folio text, since this procedure

---

[1] *a.* 1300 *Cursor Mundi:* Þis ded had euer i-wis ben hidd, if god him-self ne had it kydd.

c. 1330 *Arthour and Merlin:* The other　no might ben y-kidde Behinden hem thai werren y-hidde.

c. 1470 Harding's *Chronicle:* Vnto no manne was it kyde [rime hid].

Other instances have been cited by Zachary Grey (*Notes on Shakespeare*, Vol. I, p. 397) who, I find, proposed in 1754 the interpretation here put forward.

[2] As by J. R. Brown, 'New Arden' 1955 and Dover Wilson, 'New Cambridge', 1953.　　　　　　　　　　　　[3] *New Readings*, Vol. I, p. 140.

involves no change of the original verb *meane* which is found in both quartos and in the folio, and since also there is clear evidence in earlier Tudor English of the sense in which Jessica might intend this verb. NED shows the adjective *mean* (*a*) said of the middle condition between extremes of fortune; (*b*) said of the married state as contrasted with continence on the one hand and unchastity on the other, with an unambiguous illustration of *c.* 1540 'If he coulde not lyve chast . . . he shoulde tak a wif and lyve a meane lyf'.[1]

In Jessica's speech at this point of the play such a sense would be fully in context. The audience knows that Portia and Nerissa, in disguise, are to follow their husbands; the humour of the ring plot, with its accusations and counterthreats of infidelity, has been foreshadowed. As Portia and Nerissa leave, Launcelot has been teasing Jessica about her prospects of damnation—unless her mother was unfaithful. Lorenzo pretends jealousy of Launcelot and accuses him of getting the Moore with child. Jessica's praise of Portia, therefore, generous and sincere as it is, has reference also to Lorenzo's jesting and stresses the need for fidelity and continence in marriage—spoken as if of Bassanio, addressed by implication to Lorenzo. He answers with the claim that he is as excellent a husband as Portia is a wife.

In *Timon of Athens* (III v 22) Alcibiades asks for mercy for his friend guilty of homicide:

Nor did he soyle the fact with Cowardice, . . .
But with a Noble Fury, and faire spirit,
Seeing his Reputation touch'd to death,
He did oppose his Foe:
And with such sober and vnnoted passion
He did behooue his anger ere 'twas spent,
As if he had but prou'd an Argument.

The verb *behooue* in this passage has seemed not to 'afford any very clear meaning' and the emendation 'behave' introduced

---

[1] *mean, a.*[2] 5 c.

by Rowe in 1709 is usually substituted for it. This verb 'behave' is shown by NED in three sixteenth-century instances, used transitively, with the sense (2) 'to manage, conduct (in some specified way)', e.g.

1557 These pinchpenies do behave their persons so evil, etc.

The Shakespearean syntax is not exactly matched by that of NED's citations, but the meaning of *behave* is sufficiently apt; if the word were found occasionally with an *o* spelling, or if it were necessary elsewhere to modernise a Folio spelling *-ooue* to *-ave*, we could be content with Rowe's word rather than Shakespeare's. Unless, however, these conditions can be fulfilled, the linguist is bound to argue from the actual rather than the emended form on the hypothesis that a verb 'behove' with some such sense as 'moderate, control' was available to and understood by Shakespeare's contemporaries. External evidence of such a sense is found in the Middle English period when the Old Norse noun *hof* 'moderation, measure', taken over into English use, occurs in *Ormin* (*c.* 1200) and in *Cursor Mundi* (*a.* 1300). To quote NED's fourth and last instance, on the proverbial theme 'Too much hope deceives':

> Hop es god at hald wit houe,
> Bot til vnskil not worth a gloue.[1]

Should it be asked if I am justified in citing a noun from a northern text of 1300 as evidence for the existence of the related verb in London English three hundred years later, I must answer, as before, that instances are not infrequently found where a word 'submerges' as it were for several centuries; the written record is the unsubmerged iceberg. I would, however, readily agree that Shakespearean interpretations of this kind must be closely scrutinised. In the present instance there is almost too much evidence to handle in the space of a brief note on the single Shakespearean word. It will be convenient, first of all, to dispose of the *be-* prefix. Abbot (*Shakespearian Grammar*, 1875, § 438)

---

[1] NED: *Hove, hof, sb.*[2]

illustrates Shakespeare's use of this with nouns and adjectives to convert the nouns into verbs, as 'bemonster', 'be-sort', 'befortune', 'bemadding'. If we postulate then that the simple form *hove*, in the sense 'measure, moderation—balance, poise, control' was perhaps in living use in Shakespeare's England, we have a pattern of relationship which will take in a number of instances of *hove*, *hover* usage from the Middle English period onwards: isolated fragments of linguistic evidence, words apparently related in form but not in sense, begin to belong together. The lexical evidence is of a verb *hove*, of unknown derivation, in frequent use from the thirteenth century, but largely superseded by the verb *hover* in the sixteenth century. NED shows the principal meanings of this verb *hove*, 'to remain suspended, floating, poised; to wait, linger; to come or go floating or soaring'. One of the *hove* nouns (*c.* 1400) has the sense 'lingering, suspense'; another (also *c.* 1400) means 'lees, dregs, sediment'; a third, in the East Anglian dialect of the nineteenth century (EDD *Hove* or *hover*), is 'a floating island'. The usual senses of *hover* I need not detail; NED shows a second verb 'to pack hops lightly, in order to defraud the measure'; the noun *hover* can mean 'any overhanging stone, bank, shelter'; the adjective can be applied to light loose soil. Additional evidence that the verb *hover* implies 'measure, weigh, balance, control' is found in Latin and French dictionaries of the sixteenth and seventeenth centuries. Rider's *Dictionarie* (1626 ed.) includes 'Hoved, taried', and shows for the verb *Hover* the three senses 'flote; soare; hang over, ready to fall'. The second sense given, 'To hover, or soare', is translated by *Libro*; in his Latin-English section Rider translates this *Libro* 'To weigh, poyse leuell, ... to Counterpoise, to lift up'. Cooper's *Thesaurus* (1578 ed.) translates *libro* in similar terms: 'To weygh; to poyse; to make weightie: to houer: to leuell: to counterpoyse: to deuide equally'. Cotgrave (1632 ed.) translates *A houering* by the French 'Balancement'; the verb *houer* he subdivides: To *houer* (or stand aloofe from) he distinguishes from To *houer ouer*; the first he translates by 'Marchander'. And among the senses of *marchander*, in his French-English section are included 'to houer or stand aloofe from; to braue, or deale with, afarre off (before a closing) either circumspectly and for aduantage, or cowardly and in feare'. We are back here, I think, to what Alcibiades would claim for his friend: that, beginning the combat in noble fury, he tried, even before his anger was spent, to control his rage, to deal circumspectly with his enemy, not to close for the mortal blow. The bedazed student may complain that to offer so much evidence on the sense of the single word is to thicken rather than to clarify the meaning that Shakespeare intended. I hope, however, that it may be counted in favour of the proposed interpretation that it is difficult to set out the evidence neatly, and that the colours, one might say, run into each other. Linguistic truth is rarely tidy, and to understand what Shakespeare wrote the non-contemporary may need to take account of many small pieces of English 'text'.

A simpler instance is found in *The Taming of the Shrew* (IV i 145) when Petruchio, bringing home his wife, cries to his servants:

> Go rascals, go, and fetch my supper in. *Ex. Ser.*
> Where is the life that late I led?
> Where are those? Sit downe Kate,
> And welcome. Soud, soud, soud, soud.
> > *Enter seruants with supper.*
> Why when I say?

Johnson understood the word *soud* as 'sweet'; Mason believed it 'merely intended to denote the humming of a tune or some kind of ejaculation'; Malone thought it 'coined by our poet, to express the noise made by a person heated and fatigued'. His gloss is adopted by Schmidt (1871) and several present-day editors follow it. Hardin Craig (1951) comments: 'a nonsense syllable sung as a refrain'. The 'New Cambridge' editors (1928) give the word appropriate contextual meaning by emending *s* to *f* and Sisson in his *New Readings* follows this emendation. Certainly *f* and long *s* are easily confused; if the form *soud* occurred in the Folio text once only, and with the long *s* character, it might well be regarded as a ghost-word, intended as *foud* by the compositor, and so read by the proof-reader. The form *soud*, however, occurs four times, and there is no misreading the capital *s* of its first instance. This may well indicate that the compositor was working from a manuscript with the reading *soūd* or *sond*. *Sand* or *sond* is commonly used in Old English in the sense 'dish of food, victuals'; NED shows *sand*, *sond*, *sound* with the meaning 'a serving of food, a course', last registered *c.* 1440;[1]

> þere was fest swythe breeme; I can not telle al þe sonde,
> But rycher fest was neuer in londe.

It is possible that Petruchio, as he cries out impatiently to his servants to bring in the supper, is using a word already old-fashioned or dialectal. If so, this would help to explain why a printer's error of *u* for *n* remained uncorrected in later folios. A similar error in the First Folio text of this play, *Conlord*,[2] 'coloured' (I i 212) is corrected to *Coulord* in Folio 2.

If we are prepared to accept NED's evidence of earlier currency, emendation of the Shakespearean text in the above instances is no longer necessary; the puzzling word has unambiguous meaning wholly in accordance with the dramatic situation. Double meaning may be in play in the word *harlotry* (I *Henry IV*, II iv 437) as Falstaff takes the part of the sorrowful king rebuking his graceless son and the Hostesse commends his play-acting:

> Falstaffe.   For Gods sake Lords, conuey my trustfull Queen,
> For teares doe stop the floud-gates of her eyes.
> Hostesse.   O rare, he doth it as like one of these harlotry
> Players, as euer I see.

---

[1] Bosworth-Toller: 'a sending, mission, message; a mess (from *Latin* mitto), a dish of food, victuals'.

NED: I. The action of sending; 3. A serving of food, a course, mess. The verb *send* 'to cause (food, wine) to be handed (to a guest)' is registered only in two citations (1770 and 1825), but *to send in, up, to send to table*, 'to serve up (food)' is recorded from 1662.

[2]   Tranio at once
  Vncase thee: take my Conlord hat and cloake....

As a term of abuse 'harlotry' can mean 'filthy, worthless, trashy', senses which no doubt Shakespeare had heard levelled against his player companions and himself. But such senses are introduced here only to be set aside; the hostess, mistakenly or not, plainly intends a term of praise; her 'harlotry' then, in conjunction with 'Players', may indicate the survival into Shakespeare's time of the *harlot*, 'itinerant jester' of a century earlier.[1] If the apparently illiterate error depends on a sense which has not quite gone out of use, then the audience, enjoying the joke against the speaker, is itself caught off balance, and Shakespeare, playwright and player, has himself scored a point against his public.

3

Instances may be found in the Shakespearean text where a meaning that would be appropriate to context and situation is registered in dictionary collections only at some later date. The verb *trace* (Folio *trace*, Quarto *crush*) in *Othello* (II i 312) has not been satisfactorily explained in terms of contemporary usage. Iago hopes to injure Cassio by, in some way, inciting Roderigo against him:

> Which thing to do,
> If this poore Trash of Venice, whom I trace
> For his quicke hunting, stand the putting on,
> Ile haue our Michael Cassio on the hip . . . .

The 'hunting' image is usually understood in reference to hunting with hounds and the emendation 'trash', meaning 'to check by a cord or leash' is generally accepted. M. R. Ridley ('New Arden' *Othello*, 1958) explains it as to 'hang weights on a hound to prevent him hunting too fast'; Alice Walker in the 'New Cambridge', 1957, prefers the emendation 'leash'. In adopting the 'trash' emendation Ridley frankly and clearly points out its difficulties:

---

[1] NED: *Harlot* 2. 'An itinerant jester . . .' *a* 1340 to 1483. *Harlotry attrib.* or as *adj.* 'scurvy . . . worthless'. So in Onions with this Shakespeare reference.

the meaning produced does not seem appropriate to Iago's line of thought *at the moment*. It is true that as a rule Iago has to trash Roderigo, to slow down his impatient hunting of Desdemona; but here he is wanting to *incite* him . . .—why bother about the trashing at all? Things are not made easier by the fact that *for* in the context can either mean 'to promote' or 'to prevent'.

It seems a reasonable hypothesis that since Iago is doubtful whether Roderigo, 'this poore Trash', will be strong enough to act adequately when incited, he is tracing him so as to bring about his quicker hunting. And if the hunting is with the hawk rather than with the hound, a meaning of 'trace' can be found which is then wholly in context. In *Observations upon Hawking* (1826) J. S. Sebright gives the rule

> Hawks that want mettle must always be flown with a keen appetite (p. 56).

but in his section on the young hawk he describes how

> There is frequently to be observed in the plumage of birds of prey a defect, which goes by the name of *hunger-traces*, owing to want of food at some period during the growth of the feathers. Though the full grown falcon, when in health, may bear without injury the long fasts incident to birds of prey, . . . Young hawks should be plentifully fed, for if they are left one day without food, the hunger-traces will appear (pp. 5-7).

A fuller description of the hunger-trace is given in *The Goshawk* by T. H. White (1951):

> When we had dipped the hawk's tail in boiling water and were first able to get a better view of it, a grievous fact had come to light. Gos was suffering from a hunger trace. If a growing eyas was stinted in his food, say for a day or two, the lengthening feathers would add a weak section during those days. The stamina might be picked up again, and the feathers might continue to increase in length, healthy and strong; but always, until the next year's moult, the tell-tale weak section would lie like a semi-circular slash across the full grown plume.

It was not that it made any difference from the point of view of appearance, but the feathers were actually weak at the hunger trace, and would probably break off at it one by one (p. 47).

In trying to show by reference to the dramatic text that Iago is using a metaphor of hawking in his words 'this poore Trash of Venice whom I trace for his quicke hunting' and that this metaphor is closely interconnected with other images used by Iago of Roderigo, the commentator is at some disadvantage in that the Shakespearean image, as well as being compressed in form and swiftly utilised, is often complex in content. Here it is not simply that Roderigo is kept hungry of hope so that he may hunt the more desperately; he is hunger-traced also for the additional reason that he wastes his own means in furnishing Iago with money and jewels. In the first act of the play he is for Iago a poor 'Snipe' (i iii 391), tolerated as a source of financial supply:

Thus do I euer make my Foole, my purse: (i iii 389)

Iago's repeated prescription to him is 'Put Money in thy purse' . . . 'Go make Money'. And whereas Iago describes him here as 'this poore Trashe of Venice', 'trash' and 'purse' are once more equated by Iago in a quite different context as he tells Othello

Who steales my purse, steales trash. . . .   (iii iii 157)

It is significant also that when Roderigo complains of Iago's treatment of him (iv ii 178):

thou . . . rather . . . keep'st from me all conueniencie, then ['than'] suppliest me with the least aduantage of hope . . . I haue wasted my selfe out of my meanes

Iago approves of his spirit: 'Why, now I see there's mettle in thee'. And in the last act of the play he is made 'angry' by Iago for Iago's *gaine* (Folio) or *game* (Quarto):

I haue rub'd this yong Quat almost to the sense,
And he growes angry. Now, whether he kill Cassio,
Or Cassio him, or each do kill the other,
Euery way makes my gaine.   (v i 14)

If this interpretation of Iago's verb-image is correct, we should expect to find the noun 'hunger trace'[1] in non-figurative use at a much earlier date than 1828, when NED first registers the word. It might perhaps be argued, that is to say, that literary evidence alone, in this particular instance, would direct us to suppose that the available lexical record is incomplete.

So with the word *Shot* (2 *Henry IV*, III ii 295) when Falstaff, defending his choice of pressed-men, and letting Mouldy and Bullcalf escape service, says of Wart:

Come, manage me your Calyuer: so: very well, go-too, very good, exceeding good. O, giue me alwayes a little, leane, old, chopt, bald Shot.

Johnson noted here: '*Shot* is used for *shooter*, one who is to fight by shooting', and NED has, with this citation from the play, 'A soldier armed with a firearm'.[2] This single meaning, however, might well be judged insufficient on prosodic grounds, since each additional preceding adjective in Falstaff's sentence increases the expectation of double meaning in the noun-climax. The dramatic situation points to the appropriate second sense, a figurative use of NED's *Shot* (*sb.*[3]) . . . 'a refuse animal left after the best of the flock or herd have been selected'. Although NED's earliest citation for this noun is from a report of 1796, the wide use of the term in present-day dialect in sheep-farming counties and the long history of the verb *shoot* in a similar although less restricted sense,[3] would make it likely that the life of the noun in spoken English has been longer than the direct written evidence shows.

Earlier in the same scene the adjective *prickt* (III ii 121) seems also to require some extra meaning, when Falstaff, as a preliminary to taking a bribe for letting him escape, first selects Mouldy for military service:

---

[1] *Hunger sb.* 4e. [2] *Shot sb.*[1] 21 b.

[3] 11. f. *To shoot forth, out, away:* to drive out . . . a. 1300-1605.

Falstaffe.   Is thy name Mouldie?
Mouldie.   Yea, if it please you.
Falstaffe.   'Tis the more time thou wert vs'd.
Shallow.   Ha, ha, ha, most excellent. Things that are mouldie,
lacke vse: very singular good. Well saide Sir Iohn, very well said.
Falstaffe.   Prick him.
Mouldie.   I was prickt well enough before, if you could haue
let me alone: . . .
Falstaffe.   Go too: peace Mouldie, you shall goe. Mouldie, it is
time you were spent.

Falstaff's 'Pricke him' means 'Mark his name' and it is probable that
Mouldy's 'prickt', as he intends it, plays back to the bawdy suggestiveness he hears in Shallows 'vse'. But the third sense of the word
lies in Shakespeare's humour, not in Mouldy's. Falstaff's words
reiterate the clue, and part of the point of the joke is that Mouldy
himself does not perceive the congruity of a man with his name
claiming to be sufficiently 'turned sour'. The adjective *pricked* is
not registered in this sense by NED until 1678, although other
verbal forms are found from 1594.[1]

Macbeth, told of the 'mouing Groue', begins to grow 'a-weary
of the Sun:

I pull in Resolution, and begin
To doubt th'Equiuocation of the Fiend,
That lies like truth.

This verb *pull in* (v v 42) has been felt as 'too deliberate' so that
Johnson's emendation 'pall in', i.e. 'fail in', is not infrequently
preferred, as by Dover Wilson in his 'New Cambridge' text
(1947). NED shows *pull in* meaning 'To rein in (one's horse)'
giving this instance from *Macbeth* as the first citation. But the
Dictionary also illustrates the sense 'to withdraw from use or
view', citing from Fletcher's *The Sea Voyage* a strikingly similar
passage:

---

[1] *Prick v.* 8. Of wine, beer, &c.: To become or begin to be sour.

> How weary, and how hungry am I,
> How feeble, and how faint is all my body?
> Mine eyes like spent Lamps glowing out, grow heavy,
> My sight forsaking me, and all my spirits,
> As if they heard my passing bell go for me,
> Pull in their powers and give me up to destiny.   (III i)[1]

Earlier commentators have drawn attention to this and it is somewhat surprising that the sense 'check' or 'rein in' should continue to be preferred.[2]

4

It is sometimes possible to understand the meaning of the Shakespearean text if we are prepared to accept as current in the London English of his time, words or forms now localised in other areas. The noun 'murder' in Cordelia's speech (*Lear*, I i 230), if taken in its present-day sense, seems somehow out of place. The King of France marvels that she has so lost favour:

> sure her offence
> Must be of such vnnaturall degree,
> That monsters it

and Cordelia asks her father

> I yet beseech your Maiesty.
> ... that you make knowne
> It is no vicious blot, murther, or foulenesse,
> No vnchaste action or dishonoured step
> That hath depriu'd me of your Grace and fauour....

Where the Folio reads *murther*, the 1608 Quarto has *murde*; it seems probable, on the evidence of linguistic and dramatic context, that this is the original Shakespearean form. NED shows the verb *mird* with the sense 'To meddle. Also to sport amorously'

---

[1] I quote from the Folio of 1679.
[2] As by Kittredge (*Sixteen Plays* p. 959) who quotes Mason's citation of the passage from Fletcher, but glosses the Shakespearean *pull in* as 'rein in, check'.

found in Scottish sources from 1614; EDD illustrates the verb in Scottish usage in various senses including 'to meddle; to make amorous advances', with the related noun *mird* in the sense 'flattery, coaxing' (1865). Shakespeare's text has the form *windring* as if from the verb 'wind-er', a frequentative form of *wind*,

> You Nimphs cald Nayades of yᵉ windring brooks,
>
> > (*The Tempest*, IV i 128)

and it would not be unreasonable to suppose a verb 'mird-er' current in the spoken language of Shakespeare's time, giving an associated noun 'mirder', which, in the *Lear* text, happens to take on a more familiar, but now misleading spelling form with *u* for *i*.

There has been difficulty over Agamemnon's *sent* or *sate* in *Troilus and Cressida*, II iii 86:

> Agamemnon.   Where is Achilles?
> Patroclus.   Within his Tent, but ill dispos'd my Lord.
> Agamemnon.   Let it be knowne to him that we are here
> He *sent* our Messengers, and we lay by (Q *sate*)
> Our appertainments, visiting of him. . . .

Theobald's emendation 'shent' for Folio's *sent* has been generally accepted by present-day editors. Yet the quarto's *sate*, it may be argued, is meaningful without emendation. EDD shows the verb *sit* (13), 'To ignore, set aside, disregard' with such noun objects as 'call, summons, bidding' (Scotland, Northumberland and S. Donegal); NED shows the verb *set* (which may have a past tense form *sat*, *sate*) in the special sense (126) 'to reject, set aside', with two citations from a work on Scottish law of 1678.[1] If it be objected that Scottish usage cannot properly be cited as evidence of word-meaning in Shakespeare's London, I would answer again that a number of words and senses noted as 'Scottish' by NED are found in English parish records of Shakespeare's time.

---

[1] Thus an assizer was set . . . because he was not twenty-five Years of age. To object against a witness in our Law, is called to cast a witness, or to set him.

Retyres in Nestor's speech (*Troilus and Cressida*, I iii 54) has puzzled editors and commentators. The speaker is considering how the storms of Fortune distinguish true valour from valour's show:

> when the splitting winde
> Makes flexible the knees of knotted Oakes,
> And Flies fled vnder shade, why then
> The thing of Courage,
> As rowz'd with rage, with rage doth sympathize,
> And with an accent tun'd in selfe-same key,
> Retyres to chiding Fortune.

Among the emendations proposed are returns, replies, retorts, rechides and recries; 'retorts' has been most widely accepted and is found in number of present-day texts. This emendation, it is true, seems to give the meaning to which the context directs us but there is some evidence also that the original form could bear this required sense; it may well have been heard by Shakespeare's audience as a variant of *-tear* (v^1 8), which NED shows in the sense 'to rant and bluster; to "go on" violently' in seventeenth-century usage, with a first citation from Ben Jonson's *Poetaster*, 1601:

> Hee will teach thee to teare and rand, Rascall, to him.[1]

In the Shakespearean verb the prefix *re* offers no difficulty: Shakespeare uses the verb 'respeaking' (*Hamlet*, I ii 128); 'regreet' occurs several times in the plays. It would therefore be well within the pattern of Shakespearean word-formation if, in Nestor's speech, the thing of courage re-tears to chiding Fortune. And there is some evidence[2] that the folio/quarto spelling *-tyres/-tires* could represent the verb now found in normal spelling

---

[1] I give the quotation as NED gives it. It should, however, be noted that *teare* and *rand* are used here without a pronoun object; *to him* is imperative, the beginning of a new sentence: *to him, cherish his muse, goe.*

[2] I am glad to find further support for the interpretation here proposed in what Kökeritz has said on the meaning and pronunciation of a similar form, *tyring* (2 *Henry IV*, Prol. 37) in the sentence 'The Postes come tyring on'. He believes that this spelling is best interpreted as 'tearing' and notes that [tɪə] for the verb 'tear' is still heard in many districts. *Shakespeare's Pronunciation*, p. 208.

as 'tears': Stratford records (1605) have two instances of the spelling *sier*, 'sear' (portion of a gunlock; see p. 329). NED shows *teer* and *teear* as nineteenth-century dialect spellings of '*tear*' while the *English Dialect Dictionary* cites also a Scottish *tirr*, 'to snarl; to speak illnaturedly', relating it to the Danish verb *tirre*, 'to tease, irritate, goad'.

The form *still-peering* (*All's Well*, III ii 113) has seemed to most editors to represent a corruption of the true text and the emendation 'still-piecing', meaning 'that closes immediately, always closing again', has been generally accepted.[1] Bertram, on his way to serve the Duke of Florence, has written to his mother in France:

> I haue sent you a daughter-in-Law, shee hath recouered the King, and vndone me: I haue wedded her, not bedded her, and sworne to make the not eternall.   (III ii 21)

His wife Helena reads again the letter she has from him:

> *Till I haue no wife I haue nothing in France.*
> Nothing in France vntill he has no wife:
> Thou shalt haue none Rossillion, none in France,
> Then hast thou all againe: poore Lord, is't I
> That chase thee from thy Countrie, and expose
> Those tender limbes of thine, to the euent
> Of the none-sparing warre? . . .
> . . . O you leaden messengers,
> That ride vpon the violent speede of fire,
> Fly with false ayme, moue the still-peering aire
> That fings [sings] with piercing, do not touch my Lord. . . .

Elsewhere in Shakespeare's language the air is 'intrenchant', 'invulnerable', 'woundless'; after Hamlet's killing of Polonius, Claudius hopes to free himself from any imputation of guilt so that the 'poysned shot' of slander

> may misse our Name,
> And hit the woundlesse ayre.   (IV i 44, Q. 2)

---

[1] Halliwell notes 'Some editors retain the old reading, *still peering*, still-appearing, appearing still and silent, but which sings by means of the whizzing of the bullet'.

In Helena's speech, the context suggests, the air sings with joy as it is pierced by the bullets and comes together again unwounded. For the second part of this image earlier commentators have cited the Biblical parallel:

> As when an arrow is shot at a marke, it parteth the aire, which immediately commeth together againe, so that a man cannot know where it went thorow.
>
> (Wisdom of Solomon, Geneva version, ed. 1595)

And in Barnabe Googe's translation of Palingenius's *Zodiacus Vitae*, the elements of water, air and fire are contrasted with the earth, which is the feeblest of the four elements:

> For when that God had deckt the world, with Starres in trym aray,
> What drosse remaynde he bad the winds, to clense and sweepe away,
> Then in with hasty course they rushe their Lordes awarde to do,
> The Northwinde blowes the Southwind huffes, ye West, & East set to:
> With striuing blasts they sweepe the fieldes & round in heape they cast
> Whatsoeuer they finde, constrayning it, the earth is framd at last:
> Which, banisht from the heauens hye, straight downe to Centre fell,
> No place more farre nor base appears, wher nygher shee might dwell.
> Besyde, of weaker force it is, and eke of smaller power,
> Then all the rest of Elements are, and feblest of the fower.
> For if by feruent heate of Sunne it be constrained to gape,
> Or pearst with Plow it cannot ioyne, nor take his former shape.
> The waters if they parted be doe straight returne in one,
> And voide of all diuision seemes, as if there had bene none.
> So doth the Ayre, and Fier eke, if these diuided bee,
> At fyrst they ioyne againe, so that no signe of hurt you see.
> And why? because they are more pure, and perfect in degree,
> And of their proper force alone they alwayes moued bee.
>
> (Googe, p. 112)

Fire and Air, the ideas of piercing and of at once joining together
again, which are found in this passage, are combined in Helena's
image. The 'loud windes' and the 'still closing waters' form part
of a similar image when Ariel 'like a Harpey' causes the banquet
to vanish which has appeared before Alonso:

> you fooles, I and my fellowes
> Are ministers of Fate, the Elements
> Of whom your swords are temper'd, may as well
> Wound the loud windes, or with bemockt-at-Stabs
> Kill the still closing waters, as diminish
> One dowle that's in my plumbe. . . .   (*The Tempest*, III iii 64)

Helena's 'still-peering' would have appropriate meaning if we
assume an earlier currency and wider location for the noun and
verb *peer*, 'a match; to match, equal', shown by EDD in nineteenth-
century dialect in Scotland and the Isle of Wight. That *peer* was
current in seventeenth-century English with this range of meaning
is suggested by Cotgrave's *Dictionarie* (1632), which translates the
English noun *A Peere* by the French *Paire*, *Per*; the French adjective
Pair is translated 'Like, alike, equall, matching, euen, meet'.
NED shows the noun *peer* in the sense (3) 'One who is associated
or matched with another; a companion, mate . . .', with one
citation of *c.* 1330 for the sense 'wife'. And if this 'mate, wife'
sense were still current in Shakespeare's time, even as a poetic
archaism, the relevance of the singing air image to Helena's
situation would be the stronger.

The phrase *make rope's in such a scarre* (*All's Well*, IV ii 38) is not
easy to interpret. Diana is asked by Bertram

> Stand no more off,
> But giue thy selfe vnto my sicke desires,
> Who then recouers . . .

Although in her previous speech to him her words have dignity
and sincerity—

> Tis not the many oathes that makes the truth,
> But the plaine single vow, that is vow'd true

—she has now, in accordance with Helena's plan, to seem 'as wonne', to desire the ring and appoint him 'an encounter'. Her pretended surrender is abruptly accomplished; it occupies only a line and half of generalised quasi-proverbial observation:

> I see that men make rope's in such a scarre,
> That wee'l forsake our selues. Giue me that Ring . . .

after which in her language to Bertram she reverts at once to the style and theme of honour:

> Mine Honours such a Ring,
> My chastities the Iewell of our house

and

> When you haue conquer'd my yet maiden-bed. . . .

I suggest that internal evidence would sufficiently support for the noun 'scarre' of this Shakespearean passage the sense 'splice' which is registered by EDD in Scottish and northern dialect; if this interpretation is correct we should expect to find additional snippets of external evidence, both of this noun *scare* and of the figurative *splice*, 'to marry', in earlier records nearer to Shakespeare's time.

External evidence at present available indicates the incompleteness of our lexical collections: the verbal noun *splicing* is first registered by NED in 1524-5, but *splice*, the noun and verb, are not recorded until about a hundred years later; the figurative *splice*, 'to marry' is first noted as used by Smollett in 1751, with the noun 'marriage' in 1830 in the work of John Galt, another Scottish writer. The noun *scare* (*sb.*[4]) is noted by NED (as originally Scottish dialect, 'a joint or splice') only in the restricted sense 'the part of a golf club where the head joins the handle', 1881, 1897. EDD shows both noun and verb in Scotland and some of the northern counties of England, with the noun in a rather wider range of meaning:

A splice; a joint in carpentry; each piece or the fitted end of each piece joined by 'scaring'; one of the parts of a fishing-rod; the joint shown in consequence of imperfect welding in a forged piece of iron.

I take it that in Diana's image a woman is caught in a snare which is made in some way with a skilfully spliced rope: it is worth noting that similar 'snare' imagery is used earlier (III v 21) as Mariana cautions Diana against men's various 'promises, entisements, oathes, tokens, and all these engines of lust' (An *engine* can mean 'A contrivance for catching game, a snare, net, trap, decoy or the like', NED 5c.):

> many a maide hath beene seduced by them, and the miserie is example, that so terrible shewes in the wracke of maiden-hood, cannot for all that disswade succession, but that they are limed with the twigges that threatens them.

And a similar cunning intertwining trickery may be suggested in Diana's generalising conclusion (IV ii 73) as Bertram leaves her after the 'encounter' has been appointed:

> Since Frenchmen are so *braide*,
> Marry that will, I liue and die a Maid:
> Onely in this disguise, I think't no sinne,
> To cosen him that would vniustly winne.

The noun *braid* can mean 'an adroit turn; a trick or subtilty' as well as 'anything plaited, interwoven, or entwined'.

5

It will be convenient to include here three other instances where a knowledge of regional English may help to clarify some details of Shakespearean grammar and syntax.

In some midland dialects of the present time the perfect form *wished* does not always refer to past time, but often is temporally the same as the present, only it implies that the wish cannot be fulfilled,[1] e.g. I wished I could go there tomorrow. So, I suggest, in *Coriolanus* (IV vi 24) when the tribunes, having shown their power in expelling Coriolanus, try to 'seeme humble after it is done', and Brutus says regretfully to the citizens:

We *wisht* Coriolanus had lou'd you as we did.

For the present-day relative pronoun 'whose', there may be found in seventeenth-century local records *whom there, that their.* The accounts of Stockton (Shropsh.) 1638 record payment

to the highte constable for three Poore Children whom there Parence weare executed at Srewsbury.

The constable of Leamington Hastings (Warwicksh.) 1673 gives fourpence to a group of passengers who have a pass permitting them to travel to their friends, receiving relief as they go; his accounts show:

Giuen to John Barnes and Thomas Wattson with their wiues & children wich wr semen that their ships did misscary & sink but by the mercies of god their liues were preserued, with a passe.

A similar construction is found in *Henry V* (IV iv 76) as the Boy speaks with scorn of Pistol, *le grand Capitaine*:

The empty vessel makes the greatest sound, Bardolfe and Nym had tenne times more valour, then this roaring diuell i'th olde play, *that* euerie one may payre *his* nayles with a woodden dagger, and they are both hang'd. . . .

The adverb phrase *at once* is registered by NED in the sense 'at one time' with two citations only, 1563, 1585. The phrase is found in later local usage: I have noted in the accounts of Rushbury (Shropsh.) 1699 *att once*, 'on one occasion', with the sequent phrases *att twice, att thrice*, and in Sowtham (Warwicksh.)

---

[1] See O. Jespersen, *A Modern English Grammar*, Vol. IV, 1932, § 6.7 (whose phrasing I adapt): The pluperfect *had hoped* does not always refer to the before-past time, but often is temporally the same as the preterite *hoped*, only it implies that the (past) hope was not fulfilled.

att twice 'on two occasions'. Isabella uses this phrase *at once* in speaking to Angelo (*Measure for Measure*, II iv 106):

> Angelo. Then must your brother die.
> Isabella. And 'twer the cheaper way:
> Better it were a brother dide at once,
> Then that a sister, by redeeming him
> Should die for euer.

As a 'cheaper way' than his sister's death 'for euer' the Shakespearean *at once* may well include this local sense 'at one time', suffering death once only.

CHAPTER VIII

Contextual evidence : single meaning

In accumulating new information about Elizabethan word-form and word-meaning the non-contemporary can become more aware of the potentialities within the language medium as Shakespeare found it, more alert to the meanings that *might* be there for poet and dramatist in the single word. Our final concern, however, is not with the language that Shakespeare found but with the language that he made, with those precise directives within his dramatic text by which the wide range of potential meaning is limited and controlled. It is with such internal contextual evidence that this chapter is concerned.

Although we often find it convenient to speak of the 'meaning of a word' as though the word in isolation contains that meaning, it is a valid principle of present-day linguistics that we cannot know the actual meaning of the single word in any given text until we have first understood the whole sentence of which that word is part. So in George Herbert's lines[1]

> Onely a sweet and vertuous soul,
> Like season'd timber never gives,

it is the three words, 'season'd timber never', which direct the hearer to the required sense of 'gives' out of the forty or so possible meanings which the word might have. Obviously also the word-meanings are interdependent: out of the range of meaning otherwise available in the word 'seasoned', one particular sense is determined for it by the following 'timber'. And if it were objected against us that we are 'only guessing' at the meaning,

---

[1] 'Vertue': *Works of George Herbert*, ed. by F. E. Hutchinson, Oxford, 1941, p. 87.

we could answer with full confidence that such guesswork is safely based on a knowledge of a hundred other 'wood-not-warping' situations in language and in life. These situations are, as it were, the external evidence. Guesswork about Shakespearean word-meaning based on Shakespearean context, especially when word or meaning is no longer in general currency, requires to be checked against external evidence from the written record. So with the phrase *sound his state* in *Timon of Athens* (II i 13) when a senator calculating the sum of Timon's debts and certain that Timon's extravagance cannot long continue, wishes speedily to reclaim what he has lent:

> Senator.   And late fiue thousand: to Varro and to Isidore
> He owes nine thousand, besides my former summe,
> Which makes it fiue and twenty. Still in motion
> Of raging waste? It cannot hold, it will not.
> . . . It cannot hold, no reason
> Can sound his state in safety. Caphis hoa, . . .
> Get on your cloake, & hast you to Lord Timon,
> Importune him for my Moneyes. . . .

In this context of language and situation 'state' can well mean 'circumstances as regards means of livelihood, riches or possessions'. NED illustrates this sense (1e.) from 1389 to 1763:

> 1389 If eny brother of sister falle in pouert, . . . his state shal bene holpen, of euery brother and sister of ye gilde, w^t a ferthyng in ye woke. 1763 My Credit at last gasp, my State undone.

A complementary meaning of the verb 'sound' may be derived from the adjective in its sense (3c.) 'financially solid or safe', as illustrated by NED (1601):

> left his credite sound with the marchants, and readie money to his sonne.

And 'in safety', 'without incurring financial loss', completes the Senator's statement: 'No reasonable person can think it possible to ("no reason Can") give financial backing to Timon ("sound his state") . . .'. A satisfactory interdependence of meaning between the main words of the sentence is thus established. 'State' has probably the additional sense 'splendour, extravagance', and 'sound' may suggest the metaphorical 'fathom, test the depth of'. Those editors[1] who have taken this secondary metaphorical sense as the major statement-meaning of the verb have run into difficulties with the rest of the sentence. Johnson comments that the supposed meaning of this 'must be, —No reason, by sounding, fathoming, or trying, his state can *find it safe*. But, as the words stand, they imply that no reason can *safely sound* his state.' He accordingly emends to 'found', following an earlier suggestion.

External evidence adduced should, wherever possible, be contemporary with Shakespeare, but it may sometimes be necessary to manage with citations of earlier or later date, perhaps also from dialect rather than standard English. In some cases the Shakespearean interpretation proposed must remain provisional: the discovery of more, or more relevant, external evidence may lead us to look in a new way at the contextual directives of the dramatic text and so to modify our present 'guesses'. Sometimes, however, internal and external evidence seem perfectly to complement each other: taking the Shakespearean watch to pieces we can put it together and get it going again without having any awkward bits left over; word-meaning and sentence-meaning may be seen as satisfactorily interdependent. Where there are awkward bits left over, what appear to be difficulties of grammar or syntax may in reality be lexical problems: there are still many questions to be asked and answered on the basic problem of what the words mean in the dramatic text of our greatest literary artist. In trying to answer some of these questions it will be obvious that I come as a gleaner profiting largely from the main harvest work of the great *New English Dictionary*: the first gleaners get the best pickings. And although some of the discoveries that lie waiting

---

[1] H. J. Oliver in the 'New Arden' *Timon*, 1959, keeps the Folio reading: 'the meaning is that no person of any reason could possibly test Timon's estate and think it was safe.'

to be made are of trifling importance for our understanding of
the power and energy of Shakespeare's art, each small success can
be of value in showing the way to a swifter and more accurate
awareness of other problems of word-meaning as yet unsolved
and perhaps unnoticed; so too an initial failure to pick up the
right clues can itself be turned to profit; what was wrong in the
'guesswork' can be analysed.

2

I shall deal first with a few simple instances where internal
evidence of linguistic or dramatic context seems to suggest that a
commonly accepted Shakespearean gloss is insufficient or wrong
and where external evidence to justify this intuition is readily
available in the non-Shakespearean citations of the *New English
Dictionary*. First the evidence of linguistic context: at the beginning
of the *Merchant of Venice* (I i 19), when Salarino tells Antonio
that if he had 'such venture forth' he would always be

Peering in Maps for ports, and peers, and rodes

the present-day sense of 'pier', 'a mole projecting into the sea',
as given by Schmidt (1874)[1] and implied by Onions (1911)[2]
appears somewhat out of context. Because of its position between
'ports' and 'rodes' (*road*, 'a sheltered piece of water near the shore
where vessels may lie at anchor in safety'), it might reasonably
be expected that the Shakespearean 'pier' means some kind of safe
piece of *water*; such an expectation is confirmed by NED which
shows this noun with the now obsolete sense 'haven' in the English
of Shakespeare's time.[3] Salarino's three 'safe water' nouns are

---

[1] *Shakespeare-Lexicon*, by Alexander Schmidt; I quote from the fourth ed.,
Berlin and Leipzig, 1923.

[2] *A Shakespeare Glossary*, by C. T. Onions; I quote from the 2nd ed. of 1919.
Onions, who supplies definitions 'of words or senses of any words now obsolete
or surviving only in provincial or archaic use', gives no gloss for *pier, room, stand
in* or *malice* in the particular Shakespearean instances here considered.

[3] *pier*[2] 2b. *a.* 1552 to 1721.

thus in sequence; his list no longer provokes the reaction appropriate to the intelligence-test direction: 'Cross out the word which does not belong to this group'.

The present-day sense of *roome* (Schmidt: 'apartment') seems insufficient on linguistic grounds as well as out of keeping with the dramatic situation when Lodovico tells Othello (v ii 330)

> You must forsake this roome, and go with vs:
> Your Power, and your Command is taken off,
> And Cassio rules in Cyprus.

On the ground of situation, 'You must forsake this roome' in its modern sense would imply in Lodovico some knowledge of Othello's resolution not to leave the place where Desdemona lies dead. But Othello is apparently not free to initiate action; he has been and is to be held 'close prisoner'. Lodovico knows nothing of his resolution

> Heere is my iournies end, heere is my butt
> And verie Sea-marke of my vtmost Saile.

On linguistic grounds—'Power', 'Command', 'Cassio rules'—'roome', as the speaker intends it, would seem to represent 'office, function, appointment', a sense which NED denotes 'Exceedingly common in the sixteenth century'.[1] To appreciate the possible dramatic irony it is necessary first to understand this primary sense. A similar double meaning may be in play in *Richard II* (v v 108) where 'roome' may suggest both 'space' and 'office' as the king strikes down a second servant who is attacking him:

> Go thou and fill another roome in hell.

It is because of the office which the servant has accepted that he deserves to die.

The verb *Stand* is insufficiently vigorous if understood as 'to be in a state or condition' (Schmidt's gloss) when in *King Lear*

---

[1] *Room sb.*[1] 12. *c.* 1483-1644.

(I ii 3) Edmond the bastard declares his intention to supplant his legitimate brother.

> Thou Nature art my Goddesse, to thy Law
> My seruices are bound, wherefore should I
> Stand in the plague of custome, and permit
> The curiosity of Nations, to depriue me?

It seems to require at least as much active force as is contained in the grammatically parallel 'permit'. Further, whereas 'plague' as cliché-metaphor represents nowadays merely some constant irritant that can be, and often is, tolerated over a long period, the sense 'to *be*' in relation to 'plague' would in earlier English imply a quite abnormal lack of emotional energy. The evidence of NED suggests that Edmond's sentence should be analysed not with a verb 'stand' followed by the adverb phrase, but with the verb 'stand in', transitive, followed by its object 'the plague of custom'. This verb is shown[1] with such senses as 'to remain obstinate in an opinion, *to maintain stoutly*' in general currency in Shakespeare's time; in the rare sense 'to insist upon having' it is registered only from Shakespeare's text (*Titus Andronicus*, IV iv 105).

In *Julius Caesar* (III i 174) if *malice* is understood in its usual sense, 'hate, enmity, ill will' (as Schmidt defines it) the overtures of Brutus to Antony after the death of Caesar must seem dangerously threatening:

> For your part,
> To you, our Swords haue leaden points Marke Antony:
> Our Armes in strength of malice, and our Hearts
> Of Brothers temper, do receiue you in,
> With all kinde loue, good thoughts, and reuerence.

Through linguistic context ('leaden points') and dramatic situation Shakespeare has denied to 'malice' all sense of 'active hatred'; what is indicated is the now obsolete 'power to harm', a power which Brutus promises will not be used.[2]

---

[1] NED: *stand v*. 72. Stand in—.
[2] NED: *malice* 2. *c*. 1380-1685, Onions shows this sense, *King John*, II i 251.

3

Although from a stage performance the audience would probably understand some of the senses which I have suggested, more serious misapprehension may sometimes occur, and re-creation of printed text in dramatic form will not always suffice to illumine Shakespeare's dramatic intention; actor and producer may be misled by non-contemporary editorial comment so that in a stage performance a line of great significance may be thrown away. In such cases it is by recognising afresh those factors in the text which limit meaning that we may have available again what Shakespeare first wrote; so in the following passage from *King Lear* (IV vi 81), when Gloucester has, as he thinks, fallen from the cliff edge to which the beggar-fiend has led him:

Edgar.   What thing was that
Which parted from you? . . .
It was some Fiend: Therefore thou happy Father,
Thinke that the cleerest Gods, who make them Honors
Of mens Impossibilities, haue preserued thee.
Gloucester.   I do remember now: henceforth Ile beare
Affliction, till it do crye out it selfe
Enough, enough, and dye. That thing you speake of,
I tooke it for a man: often 'twould say
The Fiend, the Fiend, he led me to that place.
Edgar.   Beare free and patient thoughts.
                    Enter Lear.
But who comes heere?
The safer sense will ne're accommodate
His Master thus.

Accommodate here is currently interpreted 'furnish or equip' (Onions) with ' "The safer" (i.e. saner) sense' that of King Lear, as in Johnson's commentary: 'Here is Lear, but he must be mad: his sound or *sane* senses would never suffer him to be thus disguised.' I suggest instead for 'accommodate' the equally

contemporary 'adapt itself to'—more specifically here 'to maintain itself when confronted by'—and take the saner sense as that
of Gloucester. Close study of linguistic context and dramatic
situation will show, I believe, that Edgar's words are capable of
one interpretation only: 'Gloucester's newly-recovered and
precarious mental balance—his resolution to endure affliction
until death—will never be able to maintain itself against the shock
and horror of encountering Lear as he now is.' The interpretation
hitherto accepted is suspect on several counts. First it derives from
a text which at the crucial point is non-Shakespearean. The stage-
direction 'drest madly with flowers', after *Enter Lear* was inserted
by Theobald[1] (from Cordelia's description, 'Crown'd with ranke
Fenitar, and furrow weeds', IV iv 3) and has survived in variant
forms into modern editions. It is this direction only that makes us
suppose that Edgar is speaking of Lear. Next it should be noted
that it becomes necessary to change the grammar of Edgar's
words if Johnson's interpretation is accepted: Edgar says 'will
ne're accommodate', Johnson 'would never suffer'; Edgar uses
the comparative 'safer', Johnson has 'sane', dropping the comparative form.

If Shakespeare's text is accepted as it stands, it must seem that
Edgar has, at this stage of the action, no word of hope or fear for
Lear's recovery; his speech points rather to a new crisis which is to
test to breaking-point *Gloucester's* new-found sanity. Edgar
describes elsewhere how he met his father

> with his bleeding Rings,
> Their precious Stones new lost: became his guide,
> Led him, begg'd for him, sau'd him from dispaire. (v iii 191)

And on Dover cliff he has heard his words:

> O you mighty Gods!
> This world I do renounce, and in your sights
> Shake patiently my great affliction off:

---

[1] I am indebted to my friend and colleague Mrs. Nowottny for drawing my
attention to this.

If I could beare it longer, and not fall
To quarrell with your great opposelesse willes,
My snuffe, and loathed part of Nature should
Burne it selfe out.

The role of poor Tom, Lear's companion in the storm, Edgar
renounces as he saves his father. Lear's entrance 'heere' and 'thus'
affects him chiefly as it may affect his father: Gloucester is now,
unlike Edgar, to have his first encounter with the king, his
master, since 'his wits are gon', to see feelingly what the heart
could break at. As Edgar fears, Gloucester is tempted again to
self-slaughter and prays for death that he may escape from that
temptation

You euer gentle Gods, take my breath from me,
Let not my worser Spirit tempt me againe
To dye before you please.

And after the battle in which the king's party is defeated, 'in ill
thoughts againe' he could be content to rot where he lies.

Internal evidence, it may be argued, supports the gloss proposed; external evidence is found in NED[1] in an interesting citation
from Bacon's *Coulers of Good & Evill*, 1597[2] (which I give here
at somewhat greater length for its coincidental value to the
Baconians):

for in the minde of man, *gradus diminutionis* may worke a wauering
betweene hope and feare, and so keepe the minde in suspence from
setling and accommodating in patience, and resolution; hereof
the common fourmes are, *Better eye out, then alwayes ake*, make or
marre, etc.

It is noteworthy that Bacon's 'accommodating' is accompanied by
'patience' and 'resolution' even as Edgar counsels 'free and patient
thoughts'.

---

[1] NED: accommodate 2. To adapt . . . (one thing . . . *to* another) . . . 1588 onwards. 3. To adapt oneself *to*, 1597 Bacon; 1677.
[2] *Essayes*, 1597, p. 31 v.

4

In the instances so far considered the Shakespearean glosses 'guessed at' from the context can be supported by external evidence made available in NED. I come now to a second group where evidence of Shakespearean context points strongly to senses not directly confirmed by NED's authority. In such cases it is sometimes possible to rearrange or reapply the Dictionary's evidence; elsewhere it is necessary to go beyond the Dictionary to other sources.

A simple instance occurs in *Merchant of Venice* (III ii 240) when Lorenzo, Jessica and Salerio come to Portia's house; Bassanio welcomes his friend Lorenzo and Gratiano asks Nerissa to welcome Jessica:

> Nerrissa, cheere yond stranger, bid her welcom.

Even if Jessica is apprehensive of the 'shrewd contents' of Antonio's letter, Gratiano is triumphantly high-spirited; in conjunction with 'stranger' and 'welcom', his verb 'cheere', as he intends it, must imply 'greet with kindness and hospitality'. For the verb *cheer* NED does not illustrate such a sense, but 'kindly welcome or reception' is shown as a now obsolete sense of the noun; Shakespeare's Lucrece 'securely giues good cheare, And reuerend welcome to her princely guest' (l. 89).

In the same way it may be better to understand from Shakespearean context and from NED's non-Shakespearean definition the main sense of *copy* in *Comedy of Errors* (v i 62), when Adriana coming to fetch her 'poore distracted husband' from the Priorie is skilfully betrayed by the Abbesse to her 'owne reproofe'. It may be, she grants, that some love drew him so oft from home. The text continues:

> Abbesse. You should for that haue reprehended him.
> Adriana. Why so I did.

Abbesse. I but not rough enough.

Adriana. As roughly as my modestie would let me.

Abbesse. Haply in priuate.

Adriana. And in assemblies too.

Abbesse. I, but not enough.

Adriana. It was the copie of our Conference.
In bed he slept not for my vrging it,
At boord he fed not for my vrging it:
Alone, it was the subject of my Theame:
In company I often glanced [at] it:
Still did I tell him, it was vilde and bad.

Abbesse. And thereof came it, that the man was mad.

The arrangement of the dramatic dialogue directs us to understand the main sense of 'copy' as that of Latin *copia*, 'plenty', in swift rejoinder to the reproach of 'not enough'. So Theobald comments; 'we are to take it in the nearest Sense to the Latin word *copia*, from which it is derived'. NED indeed shows this as one of the earliest senses of the word, but for this actual phrase in Shakespeare's text offers the definition 'agenda or subject matter; the theme' (11 b.); a number of recent editors following the Dictionary give this possible secondary sense as their only gloss.

In the fisherman's speech in *Pericles* (ii i 156) *condolement* as defined by the Dictionary seems slightly wrong in tone. The fishermen have found in their nets an old 'rusty Armour' which Pericles, shipwrecked, recognises as his own and asks to have so that he may contend in the tournament. When Pericles promises

And if that euer my low fortune's better,
Ile pay your bounties; till then, rest your debter

the first fisherman gladly gives him this 'Coate of worth', but the second fisherman has also a word to say:

I but harke you my friend, t'was wee that made vp this Garment through the rough seames of the Waters: there are certaine Condolements, certaine Vailes: I hope sir, if you thriue, you'le remember from whence you had them (Quarto 1).

The meaning of 'Vailes' is not in doubt: NED illustrates the sense 'gratuity given to a servant'. 'Condolement' is registered by the Dictionary in the senses 'lamentation' (as in *Hamlet*, I ii 93), 'sympathy in bereavement', 'an expression of sympathy with anyone in his suffering or loss' and, for this *Pericles* instance only, 'a tangible expression of this, a solatium'. But the fisherman is not asking for sympathy for any emotional loss or suffering; physical hardship in the 'rough seames of the Waters' is the usual lot of himself and his fellows and they are not so ground down by poverty that they go hungry for 'Puddinges and Flap-iackes'. What the man wants is what Pericles promises: if he should win the tournament, the fisherman and his partner would like to be paid something for the armour; they would like a share of his good fortune: -*dole* represents 'share' rather than 'grief'. It is clear then why the fisherman puts his request indirectly as general statement: 'there are certaine Condolements, certaine Vailes'. This simple indicative is the middle term between the blunt affirmation with which he begins and the polite conditional with which he ends. As the rough friendship of 'harke you my friend' is replaced by the respectful 'I hope sir, if . . .', so too the 'condolement' earned by those who share the risks of an operation is replaced by the 'vails' received not as a right but from a social superior.

Recent editors have been puzzled by the meaning of *wrangle* in *The Tempest*, v i 174, and it is generally agreed that 'no instance has ever been brought forward, either from Shakespeare or from any contemporary author, where the word "wrangle" bears the sense required of it'[1] in this passage. Ferdinand and Miranda are playing at chess:

> Miranda.   Sweet Lord, you play me false.
> Ferdinand.   No my dearest loue,
> I would not for the world.

---

[1] Staunton, 1872. I quote from Furness *Variorum* 1897.

> Miranda.   Yes, for a score of Kingdomes, you should wrangle,
> And I would call it faire play.

Kermode[1] comments that 'there seems to be no warrant for interpreting *wrangle* as meaning "cheat"; it must mean "dispute"' and ends regretfully 'If only *wrangle* could mean "play unfairly, cheat", the solution would be much neater'. Submission to internal evidence is an important part of my procedure and I am glad therefore to note that here, as elsewhere, contextual directives can be safely followed; there *is* dictionary evidence that Miranda's 'play me false' and 'wrangle' are in some ways parallel in meaning. Cotgrave's *Dictionarie* (1632 ed.) translates the English noun 'A wrangling' by

> Noise, riote, patricotage, tintamarre, chicanerie,

and this *chicanerie* supplies the ingredient of unfairness. The French *chicanerie* is defined:

> wrangling, pettifogging, litigious, or craftie pleading; *the perplexing of a cause with trickes;* or the pestering thereof with (subtile, but) impertiment [*sic*] words.

Rider's *Dictionarie* (1626) shows that the English verb 'To wrangle' has two different senses, translated into Latin as

> 1 Alterco, ercor. 2 Tergiversor.

And Cooper's *Thesaurus* (1578) defines this last verb

> Tergiuersor . . . Cic. To turne backe: to deny: to haft: to ouerthwart: *to runne away and fight still,*

with the further citation

> Tergiuersari in re aliqua. Cice. To hafte or ouerthwarte in a marter [matter]: to wrangle.

NED shows the English *haft* (*v.*[2]), 'to use subtilty or deceit', while *overthwart* is 'to obstruct, cross, thwart' perhaps with some indirection implied.[2]

---

[1] 'New Arden', 1954.   [2] See adjective and adverb citations.

A similar difficulty occurs in *Othello*, II i 70, as Cassio comments on Iago's swift arrival in Cyprus with Desdemona:

> Ha's had most fauourable, and happie speed:
> Tempests themselues, high Seas, and howling windes,
> The gutter'd-Rockes, and Congregated Sands,
> Traitors ensteep'd, to enclogge the guiltlesse Keele,
> As hauing sence of Beautie, do omit
> Their mortall Natures, letting go safely by
> The Diuine Desdemona.

Where the Folio has *ensteep'd*, Quarto 1 has *enscerped*. NED glosses *ensteep*, found in this instance only, as 'To immerse, station under water'; the simple verb *steep*, however, in the general currency of Elizabethan English and in a number of Shakespearean instances (including *Othello*, IV ii 50) has the basic meaning 'soak' which would seem out-of-context as attaching to this 'ensteep' compound of Cassio's speech. Alice Walker ('New Cambridge' *Othello*, 1957) gives the reading 'insteeped' which she understands as 'submerged'; M. R. Ridley ('New Arden' *Othello*, 1958) notes that

> *gutter'd* can no doubt mean 'channelled', but if so, what is the point of it? A channelled rock is no more dangerous than any other. But a submerged rock is, and I suspect that *gutter'd* and *ensteep'd* both mean, in Cassio's high-flown diction, no more than 'under-water', though *ensteep'd* may have a hint of 'double-dyed'. One would feel happier if one could find a meaning for Q1's *enscerped*, . . .

The noun *escarp* is defined by NED as 'A steep bank or wall immediately in front of and below the rampart . . .' and is registered from 1688; *scarp*, having the sense of this 'escarp' is found from 1589. Cotgrave's French *escarpe* (1632 ed.) is in English

> A scarfe, or little wall without the mayne rampire of a fort.

Cassio's *enscerped* may then be understood as en-scarp-ed; it is likely that such rocks and sands as form this 'little wall' *below* the rampart—the lower outer edge of the uprising land mass—are the 'Traitors' of the Shakespearean passage. The 'Sands' are dangerous because 'Congregated'; in seventeenth-century proverb idiom many sands will sink a ship: 'Many little sands gather'd to an heape, faile not to swallow a greet vessell' (1615).[1] Sands are dangerous when congregated underwater; the rocks are similarly those of the sea-bed. They are 'Traitors' for a related but contrasted reason, not because they are 'Congregated' or piled-up, but because they are 'gutter'd' or hollowed out, forming deep channels which give a false idea of the minimum depth of water available for the 'guiltlesse Keele'. It is possible that Shakespeare is using a similar sand-bank image in *Merchant of Venice* (III ii 84) when Bassanio speaks of the deceit of outward show:

> manie cowards, whose hearts are all as false
> As stayers of sand. . . .

5

In the last five examples considered ('cheere', 'copy', 'condolement', 'wrangle', 'enscerp'd') it has been possible to 'guess' the Shakespearean meaning from language and situation directives of the immediate context; the next examples are perhaps more interesting in that the full meaning of the problem word derives from a more extended dramatic context.

In *Much Ado* (II i 214) Benedicke, who as one of the maskers has been obliged to listen to Beatrice abusing that Benedicke whom he pretends not to know, expresses to himself his anger and perplexity:

> But that my Ladie Beatrice should know me, & not know me: the Princes foole! Hah? It may be I goe vnder that title, because I am merrie: yea but so I am apt to do my selfe wrong: I am not so reputed, it is the base (though bitter) disposition of Beatrice, that putt's the world into her person, and so giues me out:

---

[1] Tilley: S 92, 1615 first cit.

His phrase *the base* (*though bitter*), found in Quarto and Folio text, is generally considered 'not intelligible', as for instance by Dover Wilson (1923), and Johnson's emendation 'the base, the bitter' is usually preferred. It may, however, be argued that the phrase has meaning as it stands and needs no emendation. The real difficulty is in the word 'base'; if it has its usual meaning 'low' or 'mean', it is hard to find sense in the concessive 'though': there seems no reason why the meanness of the attacker should reduce the bitterness felt by the attacked. If, on the other hand, 'base' means 'counterfeit', Benedicke in believing that he goes under the title of the prince's jester ('yea but so') is likely ('apt') to do himself an injustice: such a role is assigned to him only through the counterfeiting, bitter though that may be to suffer, of the bitter-natured Beatrice. The noun 'disposition', as we are invited to infer from its dual qualification 'base (though bitter)', compresses two meanings into the single word: NED illustrates the verb *dispose* as meaning (1 d.) 'to place in a particular employment, to assign, appoint' (1579-1697). And 'counterfeiting' is a deed in fashion throughout the play. Earlier in this same masking scene, Anthonio, his identity challenged by Ursula, denies that he is in fact Anthonio, 'To tell you true, I counterfeit him'. Later, the Prince and Claudio in the orchard, knowing that they are overheard by Benedicke, pretend to think that in her 'life of passion' for Benedicke—which they have invented for her—Beatrice herself 'doth but counterfeit'.

External evidence shows 'base' in this sense 'alloyed, debased, counterfeit' first registered by NED (15.) in a poem of Skelton's (*a.* 1528); in Shakespearean usage the word has this 'counterfeit' sense when Henry VIII rebukes the Bishop of Winchester for trying by words of flattery and 'sodaine Commendations' to turn away his frown: 'They are too thin, and base to hide offences' (v iii 125).

It seems reasonable to ask further if there is any factor in the Shakespearean linguistic context (rather than in the dramatic situation) which would direct the hearer to the 'base'/'counterfeit' equation; there *is* external evidence to suggest that 'putt's the

world into her person' gives this direction. What is commonly
reported is proverbially suspect in Shakespearean and later English:
'Report (or Fame) is a liar'[1]—Benedicke himself confesses in his
very next speech that he has 'played the part of Lady Fame' in
telling Claudio that the prince has won Hero for himself. And
in what would be a quite well known anecdote from classical
story it is clearly laid down that a worthless or false opinion is
not made valuable or genuine by multitude of witness. In the
Apophthegmes of Erasmus (available in the English translation of
Nicholas Udall, 1547) Socrates is quoted as using a 'coin' image
to express this truth:

> Those persones, whiche would giue credence vnto the vnlearned,
> and unexperte multitude of the people, Socrates affirmed to doe
> euen like, as if a man refusyng one peece of money of fower
> grotes, would not take it in paimente, and yet a greate nomber of
> like refuse peces, cast in an heape together, he would allow for
> curraunt, and receiue theim in paimente.

Udall adds a note:

> A counterfaict pece of coigne, be it euen in neuer so great an
> heape, is a counterfaict peece. This maketh against the estemyng of
> witnesses, by the multitude of theim . . .[2].

For the Shakespearean interpretation here proposed the argument rests firmly on the relatedness of the evidence. A second
sense of 'base', less important and less easy to prove, may have
been caught half-consciously by the alert ears of a contemporary
audience: 'base'[3] can mean 'the smallest kind of cannon', and
Beatrice, says the still-smarting Benedicke, as he repeats the
story of his discomfiture,

> told mee, not thinking I had beene my selfe, that I was the Princes
> Iester, and that I was duller then a great thaw, hudling iest vpon

---

[1] Tilley: F 44 Fame (Report) is a liar, 1594 first cit. T 99 They say so is half a
lie, 1666 first cit.: 'To have heard say, is half a lye'.
[2] My quotation is from the 1877 reprint of the 1564 ed., p. 22.
[3] NED: *base, sb.*[6].

iest, with such impossible conueiance vpon me, that I stood *like a man at a marke, with a whole army shooting at me:* shee speakes poynyards . . . .

This instance illustrates how the asking of an apparently simple question—why the Shakespearean text has 'though' instead of 'the'—may point the way to a more contemporary enjoyment of a line or two of Shakespearean dialogue. In trying to analyse why the dramatist has so written we appreciate more closely the fineness of texture which he has achieved.

The living idiom of the Elizabethan world may take on a special and individual life in the smaller world of the Shakespearean play; a swift allusion to some fragment of vivid metaphor may be pointed to a special situation in a manner particularly appropriate to the speaking character. So, with the word *py'ed* in Caliban's speech (*The Tempest*, III ii 71). Having drunk deep of Stephano's wine Caliban kneels to his 'noble Lord', asking again that Stephano take vengeance on Prospero and himself become ruler of the island. As Trinculo, under threats, discontinues his mocking interruptions of this 'poore Monster', Ariel takes over, speaking as if he is Trinculo.

> Stephano.   How now shal this be compast?
> Canst thou bring me to the party?
> Caliban.   Yea, yea my Lord, Ile yeeld him thee asleepe,
> Where thou maist knocke a naile into his head.
> Ariell.   Thou liest, thou canst not.
> Caliban.   What a py'de Ninnie's this? Thou scuruy patch:
> I do beseech thy Greatnesse giue him blowes.

Johnson believed *py'de Ninnie* an allusion to the striped coat worn by the fool Trinculo, which would be a special costume of which Caliban could have no knowledge; accordingly, in his edition, he preferred to give this line to Stephano. Other editors leave the speech to Caliban, but take *pied* also in this sense 'particoloured'. I suggest instead that it means 'chattering like a magpie'

—with the preterite participle used in an active sense, as in the Stratford phrase 'an ill lookd wooman' meaning 'having the power to look on with the evil eye' (p. 20); so too the current English 'well spoken'.[1]

Caliban's outburst comes when he has, as he thinks, been given the lie for the third time by Trinculo. At the second interruption *Thou lyest* (this time by Ariel) Caliban has turned on Trinculo with the words

> Thou lyest, thou iesting Monkey thou:
> I would my valiant Master would destroy thee.
> I do not lye.

The 'jesting monkeys' of Caliban's world are the spirits ordered by Prospero to punish him,

> Sometime like Apes, that *moe and chatter* at me,
> And after bite me (ii ii 9),

and it is to the mindless mischievous chattering of Trinculo that Caliban refers. Stephano threatens Trinculo, not for jesting at Caliban, but for interrupting him ('if you trouble him any more in's tale' and 'Interrupt the Monster one word further'), and it is for Ariel's senseless-seeming repetition ('parrot-like' in our idiom) that Trinculo is beaten. NED's citations show that one of the meanings of *pie* from the early fourteenth to the mid-nineteenth century is its habitual collocation with the verbs *chat, chatter;*[2] a magpie is still a *chatter-pie* in many dialects. So *py'de Ninnie* is parallel to *iesting Monkey*; Caliban's image is from the life he knows, and his indignation, as Johnson felt, comes from the immediate situation.

The clue in this last instance was the past experience of speaking character; elsewhere the clue may lie in a character's view of his own true humour. At the beginning of *Othello* Iago explains to

---

[1] See Henry Sweet's *New English Grammar*, Pt. II, Oxford, 1898, § 2356, for other instances.

[2] *pie, sb.*[1]; *pie, v*[1]. 1657, to repeat like a magpie.

Roderigo that he follows Othello only to serve his turn upon him:

> In following him, I follow but my selfe.
> Heauen is my Iudge, not I for loue and dutie,
> But seeming so, for my peculiar end:
> For when my outward Action doth demonstrate
> The natiue act, and figure of my heart
> In Complement externe, 'tis not long after
> But I will weare my heart vpon my sleeue
> For Dawes to pecke at; I am not what I am.

The importance which Iago gives to the 'natiue act, and figure' of his heart (i i 62) in contrast to his 'outward Action', makes us expect for his word *act* some meaning of central significance— the principle or essential energy of his nature. Such a sense, defined conjecturally as 'activity, active principle' (3) and illustrated by NED from 1398 to 1730 may be found also in later philosophical writings. To cite one instance:

> According to St. Thomas Aquinas, the physical order was essentially made up of 'natures', that is to say, of active principles, which were the cause of the motions and various operations of their respective matters. In other words, each nature, or form, was essentially an energy, an act (1938).[1]

This sense would be fully in context in Iago's speech; he wishes above all to conceal from others the guiding principle of his actions. When Roderigo would die for love of Desdemona, Iago dwells on the power of human reason, "'tis in our selues that we are thus, or thus'; love is merely 'a permission of the will' (i iii 340). His own strong ambition must be subject to reason: he has to repress his resentment that

> Preferment goes by Letter, and affection,

since men may be obliged 'for necessitie of present life' to 'show out a Flag, and signe of Loue', even though they keep 'their

---

[1] *The Unity of Philosophical Experience*, by E. Gilson, 1938, p. 205.

hearts attending on themselues'. It is easy for him to feign anger
when Othello seeks to know his thoughts of Cassio—'speake to
me, as to thy thinkings' (III iii 131)—and he denies him

> Though I am bound to euery Acte of dutie,
> I am not bound to that: All Slaues are free:
> Vtter my thoughts?

And when Othello urges again 'Ile know thy Thoughts' he answers
with quick and unpretended anger

> You cannot, if my heart were in your hand,
> Nor shall not, whil'st 'tis in my custodie.

In the final scene of the play it is to Othello's question 'Why he
hath thus ensnar'd my Soule and Body' that Iago's last answer is
made

> Demand me nothing; what you know, you know

showing the same determination to keep concealed whatever
pattern of conduct his will had figured upon his heart.

In another Shakespearean instance (*Henry V*, I ii 189) this sense
'active principle' would be fully relevant. Canterbury speaks of
the order of government

> Therefore doth heauen diuide
> The state of man in diuers functions,
> Setting endeuour in continual motion:
> To which is fixed as an ayme or butt,
> Obedience: for so worke the Hony Bees,
> Creatures that by a rule in Nature teach
> The Act of Order to a peopled Kingdome.

Eighteenth-century editors, following Pope, emended *act* to 'art';
present-day editors restore the text, glossing *act* 'operation, action'.

6

Within this chapter, since first citing the linguistic dictum
that we can know the meaning of the word only after we have

understood the sentence in which it is contained, I have considerably extended the range of this 'sentence'. My last instance, a consideration of the meaning of *achievement* (*Henry V*, III v 60) takes as the relevant context one of the main themes of the play. The French resolve to capture the English king as he marches back to the coast:

> King of France. For your great Seats, now quit you of great shames:
> Barre Harry England, that sweepes through our Land
> With Penons painted in the blood of Harflew:
> Rush on his Hoast, as doth the melted Snow
> Vpon the Valleyes, whose low Vassall Seat,
> The Alpes doth spit, and void his rhewme vpon.
> Goe downe vpon him, you haue Power enough,
> And in a Captiue Chariot, into Roan
> Bring him our Prisoner.
> Constable of France. This becomes the Great.
> Sorry am I his numbers are so few,
> His Souldiers sick, and famisht in their March:
> For I am sure, when he shall see our Army,
> Hee'le drop his heart into the sinck of feare,
> And for atchieuement, offer vs his Ransome.

'Achievement' is generally understood as 'exploit' (Schmidt), 'something won'; a more specific sense 'a heraldic device to commemorate a feat of arms' may, however, be intended. The preposition *for* can mean 'instead of'; in support of this there is the strong contrast between 'atchieue' and 'ransom' to be heard later in the play (IV iii 80, 91) when Mountjoy comes to know from King Henry

> If for thy Ransome thou wilt now compound

and the king sends back his answer

> Bid them atchieue me, and then sell my bones.

It is then in the difference which Shakespeare makes between the French and English concepts of honour that the special sense of the

noun 'atchieuement' has its place. Honour for the French derives
in birth and blood and is displayed in splendour. The battle lost,
they ask for 'charitable License' to

> wander ore this bloody field,
> To booke our dead, and then to bury them,
> To sort our Nobles from our common men.
> For many of our Princes (woe the while)
> Lye drown'd and soak'd in mercenary blood:
> So do our vulgar drench their peasant limbes
> In blood of Princes. . . .   (IV vii 81)

As the English see it, honour is achieved in the blood of battle, so
that courage of king and common soldier may be commemorated
in epitaph and emblem. If Henry cannot gain an honourable em-
pire he is content to lay his bones

> in an unworthy Vrne,
> Tombelesse, with no remembrance ouer them.   (I ii 229)

but it is his hope that upon the 'Natiue Graues' of Agincourt's
survivors

> Shall witnesse liue in Brasse of this dayes worke.   (IV iii 97)

The Welshman who fought with the Black Prince gained 'an
honourable badge of the seruice' (IV vii 106), traditionally 'worne
as a memorable Trophee of predeceased valor' (V i 76); Williams's
integrity gains him the king's glove to wear in his cap. At
Agincourt Henry declares

> he to day that sheds his blood with me . . .
> This day shall gentle his Condition.

The most vivid symbol of its honour is seen by the French as the
splendour and 'faire shew' of an army; shame in defeat is felt by
the nobles as confounding their own pageantry

> Reproach, and euerlasting shame
> Sits mocking in our Plumes.   (IV v 5)

Henry's pride in achieving Harflew they resent as if it is an
'achievement' which he has painted blood-red on his pennon; in

imagined triumph over a craven foe they would consign this
brilliance to the sink of fear.

Contemporary sources show 'achievement' as a term of heraldry
in varying forms and ranges of meaning. Hall's *Chronicle of
Henry V* (1548) speaks of *Hatchementes* borne at the king's funeral;
so Laertes cries out against the obscure buriall of his father

> No Trophee, Sword, nor Hatchement o're his bones
>
> > (*Hamlet*, iv v 214).

Bossewell's *Workes of Armorie* (1572) suggests that *achement* and
acheuement can be used interchangeably.[1]   John Ferne's *Blazon
of Gentrie* (1586) makes a distinction between 'the whole atchieuement' and 'addicions called atcheaments':

> For, the creast, tymber, mantell, or worde, bee no part of the coat-
> armour: they be addicions called atcheaments, added not manye
> hundred yeares agoe, to the coates of gentle-men, and the excellent
> noble.   (p. 185)

It is of interest that this use of *addition*[2] can be paralleled in *Troilus
and Cressida*

> I came to kill thee Cozen, and beare hence
> A great addition, earned in thy death.   (IV v 141)

Possibly also in *Hamlet* (I iv 20-1, Quarto 2) the collocation of
'addition' and 'achievements' attaches to both words some secondary sense of heraldic distinction:

> They clip vs drunkards, and with Swinish phrase
> Soyle our addition, and indeede it takes
> From our atchieuements, though perform'd at height
> The pith and marrow of our attribute . . . .

---

[1] because ye may the better vnderstande what suche achementes bee. But it
might be asked to me, what thys worde acheuement meneth. Bk. II, Folio 121 v.

[2] NED: *addition* 5. Something added to a coat of arms . . . First citation *Troilus
and Cressida*.

CHAPTER IX

Contextual evidence: the language that Shakespeare 'made'

The preceding chapter was concerned with words in the Shakespearean text which have mainly single meaning and the interpretations there proposed rest on the principle that meaning is contextual. It may be argued also, to complete the proposition, that just as the individual context is unique, so too the single word when used in different 'sentences' has never quite the same field of reference, the same total of meaning. Applying this principle to Shakespeare's work I shall try now to illustrate some of the kinds of more-than-one meaning with which he has pointed and enriched his writing and shall look especially for any slight indications within his text which might make us question the sufficiency of our present interpretations, the total of meaning we are accustomed to allow. As before, for convenience of handling, I shall speak as if this total of meaning is gathered into the single word (or phrase) and each component of this total which I believe to be evidenced in Shakespeare's verbal and dramatic context I shall seek to confirm in contemporary usage outside the play.

Sometimes it seems that what we regard as a crux may itself be the clue. Given an audience trained to quick response, Shakespeare may have found profit in holding up the speed of that response; he may have chosen on occasion to write what would be momentarily unintelligible. With the word *wit*, for example, in Portia's speech to the black Prince of Morocco (*Merchant of Venice*, II i 18) he may have intended to frustrate his hearers' expectancy so as to make them pause on the word to take in its double sense:

In tearmes of choise I am not solie led
By nice direction of a maidens eies:
Besides, the lottrie of my destenie
Bars me the right of voluntarie choosing:
But if my Father had not scanted me,
And hedg'd me by his wit to yeelde my selfe
His wife, who wins me by that meanes I told you,
Your selfe (renowned Prince) than stood as faire
As any commer I haue look'd on yet
For my affection.

Portia has complained to Nerissa 'so is the wil of a liuing daughter curb'd by the will of a dead father': here too she might be expected to say that she is 'scanted' and 'hedg'd' not primarily by her father's 'wit' (although 'holy men at their death have good inspirations') but by his 'will'. So strong indeed is this expectation that a number of editors, from the eighteenth century to the present day, have supposed the 'wit' of the original texts (Q. 1600, Q. 1619, F. 1623) to represent scribal or compositorial error and they have substituted for it the 'will', 'testament', which they are agreed that the context demands. But perhaps Shakespeare himself has given what the context demands and something over. External evidence suggests that 'testament' is one of the meanings of 'wit' in Tudor England. NED illustrates the verb *wit* 'to bequeath', in use until 1547; the noun *witword*, 'will or testament', known as far back as the laws of Ethelred, is registered by the Dictionary mainly in northern documents, until the middle of the sixteenth century.[1] The 'wit' that hedges Portia includes then both the ingenuity of the will's provisions and the wisdom that inspired them: if we ask why she is saying less than we expect, we find that she is saying more.

Although the dividend yield of detailed linguistic research tends to be somewhat slow, there are occasional bonus issues in that pieces of knowledge do not remain isolates. *Wit*, 'to bequeath', which makes sense of Portia's line (through double meaning)

---

[1] *wit, v.*[2]; *witword* Chiefly *north*.

makes good (single) sense of another Shakespearean passage which editors have long found puzzling. In 2 *Henry IV* (IV iv 104) the king, as he hears the good news of the rebels' defeat, is suddenly taken ill. The Folio has

> And wherefore should these good newes
> Make me sicke?
> Will Fortune neuer come with both hands full,
> But write her faire words still in foulest Letters?

The quarto reads 'But wet her faire words stil in foulest termes?' Because of the double variant, Dover Wilson suspects 'that F. is a makeshift of the prompter and that Q. conceals something else written by Shakespeare'. Alice Walker argues that 'although the Folio line . . . gives a superficial kind of sense it breaks the image'; the quarto reading, however, is 'nonsense' and she proposes the emendation 'mete', meaning 'to measure' for the original 'wet'.[1] I suggest that it is possible to keep the quarto text unemended, understanding *wet* as a variant spelling of 'wit'; its meaning could be 'bequeath' in the sense 'to make over, assign'. (See NED *bequeath* 4.) And it is worth noting that the verb 'wet' is found here in collocation with 'termes' which can mean 'limiting conditions'. (In Portia's speech the noun 'wit' follows the phrase 'tearmes of choise'.) Its object 'words' could mean 'that which is granted' (cf. NED *witword*). The king is then complaining that what Fortune gives with one hand she takes away with the other; her grant may be generous but the conditions accompanying the gift serve to nullify it; this is strikingly exemplified in the rest of his speech:

> Shee eyther giues a Stomack, and no Foode,
> (Such are the poore, in health) or else a Feast,
> And takes away the Stomack (such are the Rich,
> That haue aboundance, and enjoy it not.)
> I should reioyce now, at this happy newes,
> And now my Sight fayles, and my Braine is giddie.

---

[1] *Textual Problems of the First Folio*, Cambridge, 1953, p. 117.

As Portia's 'wit' makes clear the meaning of this passage, so the difficulty of Antony's *Arme-gaunt Steede* (*Antony and Cleopatra*, I v 48) may be partially solved by setting it against the word-play of the dying John of Gaunt (*Richard II*, II i 82). King Richard asks 'What comfort man? How ist with aged Gaunt?' and Gaunt replies

> Oh how that name befits my composition:
> Old Gaunt indeed, and gaunt in being old:
> Within me greefe hath kept a tedious fast,
> And who abstaynes from meate, that is not gaunt?
> For sleeping England long time haue I watcht,
> Watching breeds leannesse, leannesse is all gaunt.
> The pleasure that some Fathers feede vpon,
> Is my strict fast, I meane my Childrens lookes,
> And therein fasting, hast thou made me gaunt:
> Gaunt am I for the graue, gaunt as a graue,
> Whose hollow wombe inherits naught but bones.

In the penultimate line here the contradistinction between 'Gaunt . . . for' and 'gaunt as' points towards the possibility that the two adjectives are to be understood in differing senses. Gaunt has listed the causes of his leanness—age, grief, fasting, sleeplessness, his strict separation from his son—and in 'gaunt as' he refers again to this emaciation; in his 'Gaunt . . . for' therefore some fresh statement might be excepted: 'lean for' followed by 'lean as' would lack dramatic sharpness. The immediate context suggests that 'Gaunt . . . for' means 'fit, ready for'; it repeats his first line 'Oh how that name befits my composition:' Etymologically this meaning is very possible: NED shows the verb *gain* (adopted from ON *gegna* . . . to be meet, fit or suitable) with the by-form *gawne*, which is recorded in fifteenth-century northern English and due perhaps to the less common ON *gagna*.[1] If it is legitimate to suppose this verb-form *gawne* current in spoken English over a wider

---

[1] NED: *gain v.*[1] . . . The form *gawne* may be due to the less common ON *gagna* a derivative of *gagn = gegn*, but was perhaps influenced by the vowel of *gawin*, the northern var. of *gain sb.*[1]

area and for a longer time than NED's citations show, we have then in Gaunt's speech its past participle; he has been 'made ready' for his grave by Richard 'therin . . . hast thou made me gaunt'.

The *Arme-gaunt* of *Antony and Cleopatra* (I v 48) has aroused much conjecture. Cleopatra asks herself where Antony is

Or does he walke? Or is he on his Horse?
Oh happy horse to beare the weight of Anthony!
Do brauely Horse, for wot'st thou whom thou moou'st,
The demy Atlas of this Earth, the Arme
And Burganet of men.

Alexas describes Antony's departure

So he nodded,
And soberly did mount an Arme-gaunt Steede,
Who neigh'd so hye, that what I would haue spoke,
Was beastly dumbe by him.

A number of editors, among them Dover Wilson, think the form a textual corruption; others explain it as 'worn thin with hard service in armour'. If my interpretation of John of Gaunt's line is correct it might well have the sense 'made ready in harness, ready for armed conflict', perhaps even 'made (more) ready by the prospect of battle and by the greatness of the *Arme* it is to move'.[1] There would be no real difficulty of grammar or syntax. Abbott (§ 430) gives a number of instances from Shakespeare's text of a compound formed from noun and participle, for the understanding of which some preposition or other ellipse must be supplied: the examples include: 'many an Orphans water-standing-eye' (3 *Henry VI*, v vi 40), 'The King was weeping ripe for a good word' (*Love's Labour's Lost*, v ii 274), 'Her pittie-pleading eyes' (*Lucrece*, l. 561). Variant forms of the adjective *gain*, 'convenient, suitable, active, nimble, etc.', are common enough in present-day dialects; it is perhaps worth noting that the *English Dialect Dictionary* happens to record a '*gahin* horse' in south

---

[1] Compare *Richard II*, v ii 9.

Worcestershire: 'I niver sin no gahinier 'arse nar this un; a works copita.'

These interpretations of 'wit', 'wet' 'Gaunt' and 'Arme-Gaunt' rest on the assumption that Shakespeare was able to use the full resources of the ordinary language of his time. And it would be, I suggest, no matter for surprise that a dramatic language which has its roots in the whole life of a community should include an occasional dialect form or an old-fashioned word or meaning about to be superseded from literary use. In these cases however it might be the more difficult for the later commentator to 'prove' beyond a doubt that what Shakespeare's characters appear to use as language counters were in fact still current coin.

2

In giving to the individual word some new total of 'old' meaning Shakespeare often presents his clues with such ease and naturalness that the word-play seems to grow inevitably out of the feeling and situation of speaking-character. In such instances we may better understand what he has written if we can forget that his pen contrived it; if, hearing rather than seeing, we become identified with the one who speaks his words.

To understand what is new in the total meaning of *unbraided* (*Winter's Tale*, IV iv 204) it is necessary to enter into the humour of the speaking-character so as to appreciate the shrewdness with which he applies to his own situation the full flavour of the word in current speech. The servant tells of the arrival of the pedlar at the sheep-shearing feast:

> Seruant. He hath songs for man, or woman, of all sizes: No Milliner can so fit his customers with Gloues: he has the prettiest Loue-songs for Maids, so without bawdrie (which is strange,) with such delicate burthens of Dildo's and Fadings: Iump-her and thump-her; and where some stretch-mouth'd Rascall, would (as it were) meane mischeefe, and breake a fowle gap into the Matter,

hee makes the maid to answere, *Whoop, doe me no harme good man:* put's him off, slights him, with *Whoop, doe mee no harme good man.*
Polixenes.   This is a braue fellow.
Clowne.   Beleeee [Beleeue] mee, thou talkest of an admirable conceited fellow, has he any vnbraided Wares?
Seruant.   Hee hath Ribbons of all the colours i'th'Raine-bow . . .
Clowne.   Pre'thee bring him in, and let him approach singing.
Perdita.   Forewarne him, that he vse no scurrilous words in's tunes.
Clowne.   You haue of these Pedlers, that haue more in them, then you'ld thinke (Sister.)

Editors have long been puzzled by the meaning of 'unbraided'. To summarise some of the commentary as briefly as possible: the emendations 'braided' and 'embroided' have been proposed; the word has been taken in its literal sense to mean 'smooth and plain goods . . . not twisted into braids', 'not ornamented with braid', etc.; a later group of definitions, 'undamaged, unspoilt, unfaded, not counterfeit or adulterated', is arrived at by a consideration of three pieces of linguistic evidence—(1) 'braide' which appears to bear the sense 'deceitful' in Diana's speech (*All's Well*, IV ii 73):

> Since Frenchmen are so braide,
> Marry that will, I liue and die a Maid:
> Onely in this disguise, I think't no sinne,
> To cosen him that would vnjustly winne.

(2) *braided* 'Faded, that hath lost its colour' in Bailey's *Dictionary* (1721),[1] and (3) the collocation of 'braided' with 'ware' (as, for instance, in Middleton's *Anything for a Quiet Life* (c. 1626):[2] 'she says you vent Ware that is not warrantable, brayded Ware, and that you give not *London* measure').[3] In so far as the clown's question refers to the pedlar's haberdashery and is answered by the servant within the same range of meaning, these definitions

---

[1] *An Universal Etymological English Dictionary*, by N. Bailey, 1721.
[2] I quote from the quarto of 1662.
[3] So too in Thomas Deloney's *The Gentle Craft*, Part II (written bt. 1597 and 1600) ed. by F. O. Mann, 1912, p. 158: their loues are like braided wares, which are often showne, but hardly sold.

of the second group are satisfactory, as is attested by the later words of the clown, 'Pedler let's haue the first choice'. But the clown's words, as well as being answerable by 'Ribbons of all the colours i'th'Raine-bow,' are themselves in answer to the servant's description of the songs of Autolycus. The songs are the first interest of the clown, of Shakespeare and of the audience, 'let's first see moe Ballads: Wee'l buy the other things anon'; the clown gladly buys, as we would gladly hear, the ballad of the Usurer's wife, and of the Fish who sang against the hard hearts of maids. The servant has praised the variety of the pedlar's songs, but he describes one kind only, the kind in which the clown and some part of the audience take least interest, 'Loue-songs for Maids, so without bawdrie', in which the girl evades the scurrilous jests of her singing-partner, 'put's him off, slights him'. While admitting the wit of this kind of song, the clown would be fitted with a different glove, as Perdita well understands. *Braid* can mean 'An adroit turn; a trick or subtilty'.[1] The clown would have his love-songs without these evasions, and with a countryman's alertness, in phrasal form particularly relevant to dealings with a pedlar, he asks directly for what he wants. Shakespeare is using here a phrase of fixed form with its current sense, but at the same time he isolates and emphasises one of the elements of the phrase pattern, so that, from the personality of the speaker and from the dramatic situation, there flashes out the unique sense which characterises living language. The requisite external evidence for the meaning of *unbraided* here put forward has long been known: all that is suggested in this analysis is the need to see the Shakespearean word in a somewhat extended context, so that it refers not only forward to the 'Ribbons' but backward and forward to the songs.

I. A. Richards has spoken of metaphor as a transaction between contexts; such a phrase might well be applied to some of Shakespeare's double meaning. The crucial word, for the total

---

[1] NED: *braid sb.* 3.

meaning of which we try in vain to find parallels in other literary usage, may signify a momentary hingeing together of two senses, forming the pivot for the continuity of an argument or movement of thought. To know the word's function it is necessary then to watch how its direction changes. A simple example may be found in the word *conveyance* (*Much Ado*, II i 253) when Benedict describes how he was misused by Beatrice:

> shee told mee, not thinking I had beene my selfe, that I was the Princes Iester, and that I was duller then a great thaw, hudling iest vpon iest, with such impossible conueiance vpon me, that I stood like a man at a marke, with a whole army shooting at me.

No doubt a contemporary audience, accustomed to such verbal dexterity, would easily pick up the two senses, would see the two arms of the hinge; those glossarists I have consulted stop short at one, reading the word in incomplete citation as given for example in Bartlett's *Concordance*. 'Huddling jest upon jest with such impossible conveyance upon me', and explaining as 'sleight of hand, jugglery, manual or mental adroitness'. If the context is extended to take in 'that I stood like a man at a marke, with a whole army shooting at me', a second sense 'carriage of shot' is also required—a sense previously unregistered for the noun 'conveyance', although indicated by NED's seventeenth-century citations for the verb 'convey'.[1]

Other instances may be found where a word, unless it has something more than one meaning, might as well not be in the text at all. So with the word *weake* in *The Tempest* (II ii 148) as Trinculo marvels at Caliban for his readiness to believe that Stephano, his 'braue God', who 'beares Celestiall liquor', has come 'Out o'th Moone'; he watches the monster take a drink of Stephano's wine:

> By this good light, this is a very shallow Monster: I afeard of him? a very weake Monster:

---

[1] *Convey v.* 4b. To project to a distance, to 'carry' (a shot, etc.), 1634, 1660.

The Man i'th Moone?
A most poore creadulous Monster:
Well drawne Monster, in good sooth.

This qualifies as a good 'double or quits' instance since later
Folios have instead of 'weake' a simple repetition of the 'shallow'
of the previous line and some editors, seeing no point in 'weake'
as a variant epithet, have preferred to print the 'shallow' of these
later Folios.

It may first be argued from the given text that the phrase
'Well drawne' constitutes, as it were, a stage-direction: Caliban,
'a very shallow Monster', is yet to drink deep. The adjective
'shallow', then, which alone carries most of the meaning in the
first sentence, requires to be spoken by Trinculo with scorn for
Caliban's mental powers, but with some ironic admiration for
the drinking capacity which he is in process of demonstrating.
And it seems worth while to ask if the adjective 'weake' in the
following parallel phrase might not imply a similar irony: we
find then that 'to soak, to steep in wine' is a meaning of the verb
'weak' in mid-sixteenth century English: NED cites 1559 'Newe
herbes nede the lesse time, when they are stiept or weekt in wine
or other liquor.' If this reading of the situation is correct, Trinculo's
'weake' has three meanings: to its first sense 'feeble' we are
directed by the preceding question 'I afeard of him'. Its second
sense 'credulous'[1] derives from Caliban's acceptance of Stephano
as 'The Man i'th'Moone' and is specifically repeated in Trinculo's
subsequent judgment 'A most poore creadulous Monster'. The
third sense, the ironic 'soak', is present by implication only, not
formally on the grammatical level (weake = 'steep', not 'steeped').

I note in passing that if Trinculo's first phrase, his asseveration
'By this good light', is to refer not only to God's light but to
Trinculo's mental powers, it may be of relevance in this 'drinking'

---

[1] NED: weak a. 8b. Lacking force of intellect or strength of mind; easily
deceived, credulous. 1423 to 1885. NED does not mark this sense as obsolete, but
I cannot recall seeing or hearing the adjective weak, used absolutely, in this
sense in present-day English.

context that 'light' in Shakespearean usage can mean 'dizzy, giddy'. Perhaps too his phrase 'Well drawne . . . in good sooth' contains a further pun: 'sough' can mean both 'a deep breath' and 'a small gutter or drain'.[1] Remembering such place-name pronunciations as 'Keethly' for *Keighley*, one might hope to find 'sooth'/'sough' spelling variants in some earlier period. Trinculo's 'in good sooth' might then suggest that Caliban has a good throat for drinking and that he has been holding his breath for a long drink. This last *sooth* = sough hypothesis is of course merely an alerting of the linguist to a not-yet proven possibility; I do not wish to detract from the acceptability of those Shakespearean glosses for which there is external evidence by putting forward, as if in the same rank, those for which the external evidence is still to find. On the other hand, an occasional example of this kind may suggest the sort of inventiveness with which I believe we may properly cast about.

If this gloss of Trinculo's 'weake' is correct, its plain statement meaning hinges together the senses 'feeble' and 'credulous', while its ironic implication 'soak' would reverse the evaluation of Caliban as feeble which is made by the speaker at the same time in the same word. Here plainly the non-contemporary commentator must be content only to demonstrate the coincidence of evidence; there can be no question of *proving* with what intonation the composing-dramatist imagined his words to be spoken. And if there are directives within his text which seem to point to his intention, such directives are very swiftly given. The process of analysis, by contrast, is bound to weaken those very effects it tries to measure.

My next instance is more complex; I shall try to show that in Falstaff's phrase *horson Achitophel* (2 *Henry IV*, I ii 41), Shakespeare contrives an allusion at once tragic and comic, part of the structure

---

[1] NED: *sough*, *sb.*[1] 2. A deep sigh or breath. *Sough*, *sb.*[2] 2. A small gutter . . . a drain.

of conscious wit of an accomplished jester as well as an indication that the unpleasant reality of life is, perhaps less consciously, known and accepted. Speaking to the page whom the prince has put in his service, Falstaff talks at first of the prince himself, professing a certain annoyance with him,

> He may keepe his owne Grace, but he is almost out of mine, I can assure him,

and then continues, with apparent inconsequentialness,

> What said M. Dombledon, about the Satten for my short Cloake, and Slops?
> Page.   He said sir, you should procure him better Assurance, then.
> Bardolfe: he wold not take his Bond & yours, he lik'd not the Security.
> Falstaffe.   Let him bee damn'd like the Glutton, may his Tongue be hotter, a horson Achitophel; a Rascally-yea-forsooth-knaue, to beare a Gentleman in hand, and then stand vpon Security? The horson smooth-pates doe now weare nothing but high shoes, and bunches of Keyes at their girdles: and if a man is through with them in honest Taking-vp, then they must stand vpon Securitie. . . .

In the witty sequence of this denunciation, it is Mr. Dombledon who is condemned as an Achitophel, a type of false counsellor who has been accustomed to deceive ('beare . . . in hand') his customers with obsequious flattery ('a Rascally-yea-forsooth-knaue'), apparently content to take a gentleman's note of hand ('to beare a Gentleman in hand') but come at last to insist on ('stand vpon') security. Achitophel is the arch-deceiver of old Testament history: as the trusted counsellor of King David (Samuel 2, xv-xvii), he transferred his allegiance and supported the prince Absalom against his father. Such men as Mr. Dombledon wear the high shoes of pride, and since all of them have 'bunches of Keyes at their girdles', they may well be in league together to deny further credit to each other's defaulting clients: the proverb 'All the keys hang not at one man's girdle', first registered 1400, is defined (1721) as 'Spoken to those who refuse us their help . . .

intimating that others may afford what they deny us.'[1] This, so far, is all of a piece; the bits jig-saw together. But there is also an important bit left over, a fragment of a different picture. Detailed knowledge of Biblical narrative was part of the language currency of Shakespeare's time, and Achitophel, counsellor of the prince Absalom against his father David, would be recognised as having something in common with Falstaff, that 'villanous abhominable mis-leader' of the young Prince Hal; part of his story indeed has startling relevance to Falstaff's situation. When Achitophel lost the confidence of Absalom, when he 'saw that his counsel was not followed', he 'hanged himself and died'. Falstaff is to die when the prince, crowned king 'has kild his heart'. It cannot, I suggest, be regarded as mere coincidence that Falstaff alone of Shakespeare's characters should speak the name of Achitophel, and at this point of the play. For he and the young prince are now separated; we hear why from the Chief Justice:

> the King hath seuer'd you and Prince Harry, I heare you are going with Lord Iohn of Lancaster, against the Archbishop, and the Earle of Northumberland.

If military necessities continue, and if the prince's reformation is maintained, Falstaff can reckon their old association at an end. When the Chief Justice voices the general disapproval, 'heauen send the Prince a better companion', Falstaff replies with an irony which conceals an inner truth 'Heauen send the Companion a better Prince'. Critics are agreed that much of the humour of this scene comes from the intrusion of that reality which Falstaff so intently disregards; is not 'Achitophel' a foreshadowing of future reality? 'You must speake lowder, my Master is deafe', says his page. The Chief Justice speaks to Falstaff of the actual: 'What? you are as a candle, the better part burnt out', and again 'Is not . . . euery part about you blasted with Antiquity?' And Falstaff's complaints, although outwardly they refer to his service in the second campaign against the rebels and to lack of money, his

---

[1] See ODEP.

'Consumption of the purse', have part of their artistic effect from the unavoidable truth: 'Well, I cannot last euer 'and' Borrowing only lingers, and lingers it out, but the disease is incureable'.

To pick up the full meaning of the Shakespearean text the outsider has first to know the range of idiom available in Elizabethan London; we have, for instance, to inform ourselves, laboriously or casually according to the luck of the game, of the language-value of the 'bunches of Keyes at their girdles'. I want further to suggest that within Elizabethan spoken English there may have been ready to Shakespeare's hand another verbal linkage, which, while it could be used to refer precisely to the stage which had been reached in the relationship of Falstaff and Mr. Dombledon, might also serve as a comment by Falstaff on his own position; he has not yet reached more than the half-way mark on his sorry way to Achitophel's end. Achitophel, rejected, hanged himself; Falstaff, for the present, suffers one thing only, and that, no doubt, as a result of his enforced separation from the prince—he is refused credit by Mr. Dombledon; in the idiom of Shakespeare's day he is 'halfe hanged, that hath lost his credit'. Withals' *Dictionarie* (p. 231) translates Semi suspensus, halfe hanged, that hath lost his credite, or hath it taken from him. 'Half-hanged' itself does not come into Falstaff's speech but the unspoken sense may be hammered home with every repetition of the word *security*. And the repeated phrase to 'stand vpon Security' may be a euphemism for suicide by hanging.[1]

The difference between such an analysis of Falstaff's words and the words themselves as Shakespeare presents them is inevitably the difference between the coloured balls as they lie in their box and the living patterns which they make when manipulated by the juggler's art. While the glossarist can only set out the pieces of evidence one after another, the reader who wishes to test the validity of the proposed interpretation must break the linear sequence and let the clues present themselves again in three-dimensional stage dialogue.

---

[1] I believe that I once found evidence for this but I cannot now find it again.

3

Some quite simple instances of double meaning have their origin in the natural fluidity of language. While it is the office of the lexicographer to separate meaning into manageable and watertight compartments, the energetic speaker cannot always avoid, and will not wish to avoid, spilling over from one meaning to another. So in 1 *Henry VI* (IV iv 14), when Sir William Lucie is sent asking for help

> from bought & sold Lord Talbot
> Who ring'd about with bold aduersitie,
> Cries out for noble Yorke and Somerset. . . .

'Adversity' will certainly mean 'ill fortune', but its qualification by the adjective 'bold' (usually applied to persons, their words or actions) suggests that it is intended to bear some additional and less abstract sense; it seems as if it may refer collectively to Talbot's adversaries, the overwhelming 'force of France' which has 'intrapt' him, as well as to his own grim 'necessity' and England's 'losse'. NED shows *adversity* meaning 'opposition' in currency until *c.* 1450; and this Shakespearean instance, I suggest, illustrates a later usage of this sense.

The word *aduantage* in *King John* (II i 297), when the English and French forces take up their positions for battle prompts a similar kind of question:

> Iohn.   Vp higher to the plaine, where we'l set forth
> In best appointment all our Regiments.
> Bastard.   Speed then to take aduantage of the field.
> France.   It shall be so, and at the other hill
> Command the rest to stand, God and our right. . . .

King John's order 'Vp higher' seems to give to the noun 'aduantage' the sense of 'superior position', a rising ground, a place of vantage; the Bastard's 'Speed then to take' suggests 'a time of vantage', an opportunity or 'chance'. NED confirms these senses in Elizabethan English: in the language patterns of the time any army which hastens to take up a good position on higher ground is likely to seize the advantage in both place and time.

A noun closely related to or formed from a verb may have in earlier English either active or passive verbal sense: 'spent . . . at our Choyce' refers to the eating and drinking when the parish officers were chosen (Kenilworth parish records, 1629). So in *Midsummer Night's Dream* (v i 39) when Theseus asks

> Say, what abridgement haue you for this euening?
> What maske? What musicke? How shall we beguile
> The lazie time, if not with some delight?

the word *abridgement* may have, so to say, double voice. In its passive sense 'a shortened version of some longer work' it would have first place in the noun list continued by 'maske' and 'musicke' and would represent an interlude type of entertainment; in its active sense 'something to make the evening seem shorter' its function would be to 'beguile the lazie time'.[1] I suggest later (p. 338) that the words *pastime* and *play* (in the sense 'dramatic perform-ance') may be for Shakespeare strongly linked: this word *abridge-ment* is found again in Shakespeare's text as Hamlet, when the players enter (II ii 439), cuts short his speech to Polonius with the words

> For looke where my Abridgements come.
>   (Q. 2 where my abridgment comes).

Compass in Shakespeare's time has the meanings, among others, to 'obtain' and 'to make a circuit'. These two senses may be run together in the thumb-nail biography of Autolycus given by the rogue himself (*Winter's Tale*, IV iii 102)

---

[1] NED hesitates between the two senses 'A means of shortening' and 'A compend-ium of a larger work'. Onions equates the two: 'means of shortening or whiling away the time, pastime.'

I know this man well, he hath bene since an Ape-bearer, then a Processe-seruer (a Bayliffe) then hee compast a Motion of the Prodigall sonne, and married a Tinkers wife, within a Mile where my Land and Liuing lyes; and (hauing flowne ouer many knauish professions) he setled onely in Rogue: some call him Autolicus.

'Compast', meaning 'obtained' would be, as it were, parallel to 'married'; in the sense 'took on tour' it would go with the travelling of the tinker's wife, the ape-bearer and the process-server; the puppet show which Autolycus got hold of he would take from fair to fair.

Affection'd may well be a 'hinge' word as Maria describes Malvolio (*Twelfth Night*, II iii 160):

The diu'll a Puritane that hee is, or any thing constantly but a time-pleaser, an affection'd Asse, that cons State without booke, and vtters it by great swarths. The best perswaded of himselfe: so cram'd (as he thinkes) with excellencies . . . .

Following on the sense of 'time-pleaser' it would carry the sense 'ambitious, zealous'; followed by 'cons State without booke' it would carry the sense 'full of affectation'. NED illustrates the first sense from 1534 to 1623, including a citation of considerable relevance to this dramatic situation:

1567 To destroye all suche as be affectioned, or make claime to the same kingdome.

The second sense may be postulated from 'affection' = 'affectation', as in *Love's Labour's Lost*, V ii 407, when Berowne renounces 'Taffata phrases, silken tearmes precise, Three-pil'd Hyperboles, spruce affection'. NED cites Maria's 'affection'd' under the sense 'Passionate, wilful; self-willed, obstinate', with one earlier instance (1582) and no subsequent examples.[1] It seems to me that the possibility of this meaning is explicitly excluded by the immediately preceding phrase 'or any thing constantly but a time-pleaser'.

---

[1] Onions gives two senses: (*a*) full of affectation; (*b*) self-willed, obstinate.

21

The word *limbes* in Antony's speech over the dead body of Caesar (*Julius Caesar*, III i 262), through being understood only in its literal sense, has seemed to earlier editors to be strangely without meaning:

> O pardon me, thou bleeding peece of Earth. . . .
> Ouer thy wounds, now do I Prophesie. . . .
> A Curse shall light vpon the limbes of men;
> Domesticke Fury, and fierce Ciuill strife,
> Shall cumber all the parts of Italy:
> Blood and destruction shall be so in vse. . . .
> That Mothers shall but smile, when they behold
> Their Infants quartered with the hands of Warre. . . .

In the attempt to supply a word of greater emotional force a surprisingly large number of emendations have been proposed, including, among others: kind, line, lives, lymms ('bloodhounds'), imps, times, loins, minds, souls, heads.[1] Some of the emendations stem, no doubt, from the feeling that 'limbes' in its usual sense of 'arms and legs' would be stylistically incongruous. This fact should perhaps prompt the speculation that the word has a less exclusive meaning in Shakespearean English; so NED confirms— the sense 'any organ or part of the body', still current in dialect use, is registered by the Dictionary from *c.* 1000 to 1484, with the next and last 'written language' citation in 1642.

A further question is posed by the linguistic context, and in particular by the sentence-order, of the Shakespearean passage: are we not directed to expect some additional sense in 'limbes of men' which would have reference to the double emphasis of '*Domesticke* Fury' and 'fierce *Ciuill* strife' of the immediately following sentence? To put it in another way: has Shakespeare set down the order of ideas in Antony's speech in a non-dramatic, non-structured way (with the idea of *civil* war just happening to break into the 'wounds', 'limbes', 'Blood' sequence) or does the dramatist intend the lines to mean that civil war as it relates to

---

[1] Dover Wilson ('New Cambridge', 1956) and T. S. Dorsch ('New Arden', 1955) understand 'limbs' as subject to the physical effects of Antony's curse.

the 'limbs' of men is somehow worse than a struggle with an extra-territorial enemy. The question once formulated answers itself: Antony's speech has firm rhetorical structure; his word 'limbes' includes the sense 'member of a (metaphorical) body,'[1] the body politique of Rome of which Caesar, this 'bleeding peece of Earth', was once the effective head. Through this word 'limbes' and its associated imagery we are directed to remember also the speech of Brutus to the conspirators (II i 163); in answer to the proposal of Cassius

> Let Antony and Cæsar fall together

Brutus replies

> Our course will seeme too bloody, Caius Cassius,
> To cut the Head off, and then hacke the *Limbes*. . . .
> For Antony, is but a *Limbe* of Cæsar. . . .
> O that we then could come by Cæsars Spirit,
> And not *dismember* Cæsar!

In the death of Caesar Antony believes that the unity of the Roman state is itself dismembered.

A less important example of this telescoping of argument is found in *Antony and Cleopatra* (V ii 226) in Cleopatra's phrase *to conquer their most absurd intents*, when she resolves on 'liberty' rather than to 'be shewne In Rome':

> Nay, 'tis most certaine Iras: sawcie Lictors
> Will catch at vs like Strumpets, and scald Rimers
> Ballads vs out a Tune. The quicke Comedians
> Extemporally will stage vs, and present
> Our Alexandrian Reuels: Anthony
> Shall be brought drunken forth, and I shall see
> Some squeaking Cleopatra Boy my greatnesse
> I'th'posture of a Whore . . .
> Iras.   Ile neuer see't? for I am sure mine Nailes
> Are stronger then mine eyes.

---

[1] NED: *limb* 3a. and *member* 6.

> Cleopatra. Why that's the way to foole their preparation,
> And to conquer their most absurd intents.

Intent can mean both 'plan' and 'subject or theme'.[1] 'Absurd' contains also the ridicule to be directed against Cleopatra as the subject or theme of the Roman 'Rimers' and 'Comedians'. This Roman plan to make her the subject of their ridicule she will fool by her death.

The idea 'plan or project' used of some work of art or literary composition presupposes also a chosen 'subject or theme', and it would therefore be reasonable to expect that, at a time when the word 'intent' can have potentially either meaning, it will be likely to have both at once in an artist/composing context. So in *Timon of Athens* (v i 23) when painter and poet seek out Timon with promises of work to be presented to him. The painter 'will promise him An excellent Peece'; the poet will

> Tell him of an intent that's comming toward him. . . .
> It must be a personating of himselfe:
> A Satyre against the softnesse of Prosperity. . . .

Potential double meaning is available when etymologically different words have come to have identical form; in a dramatic situation where both meanings are fully relevant the speaking character may utilise this double sense quite simply and briefly. In *Julius Caesar* (III i 94) after the murder of Caesar, Publius is warned by Cassius to move away from the group of conspirators:

> And leaue vs Publius, least that the people
> Rushing on vs, should do your Age some mischiefe.

Brutus also urges him

> Do so, and let no man abide this deede,
> But we the Doers.

Abide as used by Brutus would seem to have two meanings: in opposition to 'leaue', it has the meaning 'stay'; with 'this deede'

---

[1] NED: *intent* 1b. Design, plan, project, scheme. 7. The subject or theme to be treated in an argument or discourse.

as its object it means 'to pay for, meet the consequence of'. Since both 'aby', the original form of this second verb, and its variant 'abide' are found elsewhere in Shakespeare's plays, we have no difficulty in understanding this double sense.

The meanings of two different verbs are combined in *lowted* (1 *Henry VI*, IV iii 13). Talbot's hard-pressed forces need relief, but there is 'strife' between the 'great Commanders'. Yorke complains

> A plague vpon that Villaine Somerset,
> That thus delayes my promised supply
> Of horsemen, that were leuied for this siege.
> Renowned Talbot doth expect my ayde,
> And I am lowted by a Traitor Villaine
> And cannot helpe the noble Cheualier. . . .

'Lowted' has been generally glossed as 'mocked' and NED cites this Shakespearean instance under that definition;[1] such a sense is supported by the 'rancorous spight' and 'iarring discord' illustrated in the previous scenes. But the sense 'delayed' is strongly suggested by the context; instead of the original *lowted*, conjectural emendations 'loiter'd' and 'letted' have been put forward. The need for haste is stressed: 'Spurre to the rescue', 'remisse Traitors', 'Long all of Somerset, and his delay', 'Sleeping neglection'; in the next scene 'It is too late' and 'Too late comes rescue'. External evidence confirms this textual directive: a verb *lout* showing as one of its connotations 'sneaking inactivity' is recorded in literary English as late as Caxton; it survives in its simple form and in an iterative variant *lowter* in some present-day midland and northern dialects.[2]

---

[1] *lout v.*[3] 1.

[2] Bosworth Toller: lutian, To lie hid, be concealed, lurk, skulk, be latent. . . . Lutode *torpebat*.

NED: *lout v*[2]. To lurk, lie hid, skulk, sneak (until 1483).

EDD: *lout v*[1]. To idle, wander idly about.

lowter v. To idle, loiter.

louther Sc. To remain in idleness, to loiter, idle.

In the examples here put forward it is the energy and sometimes the indignation of the speaker which has brought about this compression of two meanings into one word. And, if I may hazard a classification and pass rapidly on, this kind of double meaning—which is something rather different from the active point-scoring fully-intentioned ambiguity—is of special value to the dramatist as part of the never-again-ness of his language; reader and 'auditor' are kept alert and required to accept as part of the natural order of things that what a word can mean will change with the changing situations of the external world. And as Shakespeare effortlessly contrives it, we have the impression that not the speaker only, but the language also, exerts some control over what is said. Force of feeling leads the speaker to an unusual economy of expression; language and situation together enforce the manner of that economy.

CHAPTER X

Shakespeare of Stratford

Of Sir Walter Ralegh we have it on Aubrey's authority that 'he spake broad Devonshire to his dyeing day' but how far Shakespeare kept his Warwickshire dialect no one has recorded. As an actor on the London stage he would use, we may suppose, a style of speech that was clear and readily intelligible, as free as possible of recognisable regional mannerisms. As a playwright also, it has been suggested, he 'would naturally be careful to avoid any pecularities of diction which his London audiences might find obscure or ludicrous, and anything of this kind which he introduced inadvertently would probably be brought to his notice by the actors'.[1] If we agree with Bradley in this opinion, then, as Kökeritz has pointed out, 'there is actually no reason why we should expect any provincialisms at all'[2] in Shakespeare's plays. Kökeritz has the impression nevertheless that there is in Shakespeare's writing some evidence, albeit rather indefinite, of his Warwickshire background; Onions, in his *Shakespeare Glossary*, seeking 'to show the relation of the poet's vocabulary to that of the dialects of the midland area' and of Warwickshire, lists some two dozen words in Shakespeare's text which are now localised in Warwickshire or in the midlands generally. More precise evidence, however, has not been found and the general conclusion has been fairly reached that 'Shakespeare in London shows no sign of surviving local patriotism'.[3]

---

[1] 'Shakespeare's English', by Henry Bradley, in *Shakespeare's England*, Oxford 1916, Vol. II, p. 573.

[2] *Shakespeare's Pronunciation*, p. 45.

[3] 'Shakespeare and Elizabethan English' by G. D. Willcock, in *A Companion to Shakespeare Studies* 1934, pp. 120-1.

As G. D. Willcock continues:

> When he has occasion to use dialect in his plays (as in the Tom o'
> Bedlam scenes in *King Lear*) he is content with the conventional
> stage 'southern'. A number of dialect words (some of them trace-
> able to Warwickshire) have been collected from his works, but
> the contexts in which they occur (notably the Witches' scenes in
> *Macbeth*) have mostly the effect of detaching the poet from them.
> For the accents of his workaday speech we have no evidence at all.

A brief reconnaissance into the local records of Stratford in the
late sixteenth and early seventeenth century—records first
explored and calendared in the mid-nineteenth century by that
giant of Shakespearean scholarship, J. O. Halliwell (Halliwell-
Phillipps)—has yielded some linguistic detail of interest for the
study of Shakespeare's language and meaning. But the central
problem of how much, if any, of Shakespeare's purely local
language found a place in his dramatic text remains, of course,
unsolved; many years of investigation would give only a provisional answer. Meanwhile it seems likely that future research
will establish as more widely current such elements of apparently
'Stratford' language as occur in his text.

A small number of rather unusual spelling variants which
occur in the Shakespearean text can be found also in the early
records of Stratford, Warwickshire and the midland counties.
So with the spelling *hudg'd* 'hugged', in the folio text of *The
Merchant of Venice*, II vi 16

> Hudg'd and embraced by the strumpet winde[1]

Stratford Chamberlains' Accounts show payments for 'dydgen
['digging'] of v Lodes of gravell' (1601), 'for wyne and shugger'
and 'nutmedggs' (1623). Other midland parishes of about this
time have sporadic *dg* spellings for final *g*; *pedges* 'pegs' (Accts.
of the Abbey, Shrewsbury, 1596); *tadges* 'tags' (St. Mary's,

---

[1] J. G. McManaway comments (*Shakespeare Survey* 13, 1960, p. 169): 'If any
Shakespearian spelling has survived in this line, it must be Q's *hugd*', since F is
a reprint of Q, which was set from Shakespeare's foul sheets.

Shrewsbury, 1612); *ludges* 'lugs', and *twidges* 'twigs' (Pattingham, Staffs., 1642). There is no reason to doubt that such spellings indicate a variant pronunciation although it must remain for future research to determine over how wide an area this particular ripple extended.

Syllabic *r* is occasionally found in the Shakespearean text. Lavinia laments that she can find no mercy in Tamora:

> No Garace,
> No womanhood? (*Titus Andronicus*, II iii 182)

Goneril rebukes her husband

> France spreds his banners in our noyseles land,
> With plumed helme, thy state begins thereat ['threat'].
> (*Lear*, IV ii 57, 1608 Q; Folio omits; most eds. read 'to threat')

This type of pronunciation is heard in some present-day regional dialects; similar spellings are found in the early records of Stratford and other Warwickshire parishes: *matteryce*, *matterice*, 'mattress', Stratford 1602; *buckerham*, 'buckram', Southam 1631; 'for armes for the taryne ('trained') band', Solihull 1660; 'for Cerasing ['grazing'] the Cowes', Combrock 1741.

The variant *shinne* for 'chin' occurs in *Coriolanus* (II ii 95)

> When with his Amazonian Shinne he droue
> The brizled Lippes before him. . . .

In present-day educated English a *sh* for *ch* pronunciation is used, finally, by some speakers in such words as 'bunch', 'lunch'. Sporadic spelling variants of this kind occur in the early records. I have noted in a Stratford document (1617) *a shape to a sowrd*, 'a chape for a sword',[1] and a few further instances, but without the consonant in the initial position, in parish records of Shropshire and Staffordshire: *faschyng* 'fetching' 1563; *porsh*, 'porch'

---

[1] *Chape*, the mounting of a scabbard or sheath.

1668; *thashing*, 'thatching' 1703; *bounshes*, 'bunches' 1742. An interesting form in the Shakespearean text is *chapes*, 'shapes' (*Hamlet*, I ii 82, Q 2; Folio *shewes*):

> Together with all formes, moodes, chapes of griefe....

Whether this is merely a spelling variant (perhaps an inverted spelling) or whether it indicates a diaphonic overlap of the *sh, ch* consonant sounds I have not sufficient evidence to determine. It is worth remarking, however, that the variant itself within the Shakespearean context may have dramatic value; it may be intended to hint at one of the ways in which Hamlet's grief will show itself. The noun *jape*, as NED shows, is found in the fifteenth century in the form *chape* with the sense 'jest, gibe'. And if we suppose that this form and sense were still in currency in the spoken language of Shakespeare's England, then Hamlet's phrase 'chapes of griefe' may carry an oblique reference to the bitter jests with which he has answered the king's words and has, nine lines earlier, begun his part in the play:

> King.   But now my Cosin Hamlet, and my Sonne?
> Hamlet.   A little more then kin, and lesse then kinde.
> King.   How is it that the Clouds still hang on you?
> Hamlet.   Not so my Lord, I am too much i'th'Sun.

Another instance where the Folio's spelling may perhaps derive from Shakespeare's manuscript is to be found in *Antony and Cleopatra* (I iv 46) where Caesar speaks of the fickleness of the people:

> This common bodie,
> Like to a Vagabond Flagge vpon the Streame,
> Goes too, and backe, lacking the varrying tyde
> To rot it selfe with motion.

Theobald here emends *lacking* to 'lackeying' and the emendation has a rightful place in any modernised-spelling edition, yet the folio's *lacking* (noted by Halliwell 'as rather a variant of form than an error') might perhaps go back to an original *lackÿng* (or *lackijng*) in Shakespeare's manuscript. A Stratford will of 1613 includes such forms as *occupÿnge, paÿnge, lÿnge:* 'that Ursula mj louinge Wife shall haue the Use and occupÿnge of the saied twentie poundes . . . she paÿnge ye pauinge & amendinge of ye Churchwaie lÿnge betwene.' This sign ÿ, or *ij*, representing final *y* of the verb-stem together with the *i* of the *-ing* suffix, I have noted sporadically in Stratford and in one or two Stafford-shire parishes. And in midland records from the sixteenth to the eighteenth centuries there are many spellings of gerund and present participle in which the final *y* of the verb-stem is lost before the *-ing* ending. Silvius's speech in *As You Like It* (II iv 38) may show an example of this:

> Or if thou hast not sat as I doe now,
> Wearing thy hearer in thy Mistris praise,
> Thou has not lou'd.

Subsequent folio editions have *wearying*, a reading preferred by a number of modern editors.

Before considering some of the elements of vocabulary found alike in Shakespeare's text and in the Stratford records of his contemporaries it may be well to illustrate once more that the linguist working with manuscript material, in Stratford as in any other area, is bound to come upon additional vocabulary of *apparent* rarity. So, for instance, a Stratford inventory of 1602 values at three shillings 'iii plate Chells of brasse'; NED shows *chelle* 'a vessel', with two citations only, the first from King Alfred's *Orosius*, c. 893, the second a. 1240.[1] Again NED registers *chilver* 'a ewe-lamb', with a note that the word is found in OE. and is still common in southern dialects, though not evidenced in the intervening period: the first citations are of c. 1000 and a. 1100, the next of 1815; a Stratford will of 1600 has the entry 'I geve unto Thomas Hathway a chylver shepe'. Similarly words and meanings not hitherto recorded in literary works may well

---

[1] See also NED: *keel sb.*[4], 1485 to 1736.

be found in such non-literary archives. A Stratford inventory of 1627 includes 'five loade of ffirses & bangles they lie on'. This word *bangle* is not found in NED, but the *English Dialect Dictionary* shows it with the sense 'the cut branch of a tree' in Warwickshire and Worcestershire. Many such examples might be cited from the local records of the five counties (Derbyshire, Staffordshire, Shropshire, Warwickshire, and Sussex) which I have read.

Household goods and personal possessions listed in Stratford wills and inventories afford some instances of what may have been regional or country terms used by Shakespeare, yet again and again, in looking at the detail of this evidence, we are reminded afresh of the inevitable deficiencies of the lexical record. The word *Dowl*, 'one of the filaments or fibres of a feather; . . . down, fluff', is shown by NED first in an instance of *c.* 1400, then in Ariel's speech to the courtiers as they draw their swords against the 'Harpey' (*The Tempest*, III iii 65);

> the Elements
> Of whom your swords are temper'd, may as well . . .
> Kill the still closing waters, as diminish
> One dowle that's in my plumbe. . . .

A Stratford inventory of 1600 includes four instances of 'dowle' pillows; another (1602) lists 'A ffether bed, A dowle bed'; this evidence adds likelihood to NED's suggestion that the forms *dowl* and *down* are etymologically connected. So too in 2 *Henry IV*, IV v 32, 33, Prince Hal, watching by his father's side, believes that the king is dead and himself assumes the crown:

> by his Gates of breath,
> There lyes a dowlney feather, which stirres not:
> Did hee suspire, that light and weightlesse dowlne
> Perforce must moue. . . .[1]

Cradle-clothes is cited by NED only from Shakespeare's text

---

[1] Alice Walker notes the occurrence of these spellings *dowlney* (Q dowlny) and *dowlne* in this passage as the 'most striking anomaly common to the quarto and Folio'. (*Textual Problems of the First Folio*, Cambridge 1953, p. 103).

(1 *Henry IV*, 1 i 88) when King Henry, hearing of Hotspur's success in battle, envies Northumberland his son:

> O that it could be prou'd,
> That some Night-tripping-Faiery, had exchang'd
> In Cradle-clothes, our Children where they lay. . . .

A Stratford inventory of 1631 lists 'a cradle cloth, & a face clothe foure peeces of linnen clothe to use about children' (NED first registers *face cloth*, a cloth laid over the face of a corpse, in Richardson's *Clarissa*, 1748). Shakespeare has the compound *bearing-cloth*, meaning, according to NED, 'a child's christening robe' in *Winter's Tale* (III iii 119): 'Looke thee, a bearing-cloath for a Squires childe', also 'a Childs bearing Cloth' (1 *Henry VI*, 1 iii 42). NED shows one earlier instance of 1601; *bearing say* is found in Stratford (1631): 'One bearing say for a child'.

In the passage in *Henry VIII* (1 i 55), where Buckingham attacks Wolsey (the butcher's son):

> I wonder,
> That such a Keech can with his very bulke
> Take vp the Rayes o' th'beneficiall Sun,
> And keepe it from the Earth

the word *keech*, although found in literary use at this time (if we may judge from NED's citations) only in Shakespeare's text, escaped emendation by eighteenth-century editors since they still knew the word in regional dialect as 'a cake of wax or tallow'. Stratford records show this sense clearly: 'a keeche of tallow' (1595), 'A keeche of tallowe', 'ffyve keeches of Tallowe' (1602), 'A Kyche of tallowe' (1603). That 'keech' and 'tallow' commonly occur together may account for, and explain, Prince Hal's abuse of Falstaff (1 *Henry IV*, II iv 252):

> thou Clay-brayn'd Guts, thou Knotty-pated Foole,
> thou Horson obscene greasie Tallow Catch.

When Falstaff's horse is removed in the Gadshill robbery the Prince has described how he 'sweates to death, and Lards the

leane earth as he walkes along' (II ii 116); as the incident is re-
capitulated by Falstaff with Kendal green embroidery, 'tallow
keech' would be an appropriate epithet of scorn as applied by the
Prince; it offers the same basting image. And in a later scene of
2 *Henry IV* where the Prince and Poins are once more disguised,
this time as two drawers, and again, as the Prince complains, are
recognised—'you knew me, as you did when you ranne away by
Gads-hill: you knew I was at your back'—Falstaff is abused by
the Prince in similar terms, 'You whorson Candle-myne' (II iv
326). The earlier 'Tallow Catch' image, it seems to me, may
fairly represent 'tallow keech'; if so, the quarto (and folio)
spelling *catch* might be a form of 'keech' in another dialect. On
the other hand, it might be the best that scribe or compositor
could do with a dialect word wholly unfamiliar to him; if he
knew the pronunciation *citch* for 'catch' of some present-day
dialects he might well normalise to *catch* a manuscript spelling
'kyche'.

A *garner* in standard English is 'a store-house for corn, a granary';
in midland dialect it is something much smaller, 'a bin in a mill
or granary'.[1] Stratford records have 'ii payles ii garners one utyng
fate' (this latter a vat for steeping grain in the process of brewing)
1593; 'a garner of bord' 1603; 'a gardner for malt' 1631. If we
know this local usage the effectiveness of the imagery is increased
in Othello's reproach against Desdemona (IV ii 57):

> Had it pleas'd Heauen,
> To try me with Affliction, had they rain'd
> All kind of Sores, and Shames on my bare head:
> Steep'd me in pouertie to the very lippes . . . .
> I should haue found in some place of my Soule
> A drop of patience . . .
> But there where I haue garnerd vp my heart,
> Where either I must liue, or beare no life,

---

[1] EDD: Chs. Midl. A bin in a mill or granary, a partition or 'ark' in a granary.

The Fountaine from the which my currant runnes,
Or else dries vp: to be discarded thence,
Or keepe it as a Cesterne, for foule Toades
To knot and gender in.

Grain and water which Othello links as the symbols of life may have their linkage also in the domesticity of Shakespeare's Stratford.

Macbeth, preparing for battle against the English, speaks to the Doctor in medical metaphor:

If thou could'st Doctor, cast
The Water of my Land, finde her Disease,
And purge it to a sound and pristiue [pristine] Health,
I would applaud thee to the very Eccho. . . .
What Rubarb, Cyme, or what Purgatiue drugge
Would scowre these English hence:

The word *cyme* here (v iii 55) is apparently unique. It has been generally assumed to be an error for 'cynne' representing a pronunciation of 'senna'; the latter is accordingly substituted in some modernised spelling texts. A doctor's account of 1625-6, preserved among the Stratford records, gives only the normal spelling of 'senna': 'for a purgin potion w^t rubarbe agarick senna creme of tartar manna sirops and others'; but it offers also the now archaic *aposeame*: 'for Mrs Mary 2 doses of Compounded aposeames'; 'for Mrs Mary, for 2 doses of aposeame as before'. NED cites *apozem* 'a decoction or infusion', first registered in Ben Jonson's *Sejanus*, 1603; *cyme* of the *Macbeth* text might well, I think, represent a shortened form of this word.[1]

As Hamlet, with Horatio, watches for the ghost's appearance and listens for the stroke of twelve, he hears in the distance the

---

[1] So, for instance, in the records of Rye, Sussex, 1516, *sence* is found as a shortened form of 'incense'; NED (under *cense sb.*[1]) shows similar shortened forms of this last word from *a.* 1375 to 1540, with the latest instance *cense* in an inventory of Worcester Priory.

drums and trumpets of the court and comments on his nation's
custom of ceremonial health-drinking: because of this custom the
Danes are 'tradust, and taxed of other nations'; he continues with
the general reflection:

> So oft it chaunces in particuler men,
> That for some vicious mole of nature in them
> As in their birth wherein they are not guilty,
> (Since nature cannot choose his origin) . . .
> Or by some habit, that too much ore-leauens
> The forme of plausiue manners, that these men
> Carrying I say the stamp of one defect
> Being Natures liuery, or Fortunes starre,
> His vertues els be they as pure as grace,
> As infinite as man may vndergoe,
> Shall in the generall censure take corruption
> From that particuler fault: the dram of eale
> Doth all the noble substance of a doubt
> To his owne scandle.[1]

There is evidence to suggest that this *dram of eale* (*Hamlet*, I iv 36)
is to be understood as an image from the brewing of beer, the
'eale' representing the fermenting agent, the beer-yeast, the 'leauen'
of seven lines earlier. We are accustomed to think of 'leaven'
as working powerfully towards good; in earlier imagery it may
also sour and corrupt what would otherwise remain untainted.
NED gives a number of citations: 'pharisaical leauen' (1555), 'the
old leaven' (after I Corinthians, v 6, 7); Milton writes (1641)

> The soure levin of humane Traditions mixt in one putrifi'd Masse
> with the poisonous dregs of hypocrisie in the hearts of Prelates.

Gyle, meaning 'wort in process of fermentation', with such
compounds as *gyling-fat*, *gyling-house*, and with the variant
spellings *yiylyng*, *yailing* is shown by NED; in Stratford records
the usual forms are *yelyng* and *yeelinge*: 'a yelyng vessell' (1586);
'the yeelinge howse', 1596 and 1602; 'One yeelinge vate', 'Two

---

[1] I quote here from the Second Quarto, 1604; Folio omits.

yeelinge vates', 1602; 'a yelyng fatt, a Utyng fatt a boltyng whitche' 1603. Even a very small amount of 'yele' in this sense could not but bring 'corruption' to 'all the noble substance' and Hamlet's *dram* can have this sense 'a very little'.[1] That an original 'yele' might be spoken as 'eale' scarcely needs proving; NED cites *east*, for instance, as a dialect form of 'yeast' and Withals, to give another example, includes in his *Dictionarie* a little translation joke based on an *ears/years* misunderstanding; 'Eares full of corne' are *Gravidæ aristæ*, and

> After certaine yeares, I shall see my Country againe,
> Post aliquot aristas mea regna videbo (p. 106).

In Hamlet's speech this *'eale* form could have also a second value, the *e'il*, 'evil', of which the 'leaven' is the image.

For the interpretation of the rest of this 'dram of eale' sentence 'Doth all the noble substance of a doubt To his owne scandle', attention may be drawn to a closely similar metaphor found in *Cymbeline*, III iv 64. Imogen, reading the letter sent to Pisanio, sees her husband's disloyalty as tainting the good faith of all other men:

> All good seeming
> By thy reuolt (oh Husband) shall be thought
> Put on for Villainy . . .
> True honest men being heard, like false Æneas,
> Were in his time thought false: and Synons weeping
> Did scandall many a holy teare: tooke pitty
> From most true wretchednesse. So thou, Posthumus
> Wilt lay the Leauen on all proper men;
> Goodly, and gallant, shall be false and periur'd
> From thy great faile:

It is noteworthy that 'leaven' and 'scandal' are again in collocation.[2] The laying on of 'Leauen' will, as it were, bring into

---

[1] NED: *Dram, sb.*[1] 4. *fig.* = *Drachm* 3; *Drachm* 3; *fig.* A small quantity; a very little.

[2] 'Leaven' is again corrupted and corrupting when Ajax abuses the railing Thersites (? one who is given to scandalling others) as 'you whinid'st leauen' (*Troilus and Cressida*, II i 15).

suspicion 'many a holy teare'; so, I suggest, Hamlet's 'dram of eale' brings into doubt all pure virtues else which a man may have; (*Doth*, 'renders'; *of a doubt*, 'containing a doubt', modern 'doubtful'); 'all the noble substance' in his character will be thought to 'take' the same 'corruption' which scandals the 'particuler fault'. For the syntax of Hamlet's sentence, as for many other Shakespearean sentences, I cannot cite an exact parallel. The construction *to doe him dead* (3 *Henry VI*, I iv 108) shows *do*, meaning 'render' followed by direct object and predicative adjective. The two phrases 'out of doubt' and 'in a doubt' are commonly used in Shakespeare's time; NED shows an instance of the latter (1559) 'Your wordes bringe me in a doubt'. Hamlet's 'of a doubt'— if it is necessary to analyse its grammatical function—I would regard as an adjectival phrase, a blending of the negative and positive forms quoted. 'To his owne scandle', meaning 'up to the level of (or 'like') its (= the dram of eale's) own corruption and discredit' presents no difficulty; Abbott (§ 187) shows several instances of *to* in this sense ('up to', 'in proportion to', 'according to', 'like'): 'to point' (*The Tempest*, I ii 194); 'To the direction iust' (*Macbeth*, III iii 4); 'to the manner of the daies' (*Love's Labour's Lost*, V ii 365).

The 'dram of eale' is of obvious symbolic value; as the play proceeds we are to ask, with Hamlet, if it is not his own habit of doubt and scruple which is for him the 'dram of eale', the 'particuler fault', to keep him from the swift revenge he promises. And it is perhaps of some dramatic significance that the Ghost, in describing the process of his murder, uses a similar but far swifter image: the 'Hebenon' is 'swift as Quick-siluer'

> And with a sodaine vigour it doth posset
> And curd, like Aygre droppings into Milke,
> The thin and wholsome blood.... (I v 69)

It is possible also that the words 'nature' and 'taint' in the Ghost's commands to Hamlet in this later scene carry some ironically slanted reference to the 'leauen', 'eale' imagery:

If thou hast nature in thee beare it not. . . .
But howsoeuer thou pursuest this Act,
Taint not thy mind. . . .

Another 'yeast' image is used by Hamlet in an evaluation-of-action context when he laughs at the affectation of Osric and others like him; they have

> only got the tune of the time, and outward habite of encounter, a kinde of yesty collection . . . and doe but blow them to their tryalls: the Bubbles are out.   (v ii 202)

Hamlet's 'dram of eale' has long been a source of difficulty to the Shakespearean commentator, and the *Fortunes starre* of the same passage, although much less important, is also rather puzzling. In conjunction with 'fortune' the word 'star' seems somehow favourable; it does not suggest, as the dramatic context would require, 'some vicious mole of nature', 'the stamp of one defect'. A Stratford document of 1646, listing the horses sold or exchanged at a fair, shows the *starre* as a natural marking on the forehead of a horse and NED also shows a number of instances of the star, 'a spot or patch of white hair . . .'(*c.* 1380 onwards): where, however, in NED's citations, a judgment is implied, the star seems to be regarded as an asset rather than a blemish.[1] The Stratford document, on the other hand, shows that this kind of forehead marking may be thought of as a defect; in the same list there is the entry 'a brown mare a bleare in ye forehead'. This sense of *blear* NED does not illustrate, but *blur* used figuratively as 'a blemish' is shown by the Dictionary from 1548. So, in *Lucrece* (222) Tarquin speaks of his 'vile purpose' as 'This blur to youth'.

The ordinary mechanical contrivances of daily life provide some of Shakespeare's images. When Viola confesses to Orsino that she loves someone 'About your yeeres my Lord', Orsino answers with the vigorous warning

---

[1] But cf. also *star*, *sb.*[3]? A crack or fissure in the skin ? A swelling or tumour in horses. 1607, 1710.

> Too old by heauen: Let still the woman take
> An elder then her selfe, so weares she to him;
> So swayes she leuell in her husbands heart. . . .
>
> (*Twelfth Night*, II iv 32)

With the realistic acceptance of the fact that the woman ages ('weares') more quickly than the man, there is recognition also of the natural habit of loving ('so weares she to him'). The verb *swayes* may have similarly a double meaning: as she moves up slowly to the level of her husband's age, so she becomes in his heart a moving force of power equal to his own. NED shows the noun *sway* in dialect use as 'a lever, crowbar'; Stratford records show it more specifically as a pump-handle: 'for mending the swige of the chapple plumpe' (1629). The same sense is found in Wolverhampton accounts: 'for mending the sweag of ye hollo-way Pump' (1694), 'for mending ye rotten row pump sweag' (1719), 'a Sweage for ye Rott'n Roe Pump' (1720). I take it that Shakespeare's verb 'swayes' has reference to the smooth upward movement of some such lever.

When Kent abuses Oswald (*Lear*, II ii 18) as

> A Knaue, a Rascall, an eater of broken meates, a base, proud, shallow, beggerly, three-suited-hundred pound, filthy, woosted-stocking knaue

this last *knaue*, in conjunction with 'woosted-stocking', may imply a pun. 'Worsted' is 'a closely twisted yarn', and *knave*, as NED shows, can mean 'a contrivance in which a spool or spindle revolves'; the Dictionary notes this as a rare sense and gives two citations only (1564, 1688); in country speech, however, it is probably of greater frequency. A Stratford inventory of 1587 includes 'i knave to wynde yarne on'.

NED illustrates the word *sear* meaning ' a portion of a gun-lock which engages with the notches of the tumbler in order to keep the hammer at full or half cock . . . ', with citations of 1596, 1622 onwards. The metaphorical usage, as the Dictionary shows, is recorded earlier: 'lyght of the seare' (? 1560), 'tickle of the sear' (1583); *tumbler* in the literal gun-lock sense is registered by the Dictionary from 1624. Stratford officers (1605) make payment 'for making a new spring at the end of the sier in Raphe Smythes peece & mending the tumbler' . . . and in the mending of another 'peece', 'haveing a new sier made for yt'. The Stratford spelling *sier* may be of relevance for the interpretation of the phrase *Desire the Locks* in *Henry V* (III iii 35) when the King, before the gates of Harfleur, warns the townspeople to surrender:

> Take pitty of your Towne and of your People,
> Whiles yet my Souldiers are in my Command, . . .
> If not: why in a moment looke to see
> The blind and bloody Souldier, with foule hand
> Desire the Locks of your shrill-shriking Daughters:
> Your Fathers taken by the siluer Beards,
> And their most reuerend Heads dasht to the Walls. . .

This somewhat puzzling verb *Desire* of the Folio text has been generally emended, following Rowe, to 'defile'. Recent editions (e.g. 'New Cambridge', 'New Arden') still give this emended reading, through which, presumably, the actual disordering of the maidens' hair is spoken of as itself equivalent to the 'hot and forcing Violation' of the licentious soldiery. It is possible, however, that the Folio spelling *Desire* might stand for a verb 'de-sear' which would better represent this compact image. A noun *Serre-front*, meaning 'A head band, forhead-band, or forhead-cloth' is included in Cotgrave's French-English Dictionary (1632 ed.); *Serre-teste* is 'A border of Goldsmiths worke, &c; worne by gentlewomen vpon their coifes, or hoods'. The verb *Desserrer* is there translated 'To loose, or set at large; to release, discharge, open, vnshut, vndoe'. The Latin verb *sero* is in English 'To locke, or shut'; *Resero* is 'To open a thing that is locked or closed . . .' (Rider's Latin Dictionary, 1626 ed.). The English language has this noun *Sear*, of obscure history, in the restricted and particularised sense 'portion of a gunlock'. It may well be that on the evidence of dramatic context, of etymology, and of contemporary

Stratford spelling, the Shakespearean *Desire* should be printed in modernised-spelling texts as 'Desear' and should be understood as referring both to the disordering of the head-dress and to the violation of virginity. The customary emendation 'Defile', by contrast, lacks precision of reference and destroys the non-comic pun which might be present in the original for those who knew the Latin and French senses.

Shakespeare uses this 'sear' image when Hamlet speaks of how the players shall be received:

> the Louer shall not sigh *gratis* . . . the Clowne shall make those laugh whose lungs are tickled a'th'sere. . . . (*Hamlet*, II ii 337)

It is possible also that *tumble* in conjunction with *hammering* implies a half reference to this gun-lock image when the Duke of Gloucester rebukes his wife and warns her of their danger:

> And wilt thou still be hammering Treachery,
> To tumble downe thy husband, and thy selfe. . . .
>
> (*2 Henry VI*, I ii 48)

Although details such as this last are of little dramatic importance, they illustrate afresh how different from that of the present time was the language medium available to Shakespeare; the words have different filaments of meaning from those which we commonly know. So too in Stratford and elsewhere a *try*[1] may be a sieve or sifting screen; Stratford inventories include 'In the Barley howse a trye' (1603); 'iiij mault sives, the hayre a Try a mault shoule' (1613); 'i Ewing fatt, i here cloth & i Trye' (1622); and it is likely enough that this 'sieve' image attaches itself to Shakespeare's *try* as, for instance, Timon seeks to reassure his steward that his friends will help him:

> secure thy heart,
> If I would broach the vessels of my loue
> And try the argument of hearts . . . . (*Timon*, II ii 187)

---

[1] NED's citations show the noun *try* in less frequent use than the Stratford evidence would suggest.

Gaunt uses a similar image as he speaks of the reasons for his son's appeal against Mowbray (*Richard II*, I i 12):

> As neere as I could sift him on that argument . . . .

The *dey house* in Stratford is the 'dairy': 'in the dey house . . . in the lyttell chamber next the dey' (1606). So in *Love's Labour's Lost* (I ii 136), when Costard is to suffer imprisonment and fasting while Jaquenetta is allowed her freedom, a 'day'/'dey' joke is ready to Shakespeare's hand:

> the Dukes pleasure, is that you keepe Costard safe . . . hee must fast three daies a weeke: for this Damsell, I must keepe her at the Parke, shee is alowd for the Day-woman.

The milkmaid's equipment would include 'on sybolle ['sye bowl'] an milkpan,' as in a Stratford inventory of 1606.[1] And within living memory in Shakespeare's country, the 'essential instrument in milking was the see or sye bowl to strain the milk.'[2] Knowing this, we may judge it not without significance that Lucio, commiserating with Claudio in his mortal peril, chooses a milkmaid as the subject of his sighing:

> And thy head stands so tickle on thy shoulders, that a milke-maid, if she be in loue, may sigh it off. . . . (*Measure for Measure*, I ii 178)

Another sifting image is that of the *Boulting-Hutch*, used by Shakespeare as Prince Hal, pretending to be his father, rebukes Falstaff who is pretending to be the Prince:

> thou art violently carryed away from Grace: there is a Deuill haunts thee, in the likenesse of a fat old Man; a Tunne of Man is thy Companion: Why do'st thou conuerse with that Trunke of Humors, that Boulting-Hutch of Beastlinesse . . . (I *Henry IV*, II iv 495)

Of *bolting-hutch* as a compound NED cites only this Shakespearean example and one instance from Milton (1641); in the Stratford of

---

[1] NED: *Say*, *sb.*[3] A bucket with two ears.
  EDD: *Say*, *sb.*[3] Sc. Nhb.Dur. A bucket . . . a milk-pail.
[2] *Folk Lore, Old Customs and Superstitions in Shakespeare Land*, by J. H. Bloom, London 1929, p. 62.

Shakespeare's time the bolting-hutch is quite commonly found as a piece of domestic equipment, although the usual form is not '-hutch' but '-which'. The records show, for example, 'a boultyng Which' 1587; 'in the kytchyn a boultyng which' 1591; 'one mustard myll wth a bowltyng wytche' 1592; 'i Boultinge witch' 1606; 'In the backside in a leane to two vting fatts one olde bolting whitche' 1627.[1] It seems not unlikely that some such form was originally used by Shakespeare in Prince Hal's speech: 'Bolting witch' would form part of the tun, trunk, bombard image group and '-witch' as a man who practises magic would have its place also in the 'carried away', 'Deuill' sequence which is continued in the prince's next speech:

> That villanous abhominable mis-leader of Youth, Falstaffe, that old white-bearded Sathan.

Falstaff, for his part, has already complained of the prince's witchcraft (II ii 18):

> I haue forsworne his company hourely any time this two and twenty yeare, & yet I am bewitcht with the Rogues company. If the Rascall haue not giuen me medicines to make me loue him, Ile behang'd.

In 2 *Henry IV* (v i 23) Falstaff laughs at the way in which Justice Shallow's serving-men, 'by obseruing of him, doe beare themselues like foolish Iustices', as David self-importantly seeks instruction from his master about the most trivial of matters; the 'Smithes note, for Shooing' is to be cast and paid, and, says Davy, 'Sir, a new linke to the Bucket must needes bee had'. A Stratford inventory (1606) shows this 'link' and 'bucket' in a 'well' context: 'tooe utinge ffattes one buckete & lynckes wth the Curbe of well'. NED, illustrating the general use of *link* as 'Something looped, or forming part of a chain-like arrangement', shows this special sense *c.* 1440 only:

> Be þe wyndas of þi mynde, wyth þis roop made myȝty in thre lynkes schal be turnyd vp þe bokett of þi desyre (*Jacob's Well*).[2]

---

[1] NED shows *Whitch, Obs.* or *dial.* = *hutch.*   [2] *Link, sb.*[2] 2.

A knowledge of local or contemporary usage may sometimes indicate why two images are closely associated in Shakespeare's text. Just before Bassanio is to make his choice of the caskets, Portia confesses:

> I speake too long, but 'tis to peize the time,
> To ich it, and to draw it out in length,
> To stay you from election.   (*Merchant of Venice*, III ii 22)

In the general currency of Elizabethan English, a *peise* is a weight, and, specifically and pertinently, a clock weight: Portia would like to put a weight on to the time so that it should pass more slowly. In Stratford records the word is likely to collocate with rope: payment is made 'for a greate Rope for the pease of the clock' (1586), and for 'Cordes for the poise' (1588). Another type of 'rope' expenditure is also shown in Stratford: 'for a eache for the capell bell rope' (1569). NED shows this noun *Eche* as 'A piece added', with two citations only (Canterbury, 1525): For ij ropes for eches for the bell ropys. For a eche to the gret bell.[1]

A list of tools in a Stratford inventory (1603) includes 'a two Inch Auger', 'a pynne Auger', 'a wrest Auger'. Of this 'pin-auger' NED gives one instance only (1523): An axe . . . a pyn awgur, a rest awgur, a flayle. The tool, no doubt, forms part of Shakespeare's image as Richard II, in his despair, thinks of the grinning Death within the hollow crown, who

> Comes at the last, and with a little Pinne
> Bores through his Castle Walls, and farewell King.   (III ii 169)

A number of words from the wool trade find their place in Shakespeare's text. The Clown in *The Winter's Tale* (IV iii 33) is overheard by Autolycus calculating the value of the wool: 'euery Leauen-weather toddes, euery tod yeeldes pound and odde shilling: fifteene hundred shorne what comes the wooll

---

[1] See also *Lear*, IV vi 53,

Ten Masts at each, make not the altitude
Which thou hast perpendicularly fell. . . .

too?' NED shows *tod* in general use from 1425 onwards as 'a weight used in the wool trade, usually 28 pounds'. The Stratford price fluctuates a little; in 1586 'one todd of wolle' is worth seventeen shillings, in 1591 'xxi todde of Woll' is valued at £20 and 'vi todde of yearne' at seven shillings. The weight itself is known as 'tod stone' (1594); another inventory lists 'Beame Scales one Todd stone of Lead' (1602). Cloths of many kinds and colours are referred to in the Stratford records: 'musk culler brode cloth', 'Ashe culler fryseadoe', 'sea green kersye' (1596); 'heare coler penistone' (1599), 'sadde tawnie color' (1594); there are medleys of various shades; 'purpur medlow', 'russet medlow' (1568). Shakespeare's colours, by comparison, are not out of the way. The nutmeg colour of the Dauphin's horse (*Henry V*, III vii 20) could be matched by 'fyne pepper culler broode cloth' (1603). When Bottom considers in what beard to play his part, 'your orange tawnie beard, your purple in graine beard' (*Midsummer Night's Dream*, I ii 96), these two colours are found side by side in Stratford: 'orange tawnye brode cloth', 'violet in grayne' (1596). The figurative 'in grain' would come readily to Shakespeare, as to others of his time. The Victorian double-dyed villain was to them a 'knave in grain'; so too Olivia could praise her own complexion: "Tis in graine sir, 'twill endure winde and weather' (*Twelfth Night*, I v 255). *Durance*, 'a stout durable cloth' (registered by NED from 1583 to 1709), is used by the Stratford housewife to make her tight-fitting bodice: 'a pettycote of stamell, wth boddies of durance' (1594). NED shows a similar instance from the north of England in 1585: 'One petticote of house-wyfe clothe . . . An upper bodye of durance'. Is it fanciful to suppose that the joke on the double meaning of this word (durability/constraint, imprisonment) must have been known to the women of Stratford and elsewhere, as well as to the arrested debtors of London? Shakespeare links the joke to the strong buff jerkin worn by the Sheriff's officer making the arrest: 'he that went like a Base-Viole in a case of leather . . . that takes pittie on decaied men, and giues them suites of durance' (*Comedy of Errors*, IV iii 27);

'is not a Buffe Ierkin a most sweet robe of durance?' (1 *Henry IV*, 1 ii 49).[1]

A few other expressions found alike in Stratford records and in Shakespeare's writing are perhaps worth noting. The Chamberlains' accounts of 1629 include the entry 'for 2 hurdls to turne the water 0-0-8d'. Shakespeare uses this sense of *turn* both literally and metaphorically. When Hotspur complains that the Trent cuts off some of the best part of the land which is to fall to his share after the rebellion, Glendower at last concedes his claim

Come, you shall haue Trent turn'd. (1 *Henry IV*, III i 136)

And when Coriolanus warns the senators of the 'absolute' power of the tribune he describes Sicinius as one who

being but
The horne, and noise o'th'Monsters, wants not spirit

---

[1] The word 'sweet' in conjunction with 'robe' (cf. 'bona-roba') suggests the possibility of an additional meaning in this last 'Buffe Ierkin'. The prince has taunted Falstaff for his drinking and lechery; he goes on to argue that those who take purses may well be called 'the Moones men'.

Falstaffe. Thou say'st true Lad: and is not my Hostesse of the Tauerne a most sweet Wench?
Prince. As is the hony, my old Lad of the Castle: and is not a Buffe Ierkin a most sweet robe of durance?
Falstaffe. How now? How now mad Wagge? What in thy quips and thy quiddities? What a plague haue I to doe with a Buffe-Ierkin?
Prince. Why, what a poxe haue I to doe with my Hostesse of the Tauerne?
Falstaffe. Well, thou hast call'd her to a reck'ning many a time and oft.

An epigram (*c.* 1594) by Sir John Davies (1569-1626) includes an incongruous ' buffe-jerkin' comparison:

Kate being pleas'd wisht that her pleasure could
Indure as long as a buffe-jerkin would:
Content thee, Kate; although thy pleasure wasteth,
Thy pleasure's place like a buffe-jerkin lasteth,
For no buffe-jerkin hath beene oftner worne,
Nor hath more scrapings or more dressings borne.

('In Katum'; *Works of Sir John Davies*, ed. by A. B. Grosart, Vol. I, 1869, p. 319.)

If the phrase 'buffe-jerkin' could, in the right kind of context, have this connotation, what seems an abrupt transition in the conversation of the prince and Falstaffe is seen to have good reason.

> To say, hee'l turne your Current in a ditch,
> And make your Channell his. (III i 96)[1]

In a Stratford will of 1622 a bequest is made 'To m^r Thomas
Turner the outsyde of a suyte of apparell of brodcloth of the
price of ffortie shillings'. Of 'outside' in this rather unusual sense
NED cites two instances[2] (1614, a. 1625), the first from Jonson's
Bartholomew Fair:

> I ha' seene as fine outsides, as either o'yours, bring lowsie linings
> to the Brokers, ere now, twice a weeke.[3]

Shakespeare has several instances where the outside is separately
specified. Rosalind and Celia on their journey to Arden intend to
have

> a swashing and a marshall outside,
> As manie other mannish cowards haue,
> That doe outface it with their semblances.
>
> (*As You Like It*, I iii 122)

Viola, receiving Olivia's ring, exclaims:

> Fortune forbid my out-side haue not charm'd her. . . .
>
> (*Twelfth Night*, II ii 19)

And in *Winter's Tale* (IV iv 646) Camillo reassures Autolycus, who,
when they want some of his clothes for their disguise, complains
that he is 'a poore Fellow'

> Why, be so still: here's no body will steale that from thee: yet
> for the out-side of thy pouertie, we must make an exchange. . . .

Stratford inventories of household goods may end with the
item 'other smale nameles stuffe' (1603). And *nameless* with this
particular shade of meaning (not shown by NED) 'too small to be
worth detailed description' is, we may well suppose from the

---

[1] NED: shows *Turn* 13. 'to alter the course of', *c.* 1200 to 1821, with two
examples, apart from this Glendower instance, where water is turned, *c.* 1330,
1821.

[2] 2b. Outer garments; clothes.

[3] *Works*, ed. by C. H. Herford, and P. Simpson, Oxford, 1937, Vol. III, p. 53.

context, one of the meanings included by Shakespeare in *Two Gentleman* (III i 319), when Speed reads from the 'Cate-log' of the 'Condition' of the woman with whom Launce is in love

Item, she hath many namelesse vertues.

Similarly when Richard's Queen, after the departure of the king for Ireland, but before the return of Bolingbroke, speaks at length in quibbling fashion of her unaccountable sense of heavy sorrow which is to come, while Bushy tries to persuade her that her 'shapes of greefe' are 'imaginary'. The Queen talks of 'Some vnborne sorrow', some 'heauy nothing':

For nothing hath begot my something greefe,
Or something, hath the nothing that I greeue,
'Tis in reuersion that I do possesse,
But what it is, that is not yet knowne, what
I cannot name, 'tis namelesse woe I wot.   (*Richard II*, II ii 40)

The Stratford sense of 'nameless' would provide the second meaning required to complete the paradox, so that the Queen in irony agrees with Bushy's judgment that her grief is nothing just at the moment when news is brought of Bolingbroke's return.

We cannot doubt that as a boy in Stratford Shakespeare had better opportunities for seeing plays on the living stage than many a provincial of the present time; the Corporation accounts show very many payments to companies of players. In an entry of 1582-3, 'Payd to davi Jones & his companye for his pastyme at Whitsontyde xiis iiid.' 'pastime' evidently implies some kind of spectacle or dramatic entertainment. So in *Love's Labour's Lost*, IV iii 377, when Biron plans how they will entertain the girls of France:

in the afternoone
We will with some strange pastime solace them:
Such as the shortnesse of the time can shape,
For Reuels, Dances, Maskes, and merry houres,
Fore-runne faire Loue, strewing her way with flowres.

Elsewhere it is interesting to see how 'pastime' in its general sense of 'recreation, amusement' may link at once in Shakespeare's mind with 'play' and 'players'. In the Induction of *The Taming of the Shrew* the Lord promises himself 'pastime passing excellent' (l. 67) from his practice on the drunken beggar; the Huntsman undertakes that they will play their parts well; immediately after this the arrival of a company of players is heralded by their trumpet's sound. When the Queen asks Rosencrantz and Guildenstern (*Hamlet*, III i 15), 'Did you assay him to any pastime?', she is told that 'certaine Players . . . are about the Court'.

It is of special interest to try to recognise in Shakespeare's text some of the patterns of association which would come easily and perhaps inevitably to one who had grown up in Stratford. In the first scene of *The Tempest* there occurs the phrase 'give over' (I i 41). The boatswain rebukes the courtiers and cries out impatiently against their clamour

> yet againe? What do you heere? Shal we giue ore and drowne, haue you a minde to sinke?

In his scornful *giue ore* there is the energy, courage and instinctive denial of death appropriate to the active and healthy. Antonio answers for the courtiers with equal bravery and contempt

> we are lesse afraid to be drownde, then thou art.

In the homely piety of the Stratford wills the phrase *giue ouer* is linked also to courage and death, this time to the cheerful courage of acceptance:

> And first as Concerninge my bodie even Wth a good Will and free hart I giue ouer Comendinge yt to the earth Wherof yt came (1624).

NED illustrates for *give over* various separate senses in general Elizabethan currency, including to abandon (an attempt), to surrender, to pronounce incurable . . .; it seems to me that in the Stratford phrase there is a blending of these elements which might be appropriate also in the *Tempest* context; the playwright may have known and half-remembered from the wills of his fellow townsmen some such formula of courage in the face of death.

To be buried 'with ham' is now no longer a living ambition; the Stratford man or woman of Shakespeare's time hoped to make decent provision for a sufficient funeral. Urseley Loode in 1619 concludes her several bequests of 'flaxane sheetes' and her own wearing 'reparrel' by naming her 'full and whole exsecutare . . . to se me honestly brought whome'. This same phrase 'bringing home' is found in the graveyard scene (v i 256) where Hamlet asks, 'Who is that they follow, And with such maimed rites?' As Ophelia's body is placed by the graveside the Priest answers Laertes' repeated demand 'What Cerimony else?' with the words

> Her Obsequies haue bin as farre inlarg'd
> As we haue warrantis, her death was doubtfull
> . . .
> Yet heere she is allowed her Virgin Rites,
> Her Maiden strewments, and the bringing home
> Of Bell and Buriall.

NED shows the phrase 'To go home'[1] as common dialectally, and cites one instance in a will of 1528 (locality not stated)

> My wiffe to bryng me home and to pay my dettes.

One further detail of word usage in another Warwickshire parish concludes this chapter. In Kenilworth the early parish accounts are kept in two sections, since the town is geographically in two parts, the old and the new; the new part is regularly known as the 'Augmentacon'. So the gathering of the neighbours from both ends of the town to ratify the accounts at a general meeting is described as 'when both ends meet'. And in 1620, for instance, there is 'dewe to the Augmentacon by Thomas Wryght xviiis', while in the constable's book (which begins in 1675) there are listed the accounts of the 'Cunstabell for the augmentation off

---

[1] *Home, adv.* 1c.

Kenellwoth' (1676), of the constable for the 'Augmentacon of Kenelworth' and the constable 'for the Dutchy of Kenellworth' (1678). Shakespeare uses this word *augmentation* in *Twelfth Night* (III ii 85) when Maria describes how Malvolio

> does obey euery point of the Letter that I dropt, to betray him: He does smile his face into more lynes, then is in the new Mappe, with the augmentation of the Indies: you haue not seene such a thing as tis. . . .

If the Kenilworth sense were part of the day-to-day language habit of playwright and audience, Maria's comparison would be even more effective, bringing as it were the remoteness of the newly discovered world within the unity of the parish boundary.

CONCLUSION

This concludes what is rather a report of work in progress than an account of work completed. At a very rough count, new elements of meaning have been suggested for about two hundred words or phrases in the Shakespearean text; in close on forty instances it has been argued that the original text has more meaning than the emendations currently accepted. It is likely that some part of what is here set out as resulting from my own investigations has already been discovered and rediscovered. On the negative side, however, I can confidently make two claims: I have invented no new linguistic terminology and have put forward no new Shakespearean emendations.

REFERENCES

Abbott: *A Shakespearian Grammar*, by Edwin Abbott Abbott, 1875.

Apperson: *English Proverbs and Proverbial Phrases*. A Historical Dictionary, by George Latimer Apperson, 1929.

Baldwin: *William Shakspere's Small Latine and Lesse Greeke*, by Thomas Whitfield Baldwin, Univ. of Illinois Press, Urbana, 1944.

Bartlett's *Concordance: Concordance to Shakespeare*, by John Bartlett, 1953 edn.

Bosworth Toller: *An Anglo-Saxon Dictionary*. Based on the manuscript collections of J. Bosworth, edited and enlarged by T. N. Toller; Oxford, 1899; with a Supplement by T. N. Toller.

Cooper: *Thesaurus Linguæ Romanæ & Britannicæ*, by Thomas Cooper, 1578 edn.

Cotgrave: *A Dictionarie of the French and English Tongues*. Compiled by Randle Cotgrave. Wherevnto is also annexed, a most copious Dictionarie, of the English set before the French. By *R.S.L.* 1632.

Dobson: *English Pronunciation 1500-1700*, by Eric John Dobson, Oxford, 1957.

EDD: *The English Dialect Dictionary*, by Joseph Wright, 1896-1905.

Farmer: *Slang and its Analogues Past and Present*, by John Stephen Farmer and W. E. Henley, London, 1890-1904.

Googe: *The Zodiake of Life*, by Marcellus Palingenius, translated by Barnabe Googe. With an Introduction by Rosemond Tuve. Scholars' Facsimiles and Reprints, New York, 1947.

Kökeritz: *Shakespeare's Pronunciation*, by Helge Kökeritz, Yale University Press, New Haven, 1953.

Malone: *The Plays and Poems of William Shakespeare*, ed. by Edmond Malone (2nd ed.), 1790.

NED: *A New English Dictionary on Historical Principles*, Founded mainly on the materials collected by the Philological Society and edited by J. A. H. Murray, H. Bradley, W. A. Craigie, C. T. Onions. As reissued in 1933 under the title *The Oxford English Dictionary*.

ODEP: *The Oxford Dictionary of English Proverbs*. Compiled by William George Smith with an introduction by Janet E. Heseltine. Second edition, revised by Sir Paul Harvey, Oxford, 1948.

Onions: *A Shakespeare Glossary* (of words or senses of words now obsolete or surviving only in provincial or archaic use) by Charles Talbut Onions, Oxford, (2nd. ed.), 1919.

Rider's *Dictionarie:* by John Rider with additions by F. Holyoke and N. Gray, 1626 ed.

Schmidt: *Shakespeare-Lexicon*, by Alexander Schmidt. Revised and enlarged by G. Sarrazin, 4th ed., Berlin and Leipzig, 1923.

Sisson: *New Readings in Shakespeare*, by Charles Jasper Sisson, Cambridge, 1956.

Tilley: *A Dictionary of Proverbs in England in the Sixteenth and Seventeenth Centuries*, by Morris Palmer Tilley, Ann Arbor, 1950.

Withals: *A Dictionarie in English and Latine*. As first set foorth by John Withals, 1616 ed.

Index